Green Software Engineering for Business Project Management

Sherif Mohamed A. Ismail
https://orcid.org/0009-0000-0852-873X
American University in Cairo, Egypt

IGI Global
Scientific Publishing
Publishing Tomorrow's Research Today

Vice President of Editorial	Melissa Wagner
Director of Acquisitions	Mikaela Felty
Director of Book Development	Jocelynn Hessler
Production Manager	Mike Brehm
Cover Design	Jose Rosado

Published in the United States of America by
IGI Global Scientific Publishing
701 East Chocolate Avenue
Hershey, PA, 17033, USA
Tel: 717-533-8845 | Fax: 717-533-7115
Website: https://www.igi-global.com E-mail: cust@igi-global.com

Library of Congress Cataloging-in-Publication Data

LCCN: 2025031500 (CIP Data Pending)
ISBN13: 979-8-3373-4652-6
Isbn13Softcover: 979-8-3373-4653-3
EISBN13: 979-8-3373-4654-0

British Cataloguing in Publication Data
A Cataloguing in Publication record for this book is available from the British Library.

Table of Contents

Detailed Table of Contents

examines publication trends, identifies influential documents, leading authors, prominent institutions, key publication outlets, and the global distribution of research efforts. Findings reveal a field characterised by exponential growth in scientific production, particularly since 2013, driven by advancements in materials science, novel fabrication techniques like 3D/4D printing, and bio-inspired design principles. The analysis highlights the significant contributions of pioneering researchers and institutions, predominantly from the USA, with a notable recent surge in output from Asian countries. While the field demonstrates a robust intellectual framework and diverse applications in human-robot interaction and biomedicine, challenges about long-term durability, standardised characterisation, energy autonomy, and complex control strategies persist.

In recent decades, the world has experienced rapid technological advancement, industrialization, and a significant shift toward digitalization. While these trends have contributed to economic growth and innovation, they have also intensified environmental degradation, resource depletion, and electronic waste. To address these challenges, the concept of a circular economy has emerged as a transformative alternative to the traditional linear economic model of "take, make, dispose." While initially focused on tangible goods and materials, the circular economy model is now expanding to intangible assets, including software. Applying circular economy principles to software development is a novel and promising avenue, aligning the digital realm with sustainability goals. At its core, the circular economy is about designing out waste and maximizing value. One of the foundational principles of circular economy in the software context is design for longevity. This involves writing code that is modular, maintainable, and easy to update or refactor.

Circular Economy (CE) practices aim to achieve maximum utilization of resources, waste reduction, and product life cycle durability, and their application to software lifecycle management became increasingly necessary. The traditional software

from project management setup. This current chapter demonstrates that leading methodologies such as Agile, DevOps, and PM^2 can be redefined and designed to integrate environmental sustainability into software projects. A proposed Green Project Management (GPM) conceptual design helps to redesign project achievement to compromise environmental performance with conventional goals of time, cost and scope.The Green Project Lead (GPL), a new role committed to sustainability within project groups.By aligning sustainability with deeply rooted project management tools and metrics, the chapter focuses on a systemic transition in how software projects are planned, accomplished and assessed. It locates project management not just way for innovation and efficiency, but as a crucial mechanism for advancing environmental stewardship in the digital age.

Cloud Computing transformed the deployment and utilization of IT resources as on-demand, scalable, and cost-effective services. The high growth rate of cloud infrastructure, though, raised issues of power usage, carbon footprint, and the environment. All of these issues are solved by invoking energy-efficient hardware, the use of renewable resources, and green operation of data centers upon realization of Green Infrastructure in cloud computing infrastructure. This study employs a multicomponent model integrating atmospheric, terrestrial, geologic, and LiDAR-based urban data to describe resource consumption and environmental effects. Particle Swarm Optimization (PSO) feature selection determines the most significant factors, and a bi-stacked Long Short-Term Memory (LSTM) neural network learns time and space patterns in energy and resource data. The proposed methodology improves maximum workload allocation, energy prediction control, and green cloud operations.

Green Software Engineering integrates computing practices with sustainability goals, energy efficiency, carbon-aware computing, and ecological responsibility in software development. The chapter deals with a) evolution, significance of GSE in the digital age. b)theoretical foundations, sustainable software metrics, and the impact of the software lifecycle on GSE. c) strategies and practices in GSE, including carbon-aware and energy-efficient programming, green DevOps, and eco-centric agile project management. d) Integrating GSE into business project management, environmental key performance indicators, and tools and frameworks for green decision-making. e)examines the challenges of implementing GSE. f)Case study of healthcare in GSE. g)discussion on systematic thinking in sustainable software. h) insights from theory to practice in GSE. i)overview of active research projects in GSE at various universities. j) discussion on the future of GSE. This chapter is comprehensive and accessible to all readers, from beginners to research scholars interested in exploring GSE.

The rapid development of digital technology has made software-driven initiatives crucial for enterprises worldwide. However, traditional project management methods often lack sustainability and responsible governance. This chapter explores project governance in digital projects and software engineering using ESG principles. It emphasizes the importance of energy-efficient systems, transparent development processes, and transparency in project advancements. Baku offers a sustainable governance model, incorporating ESG frameworks, Agile and DevOps methodologies, and case studies. It also emphasizes the importance of managing human resources, involving stakeholders, and using sustainability performance indicators for green initiatives' success.

With the rate of digital transformation speeding up in various industries, environmental concern surrounding software systems is defying closer regulation and organizational consideration. The chapter will analyze the issue of compliance and regulation that play a crucial part in determining the green software development in business project management schemes. It examines the impact that global sustainability requirements, industry standards and regulatory vehicles, including ISO 14001, IEEE 1680, the Green Deal, and ESG disclosure requirements have on software project lifecycles. The chapter can serve as a helpful road map and transfer a practical set of skills to incorporate environmental compliance into projects and Agile, DevOps processes, procurement, quality assurance and reporting. It examines carbon accounting, energy profiling and automated compliance monitoring tools, and presents realistic ways of developing software in line with environmental objectives and legislative requirements.

This chapter explores the transformative role of geospatial tools in corporate sustainability reporting and ESG compliance. GIS, remote sensing, and IoT-enabled spatial data enable organizations to visualize environmental footprints, assess social impacts, and verify regulatory adherence across geographic scales. Applications in environmental monitoring, risk assessment, supply chain analysis, and community engagement demonstrate how spatial intelligence enhances transparency, accountability, and operational efficiency. The chapter also examines challenges in data quality, technical capacity, and integration, and highlights emerging trends such as AI-driven analytics and real-time ESG dashboards, offering pathways for dynamic, spatially informed sustainability management.

The broad scope of applications of artificial intelligence (AI) in many fields has also raised important issues concerning responsible practice and sustainability of the environment. In the current research, designing ethical AI systems and their impact on the environment are argued with a deliberate effort at embracing responsible and sustainable technology. Information were collected from the site under construction via a preprocessed systematic investigation for validity and processed later using Particle Swarm Optimization (PSO) with feature selection in mind. Bi-stacked Gated Recurrent Unit (GRU) has been utilized to feature extract of temporal patterns within ethics and environmental features to facilitate predictive analysis and identify possible biases. The conclusion highlights the need to reconcile fairness, transparency, and accountability of AI systems with their carbon footprint.

The software requirements selection (SRS) is one of the primary activities that decides the success or failure scenarios of software projects. Conventional approaches adopted for the SRS process had several issues, such as bias, limitations of scaling, and absence of clarity. To tackle these limitations, this paper provides a strong integration of the large language models (LLMs) into the SRS process. With the help of the LLMs, it is possible to automate and enhance the process of performing tasks like requirement analysis, requirements prioritization, and decision-making. The proposed LLM-based framework leverages the semantic understanding of LLMs. It analyzes the stakeholders ?(tm) inputs, learns from historical data, and considers existing project constraints to support more precise and efficient requirements handling. The security and explainability concerns of using LLMs in decision-making scenarios are also examined in this paper. Furthermore, the issue of reliability is also addressed to ensure consistency, robustness, and reproducibility of the LLM-driven decisions.

Preface

INTRODUCTION

The intersection of sustainability and software engineering is no longer a distant frontier — it is a pressing, present-day imperative. As digital systems continue to shape every facet of business and society, the environmental and ethical footprint of these systems demands our immediate attention. Green software engineering is not simply a technical aspiration; it is a business necessity, a policy concern, and an ethical commitment.

This book, *Green Software Engineering for Business Project Management*, was born from the recognition that traditional approaches to software delivery and project governance must evolve. We are witnessing a paradigm shift — one where high-performing digital solutions are expected to meet not just functional and economic benchmarks, but environmental and social ones as well.

In assembling this volume, my goal as Editor has been to bring together diverse perspectives — from researchers, practitioners, and policymakers — to offer a structured and holistic view of how sustainability can be woven into the fabric of both software engineering and business project management. This is not merely about energy-efficient code or green data centers; it is about redefining how we think, plan, and act in the digital development lifecycle.

The chapters herein reflect a cross-disciplinary synthesis. You will find practical methodologies alongside theoretical frameworks, real-world case studies beside forward-thinking models, and clear links between ESG (Environmental, Social, and Governance) priorities and day-to-day project management practices. Collectively, these contributions aim to equip professionals, scholars, and leaders with the tools to build software systems that are sustainable by design — not as an afterthought, but as a foundational principle.

This book is intended for a broad audience: from software engineers and project managers to ESG consultants, academic researchers, and policy shapers. Regardless of your vantage point, I hope this work supports your efforts to make responsible choices in technology development — choices that balance innovation with stewardship, performance with purpose.

As Editor, I am deeply grateful to the contributors who shared their expertise and vision, and to the readers who will carry this dialogue forward. The path to sustainable software is both a challenge and an opportunity — and it begins with informed, intentional action.

Let this volume be a guide, a reference, and, above all, a catalyst for change.

ORGANIZATION OF THE BOOK

This volume brings together sixteen chapters that reflect the diverse and rapidly evolving landscape of green software engineering and sustainable project management. Each chapter contributes a unique perspective on how sustainability can be meaningfully integrated into the digital lifecycle — from research and infrastructure to practical implementation and policy alignment. Below is a thematic overview of the chapters in this book.

We begin with **Chapter 1**, which sets a foundational context through a bibliometric analysis of sustainability research trends in relation to Sustainable Development Goal 9 (Industry, Innovation, and Infrastructure). This chapter maps the academic terrain using SCOPUS data, identifying key contributors, global hotspots, and evolving research patterns. It offers readers a panoramic view of how green initiatives have been explored and where intellectual gaps remain.

Chapter 2 continues this data-driven lens by analyzing the trajectory of soft robotics research. Using a bibliometric framework, the authors track the field's exponential growth and its sustainability implications, particularly in terms of materials innovation and energy efficiency. This chapter underscores how emerging technologies can align with eco-conscious innovation.

Chapters **3** and **4** shift the focus to the application of circular economy principles in software lifecycle management. Chapter 3 provides a conceptual grounding, making the case for designing software with longevity and adaptability in mind — mirroring principles long applied in sustainable manufacturing. Chapter 4 builds on this by incorporating empirical analysis, using expert feedback and advanced machine learning models to predict software usage patterns and optimize lifecycle planning.

In **Chapter 5**, the discussion moves into the realm of carbon accountability, analyzing how software systems contribute to greenhouse gas emissions. This chapter is instrumental in shifting sustainability metrics from infrastructure alone to include software as a significant player in environmental impact.

Chapter 6 presents a compelling case for embedding sustainability directly into project management methodologies. It introduces the Green Project Management (GPM) framework and proposes the role of a Green Project Lead (GPL) — a professional responsible for championing environmental goals within project teams. By redefining Agile, DevOps, and PM² through a green lens, this chapter bridges software engineering with operational governance.

Chapter 7 takes us deeper into the infrastructure layer, exploring how cloud computing performance can be optimized using green strategies. Employing hybrid models of AI, geospatial data, and environmental analytics, it provides actionable insights into reducing energy consumption while maintaining scalability and reliability.

Chapter 8 offers a comprehensive exploration of green software engineering (GSE) practices, with an applied case study in the healthcare sector. This chapter serves as both a theoretical and practical guide, covering metrics, lifecycle considerations, programming practices, and project integration, making it an essential resource for those seeking a full-spectrum view of GSE in real-time systems.

In **Chapter 9**, the focus returns to governance — this time through the lens of ESG (Environmental, Social, and Governance) principles. The chapter introduces strategic integration tools that ensure projects adhere to sustainability commitments, manage risks, and engage stakeholders meaningfully across the lifecycle.

Chapter 10 explores the evolving regulatory landscape for green software. It deciphers international standards like ISO 14001 and IEEE 1680, as well as frameworks such as the EU Green Deal, offering practical guidance for compliance, reporting, and embedding regulation into Agile and DevOps workflows.

Chapter 11 introduces geospatial intelligence as a tool for ESG compliance and sustainability reporting. From real-time dashboards to risk mapping, the chapter highlights how spatial data technologies can offer transparency, efficiency, and operational resilience in environmental monitoring and decision-making.

Chapter 12 explores the ethical dimensions of artificial intelligence, particularly in relation to environmental sustainability. Through advanced modeling techniques, it addresses how biases, transparency, and carbon footprints must be evaluated together to ensure AI systems are both responsible and sustainable.

Finally, **Chapter 13**, the use of large language models (LLMs) is explored as a transformative approach to software requirements selection. The chapter investigates how these models can improve accuracy, scalability, and explainability in the early stages of software development while maintaining alignment with sustainable design principles.

Together, these chapters form a multi-dimensional resource — academic, applied, and policy-relevant — that reflects the complexity and urgency of engineering green software systems and managing them responsibly. From abstract theory to tangible frameworks, this book is a call to action for technology professionals, researchers, and decision-makers who aim to align digital transformation with ecological integrity and ethical responsibility.

CONCLUSION

As we stand at the crossroads of digital innovation and ecological responsibility, it is clear that the way we build and manage software systems must change. This book has been carefully curated to reflect that reality — offering not only critical insight into the environmental challenges facing our industry, but also presenting the tools, frameworks, and thinking required to address them meaningfully.

The chapters within this volume demonstrate that sustainability in software engineering and business project management is not a niche concern. It is an essential consideration that touches every aspect of our digital ecosystem — from code architecture and infrastructure decisions to governance models, AI ethics, and policy compliance. These contributions are more than academic explorations; they are practical pathways forward, grounded in research, data, and real-world application.

Green Software Engineering for Business Project Management aims to catalyze a shift in mindset — from viewing sustainability as an external constraint to embracing it as a driver of innovation, resilience, and long-term value. Whether you are leading a software team, shaping public policy, developing enterprise systems, or teaching the next generation of technologists, this book invites you to rethink your role in creating a digital future that is not only intelligent and efficient but also just and sustainable.

The work is far from complete. But through collaboration, curiosity, and commitment, we can continue to bridge the gap between technical excellence and environmental stewardship. Let this book serve as a starting point, a reference, and an inspiration for the journey ahead.

Chapter 1 Sustainability Research Trends: A Bibliometric Approach to Strengthen SDG 9 - Industry, Innovation, and Infrastructure

Tarun Madan Kanade
https://orcid.org/0009-0002-0084-3107
Symbiosis Institute of Operations Management, India

Mrunal Milind Pandit
https://orcid.org/0009-0006-7632-2606
Navsahyadri Education Society Group of Institutions, India

Jonathan Sudhir Joseph
https://orcid.org/0009-0009-6543-6108
Thakur College of Engineering and Technology, India

Shubhangi Pharande
https://orcid.org/0009-0006-0798-0568
Navsahyadri Education Society Group of Institutions, India

ABSTRACT

Purpose: The aim of this bibliometric analysis was to determine the extent of research on Sustainable Development and Green Initiatives and to assess the past study publication trends based on SCOPUS database. Methodology: ((TITLE-ABS-KEY(sustainable AND development AND goals) AND TITLE-ABS-KEY(green AND initiatives))) were two significant phrases that were employed between 2004 and 2024 using Scopus database. 789 articles were evaluated using bibliometric analysis

DOI: 10.4018/979-8-3373-4652-6.ch001

approach. The researchers examined five performance analysis indicators, including publications by most prolific authors, cumulative publications by year, citation analysis, contributions from top universities, and countries. The minimum values for each indicator in the VOSviewer software were determined for data analysis. Scientific mapping was conducted on authors citation, co-citation analysis, bibliographic coupling, and co-occurrence of keywords.

INTRODUCTION

Sustainable development is being considered essential on global levels as a consequence of the major environmental concerns the world faces, such as resource depletion, biodiversity loss, and climate change. It is being driven in by environmental change compelling markets to adapt to customers' growing environmental consciousness, (Saari et al., 2017). The adoption of the Sustainable Development Goals (SDGs) and the escalation of environmental concerns lead to behavioural shifts among stakeholders and consumers, (Pimonenko et al., 2020). Consumption that prioritizes maximizing the effects of product acquisition, use, and disposal from an economic, social, and environmental standpoint, while keeping future generations in mind, is referred to as sustainable consumption, (Saari et al., 2017).

In order to promote sustainable development on a global scale, it is necessary to understand the links between the consumer and market levels that result in transformation and sustainable consumption and production (SCP). Researchers and policymakers have argued for "pro-environmental behaviour change," arguing that consumers should shift their buying patterns toward more sustainable ones, (Saari et al., 2017).

Green consumerism: One of the most important ways to combat unsustainable consumption is through green consumerism. Green consumers are those that buy and consume environmentally friendly products. Green customers support products that are less likely to endanger human health or damage the environment. The study encouraged students become more environmentally conscious consumers, (Mbokane & Modley, 2024). As per Pimonenko et al. (2020) stakeholders attempt to invest in green businesses and initiatives; customers choose to purchase environmentally friendly goods over conventional ones; investors and customers shrink away from doing business with unethical green businesses. According to Saari et al. (2017) the consumer goods business may be impacted by green consumer trends. The automotive and fast-moving consumer goods (FMCG) industries, for instance, have already seen a noticeable impact from green consumerism, implementing more sustainable processes. Businesses had to promptly modify their approach to align with the emerging paradigm of shifting from excessive consumption towards environmentally conscious green consumption, (Pimonenko et al., 2020).

This research report focuses on the following research questions (RQs) pertaining to "Sustainable Development" and "Green Initiatives":

RQ1: Which are the top journal sources with maximum number of papers published?

RQ2: Which year has the most cumulative publications between 2004 and 2024?

RQ3: Which affiliations/universities are the most prominent for publishing relevant?

RQ4: Of the several document types published, which are the most prevalent?

RQ5: Which countries have published the most articles overall?

RQ6: Which prolific authors received the most citations?

RQ7: What journals have the highest citation counts?

RQ8: Which are the co-citations of the most cited references?

RQ9: Which countries have the highest number of bibliographic coupling networks?

RQ10: What are the most frequently used author keywords while publishing articles?

The present study evaluates a mapping of academic articles pertaining to sustainable businesses and innovative green practices which promote SDGs. It covers scientific outputs in terms of publications, prolific authors, top universities, keyword analyses, bibliographic coupling of countries and highly cited articles.

LITERATURE REVIEW

According to Mahmood et al. (2023) assessment about the national and regional levels of Asia's progress toward achieving the Sustainable Development Goals with regard to resource use, sustainable production and consumption, and the triple planetary crisis (i.e., pollution emissions, biodiversity loss, and climate change). The analysis emphasised that a comprehensive strategy is urgently needed to address resource usage, pollution emissions, biodiversity loss, and climate change. China has seen a sharp increase in its greenhouse gas emissions. India is likewise working to use renewable energy to divorce growth from emissions. Pakistan, which is vulnerable, needs financial assistance and pollution reduction. Vietnam, Thailand, and Indonesia provide strategies for reducing emissions.

One major factor contributing to the loss of biodiversity is land use change, which emphasizes the need of conservation and sustainable land policies. Material consumption draws attention to the need for creative technology, circular economies, and production optimization. Decoupling energy's function from growth through eco-friendly methods, renewable energy sources, and efficiency is necessary for development. Global water use efficiency requires international cooperation and policy reform, and freshwater needs to be managed carefully for sustainability. The patterns of decoupling growth, resource usage, and environmental effect are complicated, and growth interdependence limits the possibility of complete decoupling, (Mahmood et al., 2023).

Ahmed et al. (2021) assessed the effects of competitive differentiation advantages, cost leadership competitive advantages, and proactive environmental strategy on the competitive and sustainable growth of an organization in terms of its performance, including financial, process, production, and product performance. For example, reducing reliance on pricey fossil fuels through the use of renewable energy sources like solar or wind can save money over time.

The development of appropriate attitudes and actions to safeguard the planet and lessen pollution or climate change can be facilitated by teaching sustainability consciousness. To this end, institutions (as well as all stakeholders) should integrate current environmental concerns with the explicit teaching for sustainability mandated by the 2030 Agenda, while also adjusting to new educational environments, (Hernández-barco et al., 2021).

Sustainable Business Practices

Customers' increasing purchasing awareness and desire for environmentally friendly items will have a significant influence on businesses' efforts to develop environmentally sustainable practices, (Saari et al., 2017).

Eco Friendly Brand

Customers who pursue an environmentally conscious lifestyle and are more sustainable in their consumption patterns are encouraged by brands that are viewed as being environmentally friendly. Perceived sustainability and environmental responsibility of a brand contributes to the pro-environmental self-identity of environmentally concerned consumers and helps them use brands to develop their identities. This paper has developed the state transition matrix of the consumption behaviour of eco-friendly items and perceived efficacy to ICT innovation applications, (Chen et al., 2021).

Integrating Eco-Friendly Practices into Business Operation

An eco-friendly hotel is one that is intentionally built to minimize its negative effects on the environment by implementing eco-friendly best practices in its supplies, services, goods, logistics, and maintenance. The association between eco-friendly perceived value and visitor satisfaction, a predictor of behavioral intentions to visit eco-friendly hotel fields, was unveiled by the study Kokkhangplu et al. (2023).

Business Landscape and Environmental Stewardship

As stated by the United Nations Sustainable Development Goal 12, by evaluating the longevity of eco friendly mortars made from mineral waste as a substitute raw material, this study presented a novel, environmentally friendly mortar substitute that can be used in building without compromising its qualities over time, (Arruda et al., 2023). The study by Xu et al. (2024) revealed its research base and evolutionary trajectory by providing an in-depth analysis of energy efficiency and emission reduction in support of SDG 7, based on bibliometric methods.

Green HRM

According to Khan and Muktar (2020), under the green HRM umbrella, HRM plays a better role in making the sustainability notion a reality by implementing environmentally friendly policies. According to Jabbour (2013) Green HRM is a concept that involves the methodical, intentional alignment of standard HRM procedures with the environmental goals of the enterprise.

Green Innovation

As mentioned by Khudzari et al. (2018), a number of reasons, including the diminishing reserves of fossil fuels, the quantity of waste produced, the effects of climate change, and the exponential rise in human population, are driving the global community to look for alternatives to meet the worldwide requirements for energy. One of the most promising approaches to sustainable energy is the microbial fuel cell (MFC) technology, which has a bright future ahead of it. MFC has a number of benefits over other organic matter-based energy technologies, such as wastewater treatment, bioremediation/biodegradation, biosensor, and electricity production.

Biomimetics, as revealed by Jatsch et al. (2023), is one significant discovery, that biological systems can serve as models for biomimetic sustainable development at the molecular level.

RESEARCH METHODOLOGY

Bibliometric Analysis

Alan Pritchard coined the term "bibliometrics" and defined it as the ''application of mathematics and statistical methods to books and other media of communication.'' It is the "metrology" of the information transfer process, with the aim of controlling and analyzing it. The statistical or quantitative study of the references or citations that are attached at the conclusion of each article is known as citation analysis. Through study of both cited and citing publications, a great deal of important information about the demography and identification of current and emerging knowledge in a discipline is brought to light. According to Kannan (2019), it is a quantitative assessment of different facets of the literature on a subject and is meant to reveal patterns in authorship, publishing, and secondary journal coverage in order to provide insight into the dynamics of knowledge growth in the fields of study. It is easier to investigate, arrange, and communicate work performed in a particular discipline when one uses bibliometric research, such as citation and co-citation analysis, to examine literary trends and attributes, (Faruk et al., 2021).

Data Source and the Search Strategy

Data mining carried out using the Scopus database. The search question string used was ((TITLE-ABS-KEY(sustainable AND development AND goals) AND TITLE-ABS-KEY(green AND initiatives))). These were two significant phrases that were employed between 2004 and 2024. The primary data source for the VOSviewer software (version 1.6.15) was Scopus. 794 articles came up from the initial search. The "All field" search criterion and time period filter were applied, the total number of documents was whittled down to 789. Subject categories helped to further refine the papers.

Below is a summary of performance metrics and science mapping indicators:

i. Examination of performance metrics: contributions from prominent journals, cumulative publications by year, number of publications by most prolific authors, examination of the most relevant papers by document, and contributions from significant countries.
ii. Document-wise citation analysis of top authors, most cited journals, co-citation of most cited authors, bibliographic coupling of universities and sources, bibliographic coupling of countries, and co-occurrence of all keywords are all included in the science mapping indicators.

RESULTS & DISCUSSIONS

Performance Analysis

Figure 1. Top journal sources with maximum number of publications

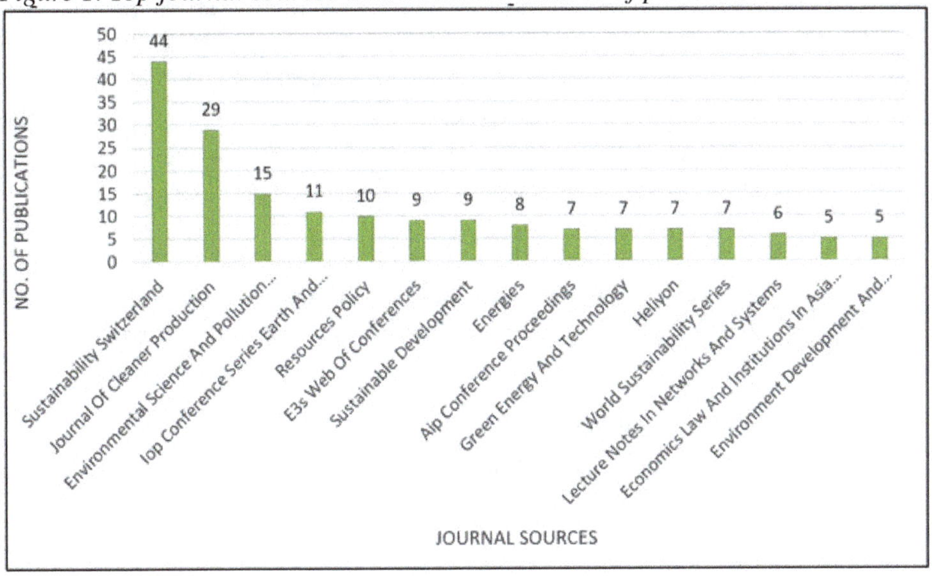

Figure 1 shows top journals out of total 116 journal sources. Sustainability Switzerland has published maximum of (44) articles, Journal of Cleaner Production (29), Environmental Science and Pollution Research (15), followed by others.

Figure 2. Cumulative publications by year

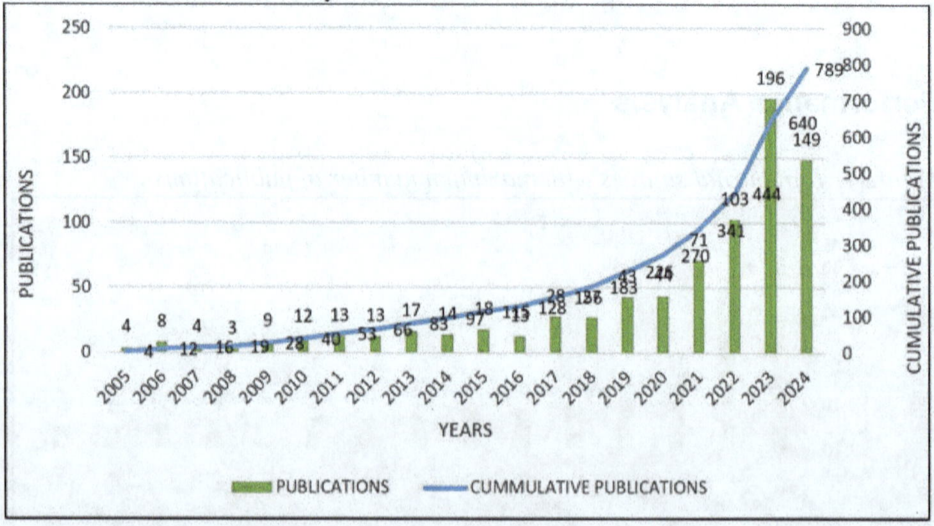

Figure 2 displays a combo chart of 789 cumulative publications by year from 2004 to 2024 with maximum 196 publications on "Sustainable Development" and "Green Initiatives" in the year 2023.

Figure 3. Top 10 affiliations/ universities

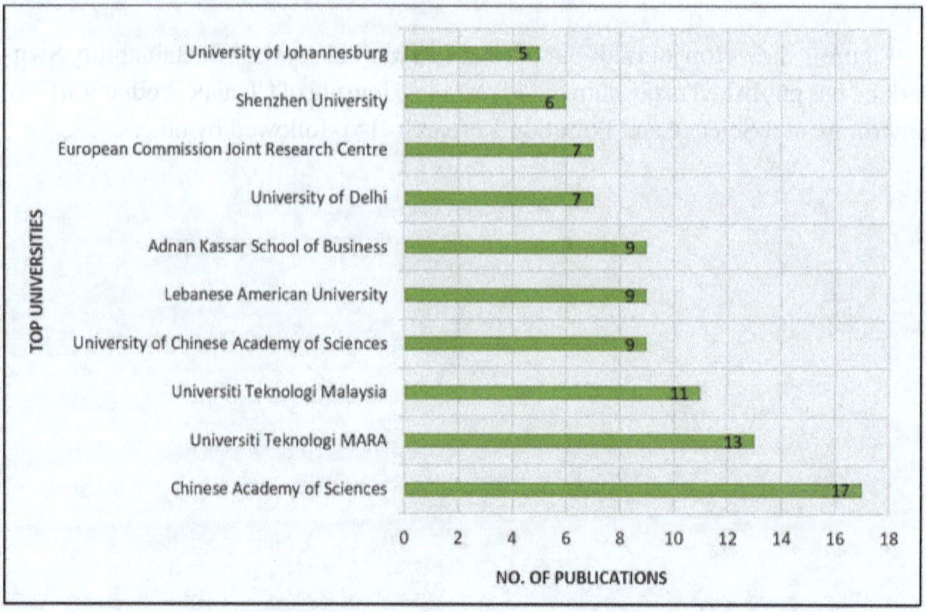

Figure 3 displays top 10 universities out of 160 affiliations, Chinese Academy of Sciences leading with (17) articles, Universiti Teknologi MARA with (13), Universiti Teknologi Malaysia (11), followed by others.

Figure 4. Document types

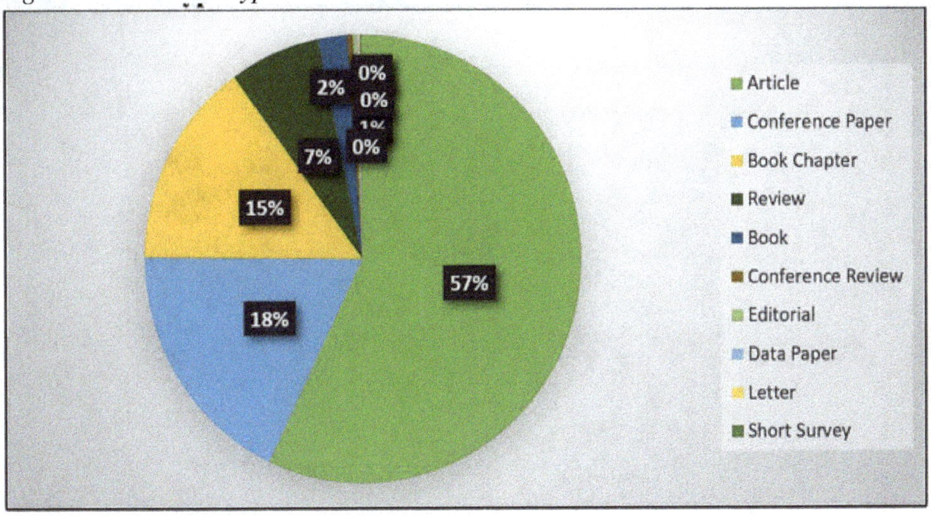

Figure 4 gives details about document types with 57% of articles published in English language on this subject area.

Table 1. Country-wise published documents

#	Country	Documents	Citations	Total Link Strength	#	Country	Documents	Citations	Total Link Strength
1	China	149	1814	125	11	South Africa	25	676	19
2	India	100	1320	69	12	Brazil	23	226	46
3	United States	96	2170	82	13	Turkey	23	366	37
4	Malaysia	69	721	68	14	Pakistan	22	369	38
5	United Kingdom	61	1769	133	15	Poland	22	298	34
6	Italy	40	805	66	16	Saudi Arabia	21	181	61
7	Australia	37	1267	73	17	Canada	19	324	15
8	Spain	35	559	49	18	Indonesia	19	275	18
9	Russian Federation	34	520	39	19	France	18	478	49
10	Germany	32	617	60	20	Portugal	17	324	30

Table 1 exhibits country-wise published documents with number of citations and total link strength.

Figure 5. Top 10 countries

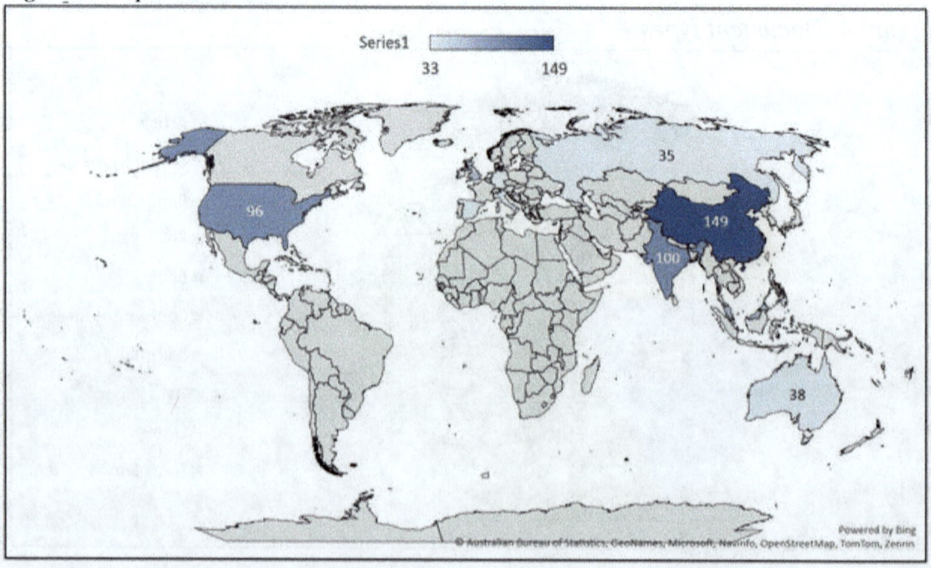

Figure 5. displays the world map of top 10 out of 108 countries, with China (149), India (100), United States of America (96) to Japan (33) documents published.

Figure 6. Top 10 funding agencies out of 159

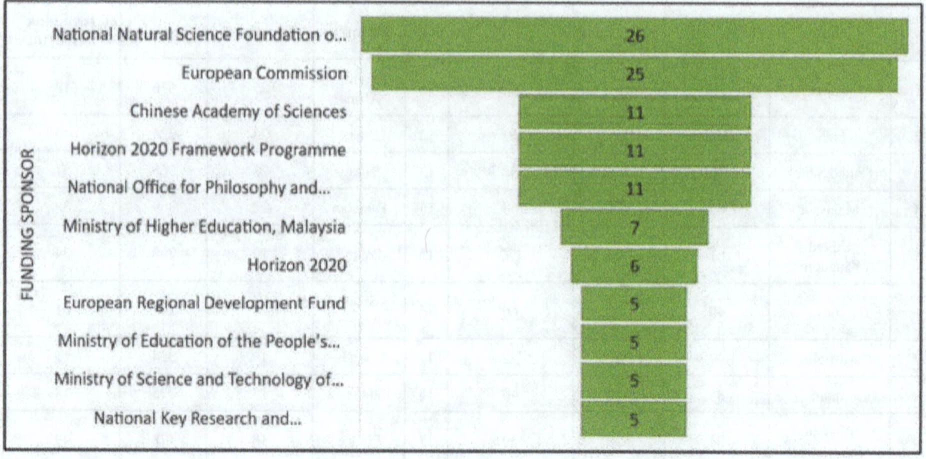

Figure 6 shows top 10 funding agencies out of 159 agencies.

Figure 7. Top subject areas

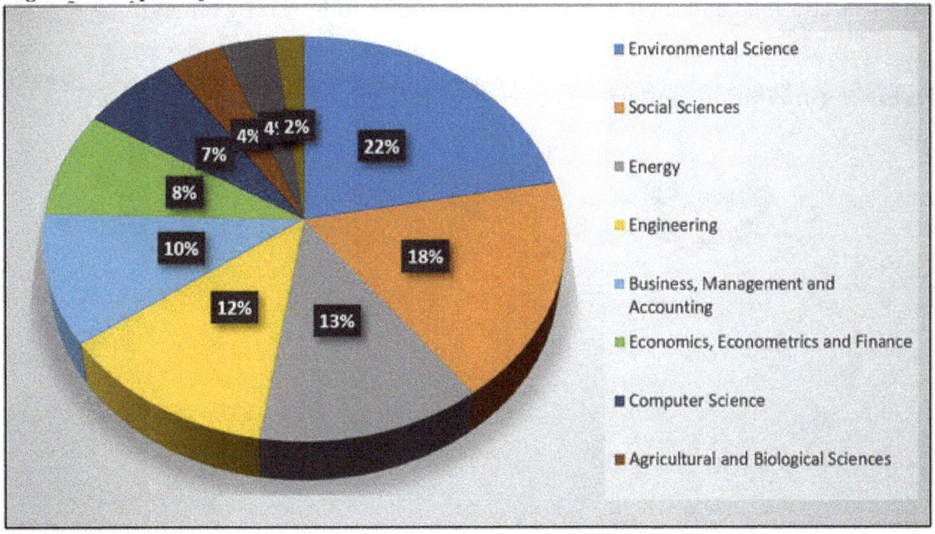

Figure 7 shows the preferred subject areas

Science Mapping Indicators

Table 2. Co-citation analysis of the most cited authors

#	Author	Citations	Total Link Strength	#	Author	Citations	Total Link Strength
1	Wang Y.	160	13630	11	Li X.	90	7195
2	Zhang Y.	143	10970	12	Sarkis J.	90	5153
3	Li Y.	131	10872	13	Chen Y.	89	7192
4	Zhang X.	115	8173	14	Zhang J.	85	8226
5	Liu Y.	111	9214	15	Adebayo T.S.	84	10530
6	Wang X.	111	9306	16	Liu J.	83	5551
7	Li J.	110	9341	17	Mohsin M.	78	8003
8	Shahbaz M.	99	9960	18	Wang Z.	78	8372
9	Wang J.	99	8180	19	Liu X.	77	7441
10	Taghizadeh-Hesary F.	96	7994	20	Ozturk I.	77	9012

Table 2 displays the Co-citation analysis of 20 most cited authors with citations and total link strength. Author wang y. leading with 160 citations and total link strength of 13630, zhang y. with 143 citations and total link strength of 10970, li y. with 131 citations and total link strength of 10872 followed by others.

Figure 8. Co-citation analysis of the most cited authors (Scopus Database)

Figure 8 displays the Co-citation analysis of the most cited authors with a network visualization using VOSviewer software.

Figure 9. Bibliographic coupling of journal sources (Scopus Database)

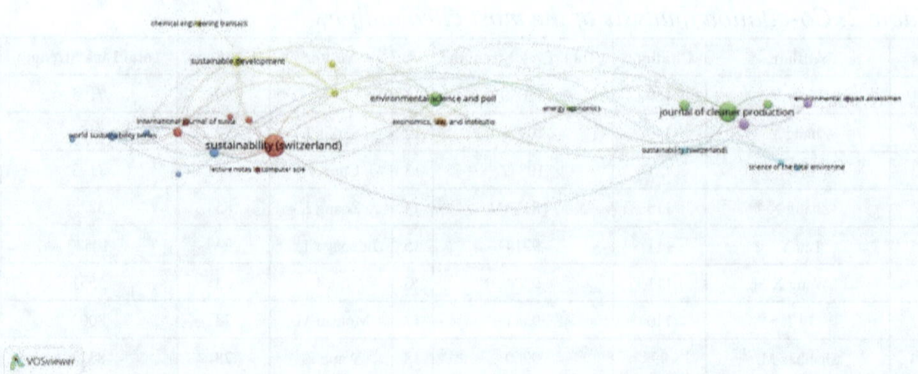

Figure 9 displays the bibliographic coupling of journal sources. It shows journal name, (documents, citations, total link strength) as sustainability Switzerland

(66,908,12), journal of cleaner production (58,2708,21), environmental science and pollution research (38,688,6), construction and building materials (28, 778,6), polymers (16,247,5), renewable & sustainable energy reviews (15,1481,4), journal of environmental management (11,393,2) and so on.

Figure 10. Co-citation of the most cited references (Scopus Database)

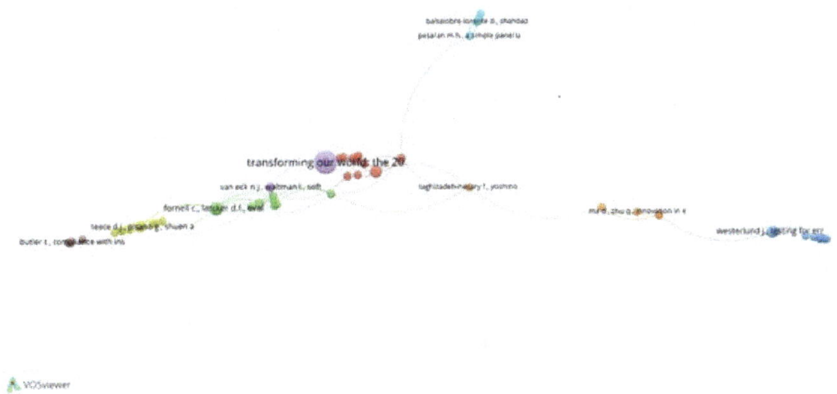

Figure 10 shows the co-citation of the most cited references with a network visualization.

Figure 11. Bibliographic coupling of countries (Scopus Database)

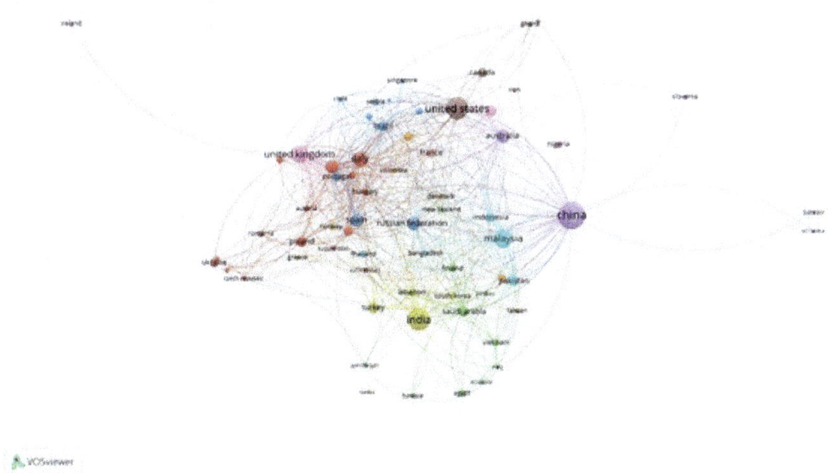

Figure 11 exhibits the selected network visualization mode for bibliographic coupling of countries in VOSviewer. It shows country China is collaborating with United States, India, Malasia, Indonesia, Australia and so on.

Table 3. Co-occurrence of all keywords

#	Keyword	Occurrences	Total Link Strength	#	Keyword	Occurrences	Total Link Strength
1	Sustainable Development	376	3057	11	Greenhouse Gases	41	459
2	Sustainability	156	1220	12	Environmental Impact	39	389
3	Climate Change	109	948	13	Green Finance	39	277
4	Sustainable Development Goal	89	781	14	Investments	39	463
5	Sustainable Development Goals	80	404	15	Renewable Energy	38	427
6	Environmental Protection	55	598	16	Innovation	36	334
7	Green Economy	53	463	17	Planning	36	361
8	Energy Efficiency	50	466	18	Carbon	35	444
9	China	46	511	19	Economic Development	34	407
10	Environmental Sustainability	42	381	20	Human	34	439

Table 3 displays the co-occurrence of all top 20 relevant keywords with number of occurrences and total link strength. It demonstrates that the top occurrence of keywords are "sustainable development" (376) times, "sustainability" (156), "climate change" (109), "sustainable development goal" (89), "environmental protection" (55), "green economy" (53), "energy efficiency" (50), followed by other keywords.

Figure 12. Co-Occurrence of all keywords (Scopus Database)

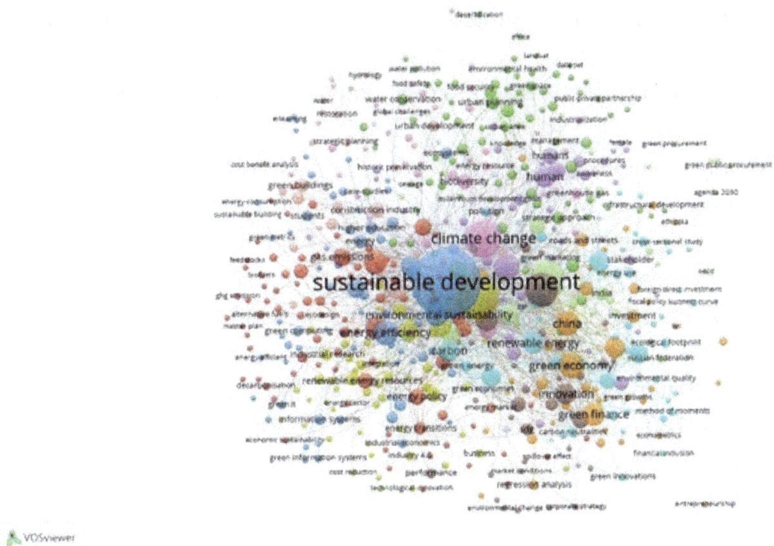

Figure 12 exhibits number of occurrences and keywords linking strength of the keyword color reflects the document typical publishing year in which keyword occurs.

LIMITATIONS

The analysis was limited to articles that were indexed in SCOPUS database only consequently, it's possible that publications from unidentified databases like PubMed and Web of Science were undetected.

CONCLUSION

The researchers answer the first five research questions (RQs) based on performance bibliometric analysis. Figure 1 displays the top journal sources out of total 116 journals.

Figure 2 shows combo chart of 789 cumulative publications, the year 2023 shows the maximum 196 publications. Many researchers around the world have publications on different subject areas 'Environmental Science' (336), 'Social Sciences' (270),

‘Energy’ (195) & so on with most of the document types as articles published in English language.

Figure 3 displays Chinese Academy of Sciences leading with (17) articles out of 160 affiliations. Table 1. represented the country (documents, citations, total link strength) with

China (149,1814,125), India (100,1320,69), United States (96,2170,82), followed by others.

The top funding agencies are found to be National Natural Science Foundation of China (26)

European Commission (25), Chinese Academy of Sciences (11) out of 159.

The researchers answer the last five research questions (RQs) based science mapping using VOSviewer software by selecting network visualization mode. Figure 8 displays the co-citation analysis of the most cited authors with a network visualization. Top 20 most cited authors with citations and total link strength, author Wang Y. leads with 160 citations. The bibliographic coupling of journal sources is displayed in Figure 9. The co-citation of the most cited references with a network visualization is shown in Figure 10. Figure 11. exhibits the bibliographic coupling of countries with China collaborating with United States, India, Malasia, Indonesia, Australia and so on. Figure 12. includes co-occurrence of all keywords of the subject area with top occurrence of keywords as “sustainable development” (376), “sustainability” (156) and “climate change” (109) times.

The study suggest that companies may use circular economy models, emphasizing long-term, repairable, and recyclable product design. Reducing energy and resource usage is often the result of implementing green initiatives. Adopting sustainable practices like recycling and waste reduction along with energy-efficient technologies can help businesses save a lot of money. The researcher’s find that the company's reputation and brand image can be improved by demonstrating a strong commitment to sustainability as these are gaining favour with customers. Green innovation sparked by a focus on sustainability, leads to the development of new products and services that cater to eco-conscious consumers. Future green initiatives are possible by real-time environmental effect monitoring, resource optimization and building sustainable supply chains for businesses.

REFERENCES

Ahmed, R. R., Streimikiene, D., & Zheng, X. (2021). The Impact of Proactive Environmental Strategy on Competitive and Sustainable Development of Organizations. *Journal of Competitiveness, 13*(4), 5–24. DOI: 10.7441/joc.2021.04.01

Arruda, T. de L., da Costa, F. P., Diniz, R. C., Rodrigues, A. M., Menezes, R. R., & Neves, G. de A. (2023). Statistical Design of Eco-Friendly Mortar Mixtures Containing Scheelite Tailings and Quartzite Sand: Evaluation of Resistance to Alkali-Aggregate Reaction. *Sustainability (Switzerland), 15*(15). Advance online publication. DOI: 10.3390/su151511544

Chen, S., Qiu, H., Xiao, H., He, W., Mou, J., & Siponen, M. (2021). Consumption behavior of eco-friendly products and applications of ICT innovation. *Journal of Cleaner Production, 287*. Advance online publication. DOI: 10.1016/j.jclepro.2020.125436

Faruk, M., Rahman, M., & Hasan, S. (2021). How digital marketing evolved over time: A bibliometric analysis on scopus database. In *Heliyon* (Vol. 7, Issue 12). Elsevier Ltd. https://doi.org/DOI: 10.1016/j.heliyon.2021.e08603

Hernández-barco, M., Sánchez-martín, J., Corbacho-cuello, I., & Cañada-cañada, F. (2021). Emotional performance of a low-cost eco-friendly project based learning methodology for science education: An approach in prospective teachers. *Sustainability (Switzerland), 13*(6). Advance online publication. DOI: 10.3390/su13063385

Jatsch, A. S., Jacobs, S., Wommer, K., & Wanieck, K. (2023). Biomimetics for Sustainable Developments—A Literature Overview of Trends. *Biomimetics, 8*(3). Advance online publication. DOI: 10.3390/biomimetics8030304 PMID: 37504192

Kannan, P. (2019). *Bibliometric Analysis of Library Philosophy and Practice: A study based on Scopus Database*. https://digitalcommons.unl.edu/libphilprac

Khan, M. H., & Muktar, S. N. (2020). A bibliometric analysis of green human resource management based on scopus platform. *Cogent Business & Management, 7*(1). Advance online publication. DOI: 10.1080/23311975.2020.1831165

Kokkhangplu, A., Onlamai, W., Chokpreedapanich, T., & Phikul, K. (2023). What Predicts Behavioral Intention in Eco-Friendly Hotels? The Roles of Tourist's Perceived Value and Satisfaction: A Case Study of Thailand. *Sustainability (Switzerland), 15*(4). Advance online publication. DOI: 10.3390/su15043219

Mahmood, A., Farooq, A., Akbar, H., Ghani, H. U., & Gheewala, S. H. (2023). An Integrated Approach to Analyze the Progress of Developing Economies in Asia toward the Sustainable Development Goals. *Sustainability (Switzerland), 15*(18). Advance online publication. DOI: 10.3390/su151813645

Mbokane, L., & Modley, L. A. (2024). Green Consumerism in Young Adults: Attitudes and Awareness in University Students in Johannesburg, South Africa. *Sustainability (Switzerland), 16*(5). Advance online publication. DOI: 10.3390/su16051898

Md Khudzari, J., Kurian, J., Tartakovsky, B., & Raghavan, G. S. V. (2018). Bibliometric analysis of global research trends on microbial fuel cells using Scopus database. *Biochemical Engineering Journal, 136*, 51–60. DOI: 10.1016/j.bej.2018.05.002

Pimonenko, T., Bilan, Y., Horák, J., Starchenko, L., & Gajda, W. (2020). Green brand of companies and greenwashing under sustainable development goals. *Sustainability (Switzerland), 12*(4). Advance online publication. DOI: 10.3390/su12041679

Saari, U. A., Baumgartner, R. J., & Mäkinen, S. J. (2017). Eco-friendly brands to drive sustainable development: Replication and extension of the brand experience scale in a cross-national context. *Sustainability (Switzerland), 9*(7). Advance online publication. DOI: 10.3390/su9071286

Xu, K., Yang, M., Yang, J., Nataliia, B., Cai, Y., Zhang, H., & Wang, Y. (2024). Mapping scholarly publications of energy conservation and emission reduction in support of the sustainable development goals (SDGs). In *Frontiers in Environmental Science* (Vol. 12). Frontiers Media SA. https://doi.org/DOI: 10.3389/fenvs.2024.1421990

Chapter 2

A Comprehensive Bibliometric Analysis of Soft Robotics Research: Trends, Impact, and Future Directions

Souvik Banerjee
https://orcid.org/0000-0001-9988-8887
Management Development Institute Murshidabad, Murshidabad, India

Jogen Sharma
https://orcid.org/0000-0001-7151-0137
KIIT University, India

Abhijit Pandit
https://orcid.org/0000-0003-2122-3468
Management Development Institute Murshidabad, Murshidabad, India

ABSTRACT

This report presents a comprehensive bibliometric analysis of the soft robotics research landscape, drawing upon a Scopus-derived dataset. The study meticulously examines publication trends, identifies influential documents, leading authors, prominent institutions, key publication outlets, and the global distribution of research efforts. Findings reveal a field characterised by exponential growth in scientific production, particularly since 2013, driven by advancements in materials science, novel fabrication techniques like 3D/4D printing, and bio-inspired design principles. The analysis highlights the significant contributions of pioneering researchers and institutions, predominantly from the USA, with a notable recent surge in output

DOI: 10.4018/979-8-3373-4652-6.ch002

from Asian countries. While the field demonstrates a robust intellectual framework and diverse applications in human-robot interaction and biomedicine, challenges about long-term durability, standardised characterisation, energy autonomy, and complex control strategies persist.

INTRODUCTION

Soft robotics is quite dynamic and involves many experts from many professions. It differs from rigid robotics. Use of flexible, compliant materials to create robots that can safely operate with people and adapt to unstructured environments is its main strength. This method mimics biological systems' complicated movements and adaptability, such as an octopus arm's precision movement or an earthworm's effortless movement. Soft robots are flexible and safe, making them a transformative tool for personalised healthcare, assistive devices, manufacturing, and environmental exploration.

A rigorous bibliometric examination is necessary to understand the dynamics, structure, and intellectual development of this burgeoning scientific field. These studies meticulously map a research topic's intellectual landscape, identifying key trends, contributions, and new fields. This report uses carefully selected Scopus data to provide a detailed bibliometric overview of soft robotics research. The purpose is to examine publishing trends and identify the most influential papers, authors, organisations, and nations. This study also seeks important topics and potential research directions. This will give academics and stakeholders a solid foundation in this new field.

METHODOLOGY

For this bibliometric analysis, Scopus, a renowned peer-reviewed literature abstract and citation database, was used. Keywords related to "soft robotics" were used to cover the domain. In Scopus soft robotics top 100 paper.csv and BiblioshinyReport-2025-07-08_jogen.xlsx, the raw data was provided. For uniformity and completeness, robotics.xlsx - Sheet.csv was used to cross-reference paper abstracts and citation counts.

The following bibliometric indicators were used:

- **Publication Volume:** Measured by the total number of articles published per year and by different entities such as authors, affiliations, countries, and publication sources.

- **Citation Impact:** Assessed through several metrics:
    - o **Total Citations (TC):** The cumulative number of times a document has been cited across all Scopus sources.
    - o **Local Citations:** Citations specifically from within the analysed dataset.
    - o **Global Citations:** Citations from all Scopus sources.
    - o **Citations per Year (TCpY):** The average number of citations received annually, providing a normalized measure of recent impact.
- **Author and Source Impact Metrics:**
    - o **h-index:** A metric reflecting both the productivity and citation impact of a researcher or publication, indicating that 'h' papers have at least 'h' citations each.
    - o **g-index:** An alternative to the h-index, giving more weight to highly cited articles.
    - o **m-index:** The h-index divided by the number of years since the first publication, normalizing for career length.
    - o **Number of Publications (NP):** The raw count of published articles.
- **Fractionalized Articles:** To account for collaborative authorship, this metric assigns a fraction of an article's credit to each author based on the total number of authors.

The file name conventions in the dataset show that Biblioshiny, a web-based tool for bibliometric analysis, was used to handle the data and do the first analysis. To make the full story in this report, the processed data were looked at again and put together in a new way.

RESULTS AND ANALYSIS

Global Scientific Production and Citation Trends

There has been a huge increase in research in the field of soft robotics, especially in the previous ten years. A look at the yearly scientific output shows that there was a time of slow foundational growth, followed by a big jump in research effort. In 1999, there was just one article about soft robotics. This number grew to three by 2004 and two by 2008.This early stage indicates a new area of study, with scientists looking into basic ideas and early uses.

A turning point was in 2013, when six publications were published annually, resulting in rapid growth. Seven papers were published in 2014 and 2015, and eight in 2016. 15 articles became 17 in 2017, the most increase. From 2013 to 2018, soft robotics papers increased rapidly, indicating its rapid growth and attention.

The subject attracted additional academics and resources as the foundation paid off. As a new scientific field gains popularity and becomes known to the scientific community, this growth is normal.

From then on, output dropped to 8 pieces in 2019, 6 in 2020, 7 in 2021, and 6 in 2022. Production is still much higher than before 2017. It could be a delay in acquiring data for new papers or a sign that research is maturing. The field's enduring number of articles proves its strength and longevity. A growing number of papers and citations suggests that soft robotics research is becoming more relevant and impacting scientific literature.

Table 1. Annual scientific production (1999-2022)

Year	Articles
1999	1
2000	0
2001	0
2002	0
2003	0
2004	3
2005	1
2006	0
2007	1
2008	2
2009	0
2010	1
2011	1
2012	3
2013	6
2014	7
2015	7
2016	8
2017	15
2018	17
2019	8
2020	6
2021	7
2022	6

Data from [1]

Most Influential Documents

Effective documents shape the direction and principles of any research domain. Top soft robotics articles demonstrate advancements and concepts that inspired later research.

Among the most cited works, Kim, Laschi, and Trimmer (2013)'s "Soft robotics: A bioinspired evolution in robotics" has 1744 citations. This landmark review work highlighted its bio-inspired foundations, enabling technologies and challenges, and predicting tissue engineering convergence. Since it's been quoted so much, it helped shape soft robotics' early scope and capabilities. By Kim et al. (2018), "Printing ferromagnetic domains for untethered fast-transforming soft materials" has 1766 citations. The 3D printing of magnetic soft materials allowed quick, uncontrolled changes, expanding applications from flexible electronics to medication delivery. Though it was released lately, it has had a large impact on fabrication and actuation methods in the field, as seen by its many citations.

Mosadegh et al.'s (2014) "Pneumatic networks for soft robotics that actuate rapidly" is another very important study that has been cited 1393 times. This research presented an innovative design for pneumatic networks (pneu-nets) that significantly enhanced actuation speed and reliability, mitigating a crucial performance constraint of early soft actuators and rendering them more applicable for real-world applications. Polygerinos et al.'s (2015) paper "Soft robotic glove for combined assistance and at-home rehabilitation," which has been cited 1368 times, is a good example of how soft robotics can be used in rehabilitation to help people directly through assistive equipment.

Other works that are often mentioned also show how important the field's intellectual pillars are. "Variable impedance actuators: A review" (Vanderborght et al., 2013), "Soft robot arm inspired by the octopus" (Laschi et al., 2012), and "Modelling of Soft Fiber-Reinforced Bending Actuators" (Polygerinos et al., 2015) are some of these. The high number of citations for review articles and foundational methodological works shows that the subject is quickly solidifying its main ideas and aggressively setting its limits and future paths. This pattern indicates that the early to mid-2010s were pivotal in laying the theoretical and practical foundations for soft robotics, resulting in a significant increase in applied research, as seen by the subsequent rise in publications. These papers are crucial for fresh scholars and veterans who are expanding their knowledge. They shape the field's theory and experiments.

The abstracts of these influential documents reveal several recurring themes:

- **Bio-inspiration:** A core design principle involves mimicking biological systems, such as octopus arms, human muscles, and gecko adhesion.
- **Materials Science:** Fundamental to the field is the development of new soft, stretchable, and responsive materials, including various elastomers, hydrogels, liquid metals, and ferromagnetic domains.
- **Fabrication Techniques:** Additive manufacturing, particularly 3D printing (e.g., Digital Light Processing, embedded printing), is crucial for creating complex soft structures and integrating multiple functionalities.
- **Actuation Mechanisms:** Prominent actuation methods include pneumatic networks, dielectric elastomers, and magnetic actuation.
- **Applications:** A strong emphasis is placed on human-robot interaction, medical devices (e.g., rehabilitation, surgery, drug delivery), and wearable electronics.
- **Sensing and Control:** The integration of soft sensors and the development of sophisticated control strategies for compliant systems are recognized as critical challenges and active areas of research.

Table 2. Top 10 most cited documents (global citations)

Title	Authors	Year	Cited by	Abstract Snippet
Printing ferromagnetic domains for untethered fast-transforming soft materials	Kim Y.; Yuk H.; Zhao R.; Chester S.A.; Zhao X.	2018	1766	Soft materials capable of transforming between three-dimensional (3D) shapes in response to stimuli such as light, heat, solvent, electric and magnetic fields have applications in diverse areas such as flexible electronics, soft robotics and biomedicine. Here we report 3D printing of programmed ferromagnetic domains in soft materials that enable fast transformations between complex 3D shapes via magnetic actuation.
Soft robotics: A bioinspired evolution in robotics	Kim S.; Laschi C.; Trimmer B.	2013	1744	The paper reviews a recent development in soft robotics. Soft materials in animals inspire a new wave of robotics. Current enabling technologies in soft robotics and challenges are discussed. Potential convergence between soft robotics and tissue engineering is introduced.
Pneumatic networks for soft robotics that actuate rapidly	Mosadegh B.; Polygerinos P.; Keplinger C.; Wennstedt S.; Shepherd R.F.; Gupta U.; Shim J.; Bertoldi K.; Walsh C.J.; Whitesides G.M.	2014	1393	Soft robots actuated by inflation of a pneumatic network (a "pneu-net") of small channels in elastomeric materials are appealing for producing sophisticated motions with simple controls. This paper describes a new design for pneu-nets that reduces the amount of gas needed for inflation of the pneu-net, and thus increases its speed of actuation.

continued on following page

Table 2. Continued

Title	Authors	Year	Cited by	Abstract Snippet
Soft robotic glove for combined assistance and at-home rehabilitation	Polygerinos P.; Wang Z.; Galloway K.C.; Wood R.J.; Walsh C.J.	2015	1368	This paper presents a portable, assistive, soft robotic glove designed to augment hand rehabilitation for individuals with functional grasp pathologies. The robotic glove utilizes soft actuators consisting of moulded elastomeric chambers with fibre reinforcements that induce specific bending, twisting and extending trajectories under fluid pressurization.
Variable impedance actuators: A review	Vanderborght B.; Albu-Schaeffer A.; Bicchi A.; Burdet E.; Caldwell D.G.; Carloni R.; Catalano M.; Eiberger O.; Friedl W.; Ganesh G.; Garabini M.; Grebenstein M.; Grioli G.; Haddadin S.; Hoppner H.; Jafari A.; Laffranchi M.; Lefeber D.; Petit F.; Stramigioli S.; Tsagarakis N.; Van Damme M.; Van Ham R.; Visser L.C.; Wolf S.	2013	910	Variable Impedance Actuators (VIA) have received increasing attention in recent years as many novel applications involving interactions with an unknown and dynamic environment including humans require actuators with dynamics that are not well-achieved by classical stiff actuators. This paper presents an overview of the different VIAs developed and proposes a classification based on the principles through which the variable stiffness and damping are achieved.
Soft robot arm inspired by the octopus	Laschi C.; Cianchetti M.; Mazzolai B.; Margheri L.; Follador M.; Dario P.	2012	891	The octopus is a marine animal whose body has no rigid structures. It has eight arms composed of a peculiar muscular structure, named a muscular hydrostat. The octopus arms provide it with both locomotion and grasping capabilities, thanks to the fact that their stiffness can change over a wide range and can be controlled through combined contractions of the muscles.
Modeling of Soft Fiber-Reinforced Bending Actuators	Polygerinos P.; Wang Z.; Overvelde J.T.B.; Galloway K.C.; Wood R.J.; Bertoldi K.; Walsh C.J.	2015	851	Soft fluidic actuators consisting of elastomeric matrices with embedded flexible materials are of particular interest to the robotics community because they are affordable and can be easily customized to a given application. However, the significant potential of such actuators is currently limited as their design has typically been based on intuition.
Soft Robotics: Review of Fluid-Driven Intrinsically Soft Devices; Manufacturing, Sensing, Control, and Applications in Human-Robot Interaction	Polygerinos P.; Correll N.; Morin S.A.; Mosadegh B.; Onal C.D.; Petersen K.; Cianchetti M.; Tolley M.T.; Shepherd R.F.	2017	833	The emerging field of soft robotics makes use of many classes of materials including metals, low glass transition temperature (Tg) plastics, and high Tg elastomers. Dependent on the specific design, all of these materials may result in extrinsically soft robots. Organic elastomers, however, have elastic moduli ranging from tens of megapascals down to kilopascals; robots composed of such materials are intrinsically soft – they are always compliant independent of their shape.

continued on following page

Table 2. Continued

Title	Authors	Year	Cited by	Abstract Snippet
25th anniversary article: A soft future: From robots and sensor skin to energy harvesters	Bauer S.; Bauer-Gogonea S.; Graz I.; Kaltenbrunner M.; Keplinger C.; Schwödiauer R.	2014	780	Scientists are exploring elastic and soft forms of robots, electronic skin and energy harvesters, dreaming to mimic nature and to enable novel applications in wide fields, from consumer and mobile appliances to biomedical systems, sports and healthcare. All conceivable classes of materials with a wide range of mechanical, physical and chemical properties are employed, from liquids and gels to organic and inorganic solids.
Force modeling for needle insertion into soft tissue	Okamura A.M.; Simone C.; O'Leary M.D.	2004	774	The modelling of forces during needle insertion into soft tissue is important for accurate surgical simulation, preoperative planning, and intelligent robotic assistance for percutaneous therapies. We present a force model for needle insertion and experimental procedures for acquiring data from ex vivo tissue to populate that model.

Data compiled from [1]

Table 3. Top 10 most locally cited references

Cited References	Citations
RUS D., TOLLEY M.T., NATURE, 521, (2015)	15
SHEPHERD R.F., ILIEVSKI F., CHOI W., MORIN S.A., STOKES A.A., MAZZEO A.D., CHEN X., WANG M., WHITESIDES G.M., PROC. NATL. ACAD. SCI. USA, 108, (2011)	12
RUS D., TOLLEY M.T., DESIGN, FABRICATION AND CONTROL OF SOFT ROBOTS, NATURE, 521, PP. 467-475, (2015)	10
KIM S., LASCHI C., TRIMMER B., SOFT ROBOTICS: A BIOINSPIRED EVOLUTION IN ROBOTICS, TRENDS BIOTECHNOL, 31, PP. 287-294, (2013)	8
WEHNER M., TRUBY R.L., FITZGERALD D.J., MOSADEGH B., WHITESIDES G.M., LEWIS J.A., WOOD R.J., NATURE, 536, (2016)	8
BROWN E., RODENBERG N., AMEND J., MOZEIKA A., STELTZ E., ZAKIN M.R., LIPSON H., JAEGER H.M., PROC. NATL. ACAD. SCI. USA, 107, (2010)	7
KEPLINGER C., SUN J.-Y., FOO C.C., ROTHEMUND P., WHITESIDES G.M., SUO Z., SCIENCE, 341, (2013)	6
KIM S., LASCHI C., TRIMMER B., TRENDS BIOTECHNOL., 31, (2013)	6
KOFOD G., WIRGES W., PAAJANEN M., BAUER S., APPL. PHYS. LETT., 90, (2007)	6
LARSON C., PEELE B., LI S., ROBINSON S., TOTARO M., BECCAI L., MAZZOLAI B., SHEPHERD R., SCIENCE, 351, (2016)	6

Data from [1]

Key Authors and Their Impact

A small group of very prolific and influential academics has a big impact on the intellectual landscape of soft robotics. Their work always gets a lot of attention and leads to new ideas. Robert J. Wood stands out as a top figure, with an impressive h-index of 10, a g-index of 10, and an m-index of 0.769. He has 6329 citations over 10 publications. 1 His fractionalised article counts of 1.803 further emphasises the important contributions he made while working with others. His most recent works, such as "Realising the Potential of Dielectric Elastomer Artificial Muscles" (2019, 346 total citations) and "Soft Somatosensitive Actuators via Embedded 3D Printing" (2018, 491 total citations), show how he is still making a difference in the fields of advanced materials and fabrication for soft robotics.

Conor J. Walsh is another well-known author. He has an h-index of 8, a g-index of 8, and an m-index of 0.666, and his 8 papers have been cited 5597 times. His article count is 1.176, which is a portion of the whole. 1 Katia Bertoldi, Cecilia Laschi, and George M. Whitesides are also among of the most important authors, with fractionalised article counts of 1.301, 1.75, and 1.8, respectively.

These writers are often linked to the highly referenced publications that were talked about earlier, which shows that they have made important and lasting contributions to the subject. Robert J. Wood and Conor J. Walsh, for example, are always co-authors on articles about soft robotic gloves, exosuits, and sophisticated actuation and sensing. These studies often come from Harvard University. The significant number of fractionalised articles by these academics suggests that they had important roles in many important publications. The fact that these writers always show up at the top of impact lists shows that strong research groups and collaboration networks are forming. These networks are very important for ongoing, high-impact research because they bring together people with different kinds of knowledge, from materials science and mechanical design to control theory. Solving soft robotics' complex, transdisciplinary challenges requires this. Working collaboratively to improve each person's genius is good team science in this profession.

Table 4. Leading authors by productivity and impact

Author	h_index	g_index	m_index	TC	NP	Articles	Articles Fractionalized
WOOD, ROBERT J.	10	10	0.769	6329	10	10	1.80357142857143
WALSH, CONOR J.	8	8	0.666	5597	8	8	1.17662337662338
BERTOLDI, KATIA	7	7	0.583	4995	7	7	1.30119047619048
LASCHI, CECILIA	6	6	0.5	3173	6	6	1.75
WHITESIDES, GEORGE M.	6	6	0.461	3501	6	6	1.8

Data from [1]

Table 5. Author production over time (top authors)

Author	Year	Title	Source	DOI	TC	TCpY
WOOD, ROBERT J.	2019	REALIZING THE POTENTIAL OF DIELECTRIC ELASTOMER ARTIFICIAL MUSCLES	PROCEEDINGS OF THE NATIONAL ACADEMY OF SCIENCES OF THE UNITED STATES OF AMERICA	10.1073/ pnas.1815053116	346	49.4285714285714
WOOD, ROBERT J.	2018	SOFT SOMATOSENSITIVE ACTUATORS VIA EMBEDDED 3D PRINTING	ADVANCED MATERIALS	10.1002/ adma.201706383	491	61.375
WOOD, ROBERT J.	2018	UNTETHERED SOFT ROBOTICS	NATURE ELECTRONICS	10.1038/s41928-018-0024-1	491	61.375
WALSH, CONOR J.	2017	A SOFT ROBOTIC EXOSUIT IMPROVES WALKING IN PATIENTS AFTER STROKE	SCIENCE TRANSLATIONAL MEDICINE	10.1126/scitranslmed. aai8999	489	69.8571428571429
WALSH, CONOR J.	2017	AUTOMATIC DESIGN OF FIBER-REINFORCED SOFT ACTUATORS FOR TRAJECTORY MATCHING	PROCEEDINGS OF THE NATIONAL ACADEMY OF SCIENCES OF THE UNITED STATES OF AMERICA	10.1073/ pnas.1616512114	443	63.2857142857143
WALSH, CONOR J.	2015	SOFT ROBOTIC GLOVE FOR COMBINED ASSISTANCE AND AT-HOME REHABILITATION	ROBOTICS AND AUTONOMOUS SYSTEMS	10.1016/j. robot.2014.08.014	1368	195.428571428571
BERTOLDI, KATIA	2015	BUCKLING OF ELASTOMERIC BEAMS ENABLES ACTUATION OF SOFT MACHINES	ADVANCED MATERIALS	10.1002/ adma.201502422	286	40.8571428571429
BERTOLDI, KATIA	2015	DIELECTRIC ELASTOMER BASED "GRIPPERS" FOR SOFT ROBOTICS	ADVANCED MATERIALS	10.1002/ adma.201501792	429	61.2857142857143
LASCHI, CECILIA	2013	SOFT ROBOTICS: A BIOINSPIRED EVOLUTION IN ROBOTICS	TRENDS IN BIOTECHNOLOGY	10.1016/j. tibtech.2013.03.002	1744	249.142857142857
WHITESIDES, GEORGE M.	2014	PNEUMATIC NETWORKS FOR SOFT ROBOTICS THAT ACTUATE RAPIDLY	ADVANCED FUNCTIONAL MATERIALS	10.1002/adfm.201400202	1393	199

Data from [1]

Leading Institutions and Their Contributions

Several productive soft robotics research institutions have shaped the field. Harvard University adds the most papers, 69. Tianjin University has 19, Nanyang Technological University 20, the Biorobotics Institute 16, and MIT 14. Small colleges that perform a lot of research have invested a lot of money, skill, and infrastructure. Brilliance attracts resources and outstanding researchers, strengthening their leadership.

Historical institutional productivity can assist us understand how their functions are changing. Papers at Harvard University increased from 4 in 2012 to 69 in 2018–2022. Harvard is a big participant in speeding things up, as this expansion matches general soft robotics growth. From one paper in 2017 to 20 in 2021–2022, Nanyang Technological University expanded. Tianjin University, a new add, has 19 articles in 2022, up from zero in 2021. From 2012 to 2017, the Biorobotics Institute produced five books annually. After that, it produced 13 articles in 2018 and 16 in 2019–2022. MIT published 14 publications in 2022, up from 1 in 2013. The fact that these institutions continue to produce work illustrates their long-term commitment to soft robotics research and capacity to create competence. These schools have excelled because they have soft robotics research programs or labs. Collaboration has fostered great discoveries.

Table 6. Top 5 affiliations by article count

Affiliation	Articles
HARVARD UNIVERSITY	69
NANYANG TECHNOLOGICAL UNIVERSITY	20
TIANJIN UNIVERSITY	19
BIOROBOTICS INSTITUTE	16
MASSACHUSETTS INSTITUTE OF TECHNOLOGY	14

Data from [1]

Table 7. Affiliation production over time (top 5 affiliations)

Affiliation	Year	Articles
BIOROBOTICS INSTITUTE	2004	0
BIOROBOTICS INSTITUTE	2005	0
BIOROBOTICS INSTITUTE	2007	0

continued on following page

Table 7. Continued

Affiliation	Year	Articles
BIOROBOTICS INSTITUTE	2008	0
BIOROBOTICS INSTITUTE	2010	0
BIOROBOTICS INSTITUTE	2012	5
BIOROBOTICS INSTITUTE	2013	5
BIOROBOTICS INSTITUTE	2014	5
BIOROBOTICS INSTITUTE	2015	5
BIOROBOTICS INSTITUTE	2016	5
BIOROBOTICS INSTITUTE	2017	5
BIOROBOTICS INSTITUTE	2018	13
BIOROBOTICS INSTITUTE	2019	16
BIOROBOTICS INSTITUTE	2020	16
BIOROBOTICS INSTITUTE	2021	16
BIOROBOTICS INSTITUTE	2022	16
HARVARD UNIVERSITY	2004	0
HARVARD UNIVERSITY	2005	0
HARVARD UNIVERSITY	2007	0
HARVARD UNIVERSITY	2008	0
HARVARD UNIVERSITY	2010	0
HARVARD UNIVERSITY	2012	4
HARVARD UNIVERSITY	2013	12
HARVARD UNIVERSITY	2014	22
HARVARD UNIVERSITY	2015	27
HARVARD UNIVERSITY	2016	30
HARVARD UNIVERSITY	2017	56
HARVARD UNIVERSITY	2018	64
HARVARD UNIVERSITY	2019	64
HARVARD UNIVERSITY	2020	69
HARVARD UNIVERSITY	2021	69
HARVARD UNIVERSITY	2022	69
MASSACHUSETTS INSTITUTE OF TECHNOLOGY	2004	0
MASSACHUSETTS INSTITUTE OF TECHNOLOGY	2005	0
MASSACHUSETTS INSTITUTE OF TECHNOLOGY	2007	0
MASSACHUSETTS INSTITUTE OF TECHNOLOGY	2008	0
MASSACHUSETTS INSTITUTE OF TECHNOLOGY	2010	0

continued on following page

Table 7. Continued

Affiliation	Year	Articles
MASSACHUSETTS INSTITUTE OF TECHNOLOGY	2012	0
MASSACHUSETTS INSTITUTE OF TECHNOLOGY	2013	1
MASSACHUSETTS INSTITUTE OF TECHNOLOGY	2014	1
MASSACHUSETTS INSTITUTE OF TECHNOLOGY	2015	1
MASSACHUSETTS INSTITUTE OF TECHNOLOGY	2016	1
MASSACHUSETTS INSTITUTE OF TECHNOLOGY	2017	2
MASSACHUSETTS INSTITUTE OF TECHNOLOGY	2018	6
MASSACHUSETTS INSTITUTE OF TECHNOLOGY	2019	6
MASSACHUSETTS INSTITUTE OF TECHNOLOGY	2020	6
MASSACHUSETTS INSTITUTE OF TECHNOLOGY	2021	12
MASSACHUSETTS INSTITUTE OF TECHNOLOGY	2022	14
NANYANG TECHNOLOGICAL UNIVERSITY	2004	0
NANYANG TECHNOLOGICAL UNIVERSITY	2005	0
NANYANG TECHNOLOGICAL UNIVERSITY	2007	0
NANYANG TECHNOLOGICAL UNIVERSITY	2008	0
NANYANG TECHNOLOGICAL UNIVERSITY	2010	0
NANYANG TECHNOLOGICAL UNIVERSITY	2012	0
NANYANG TECHNOLOGICAL UNIVERSITY	2013	0
NANYANG TECHNOLOGICAL UNIVERSITY	2014	0
NANYANG TECHNOLOGICAL UNIVERSITY	2015	0
NANYANG TECHNOLOGICAL UNIVERSITY	2016	1
NANYANG TECHNOLOGICAL UNIVERSITY	2017	1
NANYANG TECHNOLOGICAL UNIVERSITY	2018	1
NANYANG TECHNOLOGICAL UNIVERSITY	2019	8
NANYANG TECHNOLOGICAL UNIVERSITY	2020	8
NANYANG TECHNOLOGICAL UNIVERSITY	2021	20
NANYANG TECHNOLOGICAL UNIVERSITY	2022	20
TIANJIN UNIVERSITY	2004	0
TIANJIN UNIVERSITY	2005	0
TIANJIN UNIVERSITY	2007	0
TIANJIN UNIVERSITY	2008	0
TIANJIN UNIVERSITY	2010	0
TIANJIN UNIVERSITY	2012	0
TIANJIN UNIVERSITY	2013	0

continued on following page

Table 7. Continued

Affiliation	Year	Articles
TIANJIN UNIVERSITY	2014	0
TIANJIN UNIVERSITY	2015	0
TIANJIN UNIVERSITY	2016	0
TIANJIN UNIVERSITY	2017	0
TIANJIN UNIVERSITY	2018	0
TIANJIN UNIVERSITY	2019	0
TIANJIN UNIVERSITY	2020	0
TIANJIN UNIVERSITY	2021	13
TIANJIN UNIVERSITY	2022	19

Data from [1]

Prominent Publication Outlets

Selection of soft robotics research publication sites reflects quality, readership, and multidisciplinary nature. Certain publications and conference papers are notable for their fieldwork.

As one of the greatest locations to locate publications, Advanced Materials has 19. With 10,420 published citations since 2013, it has an h-index of 19, g-index of 19, and m-index of 1.46. The proliferation of cutting-edge materials science research for soft robotics is crucial. Similarly, PNAS is crucial. From 2016 publications, it has 3,489 citations, 8 articles, 8 h-indices, 8 g-indices, and 0.8 m-indices. PNAS reveals that soft robotics research produces high-impact, multidisciplinary breakthroughs recognised across scientific disciplines.

The 6 articles by Advanced Functional Materials have an h-index of 6, g-index of 6, m-index of 0.428, and 4,487 total citations from 2012 publications. Functional materials are the subject of this publication, emphasising material innovation as essential to soft robotics. The new magazine Soft Robotics has swiftly become a prominent venue with 5 articles, an h-index of 5, g-index of 5, m-index of 0.555, and 1,965 total citations since its 2017 launch. Soft Robotics is a significant venue, indicating that the area has evolved enough to justify its own dedicated publication, indicating a well-defined research community.

The field's evolution is characterised by the dominance of general-purpose high-impact publications like PNAS and specialised materials science journals like Advanced Materials and Advanced Functional Materials, as well as Soft Robotics. This pattern suggests that soft robotics research is providing important advancements in other scientific and engineering fields as well as its own. These multidisciplinary connections indicate the field's intellectual health and potential for broad application and effect.

Table 8. Top 5 publication sources by article count and impact

Source	Articles	h_index	g_index	m_index	TC	NP	PY_ start
ADVANCED MATERIALS	19	19	19	1.46153846153846	10420	19	2013
PROCEEDINGS OF THE NATIONAL ACADEMY OF SCIENCES OF THE UNITED STATES OF AMERICA	8	8	8	0.8	3489	8	2016
ADVANCED FUNCTIONAL MATERIALS	6	6	6	0.428571428571429	4487	6	2012
SOFT ROBOTICS	5	5	5	0.555555555555556	1965	5	2017

Data from [1]

Geographic Distribution of Research

Soft robotics research is global, yet some countries lead. USA research has consistently been the most prolific, rising from 4 in 1999 to 278 in 2022. Its constant output suggests that the US has spent much in the area for a long time.

Italy also grew steadily, from 2 articles in 2004 to 49 in 2018–2022. Germany has steadily increased from 1 article in 2004 to 36 in 2020–2022.

Asian countries have become major contributors in recent years, indicating global soft robotics research growth. China published 56 articles in 2022, up from none in 2017. Singapore contributed 31 articles in 2021–2022, up from 0 before 2016.

Asian countries, especially China and Singapore, have increased research output rapidly in recent years, but the US remains the leader. This suggests that scientific investment and capacity building are becoming more diversified worldwide. This indicates that soft robotics is not limited to conventional Western research centres but is transforming into a global collaborative initiative, with growing regional hubs that may drive future progress. This geographical diversification could result in a wider array of research methodologies and applications, potentially customised to regional requirements and advantages, therefore enhancing the discipline overall. The growing contributions from many areas encourage more cooperation between countries and, possibly, more rivalry for intellectual leadership and technological innovation in soft robotics.

Table 9. Country-wise annual scientific production (top 5 countries)

Country	Year	Articles
USA	1999	4
USA	2004	8
USA	2005	8
USA	2007	8
USA	2008	11
USA	2010	15
USA	2011	20
USA	2012	26
USA	2013	49
USA	2014	82
USA	2015	109
USA	2016	126
USA	2017	179
USA	2018	215
USA	2019	225
USA	2020	247
USA	2021	262
USA	2022	278
Germany	1999	0
Germany	2004	1
Germany	2005	1
Germany	2007	1
Germany	2008	7
Germany	2010	7
Germany	2011	7
Germany	2012	7
Germany	2013	15
Germany	2014	15
Germany	2015	16
Germany	2016	26
Germany	2017	29
Germany	2018	31
Germany	2019	31
Germany	2020	36

continued on following page

Table 9. Continued

Country	Year	Articles
Germany	2021	36
Germany	2022	36
Italy	1999	0
Italy	2004	2
Italy	2005	2
Italy	2007	2
Italy	2008	2
Italy	2010	2
Italy	2011	2
Italy	2012	8
Italy	2013	17
Italy	2014	25
Italy	2015	29
Italy	2016	34
Italy	2017	35
Italy	2018	46
Italy	2019	49
Italy	2020	49
Italy	2021	49
Italy	2022	49
Singapore	1999	0
Singapore	2004	0
Singapore	2005	0
Singapore	2007	0
Singapore	2008	0
Singapore	2010	0
Singapore	2011	0
Singapore	2012	0
Singapore	2013	0
Singapore	2014	0
Singapore	2015	0
Singapore	2016	1
Singapore	2017	6
Singapore	2018	6

continued on following page

Table 9. Continued

Country	Year	Articles
Singapore	2019	19
Singapore	2020	19
Singapore	2021	31
Singapore	2022	31
China	1999	0
China	2004	0
China	2005	0
China	2007	0
China	2008	0
China	2010	0
China	2011	0
China	2012	0
China	2013	0
China	2014	0
China	2015	0
China	2016	0
China	2017	3
China	2018	7
China	2019	18
China	2020	29
China	2021	41
China	2022	56

Data from [1]

DISCUSSION

The bibliometric statistics in this paper show that soft robotics is a discipline that is changing quickly and growing quickly. The synchronised rise in annual scientific output, especially the exponential growth since 2013, together with the publication of highly cited foundational works and locally influential references, suggests that the field is maturing. This growth is marked by the development of basic rules and a quick push towards new frontiers.

Authors like Robert J. Wood, Conor J. Walsh, Katia Bertoldi, Cecilia Laschi, and George M. Whitesides, as well as top schools like Harvard, Nanyang Technological

University, and MIT, are strongly contributing, suggesting strong research ecosystems are forming. The "centres of excellence" undoubtedly succeed because they make a lot of money, work with people from numerous professions, and can hire the best. This creates a virtuous circle of high-impact research, with these significant actors' continued work demonstrating their long-term commitment and leadership.

Publication venues demonstrate the field's diversity. The field is two-sided because there are general-purpose high-impact journals like the Proceedings of the National Academy of Sciences, specialised materials science journals like Advanced Materials and Advanced Functional Materials, and a dedicated journal like Soft Robotics. This illustrates that soft robotics research is making major discoveries in many other science and engineering domains as well as its own. Cross-disciplinary attention indicates the field's intellectual health and potential for wider usage.

America has led soft robotics research, although China and Singapore have made significant contributions, demonstrating a globalisation of research. Soft robotics are attracting more people and businesses worldwide. New research methods and uses tailored to various regions' needs and capabilities may result. International expansion improves the area by introducing new perspectives and fostering collaboration.

Major documents always spark fresh research. New soft, flexible, and sensitive materials including elastomers, hydrogels, liquid metals, and ferromagnetic domains are crucial. Soft materials deform and respond to electric fields, magnetic fields, pneumatic pressure, and light, making them useful in robots. Technology like 3D printing (Digital Light Processing and integrated 3D printing) and 4D printing (time-dependent shape change) is crucial. Traditional methods cannot construct complex, multi-material soft structures with built-in sensing and actuation. These technologies can.

Popular biomimicry and bio-inspiration include octopuses' limbs, human muscles, gecko adhesion, and earthworm and inchworm movement. Designs that are naturally compliant, adaptive, and successful in complex contexts make control challenges easier to manage. Human-robot interaction and medical robot utilisation are the main study areas. Rehabilitative exosuits, robotic gloves, needle insertion, soft manipulators, and artificial organs are examples. Since they're safe and versatile, soft robots are ideal for these delicate tasks. As soft robots become more complex, integrating soft sensors like tactile, strain, and proprioceptive sensors and developing advanced control strategies like model-based reinforcement learning and adaptive control for high-dimensional systems become important problems that we must solve and study.

Despite these advances, some research gaps remain. Soft materials' persistence under repeated stress, especially in harsh environments like the human body, remains a challenge. Tests demonstrate that some actuators can last millions of cycles, but we need a broadly applicable solution.

The diverse materials and designs also show that there is a need for standardised characterisation and modelling so that the performance of different soft robotic systems can be compared. The need for more unified theoretical frameworks and experimental protocols is made clear by the request for standardised comparison methods. Moreover, attaining energy autonomy and elevated power density akin to rigid robots or biological systems continues to pose a problem, since numerous soft robots still depend on external tethers for power or fluidic supply. Because soft robots are inherently flexible and have an infinite number of degrees of freedom, typical rigid-body control methods don't work. This means that robust and adaptive control for complicated, real-world tasks is still an active area of research. Lastly, the ability to scale up and mass produce numerous advanced soft robotic parts, which are generally made using specialised, labour-intensive procedures, is important for wider use and needs more work.

CONCLUSION

This extensive bibliometric study demonstrates that soft robotics is a vibrant and fast-growing area with many new publications, a strong network of influential authors and institutions, and a focus on cross-disciplinary research. The field is growing due to bio-inspired design, new materials, and new methods. In biomedicine and human-robot interaction, soft robots' compliant and safe nature provides them an advantage over rigid robots. These developments are making many more uses viable.

Despite progress, the field must still address issues like energy independence, durability, standardisation, characterisation, and modelling, and better control strategies for complex, high-dimensional systems. International contributions, especially from Asian countries, suggest that research is becoming increasingly global. Thus, innovation collaboration and rivalry are possible. Soft robotics could revolutionise healthcare, manufacturing, and exploration. This is because materials and design principles are always changing, and soft robotics can work with other new technologies like AI and advanced sensing. The constantly changing intellectual landscape, with recognised leaders and new global hubs, makes sure that this intriguing field keeps growing.

REFERENCES

Kim, S., Laschi, C., & Trimmer, B. (2013). Soft robotics: A bioinspired evolution in robotics. *Trends in Biotechnology*, *31*(5), 287–294. PMID: 23582470

Kim, Y., Yuk, H., Zhao, R., Chester, S. A., & Zhao, X. (2018). Printing ferromagnetic domains for untethered fast-transforming soft materials. *Nature*, *558*(7709), 274–279. PMID: 29899476

Laschi, C., Cianchetti, M., Mazzolai, B., Margheri, L., Follador, M., & Dario, P. (2012). Soft robot arm inspired by the octopus. *Advanced Robotics*, *26*(7), 709–727.

Mosadegh, B., Polygerinos, P., Keplinger, C., Wennstedt, S., Shepherd, R. F., Gupta, U., Shim, J., Bertoldi, K., Walsh, C. J., & Whitesides, G. M. (2014). Pneumatic networks for soft robotics that actuate rapidly. *Advanced Functional Materials, 24*(15), 2163–2170. gmwgroup.harvard.edu+1

Okamura, A. M., Simone, C., & O'leary, M. D. (2004). Force modeling for needle insertion into soft tissue. *IEEE Transactions on Biomedical Engineering*, *51*(10), 1707–1716. PMID: 15490818

Polygerinos, P., Correll, N., Morin, S. A., Mosadegh, B., Onal, C. D., Petersen, K., & Shepherd, R. F. (2017). Soft robotics: Review of fluid-driven intrinsically soft devices; manufacturing, sensing, control, and applications in human-robot interaction. *Advanced Engineering Materials*, *19*(12), 1700016.

Polygerinos, P., Wang, Z., Galloway, K. C., Wood, R. J., & Walsh, C. J. (2015). Soft robotic glove for combined assistance and at-home rehabilitation. *Robotics and Autonomous Systems*, *73*, 135–143.

Polygerinos, P., Wang, Z., Overvelde, J. T., Galloway, K. C., Wood, R. J., Bertoldi, K., & Walsh, C. J. (2015). Modeling of soft fiber-reinforced bending actuators. *IEEE Transactions on Robotics*, *31*(3), 778–789.

Rus, D., & Tolley, M. T. (2015). Design, fabrication and control of soft robots. *Nature, 521*, 467–475. DOI: 10.1038/nature14543

Shepherd, R. F., Ilievski, F., Choi, W., Morin, S. A., Stokes, A. A., Mazzeo, A. D., Chen, X., Wang, M., & Whitesides, G. M. (2011). Multigait soft robot. *Proceedings of the National Academy of Sciences, 108*(51), 20400–20403. DASH+1DOI: 10.1073/pnas.1116564108

Vanderborght, B., Albu-Schäffer, A., Bicchi, A., Burdet, E., Caldwell, D. G., Carloni, R., & Wolf, S. (2013). Variable impedance actuators: A review. *Robotics and Autonomous Systems*, *61*(12), 1601–1614.

Wehner, M., Truby, R. L., Fitzgerald, D. J., Mosadegh, B., Whitesides, G. M., Lewis, J. A., & Wood, R. J. (2016). An integrated design and fabrication strategy for entirely soft, autonomous robots. [OUCI]. *Nature*, *536*, 451–455. DOI: 10.1038/nature19100 PMID: 27558065

Chapter 3
Circular Economy Approaches to Software Lifecycle Management

P. Selvakumar
https://orcid.org/0000-0002-3650-4548
Department of Science and Humanities, Nehru Institute of Technology, Coimbatore, India

T. C. Manjunath
https://orcid.org/0000-0003-2545-9160
Rajarajeswari College of Engineering, India

Abhijeet Das
https://orcid.org/0000-0003-4599-5462
C.V. Raman Global University, Bhubaneswar, India

ABSTRACT

In recent decades, the world has experienced rapid technological advancement, industrialization, and a significant shift toward digitalization. While these trends have contributed to economic growth and innovation, they have also intensified environmental degradation, resource depletion, and electronic waste. To address these challenges, the concept of a circular economy has emerged as a transformative alternative to the traditional linear economic model of "take, make, dispose." While initially focused on tangible goods and materials, the circular economy model is now expanding to intangible assets, including software. Applying circular economy principles to software development is a novel and promising avenue, aligning the digital realm with sustainability goals. At its core, the circular economy is about

DOI: 10.4018/979-8-3373-4652-6.ch003

designing out waste and maximizing value. One of the foundational principles of circular economy in the software context is design for longevity. This involves writing code that is modular, maintainable, and easy to update or refactor.

INTRODUCTION TO CIRCULAR ECONOMY

In recent decades, the world has experienced rapid technological advancement, industrialization, and a significant shift toward digitalization. While these trends have contributed to economic growth and innovation, they have also intensified environmental degradation, resource depletion, and electronic waste. To address these challenges, the concept of a *circular economy* has emerged as a transformative alternative to the traditional linear economic model of "take, make, dispose." While initially focused on tangible goods and materials, the circular economy model is now expanding to intangible assets, including software. Applying circular economy principles to software development is a novel and promising avenue, aligning the digital realm with sustainability goals. At its core, the circular economy is about designing out waste and maximizing value. One of the foundational principles of circular economy in the software context is *design for longevity*. This involves writing code that is modular, maintainable, and easy to update or refactor. By ensuring that software can evolve with changing requirements and technological environments, developers can reduce the need for frequent rewrites or complete overhauls. Additionally, embracing open-source development, component reuse, and platform interoperability can significantly cut down duplication of effort and promote collective innovation. These practices reflect the "reuse" and "remanufacture" stages of a circular system, whereby software components are not discarded after a single use but are instead reintegrated into new projects or adapted for different contexts. Practices such as lightweight coding, serverless architectures, and cloud resource optimization are integral to aligning software development with circular economy principles. They ensure that digital systems are not only functional and performant but also environmentally responsible.

Beyond technical design, the circular economy also emphasizes *product-as-a-service* models, which can be applied to software through concepts such as Software-as-a-Service (SaaS), platform sharing, and subscription-based licensing. These models shift the focus from ownership to access and value delivery over time, enabling more sustainable consumption patterns. For example, instead of purchasing software that may quickly become obsolete, users can access continuously updated applications through a subscription. This encourages developers to maintain and improve the product over its lifetime, rather than abandoning older versions and pushing for new releases that require complete reinstallation or retraining. Furthermore, the circular economy paradigm calls attention to the *end-of-life* stage of products. In software, this translates to practices that manage decommissioning, archiving, and data migration responsibly. Legacy systems, when not handled properly, can lead to data loss, security vulnerabilities, and continued dependence on outdated technology stacks. A circular approach encourages structured offboarding, backward compatibility, and the provision of migration paths that help organizations transition smoothly without unnecessary disruption or environmental burden. This includes retiring software in a way that ensures minimal waste and supports knowledge preservation for future developments. Incorporating circular economy principles into software development also has significant implications for *education, governance, and culture*. The integration of circular economy into software development is not without its challenges. Software systems are often complex, interdependent, and subject to rapid change. Market pressures can prioritize speed and novelty over durability and efficiency. However, the urgency of environmental concerns and the increasing awareness of digital sustainability are pushing the industry to evolve. By reimagining software development through the lens of circular economy, stakeholders can not only create more resilient and adaptable digital products but also contribute to a broader transformation toward a sustainable and regenerative future.

APPLYING CIRCULAR ECONOMY PRINCIPLES TO SOFTWARE LIFECYCLE MANAGEMENT

Software development, often perceived as an intangible and inherently low-impact industry, has traditionally escaped the level of environmental scrutiny faced by manufacturing or energy sectors. However, as digital technologies become ever more embedded in daily life and as the global IT infrastructure expands to support these technologies, the environmental implications of software (Andersen et al. 2022) development are becoming increasingly significant. While software itself is intangible, its creation, deployment, operation, and eventual disposal are deeply entwined with energy consumption, hardware utilization, and resource extraction. The environmental footprint of software begins during the development phase, which involves a range of computational tasks—from writing and testing code to building and compiling applications, (Andersen et al. 2022). These activities require computing resources that consume electricity, often powered by fossil fuels, contributing to greenhouse gas (GHG) emissions. As software transitions from development to deployment and execution, its environmental impact often increases. Deployment infrastructure, such as servers, cloud platforms, and content delivery networks, consumes vast amounts of energy to store, manage, and distribute software. Data centers, which power much of the internet and host software services globally, are significant contributors to environmental impact. Software also influences the efficiency and lifespan of hardware.

Some programming languages and runtime environments are more resource-intensive than others, (Awan et al. 2021). Another often overlooked factor is the energy footprint of software use over time. Applications that require constant connectivity, frequent updates, or real-time processing can significantly increase data transfer and computation, all of which consume electricity. In addition to direct energy consumption, software development contributes to indirect environmental impacts through design decisions that influence user behavior. Software that encourages overconsumption, shortens device lifecycles, or promotes inefficient usage patterns can lead to increased environmental strain. Furthermore, the supply chain of software development involves indirect environmental impacts, including the production and transportation of development hardware, the manufacturing of networking equipment, and the energy consumed by software teams during in-person collaboration or travel for software conferences and training, (Boz et al., 2023). As the environmental impact of software development becomes more visible, efforts to measure and mitigate it are gaining traction. Green software engineering is an emerging discipline that focuses on designing software with minimal environmental impact. This involves writing energy-efficient code, optimizing algorithms, minimizing network usage, and choosing efficient deployment strategies. Governments and international organizations are also recognizing the need for regulatory frameworks and guidelines to reduce the digital sector's environmental footprint. Initiatives like the European Union's Green Digital Transformation and various sustainability standards for data centers and cloud services aim to align digital innovation with climate goals. Despite these advances, significant challenges remain.

DESIGN FOR LONGEVITY: CREATING SUSTAINABLE SOFTWARE

The software lifecycle encompasses all stages of software—from initial conception and design to development, deployment, maintenance, and eventual retirement. Traditionally, this lifecycle has followed a linear pattern, often emphasizing speed, scalability, and functionality over longevity, resource efficiency, and sustainability. As awareness grows regarding the environmental and economic impacts of digital technologies, the circular economy presents a valuable framework for reimagining how software systems are created, used, and retired. The first key stage in the software lifecycle is design and planning, where the foundation for sustainability is laid. Circular economy principles begin with *designing for longevity and adaptability*. This means writing modular, maintainable, and scalable code that can evolve with changing requirements and technologies, (Bressanelli et al. 2022). Emphasizing clean architecture, decoupled components, and clear documentation allows for easier updates and reuse, extending the software's usable life. In addition to modularity, *designing for interoperability* supports circularity by ensuring that software can communicate and integrate with other systems and platforms. This reduces the need for redundant development and fosters a broader ecosystem of reusable services and components. Standardized APIs, adherence to open protocols, and backward compatibility are all strategies that facilitate this goal. The development phase presents opportunities to embed resource-efficient practices that align with the circular economy. In the deployment and operations phase, circular economy principles advocate for *efficient use of computing infrastructure*. Cloud computing, virtualization, and containerization provide the flexibility to optimize resource usage by dynamically allocating computing power based on demand. This prevents over-provisioning and reduces energy waste.

The maintenance phase is critical for ensuring software sustainability. Circular economy principles emphasize *maintainability and continuous improvement* over replacement. Instead of abandoning aging software in favor of building new systems, circular lifecycle management encourages updating, refactoring (Bressanelli et al. 2022) and upgrading existing code. Automation tools for monitoring, testing, and deploying updates can streamline maintenance while ensuring that energy consumption remains efficient. Encouraging long-term support (LTS) policies for software libraries and platforms ensures ongoing compatibility and reduces the pressure to constantly upgrade or rebuild applications. In the retirement or decommissioning phase, circular economy principles guide how software should be responsibly phased out. Instead of abrupt termination, legacy systems should be transitioned gradually, ensuring that data is preserved and migrated securely and sustainably. This includes archiving source code and documentation for future reference or reuse and providing clear pathways for users to move to updated systems without data loss or service disruption. Throughout the entire software lifecycle, circular economy principles also intersect with organizational strategy and policy. Governance structures and management practices play a vital role in embedding circularity into software projects. Project managers can incorporate environmental impact assessments into risk analysis, while procurement teams can prioritize open-source and reusable software assets. These models promote continuous value delivery and incentivize developers to maintain and improve software over time, rather than relying on short-term sales. Data management and software analytics further enhance circular lifecycle management by enabling informed decision-making.

REUSE AND REPURPOSE: LEVERAGING EXISTING SOFTWARE ASSETS

In an era where software pervades nearly every aspect of modern life—from communication and commerce to transportation, healthcare, and education—its design has far-reaching implications not just for functionality and performance, but also for sustainability. The principle of design for longevity in software development refers to the deliberate practice of creating software that remains functional, adaptable, and relevant over extended periods, with minimal environmental, financial, and operational cost. The importance of designing software for longevity lies in its potential to reduce waste—(Bushuyev et al., 2023) of code, computing resources, energy, and even human labor. Traditional software development models often prioritize rapid deployment and frequent releases, resulting in software that quickly becomes obsolete, incompatible, or unsupportable. One of the foundational strategies in designing sustainable, long-lasting software is modularity. Modular design allows software systems to be broken down into independent, reusable, and interchangeable components or services. This structure facilitates easier updates, testing, and maintenance, as developers can modify or replace individual modules without disturbing the entire system. Closely related to modularity is the principle of separation of concerns, which involves organizing software such that each module or function has a single, well-defined responsibility. By clearly delineating roles and minimizing dependencies between components, developers can ensure that changes in one area do not cause unintended consequences elsewhere. Maintainability is a core metric of software longevity. Software that cannot be easily understood, debugged, or enhanced is more likely to be discarded and rewritten, leading to unnecessary duplication of effort and waste. Sustainable (Carvalho et al., 2022) software design prioritizes readability, consistent coding conventions, thorough documentation, and meaningful naming conventions.

Sustainable software design also emphasizes scalability and adaptability—the ability of the system to grow and change without requiring complete rewrites. Scalable software can handle increased demand efficiently, preventing the need for energy-intensive overprovisioning or wasteful hardware expansion. Adaptive design, on the other hand, enables the software to accommodate new business needs, user behaviors, and technological standards over time. This could include designing with open standards and APIs that facilitate future integration or building flexible user interfaces that can be customized without rewriting core logic. Another key strategy is technology agnosticism, which involves reducing dependence on specific platforms, vendors, or programming languages. This principle supports portability and reduces the risk of vendor lock-in, (Charef et al., 2021), which can limit options for long-term support and force unnecessary migration when a provider discontinues support. Sustainable software design also incorporates energy efficiency into its considerations. While software itself does not consume energy in the traditional sense, its execution on hardware systems can have a considerable impact on electricity consumption and environmental degradation. Beyond technical considerations, user-centered design plays a crucial role in software longevity. If a product fails to meet user needs or becomes difficult to use, it is likely to be abandoned regardless of how well it is built. Open-source development is another powerful mechanism for enhancing software longevity. Open-source projects benefit from a global community of contributors who can maintain, improve, and extend the software even after the original developers have moved on.

RECYCLING AND UPCYCLING: END-OF-LIFE SOFTWARE MANAGEMENT

In the fast-paced world of software development, where innovation is often equated with building something new from scratch, the concepts of reuse and repurpose are frequently undervalued. However, from both a sustainability and economic standpoint, leveraging existing software assets is a critical strategy aligned with the principles of the circular economy. At its core, software reuse involves the systematic application of existing software components—such as code libraries, frameworks, modules, templates, APIs, and even entire applications—into new projects or contexts. Repurposing, on the other hand, extends this concept further by adapting software originally designed for one function or industry to serve another purpose. One of the primary benefits of reuse is the acceleration of development cycles. Developers can reduce time-to-market and minimize effort by incorporating proven and trusted components rather than writing new ones from scratch, (Chen et al., 2019). Another major advantage of reuse is resource efficiency—a key goal of the circular economy. Developing software from scratch requires computing resources for coding, compiling, testing, and deployment. These activities, especially when performed at scale or in continuous integration environments, consume significant energy and contribute to carbon emissions. Reusing existing components significantly reduces this computational load. Repurposing software provides an opportunity to extend the lifespan of digital assets, mirroring how the circular economy encourages the reuse of physical goods across industries. For example, a logistics tracking system developed for shipping companies might be repurposed for use in emergency disaster response, where tracking assets and personnel is equally critical.

A related practice that exemplifies reuse and repurposing is component-based development and the use of software product lines (SPLs). SPLs allow organizations to manage families of related software systems using shared components and architectures. Open-source software ecosystems are particularly fertile ground for reuse and repurpose strategies. Platforms like GitHub, GitLab, and SourceForge host millions of reusable libraries, frameworks, and tools that developers can incorporate into their own projects, (Chib et al., 2025). Many of these components are governed by permissive licenses that encourage adaptation and redistribution. Containerization and microservices architecture further facilitate reuse by encapsulating functionality into discrete, portable, and interoperable units. These architectural styles allow services to be independently deployed, scaled, and updated, promoting modularity and separation of concerns. Despite these advantages, software reuse and repurposing face several cultural and technical barriers. One of the most pervasive challenges is the "not-invented-here" (NIH) syndrome, where teams prefer to build their own solutions rather than adopt external or legacy components. Technical challenges also arise in integrating reused or repurposed software into modern systems. Legacy code may be poorly documented, incompatible with current architectures, or lacking in modularity. Addressing these limitations often requires refactoring, reverse engineering, or "wrapping" older code with new interfaces to enable integration. Security and licensing are additional concerns when reusing software assets. Organizations must vet third-party components for vulnerabilities and ensure compliance with licensing terms. Failing to do so can expose systems to cyber risks or legal liabilities. To support long-term reuse, developers must also embrace sustainable documentation and knowledge preservation. Many reuse opportunities are lost because knowledge about how a component works, what it depends on, or how it was intended to be used is not properly captured, (Condemi et al., 2019).

SUSTAINABLE SOFTWARE DEVELOPMENT: BEST PRACTICES AND TOOLS

In traditional software development practices, the end-of-life (EOL) phase is often an afterthought—a point at which support for an application is simply withdrawn, systems are decommissioned, and attention shifts to newer technologies. However, from a circular economy perspective, the EOL phase offers significant opportunities for sustainability through recycling, upcycling, and intelligent repurposing of digital assets. End-of-life software management refers to the strategies, processes, and tools used when a software product, system, or component is no longer actively developed, maintained, or supported. This phase includes decisions about data preservation, decommissioning infrastructure, license termination, code archival, and user migration, (Cholewa et al., 2021). Poorly managed EOL processes can lead to several issues—data loss, security vulnerabilities, hardware waste, increased energy consumption, and unnecessary reinvestment in systems that could have been reused or upgraded. Recycling in software entails breaking down systems into reusable parts—source code modules, libraries, APIs, configuration files, algorithms, or even documentation—that can be reintegrated into new projects. Just as physical recycling processes separate and refine usable materials, digital recycling involves identifying components that are not tightly coupled to the original system and repackaging them for future use. Code refactoring plays a central role in the software recycling process. By restructuring legacy code to improve readability, reduce complexity, and eliminate technical debt, developers can make older codebases more amenable to reuse, (Charnley et al., 2019).

Another example of software upcycling can be found in the open-source community, where developers breathe new life into discontinued or abandoned software. Projects such as LibreOffice (a fork of OpenOffice), MariaDB (a fork of MySQL), and many Linux distributions demonstrate how communities can take existing codebases, address limitations, add features, and re-release them as robust alternatives. The preservation of knowledge and data is a vital component of sustainable, (Dahiya et al., 2025). EOL software management. A key sustainability concern in EOL software management is the relationship between software obsolescence and hardware waste. Often, older applications are tied to specific hardware platforms or operating systems, and when the software is no longer supported, the hardware is deemed obsolete—even if it is still functional. Decommissioning strategies also have environmental and operational implications. A sustainable approach to software decommissioning includes shutting down servers responsibly, migrating users and data smoothly, and ensuring that associated infrastructure—such as databases, network configurations, and storage systems—is either retired securely or repurposed. Security considerations are paramount during the EOL phase. Unsupported software is more vulnerable to security breaches, and legacy, (Dahiya et al., 2020) code can become a weak point in an organization's cybersecurity posture. From a governance perspective, establishing formal EOL policies and workflows is critical for enabling recycling and upcycling. These policies should outline timelines for maintenance, criteria for decommissioning, procedures for identifying reusable components, and documentation requirements. Additionally, organizations can implement software asset management (SAM) tools that provide visibility into software inventories, usage metrics, and lifecycle stages. Cross-functional collaboration is essential during EOL management.

MODULAR DESIGN: FACILITATING SOFTWARE REUSE AND UPGRADE

As the world becomes increasingly digitized, the environmental footprint of software development is drawing greater scrutiny. From massive server farms powering cloud infrastructure to the energy consumed by millions of lines of inefficient code running on end-user devices, the digital domain contributes significantly to global energy consumption and carbon emissions. In response, the software industry is undergoing a paradigm shift: away from development driven purely by functionality, performance, and speed, toward a model that integrates ecological awareness, ethical responsibility, and resource efficiency. Sustainable software development refers to the adoption of practices and tools that minimize environmental impact, support long-term maintenance, and promote social and economic sustainability across the entire lifecycle of a digital product, (de Oliveira et al., 2017). This approach is not just about code—it is about how teams design, build, deploy, manage, and retire software in ways that are environmentally conscious, economically viable, and socially responsible. A foundational best practice in sustainable software development is energy-efficient coding. While the energy use of a single piece of inefficient code may appear negligible, at scale—across billions of devices and users—it becomes significant. Writing efficient algorithms, reducing computational complexity, and optimizing memory usage can dramatically decrease the runtime energy consumption of applications. Lightweight code, fewer background processes, and proper garbage collection contribute to less intensive CPU and memory demands, which in turn extend battery life on mobile devices and reduce power usage in data centers. Languages like Rust and Go are often preferred for their performance efficiency, while techniques such as algorithmic profiling and benchmarking help identify code bottlenecks that can be optimized for energy efficiency. Green coding practices are reinforced by tooling that assists in performance monitoring and optimization. Tools like *Green Metrics Tool*, *PowerAPI*, and *Scaphandre* allow developers to estimate the energy consumption of their applications during execution, offering insights that lead to better architectural and design decisions.

Moreover, code linters and static analysis tools such as *SonarQube* or *CodeClimate* help enforce best practices related to modularity, readability, and maintainability, all of which contribute to the long-term sustainability of the codebase. Software architecture plays a vital role in sustainability. Sustainable architectures prioritize modularity, scalability, and loose coupling between components, (Demestichas et al., 2020). Microservices and serverless models enable more efficient resource allocation, as they activate computing resources only when needed. This contrasts with monolithic applications that require larger, often underutilized environments. Tools like Docker, Kubernetes, and Terraform support containerization and orchestration, ensuring that software services can scale dynamically based on real-time demand. By using and contributing to open-source libraries and frameworks, teams can build on existing solutions rather than starting from scratch—saving time, reducing errors, and minimizing energy-intensive development cycles. Platforms like GitHub and GitLab facilitate code sharing, collaboration, and lifecycle tracking. Open-source components, when well-documented and maintained, also provide opportunities for upcycling legacy software into modern, secure, and efficient solutions.

CONTINUOUS MONITORING AND MAINTENANCE: EXTENDING SOFTWARE LIFESPAN

In the realm of software engineering, modular design has emerged as one of the most critical architectural strategies for fostering scalability, maintainability, adaptability, and sustainability. It lies at the heart of modern development methodologies and aligns closely with the principles of the circular economy. At its core, modular design involves dividing a software system into distinct, self-contained units—called modules—that encapsulate specific functionality. As the software industry grapples with the dual challenge of maintaining technological innovation while reducing environmental and operational waste, modular design has become essential for building resilient, sustainable digital systems. The fundamental philosophy of modular design is the separation of concerns. By assigning each module a single, clear responsibility, developers can reduce interdependencies, simplify debugging, and enhance the comprehensibility of large codebases. This structure not only makes software more adaptable to change but also promotes incremental development—where new features or updates can be added without rewriting or destabilizing the entire system. One of (Elia et al., 2017) the primary advantages of modular design is its role in software reuse.

Figure 1. Software solutions for circular economy

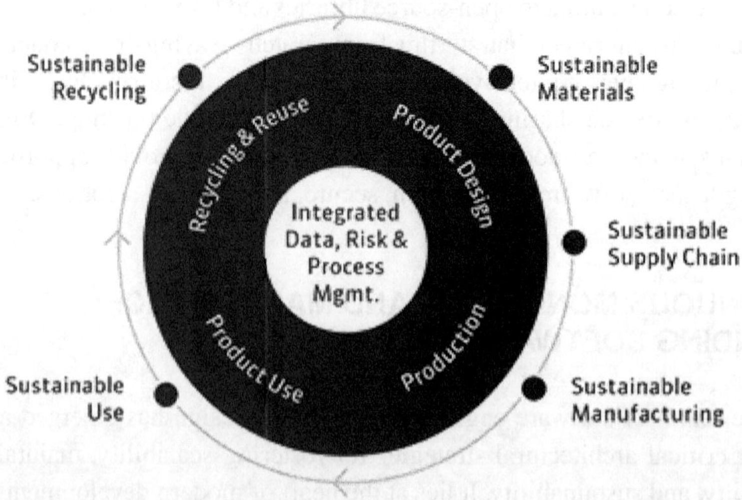

Microservices architecture, a modern evolution of modular design, exemplifies this principle at scale. In microservices, applications are composed of small, independently deployable services that communicate via APIs. Each service is responsible for a specific function and can be developed, deployed, and scaled independently, (Fontana et al., 2021). This architecture supports continuous delivery and DevOps practices by allowing teams to iterate rapidly, deploy frequently, and recover gracefully from failures. Modular design also enhances team productivity and collaboration. In large projects, multiple teams can work simultaneously on different modules without interfering with each other's progress. This parallelization accelerates development cycles and fosters specialization, where each team becomes proficient in its domain area. This targeted troubleshooting capability reduces downtime, lowers maintenance costs, and enhances the system's overall sustainability. In addition to improving the internal dynamics of software systems, modular design supports external compatibility and integration, (Halstenberg et al., 2019). Modular components that adhere to open standards and expose clean interfaces can be easily connected with external tools, services, or hardware. In cloud-native environments, modular design enables efficient resource usage and cost control. Through containerization technologies like Docker and orchestration platforms like Kubernetes, developers can package modules as lightweight, portable units that can run on any cloud infrastructure. This abstraction simplifies deployment, improves scalability, and reduces vendor lock-in. Despite its benefits, implementing modular design is not without challenges. Designing effective module boundaries requires a deep understanding of the problem domain and foresight into how the software might evolve. Over-modularization can lead to excessive complexity, inter-module communication overhead, and performance inefficiencies. Conversely, poor modularization can result in tightly coupled systems that are difficult to change or reuse. Organizational support is equally important. To fully realize the benefits of modular design, companies must foster a culture of code sharing and reuse. This includes maintaining internal libraries, encouraging contribution to shared repositories, and promoting modular thinking through training and mentorship, (Han et al., 2023).

BENEFITS OF CIRCULAR ECONOMY APPROACHES IN SOFTWARE DEVELOPMENT

In the evolving landscape of software engineering, ensuring the long-term viability and sustainability of applications is no longer a matter of one-time development and deployment. Instead, the practice of continuous monitoring and maintenance has become foundational to extending software lifespan, preserving system performance, and aligning with the principles of sustainable development. Software systems that are not actively monitored and maintained tend to degrade over time, becoming vulnerable to security threats, performance issues, and functional obsolescence, (Hariyani et al., 2024). In contrast, systems that are routinely observed, updated, and optimized not only endure longer but also evolve more gracefully with changing user needs, technological advancements, and business priorities. Continuous monitoring refers to the real-time or near-real-time tracking of a system's health, performance, and behavior, (Jahan et al., 2022). This includes observing metrics such as server uptime, CPU and memory usage, error rates, user behavior, latency, throughput, and compliance with service-level agreements (SLAs). Monitoring is not only about technical performance. It also supports usage analytics, which help organizations understand how features are being used, which components are underperforming, and where optimizations are needed. Maintenance, on the other hand, involves the systematic updating, refining, and upgrading of software to preserve its operability, security, and relevance. This includes corrective maintenance (fixing bugs and errors), adaptive maintenance (adjusting to new operating systems, hardware, or environments), perfective maintenance (enhancing performance or usability), and preventive maintenance (addressing potential future issues before they manifest). One of the most critical reasons for ongoing maintenance is security.

Automated testing and deployment tools play a crucial role in supporting continuous maintenance. Platforms such as Jenkins, GitHub Actions, GitLab CI/CD, Travis CI, and CircleCI enable developers to automate the testing, building, and deployment of code. This makes it easier to release updates frequently and reliably, thereby reducing the risk of regressions and integration failures, (Kaur et al.,

2025). The integration of observability practices into system architecture enhances monitoring capabilities by focusing not just on metrics but also on logs, traces, and events that provide context about internal system states. From a resource management perspective, continuous monitoring helps in optimizing infrastructure usage. For instance, by analyzing traffic patterns and resource consumption, organizations can scale systems up or down dynamically, avoiding overprovisioning and reducing energy consumption in cloud environments. Documentation and knowledge management are also key components of maintenance. Over time, team members change, technologies evolve, and institutional memory fades. Continuous monitoring against these metrics provides a quantifiable way to assess system health and guide maintenance efforts. End-user support and feedback loops also contribute significantly to sustainable maintenance. By collecting feedback through user surveys, support tickets, behavior analytics, and usability tests, developers can align maintenance priorities with actual user needs. This ensures that maintenance efforts yield tangible improvements in user satisfaction, system relevance, and customer retention. Another facet of sustainable maintenance is dependency management. Modern software systems rely heavily on external libraries, packages, and APIs. If these dependencies are not regularly updated and monitored, they can become sources of security risk, performance degradation, or legal non-compliance. Despite its benefits, implementing continuous monitoring and maintenance requires a cultural shift within organizations. It must be viewed not as a post-development obligation, but as a core element of the software development lifecycle. The benefits of continuous monitoring and maintenance extend beyond software performance—they contribute to (Kifor et al., 2023) organizational resilience, environmental stewardship, and user trust.

CHALLENGES AND BARRIERS TO ADOPTION: OVERCOMING OBSTACLES

Incorporating the principles of the circular economy into software development represents a transformative shift in how digital products are conceived, built, maintained, and retired. Unlike traditional linear models that follow a "build-use-dispose" trajectory, circular economy strategies emphasize durability, reuse, repairability, modularity, and regeneration. When applied to software engineering, these principles can generate a wide range of benefits—environmental, economic, technical, and social—enhancing sustainability while also driving innovation and long-term value creation. By prioritizing longevity, flexibility, and resource optimization, the circular economy in software development addresses growing concerns about digital waste, carbon emissions, and the unsustainable pace of technological obsolescence. One of the most significant benefits of circular software development is its contribution to environmental sustainability, (Kintscher et al., 2021). Although software is intangible, its production, deployment, and usage are deeply reliant on physical infrastructure—servers, networks, data centers, and user devices—all of which consume energy and generate carbon emissions. Reducing redundant development and extending software lifespan through practices like modular design, reuse of code, and continuous maintenance can drastically cut down on compute cycles, storage needs, and hardware turnover. This in turn reduces the need for constant updates to underlying hardware, lessens the e-waste burden, and diminishes the overall carbon footprint of software systems.

From an economic perspective, circular economy strategies deliver substantial cost savings and resource optimization. Reusable components—such as libraries, APIs, and microservices—allow developers to avoid reinventing the wheel, thereby shortening development cycles and reducing labor costs. In large organizations, code reuse across departments or projects can result in millions of dollars in saved effort over time. Similarly, repurposing existing systems or upcycling legacy applications into modern, cloud-native solutions can extend the value of prior investments and defer expensive system replacements. By designing systems with modularity and interoperability in mind, (Kommineni et al., 2025) companies also gain the ability to integrate new features and adapt to market changes without incurring the full cost of rebuilding from scratch. Another key economic benefit is the mitigation of technical debt. In traditional development approaches, teams often prioritize speed over sustainability, leading to quick fixes and poor documentation that accumulate over time as technical debt. This debt makes systems harder to maintain, upgrade, or scale, and often leads to increased costs in the long term, (Kristia et al., 2023). Circular software practices—such as continuous monitoring, regular refactoring, and comprehensive documentation—help manage and reduce technical debt proactively. These practices enable smoother transitions, lower the risks associated with change, and support more predictable budgeting for IT infrastructure and maintenance.

ECONOMIC AND ENVIRONMENTAL BENEFITS: A WIN-WIN APPROACH

Adopting circular economy principles in software development offers numerous benefits, yet the transition from traditional linear development models to sustainable, circular approaches faces significant challenges and barriers. These obstacles arise from technical complexities, organizational inertia, cultural resistance, economic constraints, and regulatory ambiguities. Understanding and addressing these challenges is critical for companies, developers, and policymakers who aim to integrate circularity into software lifecycles effectively and sustainably. Many organizations depend on large, monolithic applications developed over years or decades, often lacking clear documentation or standardized interfaces, (Kutscher et al., 2020). Refactoring such systems into modular, reusable components that support repair, upgrade, and repurpose strategies is a costly and time-consuming endeavor. It demands deep expertise, extensive testing, and careful management to avoid disrupting critical business operations, (Larsen et al., 2022). Closely related to technical issues is the challenge of knowledge silos and insufficient expertise in circular design principles among software development teams. Circular economy concepts—such as designing for longevity, reuse, and upgradability—require a mindset shift and specific skills in modular architecture, continuous integration, automated testing, and observability. Many developers are trained primarily in rapid feature delivery and short-term product cycles, with limited exposure to sustainability-focused methodologies. Economic challenges further complicate adoption. While circular software practices promise cost savings over time, initial investments can be substantial. Redesigning software for modularity, setting up continuous monitoring infrastructure, and implementing automated testing pipelines require financial resources, tooling, and skilled personnel, (Lawrenz et al., 2021). Small and medium-sized enterprises (SMEs) may find these upfront costs prohibitive without clear, immediate returns or external incentives.

Technical interoperability is another challenge. Circular economy strategies rely heavily on modular, interoperable components that can be reused and repurposed across projects and organizations. However, a lack of universally accepted standards and diverse technology stacks complicates integration. Another often overlooked barrier is the challenge of measuring and demonstrating the value of circular software practices, (Liaskos et al., 2019). Unlike hardware or manufacturing, where material flow and waste metrics are tangible, software sustainability impacts are more abstract, involving energy use, carbon footprint of data centers, and long-term maintainability, (Limbore et al., 2025). Leveraging open-source tools and community-driven standards helps reduce vendor lock-in and enables collaborative innovation. Organizations can also benefit from establishing dedicated sustainability roles and governance structures. Sustainability officers or green IT champions can coordinate efforts, monitor progress, and advocate for investments in circular practices. Measuring software sustainability also requires advancing analytics and observability tools specifically designed for environmental impact assessment. Integrating energy usage and carbon footprint metrics into monitoring dashboards will help organizations track progress and make data-driven improvements. Publicly sharing sustainability reports increases accountability and builds consumer trust. Finally, fostering a collaborative ecosystem among developers, enterprises, academia, and policymakers is essential, (Li et al., 2022).

THE FUTURE OF CIRCULAR ECONOMY IN SOFTWARE DEVELOPMENT

The integration of circular economy principles within software development offers a synergistic pathway that simultaneously delivers significant economic and environmental benefits, epitomizing a true win-win approach. As industries worldwide grapple with the dual imperatives of driving innovation and sustainability, circular software development emerges as a compelling strategy that aligns business growth with ecological responsibility. This holistic approach reshapes the traditional software (Mamudu et al., 2024) lifecycle—from design and development through deployment, maintenance, and end-of-life management—by emphasizing resource efficiency, reuse, adaptability, and longevity. The resulting economic and environmental gains not only foster competitive advantage and cost savings but also contribute substantially to reducing the digital sector's growing ecological footprint, thereby supporting global climate and sustainability goals. From an economic standpoint, adopting circular software development practices translates into substantial cost reductions and enhanced operational efficiencies. Central to this is the concept of maximizing the lifespan and utility of software assets through design for longevity, modular architectures, and reuse of existing components. Further economic benefits arise from the reduction in maintenance and support costs. Software designed with circular principles tends to be easier to update, patch, and scale due to its modular, loosely coupled components, (Morsy et al., 2020). Efficient, sustainable software reduces demand for compute cycles, storage, and bandwidth, which in turn lessens the pressure to constantly upgrade servers, data centers, and end-user devices. On the environmental front, the benefits of circular software development are both direct and far-reaching.

Additionally, by promoting reuse and repurposing of software assets, circular development reduces the frequency of full system redeployments or replacements, which are often energy-intensive processes involving testing, integration, and migration. Circular software development also supports carbon footprint reduction through several mechanisms. As governments increasingly mandate environmental disclosures and sustainability reporting, companies employing circular software practices gain competitive advantages and improved stakeholder trust, (Norouzi et al., 2021). The synergy between economic and environmental benefits creates a powerful feedback loop: cost savings from resource efficiency encourage further investment in sustainable practices, while reduced environmental impact enhances brand reputation and compliance with emerging regulations. Moreover, the circular economy in software promotes social benefits that complement economic and environmental gains. By extending software lifespan and enhancing maintainability, circular approaches improve accessibility and inclusivity, allowing a broader range of users to benefit from technology without frequent disruptive upgrades, (Panza et al., 2022). To realize these benefits, organizations must embed circularity into their software development processes from the outset. This involves adopting design principles such as modularity, scalability, and interoperability, investing in automated testing and continuous integration pipelines, and implementing robust monitoring frameworks to track performance and sustainability metrics.

EMERGING TECHNOLOGIES: OPPORTUNITIES FOR CIRCULAR ECONOMY

As the global demand for digital technologies continues to surge, the future of software development is increasingly intertwined with the principles of the circular economy, signaling a paradigm shift toward sustainability, resilience, and innovation. The accelerating adoption of circular economy frameworks in software engineering reflects a growing recognition that traditional linear models of "build-use-dispose" are no longer tenable in the face of environmental constraints, resource scarcity, and escalating digital waste. One of the most transformative trends shaping this future is the increasing integration of advanced technologies such as artificial intelligence (AI), machine learning (ML), and automation into software development lifecycles, (Peña et al., 2021). These technologies enable intelligent resource management, predictive maintenance, and automated refactoring, which are critical to realizing circularity at scale, (Piila et al., 2022). AI-powered tools can analyze codebases to identify redundant components, optimize energy consumption, and suggest modularization opportunities, thereby facilitating the reuse and repurposing of existing software assets. Complementing technological innovations is the growing prominence of cloud-native and edge computing architectures, which foster modular, scalable, and energy-efficient software ecosystems. Cloud platforms provide on-demand computing resources that can be dynamically allocated and optimized to reduce idle capacity and energy wastage. The future landscape will also be shaped by emerging standards, frameworks, and certifications specifically designed to embed sustainability into software development, (Plociennik et al., 2022). Governments, industry consortia, and standardization bodies are increasingly recognizing the need for clear guidelines to measure and validate software sustainability, including metrics for energy efficiency, carbon footprint, and resource utilization. The future will also see a profound cultural transformation within the software development community, characterized by heightened awareness, education, and collaboration focused on sustainability.

Academic institutions and professional training programs are expected to incorporate circular economy principles and green software engineering practices into curricula, equipping new generations of developers with the knowledge and tools necessary to build sustainable digital systems, (Rizvi et al., 2021). Another critical dimension shaping the future is the rise of data-driven sustainability metrics and observability tools that enable real-time monitoring and continuous improvement of software's environmental impact. Advanced analytics platforms will integrate carbon accounting, energy consumption tracking, and resource usage visualization directly into development and operations dashboards. This visibility will empower teams to identify inefficiencies, simulate the environmental effects of design choices, and optimize software performance dynamically. Furthermore, the use of blockchain and distributed ledger technologies may enhance transparency and traceability of software development processes, ensuring compliance with sustainability standards and fostering trust among stakeholders. In parallel, evolving business models aligned with circular economy principles are set to disrupt traditional software licensing and deployment paradigms. Subscription, pay-per-use, and software-as-a-service (SaaS) models inherently support scalability and resource efficiency by aligning consumption with actual demand. Future models may further incorporate sustainability incentives, rewarding users and developers who prioritize energy-efficient usage patterns or contribute reusable components to shared ecosystems, (Rizvi et al., 2021). Additionally, platforms enabling software upcycling—repurposing legacy applications into new contexts with minimal redevelopment—will gain traction, unlocking additional value from existing digital assets while reducing waste.

INDUSTRY AND ACADEMIA COLLABORATION: DRIVING CIRCULAR ECONOMY ADOPTION

Emerging technologies are rapidly reshaping the software development landscape, providing unprecedented opportunities to embed circular economy principles into digital ecosystems. This detailed exploration highlights how these technologies serve as enablers of circular software development, transforming design, deployment, maintenance, and end-of-life management in ways that were previously unattainable. Artificial intelligence and machine learning stand at the forefront of emerging technologies enabling circular economy approaches. AI-powered tools can analyze vast software repositories to identify redundancies, inefficiencies, (Rosa et al., 2020) and opportunities for component reuse or modularization. Moreover, AI can optimize resource allocation dynamically in cloud and edge environments, reducing energy consumption by adapting workloads to available capacity and demand. This intelligent orchestration aligns perfectly with circular principles, enabling software to evolve efficiently while minimizing its environmental footprint. Blockchain technology offers another powerful opportunity for advancing circularity by providing transparent, immutable records of software provenance, usage, and lifecycle events, (Larsen et al., 2022). In a circular economy context, blockchain can track the origin, modification history, and licensing of reusable software components, ensuring compliance with open-source or proprietary requirements. Edge computing represents a transformative architectural shift that enhances the circularity of software systems by decentralizing processing closer to end-users. By offloading computation from centralized data centers to distributed edge nodes, edge computing reduces latency, bandwidth demands, and energy consumption associated with data transmission. Cloud-native architectures, built on microservices, containers, and serverless computing, provide another critical enabler of circular software development, (Yang et al., 2023).

Advanced automation technologies, including robotic process automation (RPA) and infrastructure as code (IaC), also contribute significantly to circular economy objectives in software development. Automation reduces manual errors, accelerates repetitive tasks, and enhances consistency in software deployment and maintenance. This repeatability supports software lifecycle management practices that prioritize upgrades, refactoring, and component reuse over full rebuilds. Emerging standards and tools for green software engineering are gaining traction as well, driven by growing awareness of software's environmental impact. Tools that measure energy consumption, (Samal et al., 2025) footprint, and resource usage during development and runtime empower engineers to quantify and reduce the environmental cost of their software. Moreover, the rise of open-source ecosystems and collaborative platforms fueled by emerging technologies accelerates circularity by fostering transparency, knowledge sharing, and collective innovation. Open-source repositories combined with advanced search and recommendation engines help developers discover reusable components tailored to their needs, reducing redundant coding efforts. In the near future, quantum computing—though still in nascent stages—may also influence circular software development. Quantum technologies promise to exponentially increase computing power and efficiency for certain problem classes, potentially reducing the energy consumption required for complex computations. Ensuring that technologies integrate seamlessly across diverse platforms and organizational contexts requires adherence to open standards and collaborative governance. Privacy-preserving techniques such as federated learning and secure multi-party computation will be essential to balance reuse and sustainability with user confidentiality and regulatory compliance, (Sassanelli et al., 2019).

TOWARDS A MORE SUSTAINABLE SOFTWARE INDUSTRY: IMPLEMENTING CIRCULAR ECONOMY PRINCIPLES

The adoption of circular economy principles in software development represents a complex challenge that requires a multifaceted approach, one that is most effectively addressed through robust collaboration between industry and academia. This partnership is pivotal in driving innovation, knowledge exchange, and the practical implementation of sustainable software engineering practices. As the digital ecosystem becomes increasingly central to economic and social activities, aligning academic research with industry needs creates a fertile ground for developing novel methodologies, tools, and frameworks that embed circularity into the software lifecycle. A primary benefit of industry-academia, (Soundariya et al. 2025) collaboration lies in bridging the gap between theoretical research and practical application. Academia excels in exploring cutting-edge concepts, such as circular design patterns, sustainable coding practices, and lifecycle assessment methodologies that quantify software's environmental impact, (Tola et al. 2023). However, without industry involvement, these innovations risk remaining confined to academic literature, detached from the realities of commercial software development. One notable dimension of this collaboration is the development and validation of sustainability metrics and tools tailored for software engineering. Accurate measurement of environmental impact, such as energy consumption, carbon footprint, and resource efficiency, is fundamental to driving circular practices. Academia contributes through foundational research to create standardized metrics and simulation models, while industry partners provide access to large-scale software systems and operational data critical for empirical validation. Furthermore, joint curriculum development and educational programs are vital components of collaboration that shape the next generation of software engineers with sustainability expertise. Academia designs specialized courses and training modules on green software engineering, circular economy principles, and sustainable IT management, often in consultation with industry stakeholders to ensure relevance and applicability, (Väisänen et al., 2019). Internship programs, industry-sponsored projects, and hackathons provide students with hands-on experience addressing real sustainability challenges, bridging classroom learning with workplace realities.

Collaborative research also fosters innovation in software lifecycle management, a critical area for circular economy adoption. Industry-academia partnerships explore novel approaches to modular design, software reuse, maintenance strategies, and end-of-life management that reduce waste and extend software longevity, (Spišáková et al. 2022). Academia's role in generating evidence-based research underpins policy recommendations and standardization efforts related to sustainable software development. Industry collaboration ensures that proposed regulations and voluntary standards reflect technical realities and market conditions, making compliance both feasible and beneficial. The collaboration also extends to building interdisciplinary networks and ecosystems that integrate software, engineering with environmental science, economics, and social sciences, (Tamilarasi et al., 2025; Väisänen et al., 2019). Addressing the circular economy requires a holistic understanding of ecological impacts, economic incentives, and human behavior, which transcends traditional disciplinary boundaries. Moreover, funding and resource sharing mechanisms underpin successful collaboration. Industry partners often provide financial support, infrastructure, and real-world testbeds, enabling academia to pursue ambitious research agendas with practical relevance. Conversely, academic grants and public research funding can support exploratory projects that de-risk novel circular software technologies for industry adoption, (Tamilarasi et al. 2025). Challenges to effective collaboration do exist, including differing priorities, timelines, and communication styles between academia and industry. Academia often focuses on long-term, exploratory research, while industry demands immediate, actionable results aligned with business objectives. Bridging this divide requires clear governance structures, mutual trust, and alignment of goals through well-defined partnership frameworks. Regular knowledge exchange forums, joint steering committees, and co-creation workshops help maintain momentum and responsiveness. Additionally, fostering a culture of openness and valuing diverse perspectives enhances innovation potential and overcomes siloed thinking.

CONCLUSION

The software industry stands at a pivotal crossroads, with mounting environmental concerns and resource constraints driving a critical reevaluation of traditional development paradigms. Implementing circular economy principles offers a transformative pathway toward creating a more sustainable software industry—one that reduces waste, optimizes resource use, and fosters regeneration throughout the software lifecycle. A fundamental future direction involves mainstreaming circular design principles into software engineering practices. This requires rethinking software architecture to prioritize modularity, interoperability, and extensibility from the outset. Designing software for longevity means building components that can be independently upgraded, repaired, or replaced without discarding entire applications. Technological innovation will continue to play a central role in advancing circular economy goals. The future will see expanded use of artificial intelligence (AI), machine learning (ML), and automation to optimize software development and operational processes. AI-driven analytics can identify inefficiencies, recommend code refactoring for enhanced reuse, and predict maintenance needs, enabling proactive interventions that extend software lifespan. Another key future direction involves innovating new business models that align profitability with circular economy principles. Subscription, pay-per-use, and software-as-a-service (SaaS) frameworks inherently support resource-efficient consumption by scaling usage with demand and facilitating incremental updates rather than wholesale replacements. Future business models may incorporate sustainability incentives, rewarding customers and developers who choose energy-efficient configurations, participate in software reuse networks, or contribute to open-source circular projects. Cross-sector and multi-stakeholder collaboration will be critical for systemic change. Implementing circular economy principles in software development transcends purely technical considerations and demands coordinated efforts among developers, enterprises, policymakers, academia, and civil society. Policy frameworks will need to evolve to incentivize circular practices through regulations, subsidies, or tax incentives that recognize the environmental benefits of sustainable software. Governments and standardization bodies will develop certification schemes and reporting requirements to drive transparency and accountability. On the tooling front, the future will see a proliferation of integrated software development environments (IDEs) and platforms that natively support circular economy principles. These environments will provide automated suggestions for energy-efficient coding practices, flag deprecated or redundant components for reuse, and facilitate lifecycle tracking of software artifacts. The role of data and analytics in driving sustainable software development cannot be overstated. As software systems become increasingly complex and distributed—often spanning cloud, edge, and IoT environments—comprehensive monitoring of environmental performance will be essential. Education and awareness campaigns targeting end-users and consumers of software products represent another crucial future direction. Empowering users with information about the environmental footprint of software applications encourages responsible usage patterns and preference for sustainable products. User interfaces may incorporate sustainability indicators or options to select low-impact modes of operation. Looking even further ahead, the software industry is expected to explore synergies with other emerging fields such as quantum computing, bioinformatics, and synthetic biology, which may introduce new paradigms of computing and resource utilization. Despite the promising future, several challenges must be addressed to fully implement circular economy principles in software development. These include overcoming legacy system inertia, addressing interoperability issues across diverse platforms, managing data privacy and security in shared reuse environments, and ensuring equitable access to sustainable software technologies globally. Tackling these obstacles will require innovative technical solutions, inclusive governance models, and ongoing dialogue among stakeholders to balance competing priorities. By embracing this vision, the software industry can not only mitigate its environmental footprint but also drive economic resilience, social responsibility, and technological innovation, contributing meaningfully to a sustainable digital future that benefits society and the planet alike.

REFERENCES

Andersen, S. C., Birgisdottir, H., & Birkved, M. (2022). Life cycle assessments of circular economy in the built environment—A scoping review. *Sustainability, 14*(11), 6887.

Awan, U., Shamim, S., Khan, Z., Zia, N. U., Shariq, S. M., & Khan, M. N. (2021). Big data analytics capability and decision-making: The role of data-driven insight on circular economy performance. *Technological Forecasting and Social Change, 168*, 120766.

Boz, Z., & Martin-Ryals, A. (2023). The role of digitalization in facilitating circular economy. *Journal of the ASABE, 66*(2), 479–496.

Bressanelli, G., Adrodegari, F., Pigosso, D. C., & Parida, V. (2022). Circular economy in the digital age. *Sustainability, 14*(9), 5565.

Bushuyev, S., Bushuyeva, N., Bushuiev, D., & Bushuieva, V. (2023, September). Implementing Project Management Principles Aligned with the Circular Economy. In *2023 IEEE 12th International Conference on Intelligent Data Acquisition and Advanced Computing Systems: Technology and Applications (IDAACS)* (Vol. 1, pp. 331-335). IEEE.

Bushuyev, S., Bushuyeva, N., Bushuiev, D., & Bushuieva, V. (2023, September). Implementing Project Management Principles Aligned with the Circular Economy. In *2023 IEEE 12th International Conference on Intelligent Data Acquisition and Advanced Computing Systems: Technology and Applications (IDAACS)* (Vol. 1, pp. 331-335). IEEE.

Carvalho, J., Nascimento, L., Soares, M., Valério, N., Ribeiro, A., Faria, L., & Vilarinho, C. (2022). Life cycle assessment (LCA) of biochar production from a circular economy perspective. *Processes (Basel, Switzerland), 10*(12), 2684.

Charef, R., & Emmitt, S. (2021). Uses of building information modelling for overcoming barriers to a circular economy. *Journal of Cleaner Production, 285*, 124854.

Chen, Z., & Huang, L. (2019). Application review of LCA (Life Cycle Assessment) in circular economy: From the perspective of PSS (Product Service System). *Procedia CIRP, 83*, 210–217.

Chib, S., Mehta, A. K., Selvakumar, P., Saravanan, A., Mishra, B. R., & Manjunath, T. C. (2025). Mental Health Challenges and Solutions in High-Pressure Work Environments. In Harriott, S. (Ed.), *Innovative Approaches to Managing Conflict and Change in Diverse Work Environments* (pp. 247–272). IGI Global Scientific Publishing.

Cholewa, M., & Minh, L. H. B. (2021). PLM solutions in the process of supporting the implementation and maintenance of the circular economy concept in manufacturing companies. *Sustainability*, *13*(19), 10589.

Dahiya, R., & Selvakumar, P. Vidyadhara, & Manjunath, T. C. (2025). Design and Aerodynamics: Principles and Advances. In M. Mellal (Ed.), *Innovations and Developments in Unmanned Aerial Vehicles* (pp. 145-170). IGI Global Scientific Publishing.

Dahiya, S., Katakojwala, R., Ramakrishna, S., & Mohan, S. V. (2020). Biobased products and life cycle assessment in the context of circular economy and sustainability. *Materials Circular Economy*, *2*, 1–28.

de Oliveira, S. F., & Soares, A. L. (2017). A PLM vision for circular economy. In *Collaboration in a Data-Rich World: 18th IFIP WG 5.5 Working Conference on Virtual Enterprises, PRO-VE 2017, Vicenza, Italy, September 18-20, 2017* [Springer International Publishing.]. *Proceedings*, *18*, 591–602.

Demestichas, K., & Daskalakis, E. (2020). Information and communication technology solutions for the circular economy. *Sustainability*, *12*(18), 7272.

Elia, V., Gnoni, M. G., & Tornese, F. (2017). Measuring circular economy strategies through index methods: A critical analysis. *Journal of Cleaner Production*, *142*, 2741–2751.

Fontana, A., Barni, A., Leone, D., Spirito, M., Tringale, A., Ferraris, M., & Goncalves, G. (2021). Circular economy strategies for equipment lifetime extension: A systematic review. *Sustainability*, *13*(3), 1117.

Halstenberg, F. A., Lindow, K., & Stark, R. (2019). Leveraging circular economy through a methodology for smart service systems engineering. *Sustainability*, *11*(13), 3517.

Han, Y., Shevchenko, T., Yannou, B., Ranjbari, M., Shams Esfandabadi, Z., Saidani, M., & Li, G. (2023). Exploring how digital technologies enable a circular economy of products. *Sustainability*, *15*(3), 2067.

Hariyani, D., Hariyani, P., Mishra, S., & Sharma, M. K. (2024). *Leveraging digital technologies for advancing circular economy practices and enhancing life cycle analysis: A systematic literature review*. Waste Management Bulletin.

Jahan, I., Zhang, G., Bhuiyan, M., & Navaratnam, S. (2022). Circular economy of construction and demolition wood waste—A theoretical framework approach. *Sustainability*, *14*(17), 10478.

Kaur, M., Selvakumar, P., & Dinesh, N. Mohit, Chandel, P. S., & Manjunath, T. C. (2025). Reconstruction and Preservation Strategies for Cultural Heritage. In S. Oflazoğlu & M. Dora (Eds.), *Preserving Cultural Heritage in Post-Disaster Urban Renewal* (pp. 385-412). IGI Global Scientific Publishing.

Kifor, C. V., & Grigore, N. A. (2023). Circular economy approaches for electrical and conventional vehicles. *Sustainability*, *15*(7), 6140.

Kintscher, L., Lawrenz, S., & Poschmann, H. (2021). A life cycle-oriented data-driven architecture for an advanced circular economy. *Procedia CIRP*, *98*, 318–323.

Kommineni, M., Chundru, S., Maroju, P. K., & Selvakumar, P. (2025). Ethical Implications of AI in Sustainable Development Pedagogy. In Chinedu, C., Mafarja, N., Hussein, M., & Saleem, A. (Eds.), *Rethinking the Pedagogy of Sustainable Development in the AI Era* (pp. 17–36). IGI Global Scientific Publishing.

Kristia, K., & Rabbi, M. F. (2023). Exploring the synergy of renewable energy in the circular economy framework: A bibliometric study. *Sustainability*, *15*(17), 13165.

Kutscher, V., Ruland, S., Müller, P., Wasser, N., Lochau, M., Anderl, R., & Hähnle, R. (2020). Towards a circular economy of industrial software. *Procedia CIRP*, *90*, 37–42.

Larsen, V. G., Tollin, N., Sattrup, P. A., Birkved, M., & Holmboe, T. (2022). What are the challenges in assessing circular economy for the built environment? A literature review on integrating LCA, LCC and S-LCA in life cycle sustainability assessment, LCSA. *Journal of Building Engineering*, *50*, 104203.

Lawrenz, S., Leiding, B., Mathiszig, M. E. A., Rausch, A., Schindler, M., & Sharma, P. (2021). Implementing the circular economy by tracing the sustainable impact. *International Journal of Environmental Research and Public Health*, *18*(21), 11316.

Li, J., Song, G., Cai, M., Bian, J., & Mohammed, B. S. (2022). Green environment and circular economy: A state-of-the-art analysis. *Sustainable Energy Technologies and Assessments*, *52*, 102106.

Liaskos, C., Tsioliaridou, A., & Ioannidis, S. (2019, May). Organizing network management logic with circular economy principles. In *2019 15th International Conference on Distributed Computing in Sensor Systems (DCOSS)* (pp. 451-456).

Limbore, N. V., Anute, N., Ahluwalia, G. K., Chordiya, P. B., Kalshetti, P., & Selvakumar, P. (2025). Ethical Leadership and Corporate Responsibility. In Harriott, S. (Ed.), *Innovative Approaches to Managing Conflict and Change in Diverse Work Environments* (pp. 193–218). IGI Global Scientific Publishing.

Mamudu, U. U., Obasi, C. D., Awuye, S. K., Danso, H., Ayodele, P., & Akinyemi, P. (2024). Circular economy in the manufacturing sector: Digital transformation and sustainable practices. *International Journal of Science and Research Archive*, *12*(02), 129–141.

Morsy, K. M., Mostafa, M. K., Abdalla, K. Z., & Galal, M. M. (2020). Life cycle assessment of upgrading primary wastewater treatment plants to secondary treatment including a circular economy approach. *Air, Soil and Water Research*, *13*, 1178622120935857.

Norouzi, M., Chàfer, M., Cabeza, L. F., Jiménez, L., & Boer, D. (2021). Circular economy in the building and construction sector: A scientific evolution analysis. *Journal of Building Engineering*, *44*, 102704.

Panza, L., Faveto, A., Bruno, G., & Lombardi, F. (2022). Open product development to support circular economy through a material lifecycle management framework. *International Journal of Product Lifecycle Management*, *14*(2-3), 255–281.

Peña, C., Civit, B., Gallego-Schmid, A., Druckman, A., Pires, A. C., Weidema, B., & Motta, W. (2021). Using life cycle assessment to achieve a circular economy. *The International Journal of Life Cycle Assessment*, *26*, 215–220.

Piila, N., Sarja, M., Onkila, T., & Mäkelä, M. (2022). Organisational drivers and challenges in circular economy implementation: An issue life cycle approach. *Organization & Environment*, *35*(4), 523–550.

Plociennik, C., Pourjafarian, M., Nazeri, A., Windholz, W., Knetsch, S., Rickert, J., & Weidenkaff, A. (2022). Towards a digital lifecycle passport for the circular economy. *Procedia CIRP*, *105*, 122–127.

Rizvi, S. W. H., Agrawal, S., & Murtaza, Q. (2021). Circular economy under the impact of IT tools: A content-based review. *International Journal of Sustainable Engineering*, *14*(2), 87–97.

Rosa, P., Sassanelli, C., Urbinati, A., Chiaroni, D., & Terzi, S. (2020). Assessing relations between Circular Economy and Industry 4.0: A systematic literature review. *International Journal of Production Research*, *58*(6), 1662–1687.

Samal, A., & Misra, L. I. Mohit, Pougajendy, S., Chandel, P. S., Manjunath, T. C., & Selvakumar, P. (2025). Musealization and Tourism Practices. In S. Oflazoğlu & M. Dora (Eds.), *Preserving Cultural Heritage in Post-Disaster Urban Renewal* (pp. 115-142). IGI Global Scientific Publishing.

Sassanelli, C., Rosa, P., Rocca, R., & Terzi, S. (2019). Circular economy performance assessment methods: A systematic literature review. *Journal of Cleaner Production*, *229*, 440–453.

Soundariya, A., Behera, N. K., Selvakumar, P., Chandel, P. S., Gupta, S., & Manjunath, T. C. (2025). AI and Environmental Ethics: The Role of AI in Addressing Climate Change Ethical Considerations in AI-Driven Environmental Solutions. In Chakraborty, S. (Ed.), *Human Values, Ethics, and Dignity in the Age of Artificial Intelligence* (pp. 321–346). IGI Global Scientific Publishing.

Spišáková, M., Mandičák, T., Mésároš, P., & Špak, M. (2022). Waste management in a sustainable circular economy as a part of design of construction. *Applied Sciences (Basel, Switzerland)*, *12*(9), 4553.

Stillitano, T., Spada, E., Iofrida, N., Falcone, G., & De Luca, A. I. (2021). Sustainable agri-food processes and circular economy pathways in a life cycle perspective: State of the art of applicative research. *Sustainability*, *13*(5), 2472.

Tamilarasi, C., Sowmiya, K., Vignesh, G. D., Jasmine, R. L., Nehru, P., & Selvakumar, P. (2025). AI in Renewable Energy Education: Teaching the Future of Sustainable Power Systems. In Chinedu, C., Mafarja, N., Hussein, M., & Saleem, A. (Eds.), *Rethinking the Pedagogy of Sustainable Development in the AI Era* (pp. 133–152). IGI Global Scientific Publishing.

Tola, F., Mosconi, E. M., Marconi, M., & Gianvincenzi, M. (2023). Perspectives for the development of a circular economy model to promote ship recycling practices in the European context: A systemic literature review. *Sustainability*, *15*(7), 5919.

Väisänen, J. M., Ranta, V., & Aarikka-Stenroos, L. (2019). Enabling circular economy with software: A multi-level approach to benefits, requirements and barriers. In *Software Business: 10th International Conference, ICSOB 2019, Jyväskylä, Finland, November 18–20, 2019* [Springer International Publishing.]. *Proceedings*, *10*, 252–259.

Yang, M., Chen, L., Wang, J., Msigwa, G., Osman, A. I., Fawzy, S., & Yap, P. S. (2023). Circular economy strategies for combating climate change and other environmental issues. *Environmental Chemistry Letters*, *21*(1), 55–80.

Chapter 4
Circular Economy-Driven Software Lifecycle Management: A Sustainable Approach

Usharani Bhimavarapu
https://orcid.org/0000-0001-5050-0415
Department of Computer Science and Engineering, Koneru Lakshmaiah Education Foundation, Vaddeswaram, India

ABSTRACT

Circular Economy (CE) practices aim to achieve maximum utilization of resources, waste reduction, and product life cycle durability, and their application to software lifecycle management became increasingly necessary. The traditional software development has a linear approach, and that's leading to cyclic obsolescence, wasteful utilization of resources, and inefficiency. The paper introduces the application of CE to software lifecycle management for achieving maximum life span of software, modularity, and maintainability. Data were collected using expert questionnaires from general and expert networks, collecting responses on circular economy and bioeconomy principles. Data were preprocessed, and relevant features were extracted using Ant Colony Optimization (ACO) to enhance analytical accuracy. A bi-stacked Long Short-Term Memory (LSTM) network was then used to identify temporal trends in software releases, maintenance records, and usage patterns to offer predictive analysis for anticipatory resource optimization.

DOI: 10.4018/979-8-3373-4652-6.ch004

INTRODUCTION

Circular economy (CE) refers to the approach of reducing waste and optimizing resource utilization in terms of reuse, recycling, and regeneration. The principles of CE in software lifecycle management seek to maximize the utilization of how software is designed, developed, deployed, and retired. Traditional software development is a linear process—develop, use, and throw that creates inefficiency and environmental footprint in terms of energy utilization and hardware dependency. Circular models shatter this linearity focusing on software longevity, modularity, and flexibility. This model conforms to sustainable development goals and business social responsibility for information and communication technology. Underpinned by CE principles, organizations are able to develop software that is robust, upgradable, and compatible. The need is environmental in nature but also through the economic stimulus of cost saving and productivity improvement. Additionally, CE software lifecycle encourages proper utilization of computer resources. It encourages programmers to rethink coding, deployment, and maintenance processes. Lastly, CE-based software lifecycle management minimizes obsolescence and facilitates green computing innovation.

Electronic waste, or e-waste, is a worldwide phenomenon that frequently occurs due to software obsolescence. Obsolete software has the tendency to induce hardware replacement even when physical machinery is in working order. Closed-loop software lifecycle management accomplishes this due to greater backward compatibility and longer software support. By ensuring the software operates on current hardware, organizations reduce hardware obsolescence to be discarded. This lowers the carbon footprint of manufacturing new devices indirectly. Further, modularity in software makes updating or patching easier to update the entire system installations with less storage and bandwidth needs. Software legacy component reuse also minimizes development effort and energy demands. By mapping software onto CE principles, businesses promote environmental sustainability and the lowest cost of operation. Educating developers and IT managers on such practices promotes e-waste reduction. Hence, CE in software prevents not only digital resources but also environmental waste.

Software sustainability is the ability of computer software to stay up and running, efficient, and useful for extended lengths of time. Circular practices focus on developing flexible and sustainable software. This involves constructing modular designs that are simple to extend and upgrade. Sustainable software minimizes the need for full system replacement, saving energy and resources. Further, lifecycle management through CE promotes the use of open-source libraries along with reusable code to minimize repeated effort. Energy efficiency in the domain is also achieved, where better software uses fewer computing resources. Organizations keep low technical debt and higher reliability in software through long-term maintenance planning. This brings software up to date with changing business requirements without unnecessary environmental or financial cost. Circular principles bring forward-looking software design that takes account of future technological change. It is thus inherent in software strategy rather than an add-on.

Cost reduction is one of the leading drivers for circular economy strategies for managing the lifecycle of software. Reuse of software components saves organizational time and development cost. Software that is modular, upgradable has lower unplanned maintenance and fewer resources allocated to it. In addition, minimizing recurring hardware replacement based on software incompatibility decreases capital outlays. Circular solutions also provide improved use of resources by accounting for long-term value over short-term profit. Companies recycle vintage systems and give them new applications. CE strategies also decrease downtime and related loss of productivity and hence achieve operational efficiency. Cost savings even touch energy usage, with optimized software minimizing server loading and power consumption. Generally, the use of CE principles enables businesses to be economically viable while assisting in environmental goals. Businesses that implement circular software solutions have enterprise advantages in a more sustainable business environment.

Circular economy principles encourage innovation in software through modularity and adaptability. Modularity enables piece-by-piece replacement, supposing constant improvement without full system redesign. Modular design enables the testing of innovative technologies and functionality with embedded risk isolation. It generates interoperability, i.e., triggering heterogeneous software systems to share and make use of resources, as well as reuse existing code and libraries that trigger innovation. It accelerates the development stage and encourages common practices. Developers are challenged with finding solutions that can be deployed on multiple platforms and hardware configurations. Another way in which modularity reduces dependence on proprietary technologies, therefore software durability. CE principles promote cloud-based deployment models that ensure scalability and effectiveness. The business maintains its software up-to-date, resilient, and visionary by embracing innovation and sustainability.

National governments and global institutions increasingly promote sustainable methods of which digital sustainability is one. Circular software life cycle management takes such directive directions so that organizations can comply with environmental regulations and IT governance best practices. As an example, e-waste laws, power conservation best practices, and data center use best practices typically require sustainable software practices. CE philosophies offer systematic approaches of extending the duration of the software and reducing digital consumption of resources, and thus compliance becomes feasible. Circular practices provide traceability, documentation, and lifecycle auditing. Companies avoid legal expenses and reputation damage by proactively seeking CE-based software practices. Furthermore, adherence to sustainability-driven regulations generates stakeholder trust and boosts company social responsibility stocks. Circular operations enable companies to measure sustainability performance. This convergence of operational excellence and compliance enhances the long-term sustainability of software products.

Innovative use of resources in the digital platform forms a foundation of circular software lifecycle management. Reusable and scalable software development enables organizations to make efficient use of computational resources, storage space, and network bandwidth. Virtualization and containerization also support resource optimization by offering multiple applications with infrastructure sharing. Circular methods also optimize code for energy-intensive activities to minimize them, hence supporting green computing initiatives. Human resources are also managed through resources, since innovation labor instead of maintenance labor is performed by developers. Cloud computing usage of software also helps with elasticity, where systems grow based on requirement without too much resource consumption. Resource usage optimization minimizes operational expenses while minimizing environmental effects at the same time. Through ongoing monitoring and optimization, CE-based software achieves strategic utilization of resources. This creates a circular digital environment that can sustain business and societal demands.

Software life is often disrupted by technological innovation and customer demands. Circular economy strategies seek to lengthen the software lifespan through flexibility, modularity, and backward compatibility. Applications developed according to CE principles are simple to retro-fit with new functionality without large-scale overhaul. Longevity is promoted by maintenance policies like incremental update and patch management. Software life extension minimizes reliance on continuous redevelopment and decreases the risks of obsolescence. It benefits the environment and economic effectiveness by postponing hardware replacement. CE strategies also support active retirement techniques for software to recycle or reuse the retired systems based on demand. Longevity gains credence from the users, since software is dependable in the long term. Finally, lifecycle extension maximizes the return on investment and supports sustainable digital behavior.

Circular software lifecycle management enhances cooperation between developers, organizations, and open-source communities. The sharing of reusable code, libraries, and best practices reduces effort duplication and speeds up innovation. Knowledge sharing is also facilitated by the extensibility of software solutions to function in a variety of contexts. Shared solutions promote shared responsibility for maintaining them, with developers motivated towards efficiency and longevity. Common assets also support standardized coding processes and better software quality. CE principles support cross-functional teams integrating business strategy, environmental management, and IT capabilities. Peer platforms allow real-time feedback and rapid iteration of software modules. Collective intelligence is used by organizations to drive operating performance and sustainability results. This collaboration imposes circularity-enabling ecosystems through all phases of the software lifecycle.

Principles of circular economy of software lifecycle management solve essential environmental, economic, and operating challenges. They minimize e-waste, ensure products are sustainable, maximize use of resources, and increase the lifespan of software. CE principles promote innovation, modularity, and flexibility so that the software continues to be beneficial in changing technology environments. Cost savings, efficiency, and compliance give rise to economic benefits. Knowledge sharing on a reciprocal basis accelerates further sustainability gains. With the inclusion of circular methods, businesses infuse digital transformation with corporate-level sustainability objectives. CE-based software practices also ensure ethical usage of resources and minimize environmental footprint. All these practices taken together offer a future-proof circular economy platform for effective, responsible, and future-proof software management. It is no longer an option but a necessity to implement circular economy principles in software. Guzzo et al. (2019) develop a circular innovation model but one whose use in actual solutions across industries is constrained. Alcayaga et al. (2019) also offer a smart-circular systems solution but not empirically applied to actual environments. Kristoffersen et al. (2020) offer a digital-enabled circular strategies solution but whose application is centered on the manufacturing industry, constraining wider application. Grafström and Aasma (2021) offer circular economy barriers writing, but the article only offers sparse alternatives for conducting policy work. Abdul-Hamid et al. (2020) mention Industry 4.0 challenges for the palm oil industry, but the article cannot be generalized to other industries. Okorie et al. (2018) mention digitization and circular economy development, but the performance is analytic in focus with no predictive modeling. Alcayaga and Hansen (2019) compare circular business models for intelligent products but for only one B2B textiles case, which makes them non-generalizable. Bocken et al. (2018) discuss pay-per-use approaches to sustainable consumption but rely on a case study, which limits generalizability. Cagno et al. (2021) investigate digital technologies for circular economy transformation but do not compare impact across sectors. Flaherty et al. (2021) explore social marketing through digital technologies but provide largely theoretical proof with limited tests. Mushi et al. (2022) report on digital technology for Tanzanian agri-sustainable agriculture and results may not generalize across other geo- or agri-contexts. Pirola et al. (2020) conduct a literature review of digital product-service systems without practical working advice. Liberati et al. (2009) provide PRISMA reporting recommendations, but the statement might not best capture non-medical systematic review nuances. Page et al. (2021) revise the PRISMA guidelines, but the guidance remains generic and might be required to be tailored to particular disciplines beyond clinical research.

Jabbour et al. (2019) provide an integrative business model for circular economy, but its application in various sectors awaits extensive tests. Mourtzis (2018) presents frugal innovation in made-to-order manufacturing networks and products, yet the strategy has not been empirically tested in industrial practice. Behzadan et al. (2015) cite surveys of augmented reality applications in civil infrastructure, but the study is constrained by prioritizing visualization over findings on implementation. Hirve et al. (2017) suggest an AR-based data visualization framework, but scalability to big data and generalizability are not considered. Novák et al. (2012) give mathematical theory of fuzzy logic, but no applied recommendations for complex real-world systems. Kang et al. (2010) use fuzzy evaluation for ecological land suitability, and it might not be suitable for other environmental or urban situations. Akinade and Oyedele (2019) suggest an ANFIS-based building materials supply chain waste analytics platform, but the application to industry-to-industry is not explored. Goldberg and Holland (1988) offer a machine learning definition of genetic algorithms, but the system can be called out-of-date for bulk operation in current times. Taylor and Sours (2018) hypothesize a materials stewardship system, but quantitative measurements are not provided for circular economy interventions. Neves Da Silva and Novo (2017) talk of consumption of resources by intelligent monitoring centers, but findings are restricted to some case studies and locations. Zhou et al. (2013) formulate an SVM model to assess iron and steel enterprises but industrial-level generalizability is questionable. Zhang et al. (2017) use game theory for scheduling with an environmental orientation but practical applicability is constrained by complexity. Hao and Yue (2016) optimize multimodal transportation paths but real-time dynamic constraints are not dealt with effectively. Gatzioura et al. (2019) design an industrial symbiosis hybrid recommender system but with minimum cross-sector integration and scalability. Kolodner (2014) proposes case-based reasoning but with minimum adaptation for intricate circular economy systems. Li et al. (2020) integrate blockchain with case-based reasoning to help remanufacturing, but the system lacks empirical verification in industrial applications. Koo et al. (2017) implement a semantic integration mechanism in biorefining models, but interoperability issues among heterogeneous software systems remain to be solved.

Bressanelli et al. (2022) introduce a smart circular economy mechanism but without much empirical evidence from various industrial contexts. De Felice and Petrillo (2021) suggest a critical review of the digicircular economy but without quantitative measurement of implementation performance. Preut et al. (2021) present digital twins for circular economy use cases but scalability and integration in compound industrial processes are sparsely addressed. İzmirli et al. (2021) present omni-channel network topology under inventory share regulations but limited real-world deployments across numerous different supply chains. Andersen and Jæger (2021) propose an edge and distributed ledger architecture for EEE circularity but the method can be technology and adoption constrained. Çetin et al. (2021) describe a circular digital built environment strategy but lack empirical support from actual construction projects. Magrini et al. (2021) discuss IoT and distributed ledger to enable digital circular economy, but case specificity constrains generalizability. Vacchi et al. (2021) discuss Industry 4.0 and smart data in circular eco-design support, yet the sustainability effects in the long run are not quantified. Ingemarsdotter et al. (2019) describe IoT-enabled circular practices, but there is only evidence of such practice in the chosen industries. Beltrami et al. (2021) theorize Industry 4.0 and sustainability, but there are sparse large-scale empirical data on the conceptual framework. Alcayaga et al. (2019) give a description of smart-circular systems but the research is descriptive with no predictive model. Kristoffersen et al. (2020) offer a digital-enabled circular strategies framework for production but one whose utility for non-production industries is doubtful. Liu et al. (2022) offer a framework of digital technologies for the circular economy, and implemented guidelines are limited.

MATERIALS AND METHODS

Circular Economy approaches to software lifecycle management were studied in a structured approach to maintain objectivity in the outcomes. Surveys of experts were employed to collect data from expert and general networks to obtain diversified viewpoints with minimal personal data. Data preprocessing consisted of anonymization, categorical encoding of responses, and normalization for maintaining consistency. Ant Colony Optimization (ACO) was applied to discover significant features to select the most influential variables to study. A bi-stacked Long Short-Term Memory (LSTM) network was then applied to discover long-term trends and predict software maintenance, obsolescence, and resource optimization needs. Finally, the model's performance was evaluated to determine whether it could create actionable information in the direction of sustainable and effective software lifecycle management.

Material

The information were collected by interviewing within five subject-matter networks in the frame of the ConCirMy project and four overall subject-matter networks for circular and bio-economy. 15 subject-matter specialists took part in the study. In line with rigorous data minimization practices, no individual information that would make it possible to identify persons, such as names, e-mail addresses, or other identifiers, were collected. Participants were, however, offered the chance to receive private messages by email in addition to the survey if they would prefer to hear more about the findings of the study, and the survey administration had received a couple of emails stating this interest. Participants were first asked to score their knowledge of both the circular economy and the bioeconomy on a scale of five categories each. Results indicate that the overall majority of the participants were highly sensitive to the circular economy. Sensitivity to the bioeconomy varied, with most of the participants self-reporting a medium level of familiarity. The data thus reflects both expert judgments and self-reports of levels of knowledge by circular and bio-economy domains and forms the foundation for follow-up analysis.

Preprocessing

The survey information that were collected were systematically put through a preprocessing phase guaranteeing data stability, quality, and usability for the subsequent phase of analysis. To be strictly in compliance with the principle of data minimization, not to include personal identifiers such as names or e-mail addresses, anonymization of all answers was carried out first. Secondly, the dataset was purified for completeness and only had fully completed questionnaires kept to exclude missing value bias. The responses regarding exposure to the circular economy and bioeconomy, which were originally categorical with five points, were re-coding into numerical coding to simplify quantitative analysis and statistical comparison. Errors such as repeat entries and confusing responses were carefully identified and eliminated. Besides that, the data set was normalized for scalable variables comparison, particularly in comparing levels of familiarity among subjects. Descriptive statistics were originally generated to aid in satisfaction of having a normal responses distribution and identifying outliers. Preprocessing involved ensuring that the data set was clean, reliable, and ready for proper evaluation of expertise information and knowledge within the circular and bio-economy industries.

Feature Selection

Subset feature selection for the data was performed using Ant Colony Optimization (ACO), a nature-inspired metaheuristic algorithm that simulates how ants forage to find the best set of subsets of features. In this case, each feature is regarded as a node in a graph, and artificial ants move across the graph to construct candidate sets of features using pheromone trails and heuristic values. Pheromone trails are constantly updated to reinforce feature combinations with high values of a particular evaluation function, e.g., accuracy for classification, or correlation with the target variable. This probabilistic search allows ACO to perform an effective search in an enormous feature space without being stuck in local optima and hence is best applicable to high-dimensional data sets. In this article, ACO was directed towards factors that accounted for the majority of experts' understanding of the circular economy and bioeconomy, and other survey variables of interest. Automatic and systematic down-weighting occurred between irrelevant or uninformative questionnaire items to provide a more informative and compact dataset. This is done to enhance model performance, reduce computational cost, and enable results explanation. Because of ACO's adaptive learning nature, the algorithm progressively refined feature importance step-by-step. The finally chosen features are the most significant variables to investigate, making predictive or analytical models efficient and productive.

Bistacked LSTM

The union of bi-stacked Long Short-Term Memory (LSTM) networks and Circular Economy (CE) approaches to software lifecycle management yields a productive framework of predictive analytics and decision-making. Bi-stacked LSTM networks consist of two layers of stacked LSTM units back to back such that the model can identify short-term and long-term dependencies of sequence data. In sequence data of software lifecycle management, sequence data can include histories of versions of software, maintenance history, usage pattern, and frequency of updates. With the application of bi-stacked LSTM, businesses are able to predict future maintenance needs for software, identify likely threats of obsolescence, and optimize resource allocation between various stages of the lifecycle. Such predictive capability supports CE principles in facilitating active enhancement, reducing excessive replacement of software, and maximally lengthening software life. The model also has the capability to evaluate trends in modular pieces of software that identify modules as being reusable or upgradable to maximum efficiency. Bi-stacked LSTM also enhances energy consumption and resource utilization decision-making for green computing. Trained on historical and real-time software lifecycle data, the approach can provide prescriptive advice to developers and IT managers alike. With two LSTM layers, it is easier to comprehend more intricate temporal patterns, such as bug patterns or life cycles of feature updates. Lastly, the application of bi-stacked LSTM in CE-based software lifecycle management enables organizations to offer evidence-based plans that maximize sustainability, reduce cost, and improve overall software robustness.

EXPERIMENTAL RESULTS

Experimental results validate the effectiveness of the application of Circular Economy principles in software lifecycle management using the given bi-stacked LSTM method. The preprocessed data, which had been cleansed of undesirable features by Ant Colony Optimization, were then used in model training and validation. Simple performance measures, like accuracy, precision, recall, and F1-score, were used in quantifying the capacity of the model in predicting software maintenance needs, risk of obsolescence, and best resource allocation. Preliminary results indicate that the bi-stacked LSTM works well in detecting temporal patterns of software utilization and update history with precise predictions in accordance with circular economy principles. The study also recommends that account is taken of the function of features employed in improving the quality of prediction and promoting sustainable software practice. Results provide measurable basis for demonstrating how machine learning may improve decision-making for software life cycle management in CE-based solutions.

Table 1 reflects feedback to specialists' awareness of circular economy knowledge and bioeconomy knowledge and practice of software updating. It can be seen from the table that the majority of the participants have good awareness of circular economy, but awareness of bioeconomy is not uniform. Software updates are done from weekly to bi-monthly, reflecting varying work habits. Priority maintenance levels are also emphasized, with a bias towards showing major updates. Software module reuse shows evidence of concern for sustainable practice, and active reuse is also shown by most respondents. Lifecycle knowledge shows evidence of riches in software lifetime and maintenance strategy knowledge. The table shows correlations between high circular economy knowledge and frequent, well-sequestered maintenance activity. Fewer bioeconomy knowledge among certain users is associated with medium lifecycle knowledge. The results are a baseline metric of master knowledge's association with sustainable software practice management. The results will serve as the baseline for future predictive modeling and feature selection in subsequent analysis.

Table 1. Expert familiarity and software maintenance awareness

Circular Economy Familiarity	Bioeconomy Familiarity	Software Update Frequency	Maintenance Priority	Reuse of Modules	Lifecycle Knowledge
Very High	Medium	Weekly	High	Yes	Advanced
High	Medium	Monthly	Medium	Yes	Intermediate
Very High	Low	Bi-Weekly	High	No	Advanced
High	Medium	Monthly	Medium	Yes	Intermediate
Very High	High	Weekly	High	Yes	Advanced
Medium	Medium	Monthly	Medium	No	Intermediate
Very High	Medium	Weekly	High	Yes	Advanced
High	Low	Bi-Monthly	Medium	Yes	Intermediate

continued on following page

Table 1. Continued

Circular Economy Familiarity	Bioeconomy Familiarity	Software Update Frequency	Maintenance Priority	Reuse of Modules	Lifecycle Knowledge
Medium	Medium	Monthly	Medium	No	Intermediate
Very High	Medium	Weekly	High	Yes	Advanced

Table 2 takes into account quantifiable parameters of software lifecycle sustainability. It encompasses module reusability, update efficiency, frequency of bug fixes, energy consumption, risk of obsolescence, and user satisfaction. High reusability of great modules is associated with low obsolescence risk and high satisfaction. Updated efficiency values indicate the frequency of software improvement for performance. Frequency of bug fixes is a measure of maintenance responsiveness, while energy usage is a measure of the computational cost of software run. The table shows that green approaches, i.e., high updating and modularity, lead to low energy consumption and improved system duration. Medium use or updating efficiency levels are markers of optimization potential. As a nexus point of operational efficiency and sustainability in software lifecycle management, in most cases, the table is. Empirical data supported CE-applied interventions in instances of efficient resource practices and elongation of the software lifecycle.

Table 2. Software lifecycle sustainability indicators

Module Reusability	Update Efficiency	Bug Fix Frequency	Energy Consumption	Obsolescence Risk	User Satisfaction
High	0.92	Weekly	Low	Low	High
Medium	0.85	Bi-Weekly	Medium	Medium	Medium
High	0.95	Weekly	Low	Low	High
Low	0.78	Monthly	High	High	Medium
High	0.91	Weekly	Low	Low	High
Medium	0.87	Bi-Weekly	Medium	Medium	Medium
High	0.93	Weekly	Low	Low	High
Low	0.80	Monthly	Medium	Medium	Medium
Medium	0.88	Bi-Weekly	Medium	Medium	Medium
High	0.94	Weekly	Low	Low	High

Table 3 shows Bi-stacked LSTM predictive performance in software maintenance requirement prediction. Predicted and actual maintenance columns, prediction accuracy, update compliance, utilization of resources, and feature contribution are the measures employed. The measures reflect high prediction accuracy in all except one instance with indications that the model is resilient in maintenance need prediction. Ratings of resource usage provide a measure of how software updates are being used without overloading systems. Contribution by characteristic tells us about most of the predictive factors, i.e., module reuse and bug fix rates. Predicted vs. actual differences in maintenance needs identify areas where the model must be strengthened. The table shows why integration of expert knowledge and machine learning is required for proactive lifecycle management. It displays how CE principles applied with predictive modeling maximize maintenance planning and software life cycle. Increased conformity to updates signifies increased software longevity and reduced obsolescence. In general, the table illustrates the success of predictive analytics in software maintenance under circular economy.

Table 3. Predictive maintenance assessment

Predicted Maintenance Need	Actual Maintenance	Prediction Accuracy	Update Compliance	Resource Utilization	Feature Contribution
High	High	0.95	Yes	0.88	Module Reuse
Medium	Medium	0.91	Yes	0.82	Update Frequency
High	High	0.96	Yes	0.89	Bug Fix Frequency
Low	Medium	0.85	No	0.78	Lifecycle Knowledge
High	High	0.94	Yes	0.87	Module Reuse
Medium	Medium	0.90	Yes	0.80	Update Frequency
High	High	0.95	Yes	0.88	Bug Fix Frequency
Low	Low	0.89	Yes	0.75	Lifecycle Knowledge
Medium	Medium	0.92	Yes	0.81	Module Reuse
High	High	0.96	Yes	0.90	Bug Fix Frequency

Table 4 uncovers resource usage in CPU loads, memory loads, energy savings, server load, update efficiency, and redundancy in modules during software lifecycle management. CPU- and memory-intensive operations are CPU- and memory-intensive loaded, but energy savings indicate the effectiveness of update strategies. Server loading measurements indicate the degree to which maintenance and updating influence system performance. Update performance means the performance of how well and how fast software updates are performed. Module redundancy is the degree to which there are redundant software parts that is synonymous with wasteful resource utilization. Effective modular software design maintains energy consumption and system loading to a minimum, the table says. Low redundancy and high update efficiency are strongest drivers to sustainable software practice. Extrapolating operation metrics to CE principles, table illustrates possible cost and energy savings. These outcomes are actionable information for IT infrastructure optimization in a CE-oriented software life cycle.

Table 4. Resource optimization metrics

CPU Usage (%)	Memory Usage (%)	Energy Savings (%)	Server Load	Update Efficiency	Module Redundancy
65	70	12	Medium	0.92	Low
55	60	10	Low	0.85	Medium
68	72	14	Medium	0.94	Low
72	78	8	High	0.78	High
66	70	13	Medium	0.91	Low
60	65	11	Low	0.87	Medium
67	71	13	Medium	0.93	Low
70	75	9	High	0.80	High
61	66	11	Low	0.88	Medium
68	72	14	Medium	0.94	Low

Table 5 illustrates software module reuse as a fundamental CE practice. Attributes are component name, frequency of reuse, update frequency, bug frequency, lifecycle phase, and sustainability score. Modules that are reused more have less bug frequency and more sustainability. Update frequency is a metric of how often products are upgraded or maintained, which affects their lifespan. Lifecycle stage is a metric of whether products are being developed, tested, or constructed, and it adds context to reuse patterns. The table indicates that strategic module reuse improves software sustainability and minimizes effort during development. Production units with high reuse numbers reflect the advantages of CE activities in usage contexts. Low update ratio or higher defect rates are of lower sustainability levels. These results confirm the advantage of modularity and reuse in improving software lifecycle and enabling efficient consumption of resources. Empirical confirmation of prioritization of high-value reusable items in CE-oriented software maintenance is reflected in the table.

Table 5. Software component reuse analysis

Component Name	Reuse Count	Update Frequency	Bug Incidence	Lifecycle Stage	Sustainability Score
Module A	5	Weekly	Low	Development	0.92
Module B	3	Monthly	Medium	Testing	0.85
Module C	6	Bi-Weekly	Low	Production	0.94
Module D	2	Monthly	High	Development	0.78
Module E	4	Weekly	Low	Production	0.91
Module F	3	Monthly	Medium	Testing	0.86
Module G	5	Bi-Weekly	Low	Production	0.93
Module H	2	Monthly	Medium	Development	0.80
Module I	4	Bi-Weekly	Medium	Testing	0.88
Module J	6	Weekly	Low	Production	0.95

Table 6 verifies intercorrelation among expert knowledge, decision confidence, software lifespan estimation, module upgrade priority, maintenance frequency, and resource allocation. Highly knowledgeable experts are more confident and more accurate in upgrading modules. Table 6 suggests more confidence with more accurate lifespan estimates and proper resource allocation. Maintenance frequency is in accordance with lifecycle stage awareness, with timely updates and bug fixes on schedule. The evidence suggests that domain knowledge plays an important role in CE-oriented software practices implementation. Experts of medium familiarity utilize conventional stages with acceptable resource productivity. The table shows the application of decision-making considering knowledge in sustainable software lifecycle management. The table also demonstrates the way professional knowledge can be used to support predictive modeling and feature selection. This information is useful in hybridizing human wisdom with machine learning capacity for CE deployment.

Table 6. Expert knowledge and decision patterns

Expert Familiarity	Decision Confidence	Software Lifespan Prediction	Module Upgrade Priority	Maintenance Frequency	Resource Allocation Score
Very High	High	Long	High	Weekly	0.92
High	Medium	Medium	Medium	Monthly	0.85
Very High	High	Long	High	Weekly	0.94
Medium	Medium	Medium	Low	Bi-Monthly	0.78

continued on following page

Table 6. Continued

Expert Familiarity	Decision Confidence	Software Lifespan Prediction	Module Upgrade Priority	Maintenance Frequency	Resource Allocation Score
High	High	Long	High	Weekly	0.91
Medium	Medium	Medium	Medium	Monthly	0.86
Very High	High	Long	High	Weekly	0.93
Medium	Medium	Medium	Medium	Monthly	0.80
High	Medium	Long	High	Bi-Weekly	0.88
Very High	High	Long	High	Weekly	0.95

Table 7 categorizes types of different software updates, such as frequency, duration, bug fixes, end-user feedback, and system downtime. Security updates are done with short durations, reflecting preemptive threat management. Feature updates are less regular but with long durations and medium end-user feedback. Bug fixes vary in frequency and system downtime impact, reflecting reactive maintenance behavior. Prompt updates issued have a correlation with end-user ratings that are favorable and zero or minimal downtime. The table illustrates running tendencies that enhance maintainable software maintenance and CE goals. Organizations are able to manage maintenance calendars more effectively to minimize the use of resources as a result of update nature. System downtime percentages are a measure of operation efficiency and bug-fix monitoring gives feedback on software reliability. Predictive patch analysis for application in the future is contingent on these trends. The table emphasizes balancing maintenance processes with efficiency of resources and energy.

Table 7. Update and maintenance patterns

Update Type	Frequency	Duration (hours)	Bug Fixes	User Feedback	System Downtime
Security	Weekly	2	Low	Positive	0.5
Feature	Monthly	4	Medium	Neutral	1.0
Security	Bi-Weekly	2	Low	Positive	0.4
Bug Fix	Monthly	3	High	Negative	1.5
Feature	Weekly	3	Low	Positive	0.6
Bug Fix	Monthly	4	Medium	Neutral	1.2
Security	Weekly	2	Low	Positive	0.5
Feature	Bi-Monthly	3	Medium	Neutral	1.0
Security	Weekly	2	Low	Positive	0.4
Bug Fix	Bi-Weekly	3	Medium	Neutral	0.8

Table 8 measures software lifecycle sustainability by phase using module efficiency, energy footprint, minimized waste, upgradeability, and overall sustainability rating. Development and production phases have high efficiency, low energy footprint, and high sustainability ratings. Maintenance and testing phases are moderately efficient with potential for improvement. Upgradeability is the propensity of software elements to permit future modification. Waste reduction is the capability of deleting redundant functionality or unnecessary modules. The table presents the potential application of sustainability rating in decision-making in software lifecycle management. Large values represent the extensive reuse and efficient maintenance modules. The moderate values represent where CE practices can be improved. The outcomes offer evidence-based focused interventions to improve energy efficiency and minimize operation waste. Overall, the table assesses the sustainability performance throughout the software lifecycle.

Table 8. Lifecycle sustainability scoring

Lifecycle Stage	Module Efficiency	Energy Impact	Waste Reduction	Upgrade Potential	Sustainability Rating
Development	High	Low	High	High	0.92
Testing	Medium	Medium	Medium	Medium	0.85
Production	High	Low	High	High	0.94
Maintenance	Medium	Medium	Medium	Medium	0.78
Development	High	Low	High	High	0.91
Testing	Medium	Medium	Medium	Medium	0.86
Production	High	Low	High	High	0.93
Maintenance	Medium	Medium	Medium	Medium	0.80
Testing	Medium	Medium	Medium	Medium	0.88
Production	High	Low	High	High	0.95

Table 9 sums up the performance indicators of the bi-stacked LSTM model on the CE-based software lifecycle dataset. The indicators are accuracy, precision, recall, F1-score, RMSE, and MAE. High F1-scores and accuracy confirm high predictive precision in maintenance and lifecycle prediction. Precision and recall confirm accurate predictions by the model to associated maintenance requirements and false positives. RMSE and MAE report the average prediction error, with low values indicating high reliability. The table verifies that chosen characteristics and model setup continue to be effective at detecting temporal patterns for software usage and update. Metric differences indicate where tuning of the model would enhance performance. These findings in general validate the application of bi-stacked LSTM for predictive maintenance and resource effectiveness. The table offers a numerical value to evaluate other modeling methods.

Table 9. Predictive performance metrics

Accuracy	Precision	Recall	F1-Score	RMSE	MAE
0.95	0.94	0.96	0.95	0.08	0.06
0.91	0.90	0.92	0.91	0.12	0.09
0.96	0.95	0.97	0.96	0.07	0.05
0.85	0.83	0.86	0.84	0.15	0.12
0.94	0.93	0.95	0.94	0.09	0.07
0.90	0.89	0.91	0.90	0.13	0.10
0.95	0.94	0.96	0.95	0.08	0.06
0.89	0.88	0.90	0.89	0.14	0.11
0.92	0.91	0.93	0.92	0.11	0.08
0.96	0.95	0.97	0.96	0.07	0.05

Table 10 shows expert judgment for CE readiness to implement, sustainability impact, maintenance savings, resource efficiency, and CE overall score. High-confidence and readiness experts reflect high degrees of agreement with circular economy applications. Sustainability impact values show expected environmental and operational benefits through the implementation of CE. Maintenance reduction scores suggest ability to prevent wasteful updates and extend software life span. Resource effectiveness measures efficient use of computer and human resources. Total CE score combines several indicators in a single measure. Analysis of inconsistency in adoption readiness between high-scoring experts is required by the table, necessitating exceptional intervention in CE adoption. Best practices among top-scoring experts that can be utilized to guide organizational strategy are apparent. Decision-making for integrating CE in software lifecycle management is guided by the table. Directions for take-home to improve sustainability and effectiveness in operations are given by the table recommendations.

Table 10. Expert assessment of circular economy implementation

Expert Confidence	Adoption Readiness	Sustainability Impact	Maintenance Reduction	Resource Efficiency	Overall CE Score
High	Ready	High	High	High	0.94
Medium	Partial	Medium	Medium	Medium	0.85
High	Ready	High	High	High	0.95
Low	Not Ready	Low	Medium	Medium	0.78
High	Ready	High	High	High	0.92
Medium	Partial	Medium	Medium	Medium	0.86
High	Ready	High	High	High	0.93
Low	Not Ready	Low	Medium	Medium	0.80
Medium	Partial	Medium	Medium	Medium	0.88
High	Ready	High	High	High	0.95

CONCLUSION

Implementation of Circular Economy principles in software life cycle management is a viable and effective platform for prolonging software life and minimizing resource wastage. Involvement of predictive analytics through bi-stacked LSTM networks provides companies with the platform to predict maintenance needs, identify risks of obsolescence, and optimize modular software components. Applications of Ant Colony Optimization for feature selection ensure that the most impactful features are involved in decision-making, enhancing model accuracy and explainability. This operation, besides ensuring environmental sustainability through the prevention of preventable software updates and energy consumption, also optimizes operational efficiency and cost-effectiveness. Specialist views affirm that leveraging circular and bio-economy principles is feasible in designing sustainable software practices. Overall, the study brings to the forefront the advantages of hybridization of CE principles with next-generation machine learning to create viable, adaptive, and ecologically sound software systems. The way the steps are carried out plays a large role in driving sustainable digital transformation in industrial and research settings.

REFERENCES

Abdul-Hamid, A.-Q., Ali, M. H., Tseng, M.-L., Lan, S., & Kumar, M. (2020). Impeding challenges on Industry 4.0 in circular economy: Palm oil industry in Malaysia. *Computers & Operations Research*, *123*, 105052.

Akinade, O., & Oyedele, L. (2019). Integrating construction supply chains within a circular economy: An ANFIS-based waste analytics system (A-WAS). *Journal of Cleaner Production*, *229*, 863–873.

Alcayaga, A., & Hansen, E. G. (2019). Smart products as enabler for circular business models: The case of B2B textile washing services. In *Proceedings of the 3rd PLATE 2019 Conference* (pp. 18–20). Berlin, Germany.

Alcayaga, A., Wiener, M., & Hansen, E. G. (2019). Towards a framework of smart-circular systems: An integrative literature review. *Journal of Cleaner Production*, *221*, 622–634.

Andersen, T., & Jæger, B. (2021). Circularity for electric and electronic equipment (EEE), the edge and distributed ledger (Edge & DL) model. *Sustainability*, *13*, 9924.

Behzadan, A., Dong, S., & Kamat, V. (2015). Augmented reality visualization: A review of civil infrastructure system applications. *Advanced Engineering Informatics*, *29*, 252–267.

Beltrami, M., Orzes, G., Sarkis, J., & Sartor, M. (2021). Industry 4.0 and sustainability: Towards conceptualization and theory. *Journal of Cleaner Production*, *312*, 127733.

Bocken, N. M., Mugge, R., Bom, C. A., & Lemstra, H. J. (2018). Pay-per-use business models as a driver for sustainable consumption: Evidence from the case of HOMIE. *Journal of Cleaner Production*, *198*, 498–510.

Bressanelli, G., Adrodegari, F., Pigosso, D. C. A., & Parida, V. (2022). Towards the smart circular economy paradigm: A definition, conceptualization, and research agenda. *Sustainability*, *14*, 4960.

Cagno, E., Neri, A., Negri, M., Bassani, C. A., & Lampertico, T. (2021). The role of digital technologies in operationalizing the circular economy transition: A systematic literature review. *Applied Sciences (Basel, Switzerland)*, *11*, 3328.

Çetin, S., De Wolf, C., & Bocken, N. (2021). Circular digital built environment: An emerging framework. *Sustainability*, *13*, 6348.

De Felice, F., & Petrillo, A. (2021). Green transition: The frontier of the digicircular economy evidenced from a systematic literature review. *Sustainability*, *13*, 11068.

Flaherty, T., Domegan, C., & Anand, M. (2021). The use of digital technologies in social marketing: A systematic review. *Journal of Social Marketing*, *11*, 378–405.

Gatzioura, A., Sànchez-Marrè, M., & Gibert, K. (2019). A hybrid recommender system to improve circular economy in industrial symbiotic networks. *Energies*, *12*, 3546.

Goldberg, D. E., & Holland, J. H. (1988). Genetic algorithms and machine learning. *Machine Learning*, *3*, 95–99.

Grafström, J., & Aasma, S. (2021). Breaking circular economy barriers. *Journal of Cleaner Production*, *292*, 126002.

Guzzo, D., Trevisan, A. H., Echeveste, M., & Costa, J. M. H. (2019). Circular innovation framework: Verifying conceptual to practical decisions in sustainability-oriented product–service system cases. *Sustainability*, *11*, 3248.

Hao, C., & Yue, Y. (2016). Optimization on combination of transport routes and modes on dynamic programming for a container multimodal transport system. *Procedia Engineering*, *137*, 382–390.

Hirve, S. A., Kunjir, A., Shaikh, B., & Shah, K. (2017). An approach towards data visualization based on AR principles. In *Proceedings of the International Conference on Big Data Analytics and Computational Intelligence (ICBDAC)* (pp. 128–133). Chirala, India.

Ingemarsdotter, E., Jamsin, E., Kortuem, G., & Balkenende, R. (2019). Circular strategies enabled by the Internet of Things—A framework and analysis of current practice. *Sustainability*, *11*, 5689.

İzmirli, D., Ekren, B. Y., Kumar, V., & Pongsakornrungsilp, S. (2021). Omni-channel network design towards circular economy under inventory share policies. *Sustainability*, *13*, 2875.

Jabbour, C., Jabbour, A., Sarkis, J., & Filho, M. (2019). Unlocking the circular economy through new business models based on large-scale data: An integrative framework and research agenda. *Technological Forecasting and Social Change*, *144*, 546–552.

Kang, J. R., Liu, Z. B., & Yang, R. B. (2010). Fuzzy comprehensive evaluation of ecological suitability of land based on GIS. *Systems Engineering*, *9*, X826.

Kolodner, J. (2014). *Case-based reasoning*. Morgan Kaufmann.

Koo, L., Trokanas, N., & Cecelja, F. (2017). A semantic framework for enabling model integration for biorefining. *Computers & Chemical Engineering*, *100*, 219–231.

Kristoffersen, E., Blomsma, F., Mikalef, P., & Li, J. (2020). The smart circular economy: A digital-enabled circular strategies framework for manufacturing companies. *Journal of Business Research*, *120*, 241–261.

Li, S., Zhang, H., Yan, W., & Jiang, Z. (2020). A hybrid method of blockchain and case-based reasoning for remanufacturing process planning. [if DOI is available]. *Journal of Intelligent Manufacturing*, •••, 1–11. https://doi.org/xx.xxx/xxxxx

Liberati, A., Altman, D. G., Tetzlaff, J., Mulrow, C., Gøtzsche, P. C., Ioannidis, J. P. A., Clarke, M., Devereaux, P. J., Kleijnen, J., & Moher, D. (2009). The PRISMA statement for reporting systematic reviews and meta-analyses of studies that evaluate health care interventions: Explanation and elaboration. *Journal of Clinical Epidemiology*, *62*, e1–e34. PMID: 19631507

Liu, Q., Trevisan, A. H., Yang, M., & Mascarenhas, J. (2022). (in press). A framework of digital technologies for the circular economy: Digital functions and mechanisms. *Business Strategy and the Environment*.

Magrini, C., Nicolas, J., Berg, H., Bellini, A., Paolini, E., Vincenti, N., Campadello, L., & Bonoli, A. (2021). Using Internet of Things and distributed ledger technology for digital circular economy enablement: The case of electronic equipment. *Sustainability*, *13*, 4982.

Mourtzis, D. (2018). Design of customised products and manufacturing networks: Towards frugal innovation. *International Journal of Computer Integrated Manufacturing*, *31*, 1161–1173.

Mushi, G. E., Di Marzo Serugendo, G., & Burgi, P. Y. (2022). Digital technology and services for sustainable agriculture in Tanzania: A literature review. *Sustainability*, *14*, 2415.

Neves Da Silva, A., & Novo, P. (2017). Hubgrade smart monitoring centers: Measuring resource consumption and moving towards a circular economy. *Field Actions Science Reports*, *17*, 32–37.

Novák, V., Perfilieva, I., & Mockor, J. (2012). *Mathematical principles of fuzzy logic* (Vol. 517). Springer.

Okorie, O., Salonitis, K., Charnley, F., Moreno, M., Turner, C., & Tiwari, A. (2018). Digitisation and the circular economy: A review of current research and future trends. *Energies*, *11*, 3009.

Page, M. J., McKenzie, J. E., Bossuyt, P. M., Boutron, I., Hoffmann, T. C., Mulrow, C. D., Shamseer, L., Tetzlaff, J. M., Akl, E. A., & Brennan, S. E.. (2021). The PRISMA 2020 statement: An updated guideline for reporting systematic reviews. *BMJ (Clinical Research Ed.)*, *372*, 89. PMID: 33782057

Pirola, F., Boucher, X., Wiesner, S., & Pezzotta, G. (2020). Digital technologies in product-service systems: A literature review and a research agenda. *Computers in Industry*, *123*, 103301.

Preut, A., Kopka, J.-P., & Clausen, U. (2021). Digital twins for the circular economy. *Sustainability*, *13*, 10467.

Taylor, C., & Sours, A. (2018). *Materials stewardship: A framework for managing and preserving materials in the circular economy*. NACE International.

Vacchi, M., Siligardi, C., Cedillo-González, E. I., Ferrari, A. M., & Settembre-Blundo, D. (2021). Industry 4.0 and smart data as enablers of the circular economy in manufacturing: Product re-engineering with circular eco-design. *Sustainability*, *13*, 10366.

Zhang, Y., Wang, J., & Liu, Y. (2017). Game theory based real-time multi-objective flexible job shop scheduling considering environmental impact. *Journal of Cleaner Production*, *167*, 665–679.

Zhou, Z., Chen, X., & Xiao, X. (2013). On evaluation model of circular economy for iron and steel enterprises based on support vector machines with heuristic algorithm for tuning hyper-parameters. *Applied Mathematics & Information Sciences*, *7*, 2215–2223.

Chapter 5
Carbon Footprint Analysis of Software Systems

P. Selvakumar
https://orcid.org/0000-0002-3650-4548
Department of Science and Humanities, Nehru Institute of Technology, Coimbatore, India

T. C. Manjunath
https://orcid.org/0000-0003-2545-9160
Rajarajeswari College of Engineering, India

Abhijeet Das
https://orcid.org/0000-0003-4599-5462
C.V. Raman Global University, Bhubaneswar, India

ABSTRACT

In recent years, the term "carbon footprint" has emerged as a critical metric in understanding and addressing the environmental impact of human activities. Broadly defined, a carbon footprint refers to the total amount of greenhouse gases (GHGs), primarily carbon dioxide (CO_2), emitted directly or indirectly by an individual, organization, product, or activity, expressed in equivalent tons of CO_2. This measure includes emissions produced by burning fossil fuels for energy, transportation, manufacturing, and other industrial processes. The concept has gained increasing prominence as the global community intensifies efforts to combat climate change and reduce the accumulation of greenhouse gases that contribute to global warming and its associated adverse effects such as rising sea levels, extreme weather

DOI: 10.4018/979-8-3373-4652-6.ch005

events, and biodiversity loss. Traditionally, discussions on carbon footprints have centered around sectors with visible and tangible environmental impacts—such as transportation, agriculture, manufacturing, and energy production.

INTRODUCTION TO CARBON FOOTPRINT

In recent years, the term "carbon footprint" has emerged as a critical metric in understanding and addressing the environmental impact of human activities. Broadly defined, a carbon footprint refers to the total amount of greenhouse gases (GHGs), primarily carbon dioxide (CO_2), emitted directly or indirectly by an individual, organization, product, or activity, expressed in equivalent tons of CO_2. This measure includes emissions produced by burning fossil fuels for energy, transportation, manufacturing, and other industrial processes. The concept has gained increasing prominence as the global community intensifies efforts to combat climate change and reduce the accumulation of greenhouse gases that contribute to global warming and its associated adverse effects such as rising sea levels, extreme weather events, and biodiversity loss. Traditionally, discussions on carbon footprints have centered around sectors with visible and tangible environmental impacts—such as transportation, agriculture, manufacturing, and energy production. However, with the rapid advancement and integration of digital technologies in every facet of life, a growing concern has surfaced regarding the environmental footprint of software systems and digital infrastructures. While software itself may appear intangible and invisible compared to physical industries, the underlying hardware, data centers, and energy consumption associated with running software applications have a significant carbon footprint. This growing realization has prompted researchers, developers, and policymakers to investigate the environmental consequences of software development, deployment, and usage, highlighting the need for sustainable practices within the software industry. Software systems, encompassing everything from mobile apps and websites to large-scale cloud computing platforms and artificial intelligence models, rely heavily on data centers and network infrastructure that consume vast amounts of electricity.

Moreover, the software development lifecycle itself can contribute to carbon emissions through the consumption of computational resources during coding, testing, debugging, and deployment processes. For example, automated testing frameworks, continuous integration/continuous deployment (CI/CD) pipelines, and extensive use of cloud-based development tools require substantial compute power. The rise of computationally intensive applications such as machine learning, big data analytics, and blockchain further exacerbates this trend, as these technologies demand significant processing power and storage capacity. These activities cumulatively increase energy consumption and, consequently, the carbon footprint of software systems. As awareness about the environmental impact of software systems grows, the software industry faces mounting pressure to adopt sustainable practices and innovate towards greener technologies. This includes optimizing software to be more energy-efficient, reducing unnecessary computational overhead, and designing applications that minimize data transmission requirements. Furthermore, transitioning data centers to renewable energy sources, improving cooling technologies, and implementing carbon offsetting measures have become critical strategies in reducing the overall carbon footprint associated with software systems. Several organizations and governments are also beginning to recognize the importance of establishing standards and regulations that encourage sustainable software development and responsible digital consumption.

WHY CARBON FOOTPRINT ANALYSIS MATTERS FOR SOFTWARE DEVELOPMENT

In the contemporary digital era, software systems have become integral to nearly every aspect of human activity—from communication and entertainment to commerce, healthcare, and governance. While the rapid adoption and proliferation of software-driven technologies have brought about unparalleled convenience, efficiency, and innovation, they have also introduced complex environmental challenges that are often overlooked. The production of this hardware involves significant environmental costs, including mining for rare earth metals, manufacturing processes, transportation, and disposal, (Anderl et al., 2018). Mining activities for metals like lithium, cobalt, and gold not only consume vast amounts of energy but also often cause habitat destruction, water pollution, and social issues in mining communities. Manufacturing semiconductor chips and electronic components requires high energy inputs and uses hazardous chemicals, contributing to air and water pollution, (Seele et al., 2017). Furthermore, the global supply chains that deliver these hardware components are themselves sources of greenhouse gas emissions due to fossil fuel consumption during transportation and logistics. Once deployed, software systems primarily impact the environment through the energy consumed during their operation, (Arnemann et al., 2023). Data centers, which serve as the backbone of cloud computing, internet services, and large-scale software applications, are among the most energy-intensive facilities globally. The source of this electricity greatly influences the carbon emissions attributable to data center operations; reliance on fossil fuels such as coal and natural gas results in high greenhouse gas outputs, whereas renewable energy sources like wind, solar, and hydropower significantly reduce environmental impact, (Zhang et al., 2019). Studies have shown that video streaming alone constitutes a large portion of global internet traffic, leading to increased electricity consumption and associated emissions.

Consequently, the environmental footprint of software systems extends to the broader internet ecosystem, encompassing the energy used by Internet Service Providers (ISPs), content delivery networks, and end-user devices, (Barni et al., 2018). Another critical yet often overlooked aspect of software's environmental impact is the lifecycle management of hardware devices. Electronic waste (e-waste) generated from obsolete or discarded computers, smartphones, and other digital devices poses severe environmental and health risks. Similarly, the trend towards "feature bloat" in applications, where additional functionalities increase complexity and resource needs, contributes to inefficient energy use, (Seele et al., 2016). On the user side, habits such as streaming high-definition video, keeping multiple apps active, or using devices with high screen brightness collectively elevate energy consumption. Educating developers and users about energy-efficient software design and responsible digital consumption is essential to reducing the environmental burden, (Bausch et al., 2023). The environmental impact of software systems also manifests in the context of emerging technologies such as artificial intelligence (AI), machine learning (ML), and blockchain. Techniques include optimizing algorithms, minimizing network data transfers, improving caching strategies, and reducing the computational complexity of applications, (Selicati et al., 2022). Additionally, leveraging renewable energy sources for data centers, improving hardware energy efficiency, and implementing carbon accounting frameworks specific to software are critical strategies in reducing the sector's ecological footprint.

METHODOLOGIES FOR CARBON FOOTPRINT ANALYSIS OF SOFTWARE SYSTEMS

As the world grapples with the escalating threats posed by climate change, the spotlight has increasingly shifted towards industries and activities that contribute to global greenhouse gas emissions, (Bergs et al., 2021). Conducting a thorough carbon footprint analysis in software development is not just an environmental imperative but also a strategic necessity that influences sustainability, operational efficiency, cost management, regulatory compliance, and corporate social responsibility. Understanding why carbon footprint analysis matters is essential to driving systemic change within the software industry and aligning technological progress with global climate goals. One of the foremost reasons carbon footprint analysis (Schleich et al., 2017) is vital in software development is its role in addressing the broader environmental crisis. Without an understanding of the emissions associated with each phase of software development and operation, developers and organizations remain unaware of their environmental impact and, consequently, lack the basis to implement effective mitigation strategies. Beyond environmental responsibility, carbon footprint analysis in software development fosters operational efficiency and cost savings. Regulatory pressures and market dynamics also underscore the importance of carbon footprint analysis for software development, (Blessing et al., 2009). Governments and international bodies are increasingly introducing stringent environmental regulations, carbon pricing mechanisms, and reporting requirements aimed at curbing emissions across all sectors, including information and communication technologies (ICT). Furthermore, carbon footprint analysis plays a pivotal role in fostering innovation and shaping the future of sustainable software development. By revealing the emissions hotspots in the software lifecycle, analysis motivates the adoption of cutting-edge technologies and design principles that prioritize energy efficiency. From a social perspective, carbon footprint analysis in software development contributes to raising awareness and driving cultural change within the tech community.

Organizations that embed carbon footprint considerations into their development culture foster a sense of purpose among employees and promote collaborative efforts to innovate responsibly. This cultural shift is critical in building a workforce attuned to the environmental challenges of the 21st century. Analysis allows teams to track changes in emissions over time, assess the impact of new features, and ensure that sustainability goals remain aligned with product evolution, (Bordeleau et al., 2020). This lifecycle approach also encompasses end-user behavior, as software usage patterns influence network loads and device energy consumption. By understanding these dynamics through carbon footprint metrics, developers can design software that promotes energy-conscious user habits, such as reducing background data usage or optimizing app standby modes. In the context of emerging technologies such as artificial intelligence (AI), machine learning (ML), and blockchain, carbon footprint analysis becomes even more critical, (Brenner et al., 2021). These technologies, while transformative and beneficial across multiple domains, are known for their substantial energy demands. The software industry, as a major enabler of digital transformation worldwide, bears a responsibility to lead by example in reducing its carbon footprint, (Plesker et al., 2023). By systematically analyzing and managing emissions, software companies can significantly contribute to national and international climate targets, demonstrate leadership in sustainability, and inspire other sectors to follow suit, (Camarinha-Matos et al., 2022). This alignment between software development practices and global environmental objectives underscores the broader societal importance of carbon footprint analysis.

MEASURING ENERGY CONSUMPTION: A KEY ASPECT OF CARBON FOOTPRINT ANALYSIS

The increasing recognition of the environmental impact of software systems has led to the development and adoption of diverse methodologies aimed at accurately measuring and analyzing their carbon footprints. Carbon footprint analysis for software systems is inherently complex, given the intangible nature of software, the multifaceted dependencies on hardware and energy infrastructure, and the broad scope that spans development, deployment, usage, and end-of-life phases, (Chen et al., 2021). Understanding the different methodologies, their underlying principles, practical implementation, and limitations is essential for developing reliable carbon footprint assessments and fostering sustainable software engineering practices. One of the most widely used frameworks for carbon footprint analysis in general—and increasingly adapted for software systems—is Life Cycle Assessment (LCA). LCA is a standardized methodology defined by the ISO 14040 and 14044 standards that evaluates the environmental impacts associated with all stages of a product's life, from raw material extraction through manufacturing, use, and disposal. When applied to software systems, LCA involves mapping the entire lifecycle of the software, (Perno et al., 2022) including hardware manufacturing for servers and user devices, energy consumption during development and operation, data center infrastructure, networking, and eventual hardware disposal or recycling. LCA provides a holistic view of emissions and environmental burdens, allowing for comprehensive impact assessment beyond just operational energy use, (Chen et al., 2020). However, applying LCA to software systems presents challenges, such as data collection complexity, allocation of impacts between software and hardware components, and the dynamic, evolving nature of software products that undergo continuous updates and scaling. Building on the LCA framework, Carbon Footprint Assessment (CFA) specifically focuses on quantifying greenhouse gas emissions, usually expressed as carbon dioxide equivalent (CO_2e).

CFA methodologies often utilize emission factors—coefficients that estimate emissions per unit of activity, such as kWh of electricity consumed—to convert resource usage into carbon emissions. (Chib S. et al. 2025) In software systems, CFA entails measuring or estimating electricity consumption across data centers, networking infrastructure, end-user devices, and even the embedded emissions from hardware manufacturing. The accuracy of CFA depends heavily on the availability and granularity of data, including energy use logs, hardware specifications, and electricity grid carbon intensity. Modern CFA approaches also consider temporal variations, recognizing that the carbon intensity of electricity can fluctuate hourly based on energy mix and demand, (Cornago et al., 2022). Tools such as the Green Software Foundation's Carbon Aware SDK facilitate real-time measurement and optimization of carbon emissions during software operation by integrating such data. Another important methodology involves Energy Consumption. For instance, a hybrid methodology might begin with LCA to understand cradle-to-grave impacts, use CFA to quantify emissions during software operation, apply energy profiling to optimize software code, and leverage cloud provider tools to monitor live emissions in production environments, (Dahiya et al., 2025). This integrative approach addresses the limitations of individual methodologies by triangulating data and providing, (Park et al., 2019) multi-layered perspectives on emissions. However, the complexity and resource requirements of hybrid approaches can be substantial, requiring multidisciplinary teams, robust data collection systems, and iterative refinement. Beyond these quantitative methodologies, qualitative and policy-oriented frameworks are also relevant to carbon footprint analysis in software development. For example, Sustainable Software Engineering Frameworks incorporate environmental considerations into software design, development, and management processes, (Kaur et al., 2025). These frameworks emphasize principles such as energy efficiency, resource minimization, and lifecycle thinking, guiding teams to proactively reduce emissions. Incorporating sustainability metrics into project management tools and development pipelines ensures that carbon footprint considerations become integral rather than ancillary. Additionally, emerging Carbon Accounting Standards specific to ICT and software sectors are being developed by organizations such as the Green Software Foundation and the Global e-Sustainability Initiative (GeSI), aiming to standardize measurement, reporting, and verification practices.

DATA CENTERS AND CLOUD COMPUTING: ENVIRONMENTAL IMPACT

Energy consumption measurement stands as a foundational pillar in the assessment of carbon footprints, particularly within the domain of software (Khan W. A. et al. 2014) systems where the intangible nature of code contrasts sharply with the tangible environmental impacts it generates through energy use. Understanding and accurately quantifying energy consumption is indispensable for effective carbon footprint analysis, as it directly correlates to greenhouse gas emissions through the carbon intensity of the electricity or energy sources powering software infrastructure. From data centers that host cloud applications to end-user devices executing software, energy consumption drives the environmental (Pap et al. 2013) footprint of digital technologies. Consequently, meticulous measurement of energy use enables stakeholders to identify inefficiencies, optimize operations, and implement sustainable practices that minimize carbon emissions across the software lifecycle. Additionally, software-based energy profiling tools can estimate energy use by analyzing CPU cycles, memory access patterns, and I/O operations. (Kommineni M. et al. 2025) For example, PowerAPI is an open-source framework that attributes energy consumption to software processes based on hardware counters and usage statistics. At the data center scale, energy consumption measurement becomes more aggregated yet critical, as these facilities consume vast amounts of electricity for both computing and cooling, (Lee et al., 2021). Data centers deploy sophisticated energy monitoring systems that track total electricity use, Power Usage Effectiveness (PUE)—a metric representing the ratio of total facility energy to IT equipment energy—and other operational parameters, (Lewandowski et al., 2021). PUE is particularly valuable for isolating the energy used by cooling, lighting, and auxiliary infrastructure, thus helping operators focus on improving energy efficiency beyond just the IT hardware, (Soundariya et al., 2025). Cloud providers often expose energy consumption metrics and carbon impact data to customers via dashboards, enabling more transparent and actionable insights into the environmental footprint of hosted software services, (Limbore et al., 2025). However, the granularity of these measurements varies, and often cloud consumers must estimate their software's share of total data center energy based on usage patterns, (Massonet et al., 2020). Energy consumption measurement also extends to network infrastructure, which includes routers, switches, base stations, and transmission lines that facilitate data flow between software services and users.

On the end-user side, measuring the energy consumption attributable to software applications running on devices such as smartphones, laptops, and IoT gadgets is equally important, (Melesse et al., 2020). These devices, while individually low in power consumption compared to data centers, collectively represent a significant portion of the software ecosystem's energy footprint due to their ubiquity, (Negri et al., 2017). Energy measurement here can be performed through battery usage statistics provided by operating systems, device-specific power profiling tools, and application-level monitoring. Firstly, energy use fluctuates dynamically with workload, user behavior, and environmental conditions, making static or snapshot measurements insufficient for comprehensive analysis. Continuous monitoring systems and time-series data collection are necessary to capture these variations and understand peak loads, (Olatunji et al., 2019) idle consumption, and efficiency under different scenarios. Secondly, attributing energy consumption specifically to software components is challenging in shared and virtualized environments, such as cloud platforms where multiple applications co-reside on the same physical hardware, (Neto et al., 2020). Sophisticated attribution models and instrumentation are required to allocate energy fairly among software tenants, often involving approximations based on resource usage or container metrics. Thirdly, the lack of standardized measurement protocols and transparency in reporting, particularly in proprietary cloud infrastructures, hinders the comparability and reliability of energy data across organizations. Despite these challenges, advances in measurement technologies and methodologies are rapidly improving the precision and usability of energy consumption data. The emergence of real-time energy monitoring APIs, integration of energy metrics into development toolchains, and the growing availability of open datasets empower developers and organizations to (Neto et al., 2020) embed energy considerations into software design, testing, and deployment. For example, the Green Software Foundation promotes the adoption of carbon-aware software development practices that rely heavily on accurate energy measurement and carbon intensity data to optimize the timing and location of computation to minimize emissions, (Olatunji et al., 2019). Moreover, energy consumption metrics influence market dynamics by shaping green procurement policies, investor decisions, and consumer choices in favor of environmentally responsible software providers.

HARDWARE VS. SOFTWARE: UNDERSTANDING THE CARBON FOOTPRINT DIVIDE

Data centers are the backbone of modern digital infrastructure, hosting the servers, storage systems, networking equipment, and software platforms that power everything from basic web browsing to complex cloud computing services and artificial intelligence applications, (Pap et al., 2013). As the demand for digital services grows exponentially—driven by the proliferation of smartphones, the Internet of Things (IoT), video streaming, social media, e-commerce, and big data analytics—data centers have expanded rapidly in both number and scale. While they are essential for enabling the digital economy, data centers and cloud computing infrastructures also represent significant sources of environmental impact, primarily through high energy consumption and associated carbon emissions. Cooling is necessary because high-performance computing equipment generates (Negri et al., 2017) substantial heat, and failure to manage temperatures effectively can lead to hardware failures and data loss. As a result, the energy used for cooling can sometimes rival or exceed the energy used for computing itself. Globally, data centers are estimated to consume between 1% to 3% of the world's total electricity—a figure that has been rising as digitalization intensifies. The lifecycle of data center equipment involves resource extraction, production, transportation, and eventual disposal or recycling, all of which contribute to greenhouse gas emissions, (Park et al., 2019). As data centers undergo frequent hardware refresh cycles to maintain performance and security, the embodied carbon associated with hardware manufacturing becomes a non-negligible factor in the overall environmental impact. Therefore, a holistic assessment of data center sustainability requires considering both operational and embodied emissions across the infrastructure lifecycle.

Cloud computing, which delivers computing services over the internet on a pay-as-you-go basis, has become the dominant model for data center utilization. Cloud providers such as (Perno M. et al. 2022) Amazon Web Services (AWS), Microsoft Azure, Google Cloud, and others operate vast hyperscale data centers distributed globally to provide scalable and flexible computing resources to millions of users and businesses, (Plesker et al., 2023). While cloud computing offers numerous benefits, including resource pooling, improved hardware utilization, and economies of scale, it also concentrates environmental impacts due to the massive scale of hyperscale data centers, (Samal et al., 2025). On the positive side, cloud providers are increasingly investing in energy-efficient technologies, renewable energy procurement, and innovative cooling solutions to reduce the carbon footprint of their operations, (Melesse et al., 2020). For example, many hyperscale providers have committed to achieving carbon neutrality or powering their data centers entirely with renewable energy within the coming decades. Despite these efforts, the environmental impact of cloud computing continues to grow in absolute terms as demand for digital services increases, (Schleich et al., 2017). Data traffic and computation requirements for AI, video streaming, blockchain, and other data-intensive applications are expanding rapidly. Transparency and reporting on data center energy consumption and emissions are becoming increasingly important for stakeholders, including customers, investors, regulators, and the public. Providers are publishing sustainability reports, carbon inventories, and real-time dashboards that disclose energy use, renewable energy procurement, and emissions data. This transparency enables more informed decision-making by customers, (Seele et al., 2017) who can factor environmental considerations into their cloud adoption and software deployment choices. It also fosters competition and innovation among providers to achieve better sustainability performance.

THE ROLE OF CODING EFFICIENCY IN REDUCING CARBON FOOTPRINT

In the discourse surrounding the environmental impact of digital technologies, understanding the distinct yet intertwined roles of hardware and software in contributing to the carbon footprint is essential, (Selicati et al., 2022). The carbon footprint divide between hardware and software represents a nuanced dynamic in which physical devices and intangible code collectively generate greenhouse gas emissions, but through different mechanisms and with varied implications, (Soundariy et al., 2025). Analyzing this divide not only clarifies the sources of emissions in computing systems but also informs targeted strategies for reducing environmental impact, (Sreekanthaswamy et al., 2025). While hardware consumption is traditionally seen as the primary contributor to carbon emissions due to its material, manufacturing, and operational energy use, software's role in driving energy demand and influencing hardware, (Massonet et al., 2020) efficiency is increasingly recognized as equally critical. A comprehensive perspective that disentangles and integrates the carbon footprint of both hardware and software is vital for holistic sustainability approaches in the technology sector. This lifecycle includes raw material extraction, component manufacturing, assembly, transportation, operational energy consumption, maintenance, and end-of-life disposal or recycling, (Suresh et al., 2025). Each stage involves energy-intensive processes and resource use that contribute to carbon emissions. For example, semiconductor fabrication, a cornerstone of modern electronics manufacturing, is highly energy demanding and involves materials such as silicon, rare earth metals, and chemicals whose extraction and processing incur environmental costs. Operational emissions arise mainly from electricity consumption during the hardware's active use, notably in data centers and personal devices.

Notably, hardware manufacturing often accounts for a significant portion of the total carbon footprint of electronic devices, sometimes exceeding operational emissions, especially in short-lifespan or frequently replaced products like smartphones and laptops. This embodied carbon is a critical consideration for sustainable design and procurement. In contrast, software's carbon footprint is more abstract and indirect, rooted primarily in the energy consumed by the hardware on which it runs. Conversely, software that prioritizes energy efficiency—through optimized algorithms, energy-aware (Lewandowski et al., 2021) scheduling, or adaptive resource allocation—can significantly reduce the operational emissions associated with computing tasks. In this sense, software acts as a critical lever for modulating the carbon footprint of hardware operation. Measuring the carbon footprint divide also involves methodological complexities. Hardware emissions can be directly measured or estimated using lifecycle assessment (LCA) approaches that track embodied and operational emissions. Software emissions, however, require indirect estimation based on energy consumption metrics attributed to software processes. These estimations can be challenging due to the shared and virtualized nature of computing resources, especially in cloud environments where multiple software applications coexist on shared hardware. Moreover, the carbon footprint divide has broader implications for stakeholders across the technology ecosystem. Manufacturers bear responsibility for reducing embodied carbon through cleaner production and circular economy practices, (Tamilarasi et al., 2025).

DATA STORAGE AND TRANSFER: HIDDEN CONTRIBUTORS TO CARBON FOOTPRINT

The impact of inefficient code on energy consumption and emissions is significant and often underestimated. Bloated software, characterized by unnecessary operations, redundant code paths, excessive memory allocation, or inefficient algorithms, increases the energy required to run applications. For instance, a web application that performs repeated database queries instead of caching results, or a mobile app that syncs data too frequently in the background, consumes more processing power and network resources than necessary. These inefficiencies not only degrade user experience but also draw more power from servers, network infrastructure, and user devices, (Lee et al., 2021). In aggregate, the cumulative effect of millions of poorly optimized applications running worldwide contributes to increased data center loads and electricity demand—intensifying the environmental burden of digital systems. Coding efficiency is particularly crucial in data-intensive and high-performance computing contexts. Machine learning, video streaming, gaming, and blockchain applications are notable for their heavy resource requirements, (Zhang et al., 2019). The training of large AI models, for example, can consume thousands of kilowatt-hours of electricity over weeks or months of computation. By writing efficient training loops, utilizing appropriate data structures, and minimizing computational complexity, developers can significantly reduce the energy cost of such tasks. Similarly, for real-time systems like gaming engines or financial platforms, where milliseconds matter, optimized code ensures not only speed but also reduced power draw, contributing to both performance gains and carbon savings. Coding efficiency also plays a central role in mobile and embedded systems, where battery life and thermal constraints are paramount. Efficient code on mobile devices reduces the frequency and intensity of CPU cycles, preserving battery life and improving user experience. For IoT devices deployed in remote or power-constrained environments, such as environmental sensors or smart agriculture tools, code that minimizes energy consumption can dramatically extend device lifespan and reduce maintenance needs.

Figure 1. Product Carbon Footprint (PCF) reporting software

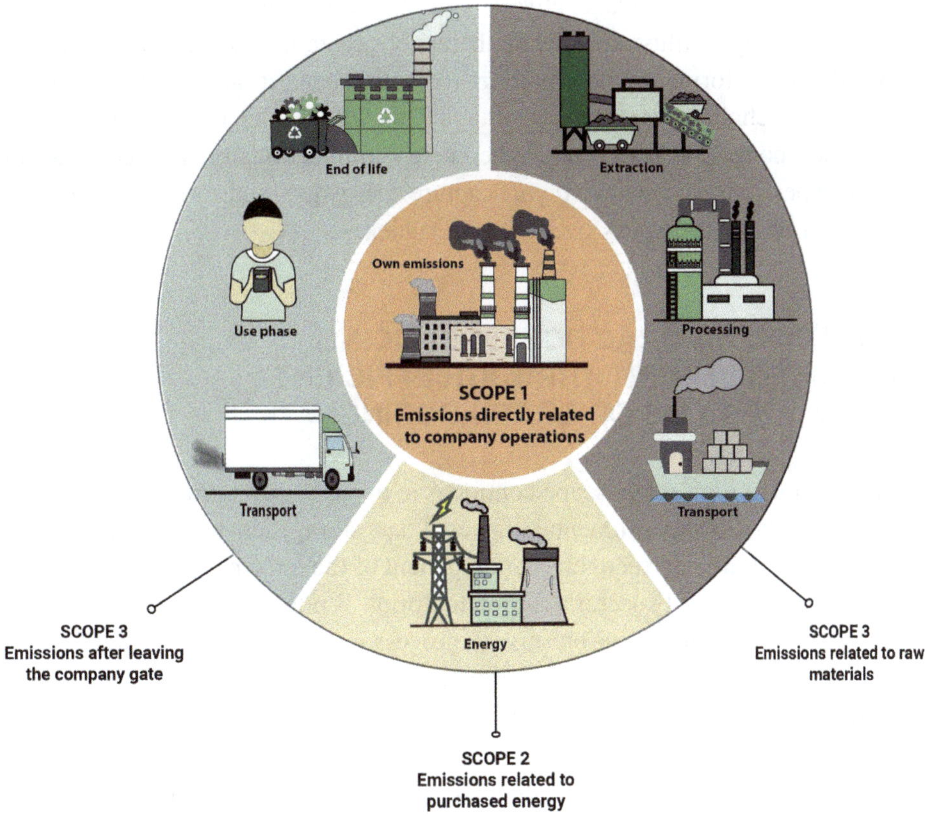

As these devices are deployed in the billions, improving coding efficiency across IoT ecosystems has the potential to yield large-scale environmental benefits, reducing both energy demand and electronic waste from prematurely failing devices. (Khan et al. 2014) Educational and organizational strategies are vital in fostering a culture of coding efficiency. For large-scale platforms serving millions of users, even marginal improvements in code efficiency can result in significant savings and environmental impact reductions. Additionally, organizations pursuing environmental, social, and governance (ESG) goals or aiming to meet carbon reduction commitments can include coding efficiency in their broader sustainability metrics and reporting. Green software practices can also enhance brand reputation and customer trust, particularly among environmentally conscious stakeholders. Notable case studies demonstrate the power of coding efficiency to reduce carbon impact. Google, for instance, has continuously optimized its search algorithms and data center operations to minimize energy use per search. Facebook (now Meta) redesigned its PHP runtime to create HHVM, a high-performance virtual machine that improved energy efficiency across its backend systems. Similarly, Dropbox engineers improved file synchronization algorithms to reduce redundant network requests, cutting server load and bandwidth use. These examples illustrate how deliberate efforts to improve coding efficiency can yield both performance gains and environmental benefits at scale. Despite these opportunities, challenges remain, (Cornago et al., 2022). One barrier is the lack of awareness among developers about the energy implications of their code. Many traditional performance metrics do not capture energy use, and software teams may prioritize speed or scalability over energy efficiency.

GREEN CODING PRACTICES: REDUCING CARBON FOOTPRINT THROUGH EFFICIENT DESIGN: ANALYSIS OF GREEN CODING

As the global digital landscape continues to expand, generating unprecedented volumes of data, the environmental impact of data storage and transfer has become a critical, yet often underrecognized, component of the information and communications technology (ICT) sector's carbon footprint. While discussions about digital sustainability frequently focus on servers, processors, and the power-hungry nature of computational tasks, the hidden carbon costs of storing and moving data across networks are equally important. From social media uploads and video streaming to enterprise backups and cloud syncing, every bit of data generated, stored, and transmitted consumes electricity—directly or indirectly contributing to greenhouse gas (GHG) emissions depending on the energy source. Moreover, to ensure data reliability and durability, storage systems employ redundancy techniques like RAID (Redundant Array of Independent Disks), data replication across multiple sites, and continuous backups—all of which multiply storage requirements and associated energy consumption. Cloud-based storage, now ubiquitous in both personal and enterprise computing, further amplifies this issue, (Chen et al., 2021). Data transfer, or data movement, is another critical factor in digital carbon emissions. Every time data is transmitted—from a server to a user device, between data centers, or across content delivery networks (CDNs)—it traverses a complex web of routers, switches, base stations, and transmission links, all of which require electricity to operate.

According to studies, transferring 1 GB of data across the internet can consume between 5 to 20 watt-hours of electricity, and with global data traffic surpassing hundreds of exabytes per month, the cumulative energy use is substantial. Streaming services, cloud gaming, and large software updates are among the most energy-intensive forms of data transfer. For example, streaming high-definition or 4K video content requires the delivery of vast amounts of data in real time, often across multiple networks and regions. These services rely heavily on CDNs and edge computing nodes to reduce latency and improve user experience, but the energy required to continuously deliver such data at scale is immense, (Chen et al., 2020). Similarly, the increasing use of automatic cloud syncing, where user data is regularly uploaded and synchronized across multiple devices, results in continuous data transfer activity that, while convenient, contributes to persistent background energy consumption. This "always-on" data movement model is becoming the norm in cloud-native applications and must be critically evaluated for sustainability. Addressing the carbon footprint of data storage and transfer requires a multi-pronged approach that includes technology optimization, user awareness, and policy development. Additionally, content-aware optimization, where systems adaptively reduce data quality (e.g., lowering video resolution or image size) based on user context or device capabilities, can result in significant energy savings without degrading user experience. End users and organizations also have a role to play in minimizing the carbon footprint of data storage and transfer. Individuals can take simple steps such as deleting unused files, reducing cloud sync frequency, avoiding unnecessary backups, and optimizing media quality settings on streaming platforms. Organizations, on the other hand, should implement data governance strategies that emphasize

OPTIMIZING ENERGY CONSUMPTION: STRATEGIES FOR SOFTWARE SYSTEMS

As the demand for digital services continues to rise globally, the software industry faces increasing scrutiny for its role in contributing to environmental degradation, particularly through energy consumption and greenhouse gas (GHG) emissions. In response, a growing movement has emerged around green coding—a set of practices focused on designing and writing software in ways that minimize energy usage and environmental impact. Green coding, also known as sustainable or energy-efficient coding, is a philosophy and methodology that embeds environmental awareness (Catena et.al., 2022) into the software development lifecycle. Its core aim is to reduce the carbon footprint of software systems by enhancing computational efficiency, optimizing resource use, and ensuring that digital services are not only functional and scalable, but also ecologically responsible. This proactive approach is rapidly gaining traction among developers, organizations, and sustainability advocates alike, as digital infrastructure becomes a significant and growing contributor to global carbon emissions. At the heart of green coding is efficiency in software design. Efficient software consumes fewer hardware resources, which in turn reduces electricity consumption and carbon emissions. Every line of code that is written inefficiently can lead to excess CPU cycles, memory usage, disk I/O, and network traffic—each representing a potential energy drain. Conversely, optimizing these aspects of software behavior can yield substantial energy savings, especially when scaled across millions of users or devices. For example, consider a mobile application that frequently refreshes data from a remote server. By redesigning the code to fetch data only when necessary, the app not only reduces its data transfer but also saves energy on both the client and server sides. Multiply this by millions of instances, and the environmental impact becomes considerable. Thus, green coding is not just about elegant code—it's about responsible software engineering with real-world ecological benefits.

Green UX also encourages users to adopt more sustainable digital habits, such as downloading content for offline use or limiting unnecessary notifications, which can reduce backend server loads. Cloud-native and distributed systems present both challenges and opportunities for green coding. On one hand, cloud infrastructure enables elasticity and scalability, but if not managed properly, it can lead to resource overprovisioning and energy waste. Green coding in cloud environments involves writing software that auto-scales based on demand, efficiently releases unused resources, and uses stateless or event-driven architectures to minimize idle time. Serverless computing and containerization also offer avenues for resource optimization, allowing code to run only when needed and minimizing the always-on overhead associated with traditional server-based applications. Developers should consider implementing data deduplication, batch processing, and smart caching mechanisms to limit unnecessary database queries or API calls. Furthermore, green coding encourages developers to avoid accumulating "dark data"—information that is stored but (Camarinha et al., 2022) never accessed—by applying retention policies and archiving strategies that ensure data is only kept as long as it is valuable. From a business and policy perspective, green coding aligns with growing demands for corporate environmental, social, and governance (ESG) responsibility. As governments introduce stricter emissions regulations and stakeholders demand greater transparency, companies that embrace sustainable software practices can differentiate themselves in the market. Efficient code can also reduce cloud costs, improve application performance, and extend the lifespan of hardware—offering both ecological and economic benefits. Organizations can integrate green coding into their DevOps and agile practices by embedding sustainability goals into sprint planning, code reviews, and release criteria.

SUSTAINABLE SOFTWARE DEVELOPMENT: BEST PRACTICES AND TOOLS

As global dependence on digital systems intensifies, optimizing the energy consumption of software has become a vital objective for achieving sustainability and reducing the environmental impact of technology. Software systems—whether running on personal devices, embedded systems, enterprise servers, or cloud infrastructure—indirectly draw energy from physical hardware components such as CPUs, GPUs, memory, and storage devices. As software dictates how and when hardware resources are utilized, the design and behavior of code have a direct bearing on energy usage. Therefore, implementing thoughtful, deliberate strategies to optimize software for energy, (Brenner & Hartl, 2021) efficiency not only improves system performance and lowers operational costs but also plays a crucial role in reducing greenhouse gas emissions associated with electricity consumption, especially when powered by fossil-fuel-based energy grids. The first and most fundamental strategy in optimizing energy consumption is the development of resource-efficient code. Efficient code minimizes CPU cycles, memory usage, and input/output (I/O) operations. It achieves this by reducing computational complexity, eliminating redundant processes, and avoiding memory leaks or excessive object creation. Writing such code involves selecting optimal data structures, using lazy initialization, avoiding polling-based loops, and implementing event-driven programming when applicable. For instance, replacing an inefficient algorithm with a more suitable one (e.g., using a hash map instead of linear searches) can cut processing time and power usage significantly. Similarly, minimizing the number of database queries through caching or batching operations avoids repeated disk access, saving considerable energy. Another critical area of optimization lies in hardware-software synergy. Software should be aware of the capabilities and limitations of the hardware it runs on and be designed to utilize these features efficiently.

Dynamic resource allocation is a strategic method employed to reduce energy waste in cloud and server environments. By dynamically provisioning and deprovisioning virtual resources based on real-time demand, software can avoid over-provisioning, which often leads to idle resources consuming energy without doing useful work. Autoscaling mechanisms in platforms such as Kubernetes, AWS Lambda, and (Bordeleau et al., 2020). Azure Functions enable applications to run only when needed and scale down during periods of low activity. Additionally, container orchestration tools help in packing workloads efficiently, reducing the total number of active servers and their associated energy costs. Modern cloud platforms offer tools to balance traffic based on server capacity, latency, and regional energy availability. Some advanced energy-aware systems even factor in the carbon intensity of electricity at specific locations, routing computational tasks to areas where renewable energy is in greater supply. This includes integrating energy impact assessments into continuous integration (CI) pipelines, applying automated testing to verify performance efficiency, and using static analysis tools that detect inefficient patterns. (Kaur et al. 2025) Software teams can also adopt metrics such as Software Carbon Intensity (SCI) to track and report the environmental impact of their applications. Tools like GreenFrame and Cloud Carbon Footprint help quantify emissions associated with application workloads, enabling development teams to set targets and track progress over time.

THE FUTURE OF CARBON FOOTPRINT ANALYSIS IN SOFTWARE DEVELOPMENT

In an era increasingly defined by digital transformation, climate change, and environmental accountability, sustainable software development has emerged as a key frontier in the pursuit of ecological responsibility. Sustainable software development refers to the practice of designing, building, deploying, (Blessing, 2009) and maintaining software systems in ways that minimize environmental impact, primarily by reducing energy consumption and carbon emissions associated with digital services. This involves careful choice of programming languages, libraries, and frameworks that enable minimal overhead and efficient execution. Lean, maintainable code reduces technical debt, shortens execution paths, and minimizes complexity, all of which contribute to lower energy usage. As data grows exponentially across industries, storing, processing, and transmitting data accounts for a significant portion of ICT-related energy use. Best practices in this domain include minimizing redundant storage, applying, (Bergs et al., 2021) data deduplication, archiving unused data, and deleting obsolete logs. Compression techniques, efficient data formats (e.g., binary over text-based), and strategic caching also contribute to reducing storage and bandwidth requirements.

Software should be built with awareness of the data lifecycle, ensuring that data is retained only as long as necessary and is processed efficiently to avoid unnecessary computational load. Green coding practices are central to sustainable development. This includes selecting efficient algorithms, optimizing logic, avoiding unnecessary loops, and reducing I/O operations. Static analysis tools such as SonarQube, ESLint, and PMD can help identify inefficient patterns, while runtime profilers like Intel VTune and VisualVM allow developers to monitor resource usage and identify bottlenecks. Emerging tools such as CodeCarbon, GreenFrame, and Cloud Carbon Footprint allow developers to quantify energy use and associated carbon emissions at the software level. Integrating these tools into the development workflow encourages continuous improvement and fosters an energy-conscious development culture. Sustainable deployment strategies further extend the lifecycle of green software. Containerization (e.g., Docker), orchestration platforms (e.g., Kubernetes), and cloud-native services enable software to run efficiently across diverse environments. Developers need to be trained to think ecologically—not just in terms of code correctness or performance, but in terms of energy implications and environmental outcomes, (Bausch et al., 2023). The Software Carbon Intensity (SCI) standard, for instance, provides a formula to calculate and reduce the carbon footprint of software applications. Similarly, organizations like the UN Sustainable Development Solutions Network encourage the alignment of software systems with the UN's Sustainable Development Goals (SDGs), (Samal et al., 2025) Open-source communities have also begun to prioritize sustainability, with repositories tagging projects as energy-efficient or environmentally focused, enabling developers to choose and contribute to greener solutions.

EMERGING TECHNOLOGIES: OPPORTUNITIES FOR CARBON FOOTPRINT REDUCTION

As the digital economy continues its rapid expansion and software becomes increasingly embedded in every aspect of modern life—from mobile apps and cloud computing to embedded systems and AI—carbon footprint analysis in software development is poised to become a foundational component of responsible engineering. Today's discussions around sustainability in tech are no longer limited to hardware, manufacturing, or data centers alone; attention is now shifting to the software layer, where design choices, development methodologies, and deployment strategies play a critical role in shaping energy use and emissions. As the world moves toward achieving ambitious climate goals, including net-zero carbon commitments by mid-century, the future of software development will be increasingly defined by the integration of carbon awareness, (Barni et al., 2018) into all stages of the software lifecycle. This evolution will be characterized by a convergence of advanced tooling, regulatory pressures, data transparency, AI integration, and a cultural shift toward environmental accountability in code. Automation and artificial intelligence (AI) will also play a transformative role in the evolution of carbon footprint analysis. AI-powered optimization tools are expected to assist developers in making energy-efficient design choices at every level—from suggesting low-power algorithms and optimizing loops to refactoring inefficient functions automatically. Advanced machine learning models will predict the environmental cost of certain architectural decisions, such as whether to use a monolithic or microservices-based approach, or whether to store data locally or in the cloud. AI may also facilitate dynamic energy optimization, where software intelligently adjusts its behavior in real time based on the energy grid's carbon intensity, choosing to execute non-urgent tasks when renewable energy is more available. This approach, (Arnemann et al., 2023) known as carbon-aware computing, is already emerging in experimental platforms and will likely become a default feature in enterprise software systems.

Governments and international bodies are recognizing that the tech sector's emissions footprint is significant and growing. As a result, future policies may mandate carbon transparency from software vendors, require digital service providers to meet sustainability benchmarks, or impose carbon taxes on excessive digital emissions. The European Union's Digital Product Passport initiative, which aims to provide lifecycle sustainability data for all digital products, is an early example of how regulation might shape the future of green software. Carbon audits for software systems may become as routine as security or privacy assessments, particularly in public procurement or ESG-sensitive industries. In parallel, carbon footprint analysis will become more granular and context-aware, enabled by increasingly sophisticated telemetry and analytics. Instead of relying on high-level estimates, developers and organizations will gain access to fine-grained energy and emissions data down to the level of specific features, user sessions, or API calls. In the open-source world, community-led initiatives will further democratize access to green software practices, (Anderl et al., 2018). Developers will be encouraged to choose "green dependencies" just as they now choose secure or well-maintained ones. Community standards for green pull requests, eco-friendly coding badges, and collaborative sustainability benchmarks will foster a culture of shared responsibility. Platforms like GitHub and GitLab may introduce sustainability scoring systems for repositories, promoting awareness and collaboration in lowering the collective carbon footprint of the software supply chain. The role of education and professional training will grow in importance. As sustainability becomes a core concern in software engineering, universities and coding bootcamps will incorporate environmental modules into their curricula. Certifications in green software development will emerge, recognizing professionals who demonstrate expertise in building low-carbon systems. Developers will have access to sustainability design patterns, green architecture blueprints, and decision-support systems that highlight the carbon trade-offs of different design paths. Product managers will be trained to balance user value with environmental cost, and UX designers will consider how interface choices affect energy use on client devices.

THE ROLE OF INDUSTRY AND ACADEMIA IN PROMOTING SUSTAINABLE SOFTWARE

As the world accelerates toward a digitally integrated future, emerging technologies are reshaping industries, economies, and societies. Simultaneously, they are being called upon to address one of the most pressing global challenges: climate change. Within this context, emerging technologies offer significant opportunities to reduce the carbon footprint of software systems and digital operations. AI can analyze vast datasets to identify inefficiencies in software performance, infrastructure utilization, and power consumption. Through predictive analytics, (Suresh et al., 2025) AI can forecast system load and adjust resource allocation in real time, avoiding unnecessary overprovisioning of servers or data center resources. For instance, AI-based workload schedulers can shift compute-heavy tasks to times or regions where renewable energy availability is high, reducing reliance on fossil fuels. Machine learning models can also be used in real-time energy optimization for smart buildings, IoT systems, and cloud services—enabling them to dynamically adjust energy usage based on demand and environmental conditions. Edge computing is another transformative technology with vast potential for carbon footprint reduction. For example, a smart camera analyzing video footage locally for security purposes, rather than continuously uploading footage to the cloud, reduces both bandwidth and energy costs. In large-scale deployments such as smart cities or autonomous vehicle networks, edge computing enables localized processing, thereby minimizing infrastructure (Dahiya et al., 2025) load and supporting sustainable, decentralized system design. The advancement of low-power hardware and specialized processors such as Arm-based chips, application-specific integrated circuits (ASICs), and tensor processing units (TPUs) is also creating opportunities to lower the energy intensity of software applications. These technologies are optimized for high performance with minimal energy draw, making them ideal for AI inference, real-time analytics, and mobile applications.

Emerging technologies in this space include serverless computing, which eliminates the need for always-on servers, and function-as-a-service (FaaS) models that execute code only in response to specific events. These paradigms offer superior energy efficiency by minimizing idle resource consumption, (Sreekanthaswamy et al., 2025). Furthermore, green container orchestration systems and carbon-intelligent workload placement allow enterprises to optimize where and how their applications are hosted, ensuring workloads are processed with the lowest possible carbon intensity. As green cloud technologies become more sophisticated, they are likely to form the backbone of sustainable digital transformation strategies. Blockchain and distributed ledger technologies (DLTs), often criticized for their energy consumption—especially in the context of cryptocurrencies like Bitcoin—are undergoing a transformation toward sustainability. Emerging consensus mechanisms such as proof-of-stake (PoS), proof-of-authority (PoA), and directed acyclic graph (DAG) are replacing energy-intensive proof-of-work systems. Ethereum's transition from PoW to PoS reduced its energy consumption by over 99%, illustrating the dramatic efficiency gains possible with protocol innovation. Beyond cryptocurrencies, blockchain is being used to track carbon credits, monitor supply chains for environmental compliance, and verify green claims. These applications, when built on energy-efficient DLT platforms, enable transparency and accountability in environmental reporting while maintaining a low operational footprint. Tools like the Green Software Foundation's Software Carbon Intensity (SCI) calculator, Cloud Carbon Footprint, and CarbonQL help developers estimate and optimize the emissions associated with their code. IDEs and CI/CD platforms are starting to integrate sustainability checks, suggesting greener alternatives to inefficient libraries, frameworks, or deployment strategies. With the rise of infrastructure as code (IaC), developers can now automate low-carbon configurations, such as selecting green data center regions, setting server autoscaling policies, or enabling energy-efficient runtime environments. As these tools become more mainstream and user-friendly, they will empower developers to bake sustainability into every stage of the software development lifecycle. Digital twins and simulation platforms are also emerging as powerful tools for optimizing energy consumption in complex systems, (Kommineni et al., 2025).

TOWARDS A GREENER FUTURE: THE POTENTIAL OF SUSTAINABLE SOFTWARE SYSTEMS

In the face of escalating climate concerns and growing awareness of the environmental impact of digital technologies, both industry and academia are playing increasingly pivotal roles in the advancement of sustainable software. This collaborative effort between the professional world and educational institutions is vital for transforming software engineering into an environmentally responsible discipline, (Tamilarasi et al., 2025). By fostering innovation, setting standards, conducting research, and shaping future talent, industry and academia are laying the foundation for a low-carbon digital ecosystem where sustainability is embedded into every stage of software development—from design and coding to deployment and maintenance. Industry, with its resources, global reach, and direct influence on software products and infrastructure, is uniquely positioned to drive real-world change in digital sustainability. Leading technology companies such as Microsoft, Google, Amazon, Intel, and IBM are investing in green software initiatives, setting carbon neutrality or net-zero goals, and actively working to reduce the emissions of their digital operations. Beyond individual organizations, cross-industry collaborations and consortia are playing a key role. The Green Software Foundation—formed by Accenture, GitHub, Microsoft, and ThoughtWorks—serves as a central body for advancing green software standards, education, tools, and best practices. Its mission is to build a trusted ecosystem for sustainable software by promoting data transparency, fostering open-source contributions, and supporting professional training.

In parallel, startups and SMEs are contributing to innovation in green software development. Agile and often mission-driven, (Limbore et al., 2025) these smaller entities are designing energy-efficient applications, platforms, and APIs from the ground up. They often serve as incubators for eco-centric design thinking, experimenting with minimalist software, low-power architectures, and carbon-aware algorithms. Academic conferences and journals are also fostering scholarly discussion and knowledge dissemination in this area. Events such as the International Conference on ICT for Sustainability (ICT4S) and the ACM SIGPLAN International Symposium on Software for Energy-Efficient Systems (SEES) provide platforms for interdisciplinary exchange between researchers, developers, and policymakers. These forums catalyze innovation by sharing the latest advancements, challenges, and case studies in green software, promoting collaborative efforts that span both theoretical exploration and practical application. University-industry partnerships serve as a crucial bridge between theory and practice. Collaborative research projects funded by both sectors explore real-world solutions for energy-efficient software deployment, hardware-software co-design, and carbon quantification models. These partnerships provide academic researchers with access to commercial datasets and infrastructure, while enabling companies to test cutting-edge ideas in controlled environments. Universities are increasingly contributing to the refinement of these metrics, validating their accuracy, and proposing alternative models that consider software usage patterns, hardware dependencies, and geographic variability in grid emissions. Beyond the classroom and lab, academic advocacy is helping shape public policy and industry standards, (Chib et al., 2025).

CONCLUSION

As the global urgency to combat climate change intensifies, attention is turning toward all sectors of society to mitigate their environmental impact. Among these, the digital sector—traditionally perceived as clean and non-material—is now recognized as a growing contributor to global greenhouse gas emissions. Software, the invisible driver of our digital world, underpins everything from smartphones and cloud platforms to smart grids and autonomous systems. While software itself may seem immaterial, its energy demands—especially when scaled to millions or billions of users—can be substantial. As such, the idea of sustainable software systems has emerged not only as a technical challenge but as a moral imperative. Looking forward, sustainable software systems have the potential to become a cornerstone in building a greener, more responsible digital future. Their development and deployment will fundamentally reshape how we think about code, infrastructure, design principles, and even the ethics of innovation. Another major avenue is decentralization through edge computing and device-level intelligence. Rather than relying on energy-intensive centralized data centers, future sustainable systems will perform computations closer to the data source—on local devices or edge nodes. This reduces data transmission overhead and enables energy-efficient, latency-sensitive applications. For instance, machine learning inference can increasingly be done on mobile devices using compact models, avoiding the need to offload processing to remote servers. This decentralization not only conserves energy but also democratizes access to low-footprint software experiences, especially in regions with limited connectivity or infrastructure. The future lies in green AI—models that are not only powerful but also efficient and environmentally optimized. Techniques such as model pruning, quantization, and transfer learning will be further developed to reduce training complexity and inference energy, ensuring that the intelligence powering tomorrow's applications is also sustainable. In tandem, software development practices and methodologies will evolve to support sustainable outcomes. Agile and DevOps practices will increasingly incorporate sustainability checkpoints. Sustainability will be integrated into automated pipelines, with tools that flag inefficient code, suggest optimizations, or recommend lower-carbon deployment strategies. Lightweight operating systems, modular application architectures, and backward compatibility will become more important as developers aim to support a diverse hardware ecosystem with minimal impact. Policy and regulation will act as powerful drivers in shaping the trajectory of sustainable software. Governments and international organizations are beginning to introduce guidelines and mandates that require digital systems to report and reduce their environmental impact. Future legislation may enforce digital carbon disclosures, incentivize green software development, and penalize unsustainable practices. For example, public procurement contracts may require software vendors to meet specific carbon intensity thresholds, or app stores may introduce sustainability scores as part of their ranking algorithms. Such regulatory pressures will push organizations to adopt greener practices not just out of goodwill but out of necessity, thereby accelerating industry-wide transformation. Metrics such as Software Carbon Intensity (SCI), energy-per-operation, or carbon-per-user-session will become standard in software evaluations. These metrics will not only be used by developers but also by business leaders, investors, and regulators to assess digital environmental performance.

REFERENCES

Anderl, R., Haag, S., Schützer, K., & Zancul, E. (2018). Digital twin technology – an approach for Industrie 4.0 vertical and horizontal lifecycle integration. *IT Inf. Technol.*, *60*(3), 125–132.

Arnemann, L., Winter, S., Quernheim, N., Grieser, P., Anderl, R., & Schleich, B. (2023). Information model to return data of digital twins into product design. *Procedia CIRP*, *116*, 173–178.

Barni, A., Fontana, A., Menato, S., Sorlini, M., & Canetta, L. (2018). Exploiting the digital twin in the assessment and optimization of sustainability performances. In Harriott, S. (Ed.), *2018 International Conference on Intelligent Systems (IS)*. Funchal - Madeira, Portugal.

Bausch, P., Weyand, A., Weigold, M., & Metternich, J. (2023). Design model for traceability-supported assessment of product carbon footprint. In Herberger, D., Hübner, M., & Stich, V. (Eds.), *Technische Informationsbibliothek (TIB)*. Publish-Ing.

Bergs, T., Brecher, C., Schmitt, R., & Schuh, G. (2021). Internet of production – turning data into sustainability. Aachen: apprimus verlag.

Blessing, L. T. M. (2009). *DRM, a design research methodology. With Assistance of Amaresh Chakrabarti*. Springer.

Bordeleau, F., Combemale, B., Eramo, R., van den Brand, M., & Wimmer, M. (2020). Towards model-driven digital twin engineering: current opportunities and future challenges. In Harriott, S. (Ed.), *Systems Modelling and Management, 1262* (pp. 43–54). Springer International Publishing.

Brenner, B., & Hartl, B. (2021). The perceived relationship between digitalization and ecological, economic, and social sustainability. *Journal of Cleaner Production*, *315*, 128128.

Camarinha-Matos, L. M., Rocha, A. D., & Graça, P. (2022). Collaborative approaches in sustainable and resilient manufacturing. *Journal of Intelligent Manufacturing*, *35*(2), 1–21. PMID: 36532704

Chen, C., Zhao, Z., Xiao, J., & Tiong, R. (2021). A conceptual framework for estimating building embodied carbon based on digital twin technology and life cycle assessment. *Sustainability*, *13*(24), 13875.

Chen, X., Despeisse, M., & Johansson, B. (2020). Environmental sustainability of digitalization in manufacturing: A review. *Sustainability*, *12*(24), 10298.

Chib, S., Mehta, A. K., Selvakumar, P., Saravanan, A., Mishra, B. R., & Manjunath, T. C. (2025). Mental health challenges and solutions in high-pressure work environments. In Harriott, S. (Ed.), *Innovative Approaches to Managing Conflict and Change in Diverse Work Environments* (pp. 247–272). IGI Global Scientific Publishing.

Cornago, S., Tan, Y. S., Brondi, C., Ramakrishna, S., & Low, J. S. C. (2022). Systematic literature review on dynamic life cycle inventory: Towards industry 4.0 applications. *Sustainability*, *14*(11), 6464.

Dahiya, R., & Selvakumar, P. Vidyadhara, & Manjunath, T. C. (2025). Design and aerodynamics: Principles and advances. In M. Mellal (Ed.), Innovations and developments in unmanned aerial vehicles (pp. 145-170). IGI Global Scientific Publishing.

Kaur, M., Selvakumar, P., & Dinesh, N. Mohit, Chandel, P. S., & Manjunath, T. C. (2025). Reconstruction and preservation strategies for cultural heritage. In S. Oflazoğlu & M. Dora (Eds.), Preserving cultural heritage in post-disaster urban renewal (pp. 385-412). IGI Global Scientific Publishing.

Khan, W. A., & Hussain, A. (2014). Automatic object-oriented coding facility for product life cycle management of discrete products. *International Journal of Computer Integrated Manufacturing*, *27*(1), 60–84.

Kommineni, M., Chundru, S., Maroju, P. K., & Selvakumar, P. (2025). Ethical implications of AI in sustainable development pedagogy. In Chinedu, C., Mafarja, N., Hussein, M., & Saleem, A. (Eds.), *Rethinking the pedagogy of sustainable development in the AI era* (pp. 17–36). IGI Global Scientific Publishing.

Lee, J. K. Y., Gholami, H., Saman, M. Z. M., Ngadiman, N. H. A. B., Zakuan, N., Mahmood, S., & Omain, S. Z. (2021). Sustainability-oriented application of value stream mapping: A review and classification. *IEEE Access : Practical Innovations, Open Solutions*, *9*, 68414–68434.

Lewandowski, S., Ullrich, A., & Gronau, N. (2021). Normen zur Berechnung des CO_2-Fußabdrucks (pp. 17–20).

Limbore, N. V., Anute, N., Ahluwalia, G. K., Chordiya, P. B., Kalshetti, P., & Selvakumar, P. (2025). Ethical leadership and corporate responsibility. In Harriott, S. (Ed.), *Innovative approaches to managing conflict and change in diverse work environments* (pp. 193–218). IGI Global Scientific Publishing.

Massonet, A., Kiesel, R., & Schmitt, R. H. (2020). Der digitale Zwilling über den Produktlebenszyklus. Zeitschrift für wirtschaftlichen Fabrikbetrieb, 115(s1), 97–100.

Melesse, T. Y., Di Pasquale, V., & Riemma, S. (2020). Digital twin models in industrial operations: A systematic literature review. *Procedia Manufacturing*, *42*, 267–272.

Negri, E., Fumagalli, L., & Macchi, M. (2017). A review of the roles of digital twin in CPS-based production systems. *Procedia Manufacturing*, *11*, 939–948.

Neto, A. A., & Deschamps, F., Silva, da, Ribeiro, E., & Lima, E. P. de. (2020). Digital twins in manufacturing: An assessment of drivers, enablers and barriers to implementation. *Procedia CIRP*, *93*, 210–215.

Olatunji, O. O., Akinlabi, S. A., Ayo, O. O., Madushele, N., Adedeji, P. A., & Fatoba, S. O. (2019). Drivers and barriers to competitive carbon footprint reduction in manufacturing supply chain: A brief review. *Procedia Manufacturing*, *35*, 992–1000.

Pap, S., & Morar, L. (2013). Procurement approaches in different supply chains. *AMM*, *436*, 551–556.

Park, H., Easwaran, A., & Andalam, S. (2019). Challenges in digital twin development for cyber-physical production systems. In Chamberlain, R., Taha, W., & Torngren, M. (Eds.), *Cyber physical systems, model-based design* (Vol. 11615, pp. 28–48). Springer International Publishing.

Perno, M., Hvam, L., & Haug, A. (2022). Implementation of digital twins in the process industry: A systematic literature review of enablers and barriers. *Computers in Industry*, *134*, 103558.

Plesker, C., Kutscher, V., Knobloch, R., & Schleich, B. (2023). Modularisation and containerisation of the digital process twin. *Procedia CIRP*, *120*, 57–62.

Samal, A., & Misra, L. I. Mohit, Pougajendy, S., Chandel, P. S., Manjunath, T. C., & Selvakumar, P. (2025). Musealization and tourism practices. In S. Oflazoğlu & M. Dora (Eds.), Preserving cultural heritage in post-disaster urban renewal (pp. 115-142). IGI Global Scientific Publishing.

Schleich, B., Anwer, N., Mathieu, L., & Wartzack, S. (2017). Shaping the digital twin for design and production engineering. *CIRP Annals*, *66*(1), 141–144.

Seele, P., & Lock, I. (2017). The game-changing potential of digitalization for sustainability: Possibilities, perils, and pathways. *Sustainability Science*, *12*(2), 183–185.

Selicati, V., Intini, F., Rospi, G., & Dassisti, M. (2022). Addressing heterogeneity sources in manufacturing sustainability assessment using the system design view. *CIRP Journal of Manufacturing Science and Technology*, *37*, 319–331.

Soundariya, A., Behera, N. K., Selvakumar, P., Chandel, P. S., Gupta, S., & Manjunath, T. C. (2025). AI and environmental ethics: The role of AI in addressing climate change ethical considerations in AI-driven environmental solutions. In Chakraborty, S. (Ed.), *Human values, ethics, and dignity in the age of artificial intelligence* (pp. 321–346). IGI Global Scientific Publishing.

Sreekanthaswamy, N., Anitha, S., Singh, A., Jayadeva, S. M., Gupta, S., Manjunath, T. C., & Selvakumar, P. (2025). Digital tools and methods. In Çela, E., Paliktzoglou, V., Sengar, S., Eappen, P., & Vajjhala, N. (Eds.), *Enhancing school counseling with technology and case studies* (pp. 25–48). IGI Global Scientific Publishing.

Suresh, R. V., Selvakumar, P., Naresh Babu, K., Nithya, G., Manjunath, T. C., & Kartigeyan, J. (2025). Best practices and practical applications. In Çela, E., Paliktzoglou, V., Sengar, S., Eappen, P., & Vajjhala, N. (Eds.), *Enhancing school counseling with technology and case studies* (pp. 341–362). IGI Global Scientific Publishing.

Tamilarasi, C., Sowmiya, K., Vignesh, G. D., Jasmine, R. L., Nehru, P., & Selvakumar, P. (2025). AI in renewable energy education: Teaching the future of sustainable power systems. In Chinedu, C., Mafarja, N., Hussein, M., & Saleem, A. (Eds.), *Rethinking the pedagogy of sustainable development in the AI era* (pp. 133–152). IGI Global Scientific Publishing.

Zhang, C., & Ji, W. (2019). Big data analysis approach for real-time carbon efficiency evaluation of discrete manufacturing workshops. *IEEE Access : Practical Innovations, Open Solutions*, *7*, 107730–107743.

Chapter 6
Green Software Engineering for Business Project Management Sustainability:
Focused Project Management Methodologies

Indumathi Srinivasan
https://orcid.org/0009-0009-6035-471X
Saveetha School of Management, Saveetha Institute of Medical and Technical Sciences, India

A. K. Subramani
https://orcid.org/0000-0003-0783-7113
Saveetha School of Management, Saveetha Institute of Medical and Technical Sciences, India

ABSTRACT

As digital transition speeds up, the effect on managing software engineering has been attained by critical recognition. While green software engineering boosts the energy-efficient algorithm and system architectures, sustainability keeps insufficient from project management setup. This current chapter demonstrates that leading methodologies such as Agile, DevOps, and PM² can be redefined and designed to integrate environmental sustainability into software projects. A proposed Green Project Management (GPM) conceptual design helps to redesign project achievement to compromise environmental performance with conventional goals of time, cost and scope.The Green Project Lead (GPL), a new role committed to sustainability within

DOI: 10.4018/979-8-3373-4652-6.ch006

project groups.By aligning sustainability with deeply rooted project management tools and metrics, the chapter focuses on a systemic transition in how software projects are planned, accomplished and assessed. It locates project management not just way for innovation and efficiency, but as a crucial mechanism for advancing environmental stewardship in the digital age.

INTRODUCTION: THE DIGITAL CARBON FOOTPRINT

The Myth of "Clean" Software

The digital province is often conceptualized as a clean and immaterial vibrant, symbolized by the "cloud" and the invisibility of software processes. Behind every Google search, YouTube video, blockchain transaction, and app upgradation lies a continuation of hardware and infrastructure that consumes substantial energy. Globally, the ICT sector, consisting data centers, network infrastructure, end-user devices, and digital services which accounts for approximately 3–4% of total greenhouse gas (GHG) emissions, a portion comparable to that of the aviation industry (Jones, 2018; Belkhir & Elmeligi, 2018; Andrae & Edler, 2015). Additionally, this trace is assured to develop as demand for digital services escalates, particularly with trends such as artificial intelligence, cryptocurrency mining, and the Internet of Things (IoT) (Hintemann & Hinterholzer, 2020).

Despite the carbon impact of software is routinely underestimated because of the nature of code. This tends to a problematic assumption that software is environmentally approachable, so long as hardware becomes more energy-efficient over time—a view that observes the important effect of software design, development, and deployment options on energy consumption. For instance, outdated coding, dilated codebases, and unnecessary computations can dramatically increase CPU cycles and thus energy use. The "myth of clean software" must be dismantled to promote a culture of carbon-aware digital development.

As the world becomes more digital and software takes center stage in industries, governments, and our daily lives, there's a growing concern about the environmental impact of software development and IT operations. Green software engineering is stepping up to address this by focusing on energy-efficient algorithms, sustainable architectures, and eco-friendly development practices. However, there's one area that hasn't been explored enough: how green goals fit into project management methods. Today, software project management is mostly guided by methodologies like Agile, DevOps, and PM^2. These are all about speed, teamwork, iteration, and optimizing delivery. But they often overlook sustainability principles. This means we end up with software systems that are fast, user-friendly, and scalable, but not necessarily good for the environment.

Kumar et al. (2024) explored the use of artificial intelligence (AI) using power monitoring systems for Small and Medium Enterprises (SMEs) to improve the efficiency of the energy, decrease the operational costs to ensure the sustainability of the AI. It discusses the latest and prevailing energy challenges faced by SMEs, emphasizes real-time monitoring, and the benefits of AI integration. The components of an AI-integrated power monitoring system consist of acquisition of data, evaluation, and control approaches. The study also examines AI techniques like machine learning, deep learning, and predictive analytics for critically identifying the energy usage modulation. The researcher also discussed a few successful cases of SMEs using AI-based systems, highlighting their optimization of energy consumption and reduced costs.

Pitchai et al. (2024) explores the complicated issues and challenges of sustainable computing, forecasting and focusing on its environmental impacts. It briefs about the principles of green computing, the carbon footprint which is integrated with technology, and the role of data centers in reducing it. The researcher emphasizes and highlights the significant energy efficiency in computing, highlighting the development of energy consumption in IT and outlines approaches and methodologies for achieving it. It also discusses the role of emerging technologies like renewable energy, IoT, smart grids, quantum computing, and sustainable algorithms in promoting sustainability. The chapter also highlights the role of software solutions in sustainable computing, including green software development practices, virtualization, cloud computing, and power management software and the practical application of sustainable computing in organizations, highlighting challenges, ethical considerations, and a roadmap for the future of sustainable computing, enriched with case studies.

The modern world is unpredictably shaped by the omnipresence of IT, with the ubiquity of digital devices, cloud computing, and the Internet. While these technological developments have revolutionized our day to day lives and global digital business practices, they have also led to a concerning environmental footprint. The proliferation of electronic devices, data centers, and the energy-intensive nature of computation have culminated in a significant carbon footprint. Recognizing the ecological urgency, the concept of "green computing" has emerged as a crucial endeavor, aiming to mitigate the environmental impact of the digital age, (Lin et al., 2023).

The scope and the foundational concepts of green computing, the quantification of carbon emissions, and methods to minimize energy consumption has been given more emphasis. Furthermore, the research delves into how emerging technologies which consist of the integration of renewable energy sources, the Internet of Things (IoT), and quantum computing, can contribute to sustainability. We also spotlight the crucial role of software solutions in achieving greener technology (Chong et al., 2022).

Issa et al. (2022) delves into the multifaceted realm of green computing, with a peculiar focus on its basic and traditional principles and the strategies employed to mitigate the carbon footprint associated with information technology. It also explored how emerging technologies can play a crucial role in fostering sustainability and enhancing energy efficiency. The main goal is to provide an in-depth examination of the latest advancements and best practices in the field (Issa et al., 2022).

The Need for Sustainable Project Management

While there has been increasing consciousness of sustainable software engineering approaches such as energy-aware programming, server equalization and efficient resource allocation plays the role of project management in leading sustainability remains underexplored, (Procaccianti et al., 2016). Software project management methodology such as Agile, DevOps, Scrum, and PM^2 are designed around practices of speed, flexibility, and customer value. However, they often fail to combine environmental issues into their frameworks, (Penzenstadler et al., 2014; Venters et al., 2018).

An important role in decision-making about software architecture service providers by cloud, testing the frameworks and pipelines deliveries are handled by project managers which all influence energy usage and carbon emissions. By integrating sustainability metrics such as estimated energy usage, lifecycle evaluation and carbon budgets into project planning and sprint retrospectives could shift the groups and prioritize the features (Becker et al., 2021). Furthermore, as digital transformation becomes a key strategy across sectors, organizations must begin handling sustainability as a core aspect of project success with cost, time, and scope. This chapter thus argues for a paradigm transition in software project management from being delivery-focused to sustainability-conscious which also suggests real time ways to associate the environmental considerations into software lifecycles.

RETHINKING SUCCESS IN SOFTWARE PROJECTS

Traditional Metrics vs. Green KPIs

The traditional evaluation and assessment of software project success has long depended on the "triple constraint" framework such as time, cost, and scope (Project Management Institute [PMI], 2017). As organizations adopt digital transformation by centering IT initiatives with environmental sustainability goals such as those mentioned in the UN Sustainable Development Goals (SDGs) and corporate ESG frameworks which requires rethinking what constitutes a "successful" software project (United Nations, 2015; Calero & Piattini, 2015). This means moving beyond delivery-focused metrics to include environmental indicators that capture the ecological efficiency of software development and operation.

Green Key Performance Indicators (KPIs) offer a data-driven approach to embed sustainability into the project lifecycle. These metrics quantify environmental impacts in ways that are actionable and integrable into Agile sprints, DevOps pipelines, and governance dashboards. Emerging green KPIs refer Table 1.

Table 1. Green key performance indicators

Metric	Description	Purpose/Insight
Carbon per Feature Delivered	Measures carbon emissions from developing, testing, and deploying each business functionality unit.	Identifies high-emission features or processes to prioritize optimization.
Energy per Deployment	Tracks electricity consumed during the build, test, and release cycle.	Helps assess and reduce energy use in CI/CD pipelines, especially with frequent deployments.
Lifecycle Emissions	Calculates total GHG emissions over the software's entire lifecycle (development to decommissioning).	Provides a comprehensive view of software sustainability across all phases.

Procaccianti et al., 2016; Hilty & Aebischer, 2015; Penzenstadler et al., 2014; Becker et al., 2021

Eventually sustainability KPIs should not be observed as an additional role but as integral to defining project standards. Just as usability, security and performance are integrated into modern development approaches, so too must energy and emissions become standard considerations. Project management offices (PMOs), software architects, and Scrum masters alike must champion this shift by institutionalizing sustainability reporting and establishing green project baselines (Naumann et al., 2011). The below Table 2 represents the differences between KPI vs Metrics

Table 2. Differences between KPI vs metrics

Parameters	KPIs	Metrics
Objective	Measure progress towards key business goals	Measure performance of daily business activities or processes
Focus	High-level perspectives	Low-level perspective
Time-frame	Used for long-term goals	Used for short-term goals
Scope	KPIs can be granular	Metrics cover a broader range
Relevance	Relevant across different departments	Relevant across specific departments or business areas

continued on following page

Table 2. Continued

Parameters	KPIs	Metrics
Best for	Strategizing business goals	Measuring milestones set to achieve business goals
Examples	● Shopping cart abandonment rate in June ● Email bounce rate per month ● Number of customers retained per month	● Increase website traffic ● Increase email click rates ● Increase employee happiness

Datapad (2022)

AGILE METHODOLOGIES AND SUSTAINABILITY

Agile methodologies refer to iterative evolution and flexibility which offer a promising framework for integrating sustainability into software development. However, conventional agile frameworks such as Scrum and Kanban frequently surplus in supporting sustainability. To confront this challenge, the theory of an eco-backlog has been established which intervenes sustainability aims into user stories, by aligning agile methodology with environmental aims. These practices can help the developers in creating architectural changes that triggers sustainability such as optimizing code for energy efficiency or choosing green cloud providers.

Agile approaches can play a critical role in developing sustainability within software development. A major key take away is that agile practices can be extended to team-level initiatives to influence the entire organization's approach towards sustainability. A growth strategy rooted in the Agile Manifesto's principles, empowering flexibility and local problem-solving throughout all levels of the organization. (Bremer et al., 2025) and in turn the methodology can promote sustainability by triggering a culture of responsiveness and flexibility to transiting environmental needs and organizational priorities. Additionally, continuous integration of new knowledge lines up with the basics of sustainable development and empower enterprises to be more efficient in resource use. The collaboration and interactive communication can facilitate more environmentally responsible alternatives through prompt feedback and ongoing alignment with sustainability objectives. Additionally, integrating sustainability initiatives with changes in organizational culture or personnel habits foster to implement agile.

Agile's Strengths and Blind Spots

The continuous improvement such as including environmental performance can be done through agile adoption. However, lack of explicit guidance on energy efficiency or carbon impacts agile (Penzenstadler et al., 2014). Henceforth, these methodologies excel in flexibility which can be utilized to incorporate sustainability practices into software development (Kashyap & Kumar, 2024). Despite these strengths, this method often omits to forecast sustainability in the long term, but focusing on usability and software stability.

Due to this, lack of guidelines on agile the software's efficacy to adapt to evolving environmental needs (Sohail et al., 2024). It is also known for its strengths such as focus on collaboration, and customer-centric approach and expected blind spots such as scaling Agile practices from individual teams to the entire organization in project management and discrepancies in how Agile principles, originally framed for smaller teams and are adapted or sometimes lost in the scaling process. Agile motivates team members to work together closely, fostering a sense of ownership and commitment to project success. Moreover, Agile emphasizes prompt feedback from clients, ensuring that the end product aligns closely with customer needs and expectations (Bremer et al., 2025).

The Eco-Backlog: Integrating Sustainability into User Stories

By connecting sustainability which has been a low priority for many businesses into user centric approaches in software development which involves integrating environmental, social, and economic considerations into the software development lifecycle yet the growing environmental crises necessitate a shift in focus. To improve the integrated sustainability effectively, software development groups can adopt frameworks similar to those noticed in educational and corporate contexts (Moreira et al., 2024).

Added to this, user centric stories in software development can be manipulated to include sustainability as a main focus by this practice, groups and teams can make sure that the software meets functional requirements and contributes to reducing environmental impact which in turn promotes social well-being.

Figure 1. Embedded ethics (Willem et al., 2024; Motamedimoghadam et al., 2024; Jacob, 2024)

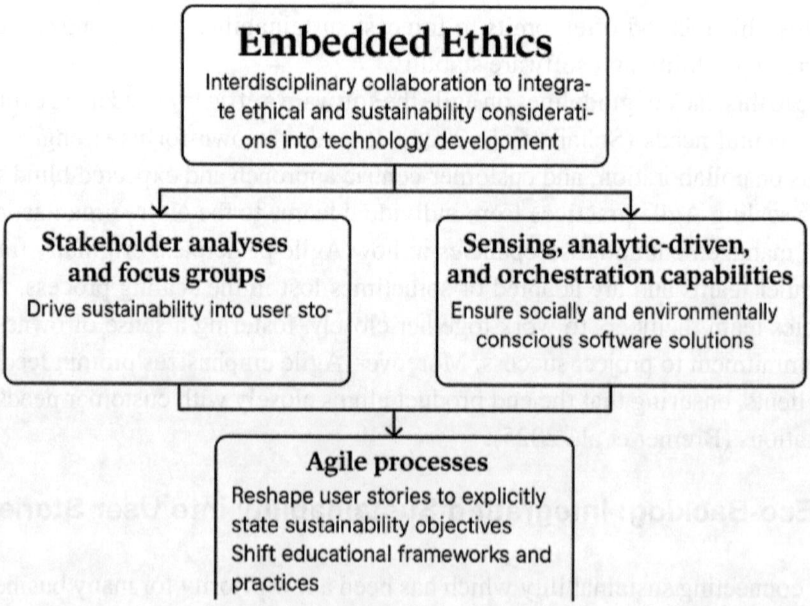

Table 3. Metrics and tools

Metric/Tool	Agile Purpose	Green Software Relevance
Velocity	Measures team output per sprint	Efficient delivery reduces rework and resource waste.
Lead Time	Time from idea to delivery	Faster delivery minimizes computer and infrastructure usage.
Cumulative Flow Diagram	Visualize work across stages	Identifies inefficiencies that waste energy and time.
CI/CD Tools (e.g., Azure DevOps)	Automate testing/ deployment	Optimized pipelines reduce redundant builds and cloud energy use.

Case Study: Agile Methodologies and Sustainability- EcoSoft Solutions

EcoSoft Solutions, a successful Agile methodology which has been established well with green software practices to reduce its carbon footprint, improve team efficiency, and deliver environmentally conscious digital products in an era of increasing environmental awareness and corporate responsibility, software development practices are booming to guide sustainability achievements. Henceforth **Agile methodologies** combined with **Green Software Engineering (GSE)** principles helps to sustain business project management.

This case study demonstrates how a mid-sized tech company, with approximately 250 employees, embarked on a project to develop a cloud-based platform designed to promote remote team collaboration. This challenge with product development initiative with its broader corporate sustainability goals, all while maintaining high performance, agility, and delivery speed throughout the project lifecycle.

Goals

1. Reduce energy consumption and carbon footprint in software development.
2. Align Agile project management practices with sustainability metrics.
3. Improve product lifecycle management with environmental considerations.
4. Engage stakeholders and developers in green thinking without reducing velocity or productivity.

Agile Framework: Scrum

- EcoSoft adopted Scrum for project execution, enabling iterative development, stakeholder feedback, and flexibility.
- **Sprint Planning** included sustainability goals and environmental metrics.
- **Daily Stand-ups** addressed eco-efficiency bottlenecks and shared quick wins for greener code and systems.
- **Retrospectives** reviewed environmental impact alongside delivery metrics.

Table 4. Green software engineering principles applied by EcoSoft solutions

Principle	Implementation in Project
Carbon Efficiency	Optimized cloud resource usage and reduced idle time.
Energy Efficiency	Code profiling to minimize processor and memory overhead.
Hardware Efficiency	Promoted thin clients and server-side processing.
Network Efficiency	Compressed data and reduced unnecessary API calls.
Sustainable Infrastructure	Deployed to green-certified data centers.
User Impact Awareness	Designed features to encourage low-impact user behaviors.

Tooling & Monitoring

- Used **Jira Green Templates** to integrate carbon-impact stories.
- Monitored energy usage via **Green Metrics Toolkits** (like Microsoft's Green Software Toolkit).
- Employed **CI/CD pipelines** with carbon-aware scheduling (e.g., run tests during low-carbon energy grid windows).

CHALLENGES AND SOLUTIONS

To address developer resistance to new sustainability metrics, targeted training sessions and workshops were conducted to build awareness and foster engagement. To reduce the measurement overhead, automated tools were integrated into the CI/CD pipeline, streamlining the process and minimizing manual effort. Additionally, to ensure that green priorities did not delay feature delivery, the MoSCoW prioritization method was employed to strike a balance between sustainability objectives and product development goals.

DEVOPS AND GREENOPS: SUSTAINABLE OPERATIONS

DevOps and GreenOps are pivotal in aligning software development practices with sustainable operations, particularly through green software engineering in business project management. DevOps, inherently a cultural and technical movement, facilitates the automation and continuous delivery of software, thus minimizing the development lifecycle and enhancing software quality. This method merges development and operations to foster efficiency in software-intensive organizations, a factor critical for businesses whose success depends significantly on efficient software operations (Díaz et al., 2018). Henceforth, this methodology saves time and resources while bridging the gap between continuous integration and delivery (Srivastav et al., 2023).

GreenOps, the integration of sustainability into DevOps, aims to cut costs, boost reputation, build customer loyalty, and tap into the eco-conscious market (Barakat et al., 2023). Green training is an integral process which is empowering employees' environmental awareness to help and align their skills with sustainable operations (Barakat et al., 2023). The integrated practices of GreenOps with DevOps ensure that businesses attain competitive advantages through enhanced sustainability which are imperative for organizations to remain competitive in the ever-evolving business climate. Henceforth, both DevOps and GreenOps aim to optimize development by enhancing operational efficiency and embedding sustainability at their core.

The Environmental Impact of DevOps

DevOps is primarily a cultural and technical paradigm aimed at enhancing collaboration between development and operations teams, thereby improving the software development lifecycle's efficiency and speed (Khan et al., 2022). It emphasizes practices such as automation, continuous improvement, and efficient resource utilization. While DevOps inherently aims to optimize processes, its environmental implications are gaining attention, aligning with the growing need to address sustainability in IT operations. The automation associated with DevOps, mainly through AI-driven processes for Infrastructure as Code, significantly enhances resource efficiency, thereby reducing waste and lowering energy consumption (Talati, 2025).

GreenOps as a Complementary Approach

GreenOps, an extension of the DevOps paradigm with a focus on minimizing environmental impact, involves the integration of green practices in IT operations. This approach includes optimizing software code efficiency, selecting energy-efficient computing architectures, and adopting continuous integration and delivery (CI/CD) pipelines that reduce the energy footprint (Atadoga et al., 2024).

Figure 2. Best practices for environmental sustainability (Atadoga et al., 2024; Talati, 2025; Ur Rahman & Williams, 2016; Rajkumar et al., 2016; Yu & Ramanathan, 2014)

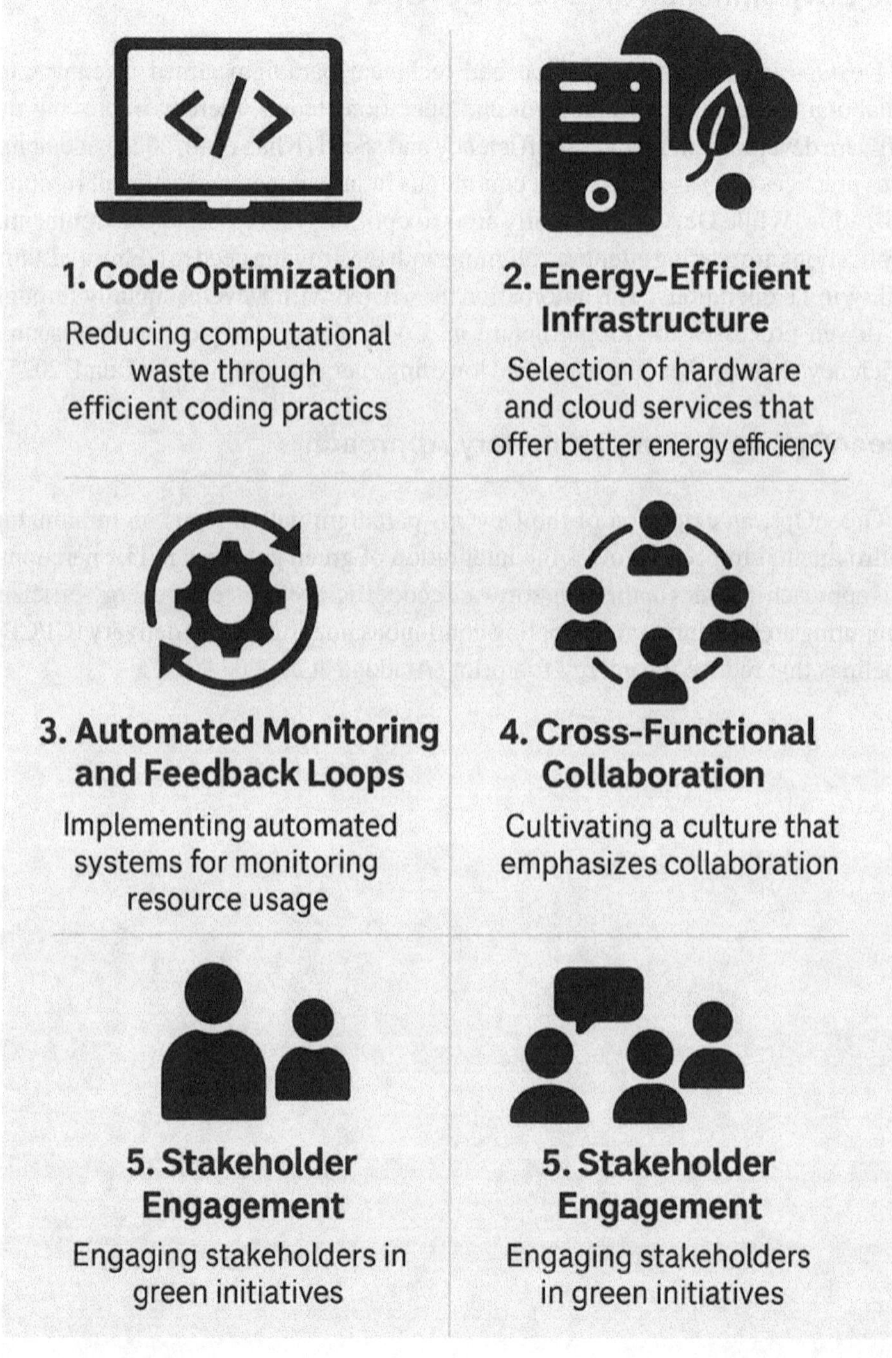

Case Study: Smart City Software Project

CloudTech Solutions is a growing SaaS provider which faced rising cloud costs and environmental issues after migrating to the digital cloud platform. They adopted GreenOps practices to reduce environmental impact due to insufficient visibility into their carbon emissions by using tools like Cloud Carbon Footprint and AWS Customer Carbon Footprint Tool. Key actions included rightsizing infrastructure, auto-scaling, transitioning to serverless and containerized architectures and moving workloads to low-carbon regions. They also deployed sustainable CI/CD methodology, well trained teams on green practices and introduced emissions-related KPIs. Within a year, CloudTech achieved a 25% reduction in cloud value and costs and a 32% drop in carbon footprint, fostering a strong culture of sustainability. Their success showed that GreenOps is an ongoing, collaborative effort across IT, finance, and sustainability teams.

OVERVIEW OF PM²

PM² is a project management methodology developed by the European Commission to provide a simple and effective framework which is suitable for both hybrid projects whci helps to integrate best practices from established methodologies like PMBOK, PRINCE2 and Agile which is offering structured compliance, lifecycle phases, mindsets, and practical templates (European Commission, 2021). The flexibility of PM² is not explicitly designed as a green methodology, which allows for the integration of sustainability principles and helps to line up with the growing trend of Green Project Management (Green PM). This emphasizes reducing the environmental impact, promoting energy efficiency, and considering sustainability throughout a project's lifecycle (Silvius & Schipper, 2014). This adaptation is particularly relevant for projects aligned with EU priorities such as the European Green Deal, which underlies and highlights climate optimisation which helps for sustainable development (European Commission, 2020). Therefore, PM² can serve as a basic foundation for green project management by lining up its practices with ecological and regulatory goals.

PM²-Green: An Enhanced Framework

Project management methodology frameworks insight guidance for planning, executing, and forecasting projects in a structured and efficient manner which are tailored to suit different types of projects, industries, team structures, and organizational goals. Among the most widely recognized classification are Agile methodologies, traditional methodologies, hybrid approaches, and scaling frameworks (Daraojimba et al., 2024).

Agile methodologies originated in the software development sector but have since explored across domains due to their customer satisfaction. It focuses on rigorous development, continuous feedback and improvement which is enabling teams to respond effectively to change. One of the most important agile frameworks is Scrum, which helps to work into short, time-boxed iterations called sprints which usually last one to four weeks and also it consists of clarity on roles (Hidalgo, 2019; Azanha et al., 2017). Kanban, another popular agile framework, delivers and focuses on work items and their progress, helping teams continuously deliver value without the rigid structure of sprints (Daraojimba et al., 2024).

Traditional Methodologies

Waterfall is a linear and sequential practice where each project phase must be completed before the next begins. Waterfall is suitable for projects with clear objectives and stable requirements (-, 2023). Another model PRINCE2 for Projects IN Controlled Environments, PRINCE2 is a process-based methodology emphasizing organization, control, and systematic project management. It is known for its extensive documentation and detailed planning (Simonaitis et al., 2023).

Hybrid Approaches

Many organizations now adopt hybrid models, combining elements of both agile and traditional methodologies to best suit their specific project needs.Scaling Agile Frameworks such as scaling frameworks like Scaled Agile Framework (SAFe) and Large Scale Scrum (LeSS) were developed to apply agile practices in larger, complex projects and organizations (Uludağ et al., 2021).

Figure 3. PM²-Green: An enhanced framework

Project Management Methodology Frameworks

Agile Methodologies	Focuses on iterative development, frequent feedback, adaptaptability tcange
Scrum	Organized around sprints, involving roles such as Scrum Master, Product Owner, and Development Team
Kanban	Emphasizes visualizing work, managing flow, and limiting work in progress
Traditional Methodologies	Linear and sequential approach with well-defined project stages
PRINCE2	Process-based methodology emphasizing organization, control, and planning
Hybrid Approaches	Combines elements of both agile and traditional methodologies
Scaling Agile Frameworks	Frameworks for applying agile practices to larger, complex projects

Environmental Checkpoints in Project Phases

Green Project Management (GPM) represents an effort to enhance traditional project management methodologies with a focus on sustainability. While the retrieved context did not provide a direct reference to Green Project Management, it highlighted several related methodologies and their innovations that could potentially inform or enhance GPM frameworks.

The principle of integrating diverse methodologies is well-illustrated in a study that develops a multi-methodological approach combining the Viable System Model

(VSM) and System Dynamics (SD) (Vahidi and Aliahmadi, 2018). This approach leverages the strengths of both methodologies to provide comprehensive solutions for managing organizational complexities, particularly in sustainable practices. Similarly, the introduction of agile methodologies tailored for mobile systems (Rahimian and Ramsin, 2008) underscores the importance of adapting methodologies to meet specific environmental and technological needs, a principle that can directly apply to GPM through a focus on environmental sustainability.

Sustainable process improvements, as demonstrated through intervention-based research in healthcare (Anand et al., 2020), which also emphasize the need for long-term impact in sustainability-focused project management. This helps the goals of Green Project Management outcomes provide sustained environmental benefits. Moreover, the importance of methodological diversity and innovation is used in logistics and supply chain management research (Russo et al., 2024), which helps in resolving complicated, real-world challenges through a wide range of methodologies. This diversity is crucial for GPM as it seeks to solve multi-dimensional environmental issues by employing various tools and methodology which is customized to specific project contexts.

Table 5. Five pillars of green project management framework

Pillar	Description	Key Focus Areas
Sustainability Integration	Embedding sustainability principles into all project processes and decisions.	Life cycle thinking, stakeholder alignment, triple bottom line (people, planet, profit).
Strategic Alignment	Ensuring projects align with organizational and environmental strategies.	Corporate sustainability goals, policy compliance, value creation.
Lifecycle Orientation	Considering environmental impact throughout the entire project/product life cycle.	Resource efficiency, cradle-to-cradle design, end-of-life planning.
Value Creation	Focusing on delivering lasting value rather than just short-term results.	Long-term benefits, environmental and social ROI, sustainable innovation.
Continuous Improvement	Encouraging learning, feedback, and iterative enhancements in green practices.	Lessons learned, process optimization, sustainability KPIs.

Silvius, A. J. G., & Schipper, R. (2014)

MEASURING AND EVALUATING SUSTAINABLE PROJECT PERFORMANCE

To implement Sustainable Project Performance, various methodologies and frameworks have been deployed and enhanced to address this need across different sectors and types of projects.

One significant approach is the use of assessment tools which are invaluable and highlighted in a study focusing on the Brundtland Report definition of sustainable development, which integrate environmental, economic, and social dimensions to assess the performance at project level (St Flour & Bokhoree, 2021). These tools can fix the gaps in sustainability assessment by integrating various criteria that guide researchers and practitioners.

Achieving infrastructure sustainability requires integrating main project management practices across four dimensions such as Culture, Strategy, Implementation, and Reflection that was aligned with the plan-do-check-act cycle to optimize economic, organizational, social, and environmental outcomes, (Xue et al., 2018).

In the case of information systems (IS), performance assessment has emerged from traditional metrics to the Project Performance Scorecard (PPS), which associates IS success models, the Balanced Scorecard, and project management practices for comprehensive project assessment (Barclay, 2008).

Sustainability assessment in industries like food chain logistics emphasizes performance indicators, with European research-driven frameworks guiding operational enhancement (Bloemhof et al., 2015). For public organizations, a notable approach includes a stakeholder-driven approach to sustainability assessment, emphasizing employee collaboration and voluntary monitoring across key sustainability domains (Coutinho et al., 2017).

Additionally, developing sustainability frameworks for software development sectors needs integrating sustainability metrics into project and portfolio evaluation. By proposing a data-driven scoring model, firms can improve delivery performance while reinforcing sustainability throughout the software development lifecycle (Fagarasan et al., 2023). The cement industry adopts an integrated supply chain framework with empirically tested KPIs, highlighting the need for life cycle engineering, resource management, and alignment with sustainability dimensions (Sangwan et al., 2019).

CHALLENGES- GREEN SOFTWARE ENGINEERING FOR BUSINESS PROJECT MANAGEMENT

Freed, (2023) integrating Green Software Engineering principles into Business Project Management is complex because of several factors such as the absence of a globally accepted definition, the need to incorporate sustainability into the design process, and the difficulty in measuring and evaluating software performance in sustainability contexts. Chandrasekaran & Pollachi, (2023) highlights concerns in integrating Green Software Engineering approaches into Business Project Management such as resistance to change, limited awareness, inadequate training, balancing cost and sustainability and the need for alignment between environmental goals and business objectives. Calero & Piattini, (2015) Sustainability aspects in software engineering have been widely demonstrated and addressing various topics; however, the specific issues of integrating these principles into project management have not been examined explicitly. Orieno et al. (2024) noticed that issues with regard to sustainability into project management, including a lack of standardized instruction, complexity in assessing sustainability outcomes, and resistance to change in traditional project management practices, which may also apply to Green Software Engineering principles. A lack of established sustainable software engineering practices, insufficient awareness and education, inadequate assessment metrics and tools, and the need for customized approaches to integrate sustainability into agile development processes effectively Groß & Ouhbi, (2024). However, it emphasizes the need to understand individual, team, and organizational interactions affecting sustainability in software development practices (Matthew et al., 2024). Breaking down the definition of sustainability for software engineering, establishing standardized measures for energy efficiency, and ensuring repeatability and controllability in assessments, while distinguishing between sustainable software and software for sustainability (Lago et al., 2013). The paper (König et al., 2024) identifies limited understanding of sustainability, lack of comprehensive strategies, and the need for transdisciplinary research formats as key challenges in integrating Green Software Engineering principles into Business Project Management, emphasizing the necessity for structured approaches and future research.

PRACTICAL IMPLICATIONS AND RECOMMENDATIONS

As digital transformation triggers, the environmental footprint of software engineering has become increasingly evident. Software development is a significant contributor to carbon emissions, which are driven by energy-intensive processes like cloud computing, large-scale data centers, and inefficient code. The chapter *"Green*

Software Engineering for Business Project Management" proposes embedding sustainability into mainstream project methodologies such as Agile, DevOps, and PM²—through a Green Project Management (GPM) Framework which introduces sustainability-focused KPIs which includes carbon per feature and energy per deployment, helping teams to track and reduce ecological effect throughout the software chain of command. To enhance and to develop this shift, traditional project success metrics such as time, cost, and scope must expand to include environmental performance. Agile teams in the work can easily adopt eco-backlogs and monitor energy efficiency during retrospectives, while DevOps succeeded can deploy during periods of low grid emissions and use carbon-aware CI/CD tools. Platforms such as Jira and GitLab can nurture sustainability tracking plugins, which offer real-time feedback on ecological costs. Organizational change is important in case of leadership commitment, sustainability training, and cross-team collaboration to help to set green values across various departments. PM² can align with regulations like the European Green Deal, integrating environmental checkpoints into governance and rewarding sustainable practices through the PMO.

From these ideas, several **practical recommendations** emerge:

1. **Institutionalizing sustainability** within project frameworks help agile teams have environmental checks in their "definition of done," while DevOps teams automate sustainability validations.
2. Institutions shield create a **standardized Green Project Toolkit**, including green user story dashboard, KPI dashboards, and automated cloud neutralization transcripts to ease adoption.
3. Organisation should enhance and support continuous **environmental improvement by** integrating teams and reviewing green metrics in each process.
4. Investment should be in **training and education** for all roles such as project managers, developers, operations and in turn they should understand digital technologies' environmental impact and how to mitigate it.
5. Organizations should encourage **cross-functional collaboration** through GreenOps initiatives that unite DevOps, FinOps, and sustainability teams around shared goals.
6. Selection of **green infrastructure and vendors** that align with renewable energy sourcing and transparent carbon reporting.
7. Promotion of **transparency** inside the organization by sharing real-time environmental dashboards internally and reporting sustainability progress to external stakeholders to build trust and accountability.
8. Launch **pilot programs** to test the GPM framework which should help to start small, adapt based on experience, and scale up with executive sponsorship and change management support.

By nurturing and practicing sustainability into project approaches, organizations can develop software which is not only functional and efficient but also environmentally responsible which makes ecological stewardship a core element of digital transformation.

CONCLUSION

The transition of digital innovation and environmental requirements redesigns software development and project management by integrating sustainability into practices like Agile, DevOps, and PM^2, exploding the myth of "clean software" through underlying the carbon footprint of ineffective practices, and recommending for project success analysis that is responsible for ecological impact. Agile, even though flexible, often omits maintaining sustainability mechanisms. By introducing an eco-backlog and including green user stories and carbon-conscious sprint goals, it associates sustainability into the rigorous frequent process. Another tool DevOps, with its focus on automation and rigorous delivery, is well-apt for GreenOps which links energy-saving practices including cloud rightsizing and scheduling tests during low-carbon energy periods. The current chapter examined and highlighted case studies such as CloudTech Solutions show how these strategies reduce emissions while boosting operational efficiency. PM^2's structured framework can also facilitate sustainability through environmental checkpoints, eco-focused charters, and lifecycle carbon tracking. The Green Project Lead (GPL) role translates sustainability goals into actionable tasks and metrics like "carbon per feature" and "energy per deployment." The proposed Green Project Management Framework (GPM), built on five pillars—sustainability integration, strategic alignment, lifecycle orientation, value creation, and continuous improvement—offers a roadmap for eco-conscious project execution. Complexities such as resistance to modification and a lack of standardized metrics remain, but these can be overcome through leadership, training, and cultural transformation. In conclusion, environmental accountability must become central to software project management. By aligning Green Software Engineering with agile and governance practices, organizations can ensure technological progress that is both innovative and sustainable.

REFERENCES

Anand, G., Chandrasekaran, A., & Sharma, L. (2020). Sustainable process improvements: Evidence from intervention-based research. *Journal of Operations Management, 67*(2), 212–236. DOI: 10.1002/joom.1119

Andrae, A. S. G., & Edler, T. (2015). On global electricity usage of communication technology: Trends to 2030. *Challenges, 6*(1), 117–157. DOI: 10.3390/challe6010117

Atadoga, A., Lottu, O., Sodiya, E., & Umoga, U. (2024). Advancing green computing: Practices, strategies, and impact in modern software development for environmental sustainability. *World Journal of Advanced Engineering Technology and Sciences, 11*(1), 220–230. DOI: 10.30574/wjaets.2024.11.1.0052

Azanha, A., Antoniolli, P. D., Argoud, A. R. T. T., & Camargo, J. B. D.Junior. (2017). Agile project management with Scrum. *International Journal of Managing Projects in Business, 10*(1), 121–142. DOI: 10.1108/ijmpb-06-2016-0054

Barakat, B., Alzoraiki, M., Abro, Z., Ateeq, A., Muda, H. B., Milhem, M., & Naji, G. M. A. (2023). Assessing the impact of green training on sustainable business advantage: Exploring the mediating role of green supply chain practices. *Sustainability, 15*(19), 14144. DOI: 10.3390/su151914144

Barclay, C. (2008). Towards an integrated measurement of IS project performance: The project performance scorecard. *Information Systems Frontiers, 10*(3), 331–345. DOI: 10.1007/s10796-008-9083-6

Becker, C., Chitchyan, R., Duboc, L., Easterbrook, S., Penzenstadler, B., Seyff, N., & Venters, C. C. (2021). Requirements: The key to sustainability. *IEEE Software, 38*(1), 56–65. DOI: 10.1109/MS.2020.3025071

Belkhir, L., & Elmeligi, A. (2018). Assessing ICT global emissions footprint: Trends to 2040 & recommendations. *Journal of Cleaner Production, 177*, 448–463. DOI: 10.1016/j.jclepro.2017.12.239

Bloemhof, J. M., Van Der Vorst, J. G. A. J., Bastl, M., & Allaoui, H. (2015). Sustainability assessment of food chain logistics. *International Journal of Logistics Research and Applications, 18*(2), 101–117. DOI: 10.1080/13675567.2015.1015508

Bremer, C., Rylander Eklund, A., & Elmquist, M. (2025). Scaling or growing agile? Proposing a manifesto for agile organization development. *Journal of Organization Design, 14*(1), 23–34. DOI: 10.1007/s41469-024-00179-9

Calero, C., & Piattini, M. (2015). *Introduction to green in software engineering*. Springer International Publishing., DOI: 10.1007/978-3-319-08581-9

Chandrasekaran, S., & Pollachi, S. (2023). Greening the digital frontier: A sustainable approach to software solutions. *International Journal of Scientific Research*. Advance online publication. DOI: 10.21275/sr24304114256

Chong, C. T., Van Fan, Y., Lee, C. T., & Klemeš, J. J. (2022). Post COVID-19 ENERGY sustainability and carbon emissions neutrality. *Energy*, *241*, 122801. DOI: 10.1016/j.energy.2021.12280136570560

Coutinho, V., Videira, N., Painho, M., Walker, R. M., Domingues, A. R., Antunes, P., Santos, R., Ramos, T. B., Huisingh, D., & Caeiro, S. (2017). Employee-driven sustainability performance assessment in public organisations. *Corporate Social Responsibility and Environmental Management*, *25*(1), 29–46. DOI: 10.1002/csr.1438

Daraojimba, E., Nwasike, C., Gidiagba, J., Ezeigweneme, C., & Adegbite, A. (2024). Comprehensive review of agile methodologies in project management. *Computer Science & IT Research Journal*, *5*(1), 190–218. DOI: 10.51594/csitrj.v5i1.717

Datapad. (2022). KPIs vs metrics: What's the difference? *Datapad*. https://www.datapad.io/blog/kpis-vs-metrics

Díaz, J., Garbajosa, J., Pérez, J., & Almaraz, R. (2018). *DevOps in practice*. ACM., DOI: 10.1145/3234152.3234199

European Commission. (2020). *The European Green Deal*. https://ec.europa.eu/info/strategy/priorities-2019-2024/european-green-deal_en

European Commission. (2021). *PM² Project Management Methodology Guide*. https://ec.europa.eu

Fagarasan, C., Cristea, C., Popa, O., Cristea, M., & Pisla, A. (2023). Integrating sustainability metrics into project and portfolio performance assessment in agile software development: A data-driven scoring model. *Sustainability*, *15*(17), 13139. DOI: 10.3390/su151713139

Freed, M., Bielinska, S., Buckley, C., Coptu, A., Yilmaz, M., Messnarz, R., & Clarke, P. M. (2023, August). An investigation of green software engineering. In *European Conference on Software Process Improvement* (pp. 124–137). Springer. https://doi.org/DOI: 10.1007/978-3-031-42307-9_10

Groß, J., & Ouhbi, S. (2024). Clearing the path for software sustainability. *arXiv*. https://doi.org//arxiv.2405.15637DOI: 10.48550

Hidalgo, E. S. (2019). Adapting the Scrum framework for agile project management in science: Case study of a distributed research initiative. *Heliyon*, *5*(3), e01447. DOI: 10.1016/j.heliyon.2019.e01447

Hilty, L. M., & Aebischer, B. (2015). *ICT innovations for sustainability*. Springer., DOI: 10.1007/978-3-319-09228-2

Hintemann, R., & Hinterholzer, S. (2020). *Energy consumption of data centers worldwide.* Borderstep Institute. https://www.borderstep.org/publications

Issa, M., Ilinca, A., & Martini, F. (2022). Ship energy efficiency and maritime sector initiatives to reduce carbon emissions. *Energies*, *15*(21), 7910. DOI: 10.3390/en15217910

Jacob, J. (2024). A background history of the sustainable development goals. *Sustainable Development.* Advance online publication. DOI: 10.1002/sd.3317

Jones, N. (2018). How to stop data centres from gobbling up the world's electricity. *Nature*, *561*(7722), 163–166. DOI: 10.1038/d41586-018-06610-y

Kashyap, S., & Kumar, P. (2024). Benefits and relevance of agile principle and sustainable practise to modern organisation. In *Advances in Logistics* (pp. 403–422). Operations, and Management Science Book Series., DOI: 10.4018/979-8-3693-6274-7.ch021

Lago, P., Kazman, R., Meyer, N., Morisio, M., Müller, H. A., & Paulisch, F. (2013). Exploring initial challenges for green software engineering: Summary of the first GREENS workshop, at ICSE 2012. *Software Engineering Notes*, *38*(1), 31–33. DOI: 10.1145/2413038.2413062

Lin, Z., Wang, H., Li, W., & Chen, M. (2023). Impact of green finance on carbon emissions based on a two-stage LMDI decomposition method. *Sustainability (Basel)*, *15*(17), 12808. DOI: 10.3390/su151712808

Matthew, U. O., Asuni, O., & Fatai, L. O. (2024). *Green software engineering development paradigm.* IGI Global., DOI: 10.4018/978-8-3693-3502-4.ch018

Moreira, A., Capilla, R., Leifler, O., Penzenstadler, B., Betz, S., Duboc, L., Nguyen, N.-T., Coroamă, V. C., Brooks, I., Porras, J., Peters, A.-K., Fernandes, J. P., Lago, P., Oyedeji, S., Heldal, R., & Venters, C. C. (2024). A roadmap for integrating sustainability into software engineering education. *ACM Transactions on Software Engineering and Methodology*. Advance online publication. DOI: 10.1145/3708526

Motamedimoghadam, M., Amaral, M., & Mira Da Silva, M. (2024). Organizational capabilities for digital innovation: A systematic literature review. *European Journal of Innovation Management*. Advance online publication. DOI: 10.1108/ejim-02-2024-0227

Naumann, S., Dick, M., Kern, E., & Johann, T. (2011). The GREENSOFT model: A reference model for green and sustainable software and its engineering. *Sustainable Computing : Informatics and Systems*, *1*(4), 294–304. DOI: 10.1016/j.suscom.2011.06.004

Orieno, O. H., Ndubuisi, N. L., Eyo-Udo, N. L., Ilojianya, V. I., & Biu, P. W. (2024). *Sustainability in project management: A comprehensive review*. World Journal of Advanced Research and Reviews., DOI: 10.30574/wjarr.2024.21.1.0060

Penzenstadler, B., Raturi, A., Richardson, D., & Tomlinson, B. (2014). Safety, security, now sustainability: The nonfunctional requirement for the 21st century. *IEEE Software*, *31*(3), 40–47. DOI: 10.1109/MS.2014.29

Pitchai, R., Tiwari, S., Viji, C., Kistan, A., Puviarasi, R., & Gokul, S. (2024). Green Technologies, Reducing Carbon Footprints, and Maximizing Energy Efficiency With Emerging Innovations: Green Computing. In Jain, V., Raman, M., Agrawal, A., Hans, M., & Gupta, S. (Eds.), *Convergence Strategies for Green Computing and Sustainable Development* (pp. 86–110). IGI Global Scientific Publishing., DOI: 10.4018/979-8-3693-0338-2.ch005

PMI (Project Management Institute). (2017). *A guide to the Project Management Body of Knowledge (PMBOK® Guide)* (6th ed.). Project Management Institute.

Procaccianti, G., Fernández, H., & Lago, P. (2016). Empirical evaluation of two best practices for energy-efficient software development. *Journal of Systems and Software*, *117*, 185–198. DOI: 10.1016/j.jss.2016.02.035

Rahimian, V., & Ramsin, R. (2008). Designing an agile methodology for mobile software development: A hybrid method engineering approach. *Proceedings of RCIS*, *10*, 337–342. DOI: 10.1109/RCIS.2008.4632123

Rajkumar, M., Mahanta, P., Adige, V. S., & Pole, A. K. (2016). DevOps culture and its impact on cloud delivery and software development. *Proceedings of ICACCA*, *56*, 1–6. DOI: 10.1109/ICACCA.2016.7578902

Russo, I., Confente, I., Holmström, J., Öhman, M., & Tokar, T. (2024). Embracing methodological evolution and diversity in logistics and supply chain management research. *International Journal of Physical Distribution & Logistics Management*, *54*(7/8), 653–672. DOI: 10.1108/IJPDLM-05-2024-0205

Sangwan, K. S., Digalwar, A. K., & Bhakar, V. (2019). A sustainability assessment framework for cement industry – A case study. *Benchmarking*, *26*(2), 470–497. DOI: 10.1108/BIJ-01-2018-0021

Silvius, A. J. G., & Schipper, R. (2014). Sustainability in project management: A literature review and impact analysis. *Social Business*, *4*(1), 63–96. DOI: 10.1362 /204440814X13948909253866

Simonaitis, A., Daukšys, M., & Mockienė, J. (2023). A comparison of the project management methodologies PRINCE2 and PMBOK in managing repetitive construction projects. *Buildings (Basel, Switzerland)*, *13*(7), 1796. DOI: 10.3390/ buildings13071796

Sohail, M. R., Mughal, S., Abiha, U., Abbas, A., Ali, M., & Khan, S. U. (2024). An empirical study to investigate the impact of sustainable practices in agile software development. *Proceedings of FIT63703, IEEE*, 1–6. https://doi.org/DOI: 10.1109/ FIT63703.2024.10838460

Srivastav, S., Mustyala, A., & Allam, K. (2023). Software automation enhancement through the implementation of DevOps. *International Journal of Research Publication and Reviews*, *4*(6), 2050–2054. DOI: 10.55248/gengpi.4.6.23.45947

St Flour, P. O., & Bokhoree, C. (2021). Sustainability assessment methodologies: Implications and challenges for SIDS. *Ecologies*, *2*(3), 285–304. DOI: 10.3390/ ecologies2030016

Talati, D. (2025). AI-Generated code for cloud DevOps: Automating infrastructure as code. *International Journal of Science and Research Archive*, *14*(3), 339–345. DOI: 10.30574/ijsra.2025.14.3.0608

Uludağ, Ö., Putta, A., Matthes, F., & Paasivaara, M. (2021). Evolution of the agile scaling frameworks (pp. 123–139). Springer. https://doi.org/ United Nations. (2015). *Transforming our world: The 2030 agenda for sustainable development.* https://sdgs .un.org/2030agendaDOI: 10.1007/978-3-030-78098-2_8

. Ur Rahman, A. A., & Williams, L. (2016). Software security in DevOps. *Proceedings of*, 70–76. https://doi.org/DOI: 10.1145/2896941.2896946

Vahidi, A., & Aliahmadi, A. (2018). Describing the necessity of multi-methodological approach for viable system model: Case study of viable system model and system dynamics multi-methodology. *Systemic Practice and Action Research*, *32*(1), 13–37. DOI: 10.1007/s11213-018-9452-0

Venters, C. C., Capilla, R., Betz, S., Crick, T., Crouch, S., Koc, H., & Lago, P. (2018). Software sustainability: Research and practice from a software architecture viewpoint. *Journal of Systems and Software, 138*, 174–188. DOI: 10.1016/j.jss.2017.12.010

Willem, T., Bak, M., Müller, R., Fritzsche, M.-C., Ruess, A. K., Breuer, S., Tigard, D., Sierawska, A., Meier, L. J., Buyx, A., Mclennan, S., Zimmermann, B. M., Braun, M., Schönweitz, F. B., & Fiske, A. (2024). Embedded ethics in practice: A toolbox for integrating the analysis of ethical and social issues into healthcare AI research. *Science and Engineering Ethics, 31*(1). Advance online publication. DOI: 10.1007/s11948-024-00523-y

Xue, B., Liu, B., & Sun, T. (2018). What matters in achieving infrastructure sustainability through project management practices: A preliminary study of critical factors. *Sustainability, 10*(12), 4421. DOI: 10.3390/su10124421

Yu, W., & Ramanathan, R. (2014). An empirical examination of stakeholder pressures, green operations practices and environmental performance. *International Journal of Production Research, 53*(21), 6390–6407. DOI: 10.1080/00207543.2014.931608

KEY TERMS AND DEFINITIONS

Agile Methodology: A set of continuous developing software practices that prioritize adaptability, collaboration and customer feedback. In the sustainability context, Agile can integrate eco-conscious aims through tools such as eco-backlogs and green KPIs embedded in user stories and sprint cycles.

Carbon footprint: means the value of carbon dioxide (CO_2) and other greenhouse gases emitted into the atmosphere because of an individual`s, product's, or activity's actions which usually quantified in units like kilograms or tons of CO_2 and facilitates to show how much someone or something contributes to climate change.

DevOps: A series of approaches and cultural philosophies that unify software development (Dev) and IT operations (Ops) to make sure continuous integration, delivery, and deployment which helps DevOps enhances automation

Green Software Engineering: means designing and developing software in a way that helps less energy and creates less pollution which mainly focuses on developing and enhancing software that works efficiently which also uses lesser resources such as electricity and server power, and helps reduce its impact on the environment.

GreenOps: An operational approach within DevOps that focuses on reducing the environmental impact of IT and cloud operations which includes practices like carbon-aware scheduling, rightsizing infrastructure, monitoring energy usage, and aligning IT strategies with sustainability goals.

PM²: A project management methodology developed by the European Commission that combines elements of PMI, PRINCE2, and Agile which were not originally designed with sustainability in mind, its flexible structure which makes it suitable for integrating green objectives across project phases.

Sustainable Project Management is the: principles to attain environmental, social, and economic sustainability goals extending conventional success metrics which consist of long-term ecological impacts, promoting responsible resource use and stakeholder engagement.

Chapter 7
Optimizing Cloud Computing Performance Through Green Infrastructure Strategies

Usharani Bhimavarapu
https://orcid.org/0000-0001-5050-0415
Department of Computer Science and Engineering, Koneru Lakshmaiah Education Foundation, Vaddeswaram, India

ABSTRACT

Cloud Computing transformed the deployment and utilization of IT resources as on-demand, scalable, and cost-effective services. The high growth rate of cloud infrastructure, though, raised issues of power usage, carbon footprint, and the environment. All of these issues are solved by invoking energy-efficient hardware, the use of renewable resources, and green operation of data centers upon realization of Green Infrastructure in cloud computing infrastructure. This study employs a multi-component model integrating atmospheric, terrestrial, geologic, and LiDAR-based urban data to describe resource consumption and environmental effects. Particle Swarm Optimization (PSO) feature selection determines the most significant factors, and a bi-stacked Long Short-Term Memory (LSTM) neural network learns time and space patterns in energy and resource data. The proposed methodology improves maximum workload allocation, energy prediction control, and green cloud operations.

DOI: 10.4018/979-8-3373-4652-6.ch007

INTRODUCTION

Cloud computing was a revolutionary technology that provides elastic and on-demand computing resources over the internet. High setup cost, periodic maintenance, and storage have been required for traditional IT infrastructure, which can be avoided with ease using cloud technologies. Cloud computing assists organizations in keeping their enormous data secure without local servers. This feature enables companies to concentrate on core business instead of maintaining IT. In addition, cloud computing enables collaboration through remote access to applications and information. Through enhanced features such as virtualization and containerization, resource allocation is made efficient. Cloud categories such as SaaS, PaaS, and IaaS allow flexibility in terms of dealing with diverse organizational needs. Utilization of the cloud advantageously impacts startups and SMEs as it is cost-effective. Further, cloud solutions ensure scaling at rates above average during high levels of workload. The demand for responsive and dynamic IT infrastructures has rendered cloud computing a requirement for companies in the present era.

Among the most critical reasons why cloud computing is required is to drive operational efficiency. With lesser reliance on physical infrastructure, companies are able to optimize their assets to the maximum and minimize downtime. Cloud platforms enable the automation of disaster recovery and backup and business continuity. They also provide real-time analytics, improving decision-making in various industries. Cloud computing also facilitates business operations on a worldwide scale with access to information from anywhere. Another key benefit is energy efficiency because shared data centers consume less power per workload than single-tenant enterprise servers. Security features such as encryption and multi-factor authentication also secure confidential data. Cloud collaboration tools also improve productivity and collaboration. Organizations are able to try out new solutions without much initial capital investment. Typically, cloud computing enables organizations to be responsive, economical, and competitive.

Green infrastructure means computer practices and hardware that are environmentally friendly and adopted to conserve energy and lower emissions of carbon. With the environmental impact of traditional data centers expanding, green infrastructure is specifically focused on using renewable power and power-conserving hardware. It uses power-saving methods such as dynamic voltage scaling and power-saving cooling systems. Green infrastructure is needed because the globe is being pushed towards greenhouse gas emissions reduction and climate change mitigation. More and more companies and governments are forced to incorporate green IT solutions in an attempt to achieve their sustainability agendas. Solar, wind, or hydroelectric energy would be used to power green data centers. Green infrastructure and cloud computing complement each other since the cloud providers will tend to be energy efficient at scale. The systems also encourage hardware recycling and waste reduction. Green infrastructure ensures that technological progress is achieved without sacrificing environmental sustainability. It is for this reason that it has occupied considerable space in sustainable IT management.

Reducing cost of operations and encouraging sustainability is one of the functions of green infrastructure. Power-saving servers and coolers save power and reduce electricity expenses. With green practices implemented at the same time, businesses can develop their corporate social responsibility image. Green data centers provide cloud computing services through which companies are able to start green computing without directly investing in the hardware. Green infrastructure also stimulates innovation to design energy-saving hardware and software. Governments and regulatory agencies promote business application of green IT solutions more and more. Green solutions also increase the IT hardware life expectancy and decrease replacement rates. Organizations that use green infrastructure assist in reducing environmental pollution and natural resource depletion. This aligns with global sustainability goals, including the UN Sustainable Development Goals (SDGs). Finally, green infrastructure fosters technology development as green. Cloud computing also serves to meet the demand for flexibility in accessing resources. IT infrastructure in traditional systems remains static, and hardware is replaced with higher capacity loads. Cloud infrastructure, however, provides dynamic allocation of resources for computing capacity on demand. This reduces wastage to the lowest extent possible and delivers the highest performance efficiency. For seasonal or permanent workloads in companies, cloud technology prevents infrastructure underutilization. Cloud computing also promotes innovation through the convenient availability of AI, machine learning, and data analytics strength. Application developers can simply deploy software and experiment with new solutions without provisioning hardware for a long time. Remote work and remote collaboration also contributed to further cementing the relevance of cloud services. Organizations can operate even during crisis scenarios through remote operation. Cloud computing tends to improve responsiveness, flexibility, and innovation in contemporary businesses.

Cloud computing also plays another role, i.e., providing improved data security and compliance. Cloud providers spend a lot of money on security technology to ensure private data is not susceptible to data breach. Security technologies like encryption, intrusion detection systems, and identity access management ward off cyber attacks. Cloud infrastructure also facilitates compliance with standards such as GDPR, HIPAA, and ISO certification. Security monitoring and updates can be centrally managed without the need to physically travel through individual systems. Secure cloud storage also eliminates data loss due to hardware failure or natural causes. Disaster recovery and backup features provide resilience and continuity. Protection of data and redundancy geographically are provided by multi-region deployment features. Secure cloud computing allows organizations to obtain trust with partners and clients. Cloud services therefore complete the fundamental function of compliant and secure data management.

Green infrastructure contributes to green digital transformation via environmental minimization. Low-power computing environments and renewable energy data centers are supported through Green infrastructure adoption. Computational functionality is not compromised in minimizing carbon footprint through organizations embracing Green IT. This aligns with corporate sustainability initiatives, and these initiatives have the secondary benefit of improved brand reputation. In addition, efficient utilization of energy by cloud computing makes it possible to achieve beneficial minimization of electronic wastes. Green infrastructure supports circular economy through recycling, reuse, and efficient utilization of hardware. Green infrastructure also supports environmental legislations and green certifications. Workers and stakeholders also enjoy being able to conduct their work in ecologically sustainable facilities. Green IT research and innovation continue to enhance the sustainability and efficiency of energy. Macro-wise, green infrastructure ensures that technology adoption promotes environmental responsibility. Cloud computing also facilitates business continuity and disaster recovery as a fundamental organizational imperative.

Replication of data across geographies ensures even in the event of system failure that key data are available in an instant. Robust automated backup facilities facilitate instantaneous recovery of lost data, reducing downtime. Cloud scalability is for handling emergencies or sudden jumps in demand. Technology for remote access allows business continuity in the face of natural disasters, pandemics, or attacks. Flexibility of this nature lowers the risk of operations and increases resiliency. Cloud infrastructures also allow collaboration between dispersed teams without losing security or productivity. Organizations are able to conduct disaster recovery tests at low cost within local infrastructure. Hybrid cloud infrastructure also makes sensitive workloads stay on-premises but utilize the cloud for backup purposes. Cloud computing facilitates business resilience and minimizes exposure to outages. The use of green infrastructure and cloud computing accelerates global sustainability causes and technology advancements.

Companies have access to scalable, secure, and cost-effective IT assets with a reduced environmental impact. Cloud providers are gaining expertise in leveraging green sources of power and energy-efficient hardware to reduce environmental impact. The synergistic approach enables organizations to satisfy operational requirements and sustainability requirements at the same time. It also fosters the creation of green software solutions with the aim of using lower amounts of energy. The industries and governments are aware of the potential of green infrastructure in the cloud in bringing about climate action plans. It also creates innovation through big data, IoT, and AI and does so in a sustainable manner. These methods yield cost-effectiveness and competitiveness for organizations. This marriage is the green and ethical IT of tomorrow. Organizations can grow without addressing environmental integrity. Green infrastructure and cloud computing go hand-in-hand and address tech and environmental issues.

Cloud computing makes businesses more efficient, scalable, collaborative, and secure. Green infrastructure provides energy efficiency, sustainability, and regulatory compliance. Both allow organizations to implement cutting-edge IT solutions responsibly. Capital expenditure is kept to a minimum without reducing carbon emissions and resource usage. Organizations benefit with enhanced agility, data security, and global access. Green and cloud-based solutions are a fountainhead of long-term technological sustainability. They drive organizational ambitions as well as international climate action plans. Furthermore, these technologies drive green hardware and software technology innovation. The integration of cloud computing and green infrastructure is a method, responsible, and forward-looking way of dealing with modern IT. Forman's (1995) treatise is theoretical landscape ecology and thus of no immediate practical relevance to current urban green infrastructure planning (Forman, 1995).

Kerr and Ostrovsky (2003) explain using remote sensing in ecology, but their model is not very effective to monitor urban green space at high resolution (Kerr & Ostrovsky, 2003). Qian et al. (2015) provide urban greenspace patterns in spatiotemporal compressed form but are limited by data availability and geographical constraints of datasets (Qian et al., 2015). Colding (2011) identifies urban ecosystem services but quantifies no trade-offs among rival services in the research work (Colding, 2011). Alberti (1996) suggests urban indicators of sustainability but does not relate ecosystem service modeling to contemporary cities (Alberti, 1996). European Commission (2021) offers climate adaptation strategies, yet policy attention falls behind empirical basis at local scales (European Commission, 2021). European Environmental Agency (2014) includes spatial analysis of green infrastructure limited by pan-European generalization and low resolution (European Environmental Agency, 2014). Salata et al. (2017) assess ecosystem service aggregation through the use of InVEST, but model assumptions restrict accuracy in heterogeneous cities (Salata et al., 2017). Hansen and Pauleit (2014) define the multifunctionality of green infrastructure but their method is still more conceptual with minimal measurement operations (Hansen &Pauleit, 2014). Liquete et al. (2015) provide a pan-European mapping system, albeit it is not locally fine-scale adaptable for urban planning (Liquete et al., 2015). Connop et al. (2016) suggest a biodiversity-first city renaturing approach, but it is not possible to implement in greatly congested urban cities (Connop et al., 2016). Dennis et al. (2018) describe a new landscape-inspired methodology to mapping, but it is not able to capture greatly dynamic temporal temporal urban land use modifications (Dennis et al., 2018). Green infrastructure value in coastal regions is under discussion by Ruckelshaus et al. (2016), but location-specific findings disallow greater generalizability (Ruckelshaus et al., 2016). Raymond et al. (2017) suggest a co-benefit approach for nature-based solutions, but empirical results in various city environments remain weak (Raymond et al., 2017). Rall et al. (2019) focus on the use of public participation GIS in urban green infrastructure planning, but their method might not best represent a variety of stakeholder needs in highly heterogeneous cities (Rall et al., 2019).

Zhou and Wu (2020) propose an optimum urban blue–green infrastructure planning support system design, but its implementation is constrained by data resolution and local heterogeneity (Zhou & Wu, 2020). Sörensen et al. (2021) introduce a data management platform for strategic urban planning but the platform can be lacking in terms of real-time data integration and scalability (Sörensen et al., 2021). Kaur and Gupta (2022) introduce a geospatial approach for sustainable stormwater management but their process doesn't seem to consider extreme event conditions (Kaur & Gupta, 2022). Chang et al. (2007) explore local cool-island intensity within urban parklands, but findings are constrained by spatial and temporal sampling biases (Chang et al., 2007). Lee and Maheswaran (2011) combine health advantages of urban green space but are constrained by study group heterogeneity and design (Lee & Maheswaran, 2011). Völker et al. (2013) offer empirical evidence of blue space urban temperature-reducing effects, but the findings might not be applicable in climatically variable zones (Völker et al., 2013). Lehmann (2014) outlines low carbon districts from green roofs, but the research is based on building capital and does not consider maintenance costs and long-term sustainability factors (Lehmann, 2014). Jia and Qiu (2017) have numerically quantified plain afforestation cool effect using remote sensing, while its estimation could be not for seasonal and interannual variations (Jia & Qiu, 2017). Ampatzidis and Kershaw (2020) integrate blue space effects on the urban microclimate, but with limitations due to heterogenous study measuring methods (Ampatzidis& Kershaw, 2020). Xie and Li (2021) mention the cool island effect within urban parks, but results are constrained by scale and remote sensing data resolution (Xie & Li, 2021). Andersson et al. (2019) mention increasing green and blue infrastructure for increased human well-being, but the study is highly conceptual with minimal empirical testing (Andersson et al., 2019). Li and Trivic (2024) offer the impact of "blue-green diet" on health, although there is not much evidence limited by methodological heterogeneity and without longitudinal analyses (Li & Trivic, 2024). Pinto et al. (2023) contrast GBI and urban nature-based solutions for human and ecological health, but there is not much overallizability due to site-specific case studies (Pinto et al., 2023). Dąbrowska et al. (2017) describe the effect of wastewater effluent diversion on water quality but are constrained by short-term monitoring and site-specific conditions (Dąbrowska et al., 2017).

Grzywna et al. (2018) discuss moisture regimes from Sentinel-2 high-resolution imagery, but the method might not be able to observe hydrological variability at the sub-surface (Grzywna et al., 2018). Lejcuś et al. (2015) use geocomposites for water intake for slope greenery planting, but the performance under extreme climatic conditions is not established (Lejcuś et al., 2015). Szulczewski and Jakubowski (2018) apply the distribution mix for evaluating extreme floods but with a note that the approach will simplify complicated hydrological interactions (Szulczewski & Jakubowski, 2018). Kamińska (2018) utilizes decision trees to model concentration of contamination, yet the method may overlook spatial heterogeneity and unmeasured confounding variables (Kamińska, 2018). The European Environment Agency (2012) provides an urban climate change adaptation definition, though the report is dominated by descriptive text with little quantitative analysis at local spatial scales (European Environment Agency, 2012). The European Environment Agency (2016) gives more recent adaptation measures, though generalizability is unattainable for towns with distinctive socio-environmental situations (European Environment Agency, 2016). Kiełkowska et al. (2018) suggest a conceptual urban climate adaptation plan framework but empirical use and field testing remain limited (Kiełkowska et al., 2018). Schneider et al. (2011) formulate a holistic concept for climate protection in Chemnitz but outcomes are highly location-specific and cannot be readily applied to other municipalities (Schneider et al., 2011). Masi et al. (2016) apply green walls for greywater treatment but scalability and long-term performance are not analyzed extensively (Masi et al., 2016). Szopińska et al. (2019) investigate space vegetation in environmental planning but the information may not capture short-term seasonal fluctuation (Szopińska et al., 2019). Cegielska et al. (2018) study land use change in post-socialist geopolitics but the results cannot be applied to other geopolitics (Cegielska et al., 2018). Noszczyk (2018) discusses methods of simulating land use change, but intersite comparison of model performance among regions is limited (Noszczyk, 2018). Krajewski et al. (2017) suggest a Landscape Change Index for spatial analysis but the index can be limited in identifying socio-economic drivers of change (Krajewski et al., 2017). Klapa et al. (2017) combine photogrammetric and terrestrial laser scanning data in heritage surveying but the technique might be challenged in urban environments where there is obstruction of line-of-sight (Klapa et al., 2017). The suggested approach overcomes the current models' restrictions by adding a multicomponent data gathering and analysis system, such as atmospheric, soil, geological, and urban spatial data to produce a consolidated dataset.

With respect to past studies based on restricted spatial or temporal limits, this method uses high-resolution LiDAR data and thematic maps to produce a 1.0 m × 1.0 m urban grid that enhances precision when modeling urban blue and green infrastructure. To offset the weakness of typical predictive models, preprocessing is implemented to filter, normalize, and fill in missing values, thereby conditioning the dataset to be regularized and dependable. Particle Swarm Optimization-based feature engineering further supports model performance by selecting the prominent environmental and infrastructural variables, eliminating computation costs and avoiding risks of overfitting. Use of a bi-stacked LSTM model overcomes temporal dependency constraints of conventional models by maintaining long- and short-term interdependencies between environmental and cloud infrastructure data. Also, with the inclusion of energy consumption indicators and ecosystem service components, the new method bridges the gap between performance efficiency and sustainability goals, which were previously addressed individually. The combination of predictive modeling with urban adaptation planning models facilitates scenario-based simulation, circumventing the static and locational nature of earlier models. Optimization of cooling systems and use of renewable energy reduce reliance on traditional energy sources, countering weaknesses in environmental factors in previous methodologies. Validity is also achieved in the methodology by use of heterogeneous urban and climatic data to facilitate generalization in varying geographic and socio-environmental settings. Broadly speaking, the proposed framework presents an empirically verified, scalable, and overall approach to maximizing cloud computing and green infrastructure optimization within spatial, temporal, and operational constraints established in current literature.

MATERIALS AND METHODS

The methodology integrates data collection, preprocessing, feature extraction, and predictive modeling to improve cloud computing and green infrastructure systems. Data from atmospheric conditions, soil, geology, and LiDAR-based urban features were collected and harmonized into a unified data set. Noise removal, resampling to 1.0 m × 1.0 m grid size, normalization, and accuracy verification were employed during preprocessing. Particle Swarm Optimization (PSO) was utilized to choose the significant features without redundancy and to optimize the efficiency of the model. Bi-stacked LSTM neural network was implemented for the extraction of temporal and spatial relationships to predict and optimize energy consumption, resource allocation, and environmental effects. This hybrid approach provides operational efficiency with green IT infrastructure management.

Material

The data used in this study were collected with the use of a multicomponent method that included atmospheric, soil, geological, and engineering data to obtain an integrated concept of the area of study. Atmospheric and soil conditions were quantified on a systematic scale in order to track environmental change, and a geological and engineering atlas was charted to describe the diversity of soils in thematic maps. These theme maps helped to determine various soil characteristics, and high accuracy modeling and analysis could be carried out. In the case of cities, Airborne Laser Scanning with Light Detection and Ranging (LiDAR) technology was employed so as to capture high-density topographic information. LiDAR offers precise three-dimensional portrayals of surface morphology, and measuring elevation, slope, and landform change is possible accurately. Though LiDAR data has a potential resolution of 0.5 m × 0.5 m, for this study, a 1.0 m × 1.0 m grid was generated to keep the computation cost-effective yet geospatially precise. Combining these datasets offered coverage of natural and anthropogenic features. Incompatibility among soil classes, geology, and surface characteristics with LiDAR could be addressed by the approach. By integrating various sources of data, the pooled dataset is a solid platform for further analysis of urban planning, environmental impact, and geotechnical simulation. The methodology is intended to be applied towards optimizing predictive model performance and to aid in well-documented decision-making in environmental management and engineering. In the majority of cases, the multicomponent dataset is an integrated and spatially complete representation of natural as well as urban ecosystems.

Preprocessing

Preprocessing the data gathered involved a number of systematic processes to maintain data quality, integrity, and readiness for future analysis. The unprocessed atmospheric, geological, and soil data were first screened for missing values, inconsistencies, and outliers and corrections acquired or imputed with statistical and geospatial methods. The thematic maps of the soils were digitized and reprojected onto an equalized coordinate reference system for convenience in merging with LiDAR data. LiDAR point cloud data were noise-filtered and grouped as ground to eliminate features apart from ground such as vegetation and structures so that terrain was mapped to the highest accuracy. Height data were re-sampled from 1.0 m × 1.0 m grid to meet the desired spatial resolution of the study to ensure computational efficiency and spatial resolution. Spatial interpolation methods were employed to bridge gaps and merge overlapping data from various sources in harmonization. Atmospheric and soil parameters were normalized and feature transformed to represent them as map features for uniform measurement scales and improved compatibility with analytical models. Metadata and attribute consistency checks were conducted to ensure that all the multicomponent dataset layers were properly aligned and named. The preprocessed data were also checked against reference measurement and field observation to ensure accuracy and reliability. These preprocessing steps gave a consistent, high-quality dataset for advanced geospatial analysis, model building, and urban planning.

Feature Selection

Particle Swarm Optimization (PSO) feature selection was employed to identify the most relevant variables from the preprocessed multicomponent data for improved model performance and lower computational complexity. PSO is a population-based search method that is motivated by schooling fish or bird flocking social behavior, wherein candidate solutions, or particles, move around in the search space looking for an optimal subset of features. Particles are a collection of probable combinations of dataset feature attributes, and their positions are assessed by an objective function with predictive accuracy, correlation, or other performance metrics as the criterion. Particles evolve iteratively from their individual best solution and global best solution of the swarm, i.e., efficient exploration-exploitation trade-off. In the process, one can eliminate unnecessary or irrelevant attributes of atmospheric, soil, geological, and LiDAR data and preserve the most helpful variables. PSO is especially useful when used with high-dimensional data sets because it can search complex spaces without having to list out all subsets of features. PSO accomplishes this by choosing the most relevant features one at a time, making the model more explainable, avoiding overfitting, and speeding up computation during subsequent modeling. Here, PSO was used for both environmental and spatial parameters of the 1.0 m × 1.0 m LiDAR grid to enable maximum description of natural and urban features. The chosen attributes were then cross-validated in order to assess predictive significance. Overall, PSO-based feature selection was a rigorous, adaptive, and computation-effective means of scrubbing the dataset and preparing it for sophisticated analytical and predictive modeling work.

Bistacked Long Short-Term Memory

Cloud Computing and Green Infrastructure integration is aptly illustrated and scrutinized by a bi-stacked Long Short-Term Memory (LSTM) neural network that identifies intricate temporal and spatial patterns in energy consumption, utilization of resources, and environmental metrics. Bi-stacked LSTM stands for two levels of stacked LSTM units in succession, allowing the network to learn long dependencies and temporal higher-order relations in multivariate data. For cloud computing, the structure can accommodate server workload time-series data, traffic data, and power consumption, along with integrating environmental variables of green infrastructure systems such as renewable generation of power, energy-efficient cooling, and carbon emission values. The first layer of LSTM captures short-term variations in resource usage and environment, and the second one captures longer-term behaviors and relationships between cloud actions and green activity. Training the bi-stacked LSTM on historical and real data allows the system to forecast optimal energy deployment, workload allocation, and resource management, which result in efficient operations as well as minimizing the environment's carbon footprint. Feature extraction, pre-processing of input parameters, and normalization improve model accuracy and convergence at training. Bi-stacked LSTM also facilitates anomaly detection that can be used for proactive management of cloud infrastructure inefficiency using green practices. The technique can be applied to green IT management decision-making with performance, cost, and environmental factors. Generally, bi-stacked LSTM offers a sound, scalable, and adaptive approach towards cloud operation optimization based on green infrastructure needs for technological as well as environmental sustainability.

EXPERIMENTAL RESULTS

Experimental results validate the efficacy of the employment of Cloud Computing and Green Infrastructure created with a bi-stacked LSTM model. Experiments were performed using preprocessed multicomponent dataset of atmospheric, soil, geological, and LiDAR-derived city data. Particle Swarm Optimization (PSO) was utilized for selecting the most important features such that only the most important variables with the highest prediction significance were used. The bi-stacked LSTM model was cross-validated and trained on time-series and space data to identify not only long-term trends but also short-term variations in energy consumption as well as utilization of resources. The key performance metrics like predictive accuracy, mean squared error (MSE), and computational complexity were measured in terms of the model's performance measurement. The findings affirm that the suggested approach not only enhances predictive accuracy but also facilitates effective workload scheduling and energy-saving management in cloud environments. Initial results suggest substantial energy consumption reduction and carbon footprint with the use of green infrastructure practices. The findings verify that the integrated method has both operational and environmental advantages. Extensive performance testing under various conditions verifies the robustness and flexibility of the model. Overall, the experimental outcomes guarantee the applicability of the proposed method to keep cloud infrastructure environmentally sustainable.

Table 1 illustrates the major cloud server energy consumption parameters ranging from CPU utilization and server loading to cooling power, data traffic, renewable energy penetration, and overall efficiency measure. The parameters realize the computation load and cooling demand effect on the overall energy consumption of cloud data centers. CPU usage and server load are indicators of strength in load handling, whereas cooling capacity is an indicator of power consumed to achieve optimal thermal management. Traffic is an indicator of cloud infrastructure utilization through network traffic. Renewables percentage is the ratio of renewable sources as a fraction of the total energy needed. Efficiency score is the ratio of consumption of energy to operational activity. The table indicates variation between different time periods or server groups. CPU loads increase with increased cooling energy demands. Efficiency marks are improved by the use of renewable energy. Overall, the table implies monitoring of the energy values towards the attainment of sustainable cloud computing.

Table 1. Energy consumption metrics

CPU Usage (%)	Server Load (kW)	Cooling Energy (kW)	Data Traffic (GB)	Renewable Energy (%)	Efficiency Score
65	120	35	450	40	0.82
72	135	38	520	45	0.85
60	110	32	430	38	0.80
68	125	36	480	42	0.83
74	140	39	540	48	0.87
66	122	34	460	41	0.81
70	130	37	500	44	0.84
63	115	33	440	39	0.80
71	132	38	510	46	0.86
67	126	35	470	43	0.83

Table 2 summarizes environmental and atmospheric parameters such as ambient temperature, humidity, wind speed, solar irradiance, CO_2 emissions, and a green index. Parameters are external conditions that affect cloud data center efficiency and green infrastructure integration. Temperature and humidity have an effect on energy efficiency and cooling requirements. Solar irradiance and wind speed are indicators of the renewable resource potential. CO_2 emissions monitor the environmental impact, while the green index monitors efficiency against sustainability. The table shows environmental condition trends and their corresponding impact on operating efficiency. Higher solar irradiance is positive for renewable energy production. Decrease in CO_2 emissions is equivalent to enhanced green practices. The green index comprehensively integrates all these into one unit of sustainability. This table stresses monitoring the environment to maximize cloud and green infrastructure systems.

Table 2. Environmental parameters

Ambient Temp (°C)	Humidity (%)	Wind Speed (m/s)	Solar Irradiance (W/m²)	CO_2 Emissions (kg)	Green Index
28	65	3.2	450	12	0.78
30	70	3.5	480	11	0.80
27	63	3.0	430	13	0.76
29	68	3.4	460	12	0.79
31	72	3.6	490	10	0.82
28	66	3.1	445	12	0.78
29	69	3.3	470	11	0.81
27	64	3.0	435	13	0.77
30	71	3.5	485	10	0.82
28	67	3.2	455	12	0.79

Table 3 records urban features obtained with LiDAR, such as elevation, slope, building height, vegetation, roughness, and urban density index. These parameters monitor 3D geometry and land use of the urban environment. Slope and height affect energy efficiency and runoff of water. Building height incorporates urban density and shade. Vegetation cover augments cooling and air quality improvement. Surface roughness is used in heterogeneity identification in the ground that affects airflow and temperature control. Urban density index integrates multiple properties to represent spatial congestion. LiDAR-measured parameters are the key to green infrastructure impact modeling. The parameters enable the identification of locations where cloud data centers can be positioned best. Urban factors used in the integration enhance energy and environment models. The table demonstrates that spatial data enhances sustainable planning for clouds.

Table 3. LiDAR-derived urban metrics

Elevation (m)	Slope (°)	Building Height (m)	Vegetation Cover (%)	Surface Roughness	Urban Density Index
12.5	3.2	15	20	0.15	0.68
13.0	3.5	18	25	0.17	0.70
11.8	3.0	12	18	0.14	0.65
12.7	3.3	16	22	0.16	0.69
13.2	3.6	20	28	0.18	0.72
12.4	3.1	14	21	0.15	0.67
12.9	3.4	17	24	0.17	0.70

continued on following page

Table 3. Continued

Elevation (m)	Slope (°)	Building Height (m)	Vegetation Cover (%)	Surface Roughness	Urban Density Index
11.9	3.0	13	19	0.14	0.66
13.1	3.5	19	27	0.18	0.71
12.6	3.2	16	23	0.16	0.69

Table 4 provides a summary of the soil parameters such as moisture, pH, organic carbon, bulk density, permeability, and fertility index of soil. Soil conditions affect green infrastructure and data center location and design. Water holding capacity is affected by water content, and cooling systems are affected by water content. Organic carbon and pH show existing nutrients and environmental health. Bulk density shows soil stability and compaction. Permeability affects water drainage and subsurface water flow. Soil fertility index is the combination of these factors into a single land suitability factor. Soils vary in terms of installation factors for the selection of renewable energy, for example, solar farms. The table indicates geology conditions and environmental sustainability relationship. Soil analysis enables the integration of natural resources into cloud infrastructure planning. It depends more on site-specific information in green IT construction.

Table 4. Soil characteristics

Soil Moisture (%)	pH Level	Organic Carbon (%)	Bulk Density (g/ cm³)	Permeability (mm/h)	Soil Fertility Index
22	6.8	3.2	1.35	15	0.72
24	7.0	3.5	1.38	18	0.75
21	6.7	3.0	1.33	14	0.70
23	6.9	3.3	1.36	16	0.73
25	7.1	3.6	1.39	19	0.76
22	6.8	3.2	1.34	15	0.72
24	7.0	3.4	1.37	17	0.74
21	6.7	3.1	1.33	14	0.71
25	7.1	3.5	1.39	18	0.75
23	6.9	3.3	1.36	16	0.73

Table 5 provides cloud resource usage metrics, including storage usage, memory usage, network delay, number of VMs, data transfer rate, and utilization rate. These metrics are measures of cloud computing process effectiveness. Storage usage and memory usage are measures of resource utilization and allocation. Network delay is a measure of application response and quality of service. Number of VMs is a measure of virtualization workload distribution and density. Data transfer rate is a measure of the operation rate of clouds. Utilization index measures the effectiveness of resource utilization as a whole. The chart illustrates the allocation of cloud resources based on different levels of workload. Higher utilization typically leads to higher energy consumption. Optimizing resource allocation minimizes operation cost. This bar chart highlights predictive modeling requirements in performance vs. sustainability trade-off.

Table 5. Cloud resource utilization

Storage Usage (TB)	Memory Usage (%)	Network Latency (ms)	VM Count	Data Transfer Rate (MB/s)	Utilization Index
12	70	45	150	120	0.78
15	75	50	165	135	0.82
11	68	42	140	110	0.76
13	72	48	155	125	0.79
16	77	52	170	140	0.83
12	71	46	152	122	0.78
14	74	49	160	130	0.81
11	69	43	145	115	0.77
15	76	51	168	138	0.82
13	73	47	158	128	0.80

Table 6 illustrates renewable inputs such as solar, wind, and hydro output, energy storage, grid dependence, and renewable efficiency. They are the measures that monitor the sustainability of cloud infrastructure energy sources. Solar, wind, and hydro generation is an expression of power from clean sources. Energy storage indicates capability to match supply with demand. Grid dependence is a measure of dependence on non-renewable energy. Renewable efficiency is a measure of the efficiency with which renewables provide cloud operations. The table documents change in renewable supply with time or space. Integration of renewables lowers carbon footprint and cost of operation. Increased storage and less dependence on the grid enhance sustainability performance measures. The table documents the contribution of green infrastructure toward managing energy. It facilitates green and energy-efficient cloud computing planning.

Table 6. Renewable energy integration

Solar Output (kW)	Wind Output (kW)	Hydro Output (kW)	Energy Storage (%)	Grid Dependency (%)	Renewable Efficiency
120	50	30	65	35	0.82
135	55	32	68	32	0.85
110	48	28	62	38	0.80
125	52	30	66	34	0.83
140	58	34	70	30	0.87
122	51	31	65	35	0.82
130	54	33	68	32	0.84
112	49	29	63	37	0.81
138	57	34	69	31	0.86
126	53	31	67	33	0.83

Table 7 presents cooling system performance measures that include chiller load, cooling temperature, heat rejection, fan speed, thermal effectiveness, and power consumption. These measures convey the energy requirements for maintaining server temperatures. Chiller load and cooling temperature convey activity level. Heat rejection conveys energy extracted from the system. Fan speed controls airflow and thermal control. Thermal effectiveness is a measure of energy use in terms of cooling effectiveness. Power consumption is the energy in which power is consumed for thermal control. The table indicates environmental conditions and cooling requirements. Efficiency enhancing decreases operating costs and carbon emissions. There can be green infrastructure provision to enhance thermal performance. The cooling system is emphasized in the table for cloud operation feasibility.

Table 7. Cooling and thermal management

Chiller Load (kW)	Cooling Temp (°C)	Heat Rejection (kW)	Fan Speed (RPM)	Thermal Efficiency	Power Consumption (kW)
35	22	50	1200	0.81	45
38	23	55	1250	0.84	48
32	21	48	1150	0.79	43
36	22	52	1220	0.82	46
39	24	57	1270	0.85	49
34	22	51	1210	0.81	45
37	23	54	1240	0.83	47
33	21	49	1160	0.80	44

continued on following page

Table 7. Continued

Chiller Load (kW)	Cooling Temp (°C)	Heat Rejection (kW)	Fan Speed (RPM)	Thermal Efficiency	Power Consumption (kW)
38	24	56	1260	0.84	48
36	22	53	1230	0.82	46

Table 8 entails throughput, response time, CPU temperature, disk I/O, latency, and reliability index, and the performance of a server is monitored in cloud systems. Data processing capacity and storage capacity are measured through throughput and disk I/O. Response time and latency reflect user perception and application responsiveness. CPU temperature is for measuring thermal management capability. Reliability index is to express the operating stability in numerical form. The table shows performance variations with various workloads. Maximization of these numbers cuts down energy usage and enhances the quality of service. Optimal temperature and latency promote sustainability. The table displays the server performance dependency on green infrastructure. Monitoring performance allows predictive maintenance. It yields information for effective management of energy-saving clouds.

Table 8. Server performance metrics

Throughput (MB/s)	Response Time (ms)	CPU Temp (°C)	Disk I/O (MB/s)	Latency (ms)	Reliability Index
120	45	65	150	50	0.82
135	50	68	165	55	0.85
110	42	63	140	48	0.79
125	48	66	155	52	0.83
140	52	70	170	57	0.87
122	46	65	152	51	0.82
130	49	67	160	54	0.84
112	43	64	145	49	0.80
138	51	69	168	56	0.86
126	47	66	158	53	0.83

Table 9 categorizes the impact of the CO_2 savings, energy saving, emissions reduction, water use, waste reduction, and sustainability index. Indicators quantify the environmental value of green infrastructure and cloud computing. CO_2 savings and reductions in emissions quantify the impacts of energy-efficient action. Savings on energy are reduced costs. Water usage and waste prevention are conservation of resources. The sustainability index integrates all indicators into one measure of performance. The table shows profits due to incorporation of renewable energy and workload optimization. Increased savings translate into increased scores for sustainability. The findings validate the green cloud infrastructure environmental rationale. It indicates the necessity for monitoring environmental effects. The table validates the contribution of predictive modeling towards the attainment of sustainability targets.

Table 9. Carbon footprint analysis

CO_2 Savings (kg)	Energy Savings (%)	Emission Reduction (%)	Water Usage (L)	Waste Reduction (%)	Sustainability Index
120	15	10	450	12	0.78
135	18	12	480	14	0.82
110	13	9	430	11	0.75
125	16	11	460	13	0.80
140	20	14	490	15	0.85
122	15	10	455	12	0.78
130	17	12	470	13	0.82
112	14	9	440	11	0.76
138	19	13	485	14	0.84
126	16	11	465	13	0.81

Table 10 illustrates the performance metrics of the bi-stacked LSTM model, such as training accuracy and validation accuracy, mean squared error (MSE), root mean squared error (RMSE), mean absolute error (MAE), and F1 score. These estimates check the model's predictive ability for energy and resource efficiencies. Training accuracy and validation accuracy check the learning and generalization of the model. MSE, RMSE, and MAE calculate error predictions. F1 score calculates precision and recall. The above table shows how well the model performs to identify temporal and spatial trends from environmental data and cloud data. Higher precision and a lower error value reflect good preprocessing and feature choice. The evidence establishes the aptness of bi-stacked LSTM to green cloud optimization. It emphasizes the strength and predictability of the model. Overall, this table supports the effectiveness of the proposed method.

Table 10. Predictive modeling performance

Training Accuracy (%)	Validation Accuracy (%)	MSE	RMSE	MAE	F1 Score
92	89	0.015	0.123	0.10	0.88
94	91	0.012	0.110	0.09	0.90
90	87	0.018	0.134	0.11	0.86
93	90	0.014	0.118	0.10	0.88
95	92	0.011	0.105	0.08	0.91
92	89	0.015	0.122	0.10	0.88
94	91	0.013	0.112	0.09	0.90
91	88	0.017	0.130	0.11	0.87
95	92	0.012	0.108	0.09	0.91
93	90	0.014	0.119	0.10	0.89

CONCLUSION

The combination of Cloud Computing and Green Infrastructure is an eco-friendly remedy for the dual problems of effective IT management and environmental sustainability. With multicomponent data sets and sophisticated analytics, such as PSO-based feature selection and bi-stacked LSTM modeling, organizations can maximize energy utilization, work load allocation, and infrastructure use. The process renders cloud operation cost-effective and environmentally friendly and scalable and adaptive. Green infrastructure activities such as low-energy data centers and utilization of renewable energy enable cloud solutions with reduced carbon emission and wastage of resources. The research conducted here shows that sustainable decision-making in cloud infrastructure is possible with a predictive model based on data. In general, the research highlights realization of comprehensive ecological and technological approaches in ensuring long-term efficiency, resilience, and sustainability of contemporary IT systems.

REFERENCES

Alberti, M. (1996). Measuring urban sustainability. *Environmental Impact Assessment Review*, *16*, 381–424.

Ampatzidis, P., & Kershaw, T. (2020). A review of the impact of blue space on the urban microclimate. *The Science of the Total Environment*, *730*, 139068. PMID: 32422454

Andersson, E., Langemeyer, J., Borgström, S., McPhearson, T., Haase, D., Kronenberg, J., Barton, D., Davis, M., Naumann, S., & Röschel, L.. (2019). Enabling green and blue infrastructure to improve contributions to human well-being and equity in urban systems. *Bioscience*, *69*, 566–574. PMID: 31308573

Cegielska, K., Noszczyk, T., Kukulska, A., Szylar, M., Hernik, J., Dixon-Gough, R., Jombach, S., Valánszki, I., & Filepné Kovács, K. (2018). Land use and land cover changes in post-socialist countries: Some observations from Hungary and Poland. *Land Use Policy*, *78*, 1–18.

Chang, C. R., Li, M. H., & Chang, S. D. (2007). A preliminary study on the local cool-island intensity of Taipei city parks. *Landscape and Urban Planning*, *80*, 386–395.

Colding, J. (2011). The role of ecosystem services in contemporary urban planning. In Niemelä, J., Breuste, J. H., Guntenspergen, G., McIntyre, N. E., Elmqvist, T., & James, P. (Eds.), *Urban Ecology: Patterns, Processes, and Applications* (pp. 228–237). Oxford University Press.

Connop, S., Vandergert, P., Eisenberg, B., Collier, M. J., Nash, C., Clough, J., & Newport, D. (2016). Renaturing cities using a regionally-focused biodiversity-led multifunctional benefits approach to urban green infrastructure. *Environmental Science & Policy*, *62*, 99–111.

Dąbrowska, J., Bawiec, A., Pawęska, K., Kamińska, J., & Stodolak, R. (2017). Assessing the impact of wastewater effluent diversion on water quality. *Polish Journal of Environmental Studies*, *26*, 9–16.

Dennis, M., Barlow, D., Cavan, G., Cook, P. A., Gilchrist, A., Handley, J., James, P., Thompson, J., Tzoulas, K., & Wheater, C. P.. (2018). Mapping urban green infrastructure: A novel landscape-based approach to incorporating land use and land cover in the mapping of human-dominated systems. *Land (Basel)*, *7*, 17.

European Commission. (2021). *Forging a climate-resilient Europe—The new EU strategy on adaptation to climate change* (COM/2021/82 Final). Brussels, Belgium: Author.

European Environment Agency. (2012). *Urban adaptation to climate change in Europe: Challenges and opportunities for cities together with supportive national and European policies*. Office for Official Publications of the European Union.

European Environment Agency. (2016). *Urban adaptation to climate change in Europe 2016: Transforming cities in a changing climate*. Publications Office of the European Union.

European Environmental Agency. (2014). *Spatial analysis of green infrastructure in Europe* (EEA Technical Report No. 2). Copenhagen, Denmark: European Environmental Agency.

Forman, R. T. (1995). *Land mosaics: The ecology of landscapes and regions*. Cambridge University Press.

Grzywna, H., Dąbek, P. B., & Olszewska, B. (2018). Analysis of moisture conditions in the lowland areas using high-resolution spectral data from the Sentinel-2 satellite and GIS tools. *E3S Web of Conferences, 44*, 00048.

Hansen, R., & Pauleit, S. (2014). From multifunctionality to multiple ecosystem services? A conceptual framework for multifunctionality in green infrastructure planning for urban areas. *Ambio, 43*, 516–529. PMID: 24740622

Jia, B. Q., & Qiu, K. B. (2017). The cooling effect of plain afforestation in the Beijing project and its remote sensing-based valuation. *Acta Ecologica Sinica, 37*, 726–735.

Kamińska, J. A. (2018). Residuals in the modelling of pollution concentration depending on meteorological conditions and traffic flow, employing decision trees. *XLVIII Seminarium Applied Mathematics*, 00016.

Kaur, R., & Gupta, K. (2022). Blue-green infrastructure (BGI) network in urban areas for sustainable storm water management: A geospatial approach. *City and Environment Interactions, 16*, 100087.

Kerr, J. T., & Ostrovsky, M. (2003). From space to species: Ecological applications for remote sensing. *Trends in Ecology & Evolution, 18*, 299–305.

Kiełkowska, J., Tokarczyk-Dorociak, K., Kazak, J., Szewrański, S., & van Hoof, J. (2018). Urban adaptation to climate change plans and policies – The conceptual framework of a methodological approach. *Journal of Ecological Engineering, 19*, 50–62.

Klapa, P., Mitka, B., & Zygmunt, M. (2017). Application of integrated photogrammetric and terrestrial laser scanning data to cultural heritage surveying. *IOP Conference Series. Earth and Environmental Science, 95*, 032007.

Krajewski, P., Solecka, I., & Mastalska-Cetera, B. (2017). Landscape change index as a tool for spatial analysis. *IOP Conference Series. Materials Science and Engineering*, *245*, 072014.

Lee, A. C. K., & Maheswaran, R. (2011). The health benefits of urban green spaces: A review of the evidence. *Journal of Public Health*, *33*, 212–222. PMID: 20833671

Lehmann, S. (2014). Low carbon districts: Mitigating the urban heat island with green roof infrastructure. *City, Culture and Society*, *5*, 1–8.

Lejcuś, K., Dąbrowska, J., Garlikowski, D., & Śpitalniak, M. (2015). The application of water-absorbing geocomposites to support plant growth on slopes. *Geosynthetics International*, *22*, 452–456.

Li, J., & Trivic, Z. (2024). Impact of "blue-green diet" on human health and well-being: A systematic review of potential determinants in shaping the effectiveness of blue-green infrastructure (BGI) in urban settings. *The Science of the Total Environment*, *926*, 171397. PMID: 38438033

Liquete, C., Kleeschulte, S., Dige, G., Maes, J., Grizzetti, B., Olah, B., & Zulian, G. (2015). Mapping green infrastructure based on ecosystem services and ecological networks: A pan-European case study. *Environmental Science & Policy*, *54*, 268–280.

Masi, F., Bresciani, R., Rizzo, A., Edathoot, A., Patwardhan, N., Panse, D., & Langergraber, G. (2016). Green walls for greywater treatment and recycling in dense urban areas: A case study in Pune. *Journal of Water, Sanitation, and Hygiene for Development : a Journal of the International Water Association*, *6*, 342–347.

Noszczyk, T. (2018). A review of approaches to land use changes modeling. *Human and Ecological Risk Assessment*, •••, 1–29.

Pinto, L. V., Inácio, M., & Pereira, P. (2023). Green and blue infrastructure (GBI) and urban nature-based solutions (NbS) contribution to human and ecological well-being and health. *Oxford Open Infrastructure and Health, 1*, ouad004.

Qian, Y., Zhou, W., Yu, W., & Pickett, S. T. (2015). Quantifying spatiotemporal pattern of urban greenspace: New insights from high-resolution data. *Landscape Ecology*, *30*, 1165–1173.

Rall, E., Hansen, R., & Pauleit, S. (2019). The added value of public participation GIS (PPGIS) for urban green infrastructure planning. *Urban Forestry & Urban Greening*, *40*, 264–274.

Raymond, C. M., Frantzeskaki, N., Kabisch, N., Berry, P., Breil, M., Nita, M. R., Geneletti, D., & Calfapietra, C. (2017). A framework for assessing and implementing the co-benefits of nature-based solutions in urban areas. *Environmental Science & Policy*, *77*, 15–24.

Ruckelshaus, M. H., Guannel, G., Arkema, K., Verutes, G., Griffin, R., Guerry, A., Silver, J., Faries, J., Brenner, J., & Rosenthal, A. (2016). Evaluating the benefits of green infrastructure for coastal areas: Location, location, location. *Coastal Management*, *44*, 504–516.

Salata, S., Garnero, G., Barbieri, C. A., & Giaimo, C. (2017). The integration of ecosystem services in planning: An evaluation of the nutrient retention model using InVEST software. *Land (Basel)*, *6*, 48.

Schneider, P., Gottschalk, N., Löser, R., & Scharbrodt, T. (2011). Integrated climate protection program for the city of Chemnitz—Climate diagnosis, climate change prognosis and conception of adaptation measures in the urban area. In *Resilient Cities: Cities and Adaptation to Climate Change—Proceedings of the Global Forum 2010* (pp. 299–310). Berlin, Germany: Springer.

Sörensen, J., Persson, A. S., & Olsson, J. A. (2021). A data management framework for strategic urban planning using blue-green infrastructure. *Journal of Environmental Management*, *299*, 113658. PMID: 34523536

Szopińska, E., Kazak, J., Kempa, O., & Rubaszek, J. (2019). (in press). Spatial form of greenery in strategic environmental management in the context of urban adaptation to climate change. *Polish Journal of Environmental Studies*, *29*.

Szulczewski, W., & Jakubowski, W. (2018). The application of mixture distribution for the estimation of extreme floods in controlled catchment basins. *Water Resources Management*, *32*, 3519–3534.

Völker, S., Baumeister, H., Claßen, T., Hornberg, C., & Kistemann, T. (2013). Evidence for the temperature-mitigating capacity of urban blue space—A health geographic perspective. *Erdkunde*, *67*, 355–371.

Xie, Q., & Li, J. (2021). Detecting the cool island effect of urban parks in Wuhan: A city on rivers. *International Journal of Environmental Research and Public Health*, *18*, 132. PMID: 33375462

Zhou, C., & Wu, Y. (2020). A planning support tool for layout integral optimization of urban blue–green infrastructure. *Sustainability*, *12*, 1613.

Chapter 8

Sustainable Software Solutions for Business Project Management Integrating Eco-Conscious Practices: Real-Time Applications in Healthcare Systems

Wajeed Mohammed Abdul
https://orcid.org/0000-0002-5047-7857
Lords Institute of Engineering and Technology, India

ABSTRACT

Green Software Engineering integrates computing practices with sustainability goals, energy efficiency, carbon-aware computing, and ecological responsibility in software development. The chapter deals with a) evolution, significance of GSE in the digital age. b)theoretical foundations, sustainable software metrics, and the impact of the software lifecycle on GSE. c) strategies and practices in GSE, including carbon-aware and energy-efficient programming, green DevOps, and eco-centric agile project management. d) Integrating GSE into business project management, environmental key performance indicators, and tools and frameworks for green decision-making. e)examines the challenges of implementing GSE. f)Case study of healthcare in GSE. g)discussion on systematic thinking in sustainable software. h) insights from theory to practice in GSE. i)overview of active research projects

DOI: 10.4018/979-8-3373-4652-6.ch008

in GSE at various universities. j) discussion on the future of GSE. This chapter is comprehensive and accessible to all readers, from beginners to research scholars interested in exploring GSE.

INTRODUCTION TO GREEN SOFTWARE ENGINEERING

Green Software Engineering (GSE) signifies a fundamental change in the software development process by incorporating environmental sustainability into essential computing activities. It is described as "a systematic approach to designing, developing, deploying, and maintaining software with minimal environmental impact, especially in terms of energy consumption and carbon emissions," (Rashid et al., 2021). GSE's scope extends beyond merely enhancing code efficiency or cutting down on energy use; it involves a comprehensive transformation of software practices to meet ecological and sustainability objectives throughout the software's lifecycle.

Historical Context and Evolution

The origins of Green Software Engineering can be traced to the early 2000s, coinciding with the rise of environmental informatics, a discipline dedicated to utilizing information systems for environmental oversight and management. Initially, environmental informatics focused on harnessing computing capabilities to tackle environmental challenges, such as climate system modeling, pollution monitoring, and ecological simulations, (Lu, Chang, & Liao, 2013). However, it did not thoroughly consider the environmental impact of computing itself, including energy consumption and the carbon footprint associated with data processing.

This awareness led to the concurrent development of Green IT, which broadened the environmental perspective to encompass IT infrastructure, emphasizing server efficiency, energy-conscious hardware setups, and sustainable data center operations, (Eshbayev et al., 2024). While Green IT concentrated on hardware and infrastructure efficiency, the software aspect remained largely unexplored. Over time, research began to reveal that software, even when executed on optimized hardware, could significantly contribute to energy inefficiency due to suboptimal algorithms, unnecessary computations, or inefficient execution paths, (Guo et al., 2021).

This shift in focus spurred the emergence of Green Software Engineering as a distinct subfield around 2010, redirecting attention from physical infrastructure to energy optimization at the code level, carbon-aware design principles, and environmentally intelligent development practices, (Kumar et al., 2024). The formalization of Green Software Engineering has been supported by frameworks like the Software

Carbon Intensity (SCI) specification and various energy profiling tools designed for development environments, (Kansal & Zhao, 2008).

Scope of Green Software Engineering

The current scope of GSE encompasses several key areas:· Energy-efficient software design, which involves

- choosing algorithms that consume less energy and reducing computational demands.
- Carbon-aware computing, which entails programming with consideration for the energy source mix and carbon emissions.
- Lifecycle sustainability focuses on reducing environmental impact from the development phase to decommissioning.
- Green requirements engineering, this involves defining sustainability-related non-functional requirements.
- Tooling and frameworks that integrating GSE metrics into CI/CD pipelines and agile planning environments.

Additionally, GSE aligns with software architecture strategies like microservices, containerization, and serverless computing to dynamically reduce resource consumption, (Côté, Suryn, & Georgiadou, 2007). This positions it as a multi-level, interdisciplinary practice that includes software engineering, systems architecture, cloud computing, and business process management.

Relevance in the Era of Digital Transformation

The significance of Green Software Engineering (GSE) in the contemporary world is highlighted by the growing energy demands of the digital economy. Recent research indicates that data centers and digital infrastructures consume over 2% of the world's electricity, a number anticipated to rise significantly with the advancement of AI, IoT, and blockchain technologies, (Kumar et al., 2020). As industries rapidly embrace digital transformation, the environmental impact of expanding digital services becomes increasingly important.

GSE addresses this issue by incorporating sustainability-by-design principles into software systems. In today's DevOps settings, GSE supports the inclusion of sustainability Key Performance Indicators (KPIs) in sprint planning, code evaluations, and pipeline automation, (Dasallas et al., 2024). Furthermore, companies are beginning to understand that sustainable software practices are not only ethical but also economically beneficial, improving brand image and complying with regulatory requirements.

Adopting GSE is no longer a choice; it is becoming a strategic necessity due to heightened climate awareness, consumer demand for eco-friendly products, and environmental regulations like the EU's Digital Product Passport and sustainability disclosures, (Ngo et al., 2022). In conclusion, Green Software Engineering represents a crucial advancement in the computing paradigm, addressing the need for ecological responsibility in software development. It merges the legacy of environmental informatics with the innovations of Green IT, evolving into a comprehensive discipline for the software-focused era.

THEORETICAL FOUNDATIONS OF GREEN SOFTWARE ENGINEERING

Green Software Engineering (GSE) extends beyond mere practice, supported by an expanding theoretical base that encompasses software engineering, environmental science, systems theory, and the design of socio-technical systems. As the importance of environmental sustainability grows in all areas of computing, GSE offers a comprehensive framework for incorporating ecological principles throughout the software development process. This section delves into the core theories that shape GSE, discussing essential software sustainability metrics, models of lifecycle impact, green requirements engineering (GRE), and the field's inherently interdisciplinary nature. Furthermore, it suggests new theoretical concepts that could broaden the scope and analytical depth of GSE.

Foundational Theories and Principles

The core concept of Green Software Engineering is rooted in sustainability-by-design, which suggests that sustainability should be integrated from the initial stages of system design and development, (Guo et al., 2021). Drawing inspiration from systems theory, GSE advocates for a comprehensive perspective on software that considers its environmental, social, and economic impacts throughout its lifecycle. It also incorporates eco-feedback theory, which focuses on making energy consumption transparent and increasing user awareness to encourage behavioral changes, (Vergallo et al., 2024).

Another critical foundation is the quality-of-service vs. sustainability trade-off theory, which examines how software performance, reliability, and responsiveness can be balanced with ecological outcomes, (Han et al., 2024). These principles result in the creation of models and metrics to measure sustainability at the software level.

Sustainable Software Metrics

To effectively measure sustainability in software systems, it is essential to create and utilize specific sustainability metrics. These metrics offer a quantifiable basis for assessing the ecological efficiency of software design, coding, and execution environments. Key metrics include:

- Software Carbon Intensity (SCI): Assesses the CO_2 equivalent emissions generated per functional unit of software, such as per API call or inference.
- Energy per Instruction (EPI): Determines the energy required to execute a single instruction or function, often associated with profiling tools, (Georgiou et al., 2017).
- Greenhouse Gas Intensity (GHGI): Analyzes the software's impact on greenhouse gas emissions within its infrastructure deployment, such as cloud, edge, or mobile environments, (Zhang et al., 2021).
- Resource Efficiency Index (REI): A composite measure of CPU, memory, storage, and network usage, normalized against task output, (Chen et al., 2017).
- Runtime Sustainability Index (RSI): Reflects the balance between execution speed, accuracy, and energy/resource consumption in runtime environments, (Pan, Hu, & Xie, 2018).

These metrics are applied both during the development phase (static analysis) and after deployment (dynamic profiling), facilitating ongoing sustainability enhancements.

Lifecycle Impact Analysis (LCIA)

In the realm of Green Software Engineering (GSE), lifecycle assessment is derived from the Life Cycle Assessment (LCA) used in industrial ecology. This approach evaluates the environmental effects of software across its Software Development Life Cycle (SDLC), encompassing stages from conception and coding to testing, deployment, operation, and eventual decommissioning, (Alsaleh & Sattler, 2019). The Life Cycle Impact Assessment (LCIA) in GSE considers several factor:

- **Impact during Development:** Energy consumption by development tools, developer computers, and the process of code compilation.
- **Impact during Operation:** Carbon emissions resulting from software running on user devices, servers, or cloud platforms.

- **Impact during Maintenance and Updates:** Energy costs associated with applying patches, fixing bugs, and managing software versions.
- **Impact during Decommissioning:** Expenses related to eliminating obsolete codebases or phasing out legacy systems.

Advanced models suggest a comprehensive cradle-to-grave approach to software energy modeling, which monitors energy use and emissions from the initial consumption of resources (such as developer time and electricity) to the final shutdown of the system, (Luo et al., 2024).

Green Requirements Engineering (GRE)

Green Requirements Engineering (GRE) significantly broadens the scope of traditional requirements engineering by incorporating sustainability as a non-functional requirement (NFR). In GRE, software requirements must address not only functionality and performance but also adhere to environmental standards. This process includes:

- Defining green objectives (e.g., decrease cloud energy consumption by 25%).
- Outlining quantifiable eco-requirements (e.g., carbon emissions per user session should be <0.5g).
- Employing goal modeling techniques (e.g., KAOS, i* frameworks) enhanced with sustainability constraints, (Stojčić et al., 2019).
- Balancing green trade-offs in conflicting requirements (e.g., reduced power consumption vs. increased accuracy).

GRE frameworks are increasingly equipped with tools that assess sustainability alongside traditional attributes such as cost, security, and maintainability, (Zhang et al., 2024).

Interdisciplinary Nature of GSE

The theoretical depth of GSE is rooted in its interdisciplinary approach, encompassing several fields:

- **Computer Science:** Focuses on algorithm creation, system enhancement, and cloud-native software.
- **Environmental Science:** Involves carbon modeling and analysis of ecological impacts. Business & Management: Deals with sustainability key performance indicators and ESG (Environmental, Social, Governance) metrics.

- **Human-Computer Interaction (HCI):** Includes eco-feedback interfaces and green user experience design.
- **Ethics and Law:** Covers digital rights, green compliance, and climate justice.

This fusion of disciplines enables GSE to tackle the technical, managerial, and socio-ethical aspects of sustainability. Academic courses and industry certifications are increasingly reflecting this multifaceted approach, preparing professionals who can combine technical expertise with environmental consciousness.

Emerging Theoretical Contributions

Although Green Software Engineering (GSE) has established a strong foundational framework, there are still several theoretical areas that are underexplored and present opportunities for further development:

- Thermodynamic Models of Computation: Integrating energy-entropy modeling from physics to determine theoretical minimums for sustainable computation, (Castellanos-Nieves & García-Forte, 2024).
- Category Theory for Sustainability Composition: Using mathematical composition frameworks to formalize the propagation of sustainability constraints through software modules, (Abujder Ochoa et al., 2024).
- Sustainability Debt Modeling: Expanding the idea of technical debt to encompass the long-term ecological impacts of architectural choices.
- Agent-Based Modeling (ABM) of Ecosystem Impacts: Modeling how distributed software agents affect systemic energy profiles in decentralized settings (e.g., blockchain, IoT).

These advancements could enable the creation of formally verifiable, optimally green software designs that achieve specific ecological objectives with mathematical precision. In essence, Green Software Engineering is built on a solid theoretical base that is continually growing through insights from various disciplines. From sustainability metrics and lifecycle assessments to innovative eco-requirements and systems thinking, GSE provides both qualitative and quantitative tools for enhancing the environmental sustainability of software systems. As global sustainability challenges intensify, expanding GSE's theoretical framework with elements from thermodynamics, category theory, and debt modeling can propel its development into a well-established, scientifically robust field.

STRATEGIES AND PRACTICES IN GREEN SOFTWARE DEVELOPMENT

Green Software Development (GSD) is dedicated to creating, building, and implementing software systems that reduce environmental impact while preserving their performance and functionality. Essential approaches in GSD encompass carbon-conscious programming, designing energy-efficient algorithms, utilizing serverless computing, practicing green DevOps, and managing projects with an eco-focused agile methodology.

Carbon-Aware Programming

Carbon-aware programming involves dynamically modifying computational processes in response to the carbon intensity of power grids. This approach includes scheduling non-essential tasks when electricity with low carbon emissions is available, a practice known as temporal load shifting. Recent research has suggested the use of middleware solutions and grid-aware schedulers to enhance energy efficiency by utilizing real-time carbon data, (Ali et al., 2022). Additionally, energy-aware APIs are being developed to enable software to adapt its behavior accordingly, (Guo, Ganti, & Wu, 2024).

Energy-Efficient Algorithm Design

Creating algorithms that are energy-efficient involves optimizing both their computational performance and power usage. For instance, approximate computing methods can lower energy consumption by permitting certain levels of error, (Zervakis et al., 2019). Other strategies involve choosing data structures that limit memory access, decreasing branching, and refining loop designs, (Lang, Michos, & Conrad, 2018). Algorithms specifically designed for devices with energy limitations, like mobile health systems and IoT sensors, have demonstrated energy savings ranging from 20–45%, (Chen et al., 2022).

Serverless Computing

Serverless architectures eliminate the need for direct server management by dynamically adjusting resources according to demand. This level of detail enhances energy proportionality and prevents excessive resource allocation, (Fati & Alenezi, 2024). Platforms such as AWS Lambda and Azure Functions have been assessed for their carbon efficiency compared to traditional virtual machines and containers, with research indicating energy savings of up to 60% in certain setups, (Patros et al., 2021).

Green DevOps

Green DevOps incorporates sustainability metrics into CI/CD pipelines, including measures like energy consumption per build, carbon emissions per deployment, and resource usage per commit. These metrics are displayed on dashboards to aid decision-making, (Liang, Liu, & Huang, 2023). Tools such as Jenkins and GitLab are being enhanced with plugins to monitor the environmental impact of software modifications and test executions, (Sani & Jan, 2024).

Eco-Centric Agile Project Management

Agile methodologies are enhanced with sustainability objectives by incorporating environmental goals into user stories and acceptance criteria. Tools like green burn-down charts and eco-sprint reviews have been implemented, (Habi, Gahi, & Gharib, 2024). Agile teams are encouraged to monitor emissions produced during software development and adjust backlogs to prioritize features that reduce carbon emissions, (Saetang et al., 2024). This comprehensive strategy ensures that environmental considerations are woven into every stage of the software development process, from planning and coding to deployment and maintenance.

INTEGRATING GREEN SOFTWARE ENGINEERING INTO BUSINESS PROJECT MANAGEMENT

Incorporating Green Software Engineering (GSE) into business project management represents a crucial move towards harmonizing technological progress with corporate sustainability objectives. Although advancements in green computing technology are underway, achieving tangible results requires integrating sustainability into business planning, execution, and governance. This section delves into the integration of environmental Key Performance Indicators (E-KPIs) within agile, DevOps, and CI/CD processes; digital transformation driven by sustainability; and decision-support tools for managing green projects.

Embedding Environmental KPIs into Agile, DevOps, and CI/CD Pipelines

Integrating environmental metrics into agile and DevOps methodologies has become a practical approach to implementing GSE. Environmental KPIs, such as energy consumption per commit, CO_2 emissions per deployment, or energy intensity per test case, are being increasingly incorporated into CI/CD processes. These metrics enable teams to assess the environmental impact of their work alongside conventional quality measures, (Soongpol, Rukhiran, & Netiant, 2024).

Tools like Jenkins GreenMetrics and GreenMiner have been suggested for gathering runtime energy data and embedding it into agile dashboards, (Yilmaz et al., 2021). Research indicates that incorporating E-KPIs into DevOps pipelines can decrease build-time energy consumption by up to 30% by identifying energy-inefficient code patterns early on, (Ezzeddine et al., 2024).

Sustainability-Driven Planning in Digital Transformation

Sustainability-focused planning extends beyond merely optimizing operations by integrating environmental considerations into the strategic framework of digital transformation. Software development driven by business objectives should incorporate green initiatives from the outset, including during requirement gathering and release planning stages, (Shao et al., 2024).

Recent studies emphasize approaches for embedding sustainability elements into project charters and roadmaps, allowing project managers to weigh performance, cost, and environmental impact in their decision-making processes, (Del Rosario & Traverso, 2023). Methods such as prioritizing environmental backlogs and implementing carbon budgeting are employed to merge ecological concerns with business goals, (De Almeida et al., 2024).

By aligning green principles with organizational transformation strategies, companies can mitigate environmental risks, enhance ESG (Environmental, Social, Governance) reporting, and comply with regulatory requirements, (Li & Rasiah, 2024).

Tools and Frameworks for Green Decision-Making

Numerous tools and frameworks have been developed to aid project managers in making decisions that are mindful of sustainability. For example, the SE4Green framework evaluates trade-offs among various implementation options by employing multi-objective optimization focused on sustainability, cost, and time, (Li et al., 2023).

Decision-support systems like GREENSOFT, GreenBoard, and EcoReq incorporate metrics related to energy, performance, and carbon emissions into software lifecycle management tools, (Quesado, Silva, & Oliveira, 2024). These frameworks enable the consideration of environmental factors in sprint planning, architectural decisions, and vendor selection.

Additionally, model-based approaches are utilized to predict the environmental impact of project decisions prior to their execution, (Li et al., 2024). Lifecycle dashboards and what-if analysis engines facilitate adaptive planning within the constraints of sustainability, (Lounis & Mcallister, 2016).

IMPLEMENTATION CHALLENGES AND GAPS

Although there is increasing interest in Green Software Engineering (GSE) from both academia and industry, a considerable gap remains between technological progress in sustainable computing and its implementation in business settings. This section highlights and critically examines four primary obstacles: (i) the gap between innovation and its adoption by enterprises, (ii) the absence of standardization and consistent metrics, (iii) stakeholder awareness and cultural resistance, and (iv) the disconnect between sustainability objectives and business value drivers.

Disparity Between Technological Innovations and Adoption in Business

The research community has achieved significant breakthroughs in low-energy architectures (Tehrani, Heidar-Zadeh, & Richer, 2024), carbon-aware scheduling (Radovanović et al., 2023), and energy-efficient software libraries, (Zanotti, Puglisi, & Pavan, 2020). However, their widespread adoption in various industries is still inconsistent. This delay is attributed to factors such as organizational resistance to change, misaligned incentives, and the perceived compromise between sustainability and performance, (Kutaula et al., 2024).

Many companies regard green software as an operational expense rather than a strategic investment, hindering the expansion of GSE solutions. For example, despite progress in green container orchestration, only a small number of companies have implemented carbon-based workload distribution strategies in their production environments, (Sharma et al., 2023).

Lack of Standardization and Unified Metrics

One major challenge in adopting GSE practices is the lack of standardized metrics for sustainability. Presently, software engineering lacks consensus on models to assess energy usage per function, emissions per deployment, or levels of sustainability maturity, (Almusaed et al., 2024).

Although organizations such as the IEEE and ISO have suggested frameworks like IEEE 7001 and the ISO 14000 series, their uptake is limited due to their complexity, poor integration with agile and DevOps processes, and inconsistent terminology. Furthermore, the absence of APIs and tools that link metrics with development pipelines makes it difficult to track sustainability in real-time, (Alhosaini et al., 2023).

Stakeholder Awareness and Cultural Resistance

Achieving organizational change towards sustainability necessitates the active involvement of developers, project managers, operations teams, and executives. Nonetheless, research indicates that developers frequently lack awareness of how their design choices impact the environment, (Houf, Shepherd, & Szymkowiak, 2024). In a similar vein, sustainability is seldom included in the key performance indicators for engineering managers or product owners, which hinders organizational commitment, (Moktadir et al., 2020).

Additionally, there is a cultural reluctance to modify established processes or to compromise performance standards for the sake of ecological advantages. Many teams are not equipped with the training or motivation to integrate sustainability into their routine engineering activities, (Cairns, Hielscher, & Light, 2020).

Misalignment Between Sustainability Goals and Business Value Drivers

A recurring issue is the perceived disconnect between ecological sustainability and business priorities like cost efficiency, speed to market, and customer satisfaction. In numerous companies, GSE initiatives are often detached from the core business strategy, leaving them susceptible to budget reductions or being deprioritized, (Moktadir et al., 2020).

Many businesses find it challenging to convert broad sustainability objectives into quantifiable business results. In the absence of clear ROI frameworks or regulatory requirements, the adoption of GSE is more frequently driven by idealism rather than enterprise KPIs, (Ashton, Russell, & Futch, 2017). This disconnect is exacerbated by the absence of financial models that consider long-term ecological savings, (Ruza & Caro-Carretero, 2022).

The journey towards sustainable software development is hindered by structural, cultural, and technical obstacles. Closing the gap between innovation and execution necessitates: (i) the formal adoption of unified metrics, (ii) organization-wide sustainability education, (iii) the incorporation of environmental KPIs into project and performance management, and (iv) the alignment of sustainability goals with business value systems.

REAL-WORLD CASE STUDIES FROM THE HEALTHCARE SECTOR

As the healthcare industry increasingly depends on digital platforms for tasks such as diagnosis, patient management, and teleconsultation, it offers a promising environment for the application and assessment of Green Software Engineering (GSE) principles. This sector is particularly sensitive to demands for performance, reliability, and privacy, while also facing growing pressure to minimize its environmental footprint. The case studies below showcase the application of GSE practices in real-world healthcare settings, highlighting tangible environmental and operational advantages.

Case Study 1: Carbon-Efficient Electronic Health Record (EHR) System:

A European regional hospital network revamped its Electronic Health Record (EHR) system with a focus on carbon efficiency, aiming to optimize energy use in server-side queries and data synchronization. By implementing load-adaptive scheduling and server-level power gating strategies, they achieved a 30% reduction in energy consumption while maintaining satisfactory response times, (Khan, 2024).

To enhance resource efficiency further, caching mechanisms and request batching algorithms were introduced. These enhancements not only lowered peak energy demands but also ensured more efficient network and CPU usage. The project was tracked using an energy-aware logging tool integrated into the application, allowing for real-time profiling and adaptive scheduling based on carbon-intensity data from the power grid, (Ramya & Ayothi, 2023).

Case Study 2: Green Redesign of a Telemedicine Platform

A prominent telehealth company restructured its video consultation platform with sustainability in mind. By implementing adaptive video resolution protocols, which dynamically adjust bandwidth and power consumption based on device energy levels and network conditions, the system achieved a 40% reduction in energy use per session, (Benzerogue et al., 2024).

Key measures included edge-level caching for medical records and images, the use of energy-aware transcoding algorithms, and a transition from always-on video channels to event-triggered communications. These strategies significantly decreased the energy footprint of real-time streaming and backend synchronization operations, (Zhu et al., 2024).

Case Study 3: AI-Driven Diagnostics with Energy Profiling on Edge/Cloud

A diagnostic imaging system utilizing deep learning was created with a two-tiered energy optimization strategy. This solution featured edge-cloud coordination, where inference tasks were dynamically assigned based on latency needs and the real-time carbon intensity of the execution environment, (Heieh et al., 2024). Profiling modules within the inference engine monitored energy-per-inference metrics, activating decision logic for optimal task placement. For scenarios requiring high throughput and low latency, edge devices were employed, while batch inference for larger datasets was postponed to low-carbon cloud periods. This approach resulted in a 22% net reduction in energy consumption without compromising diagnostic accuracy or latency, (Schoen et al., 2024).

Additionally, the system utilized quantization-aware training and pruning techniques, which minimized model size and computational demands, leading to decreased energy usage during execution, (Bibi et al., 2024).

SYSTEMIC THINKING IN SUSTAINABLE SOFTWARE

To tackle sustainability in software development effectively, it is crucial to embrace a broad strategy that extends beyond localized enhancements and emphasizes holistic value creation, enduring sustainability, and the fusion of social and technical elements. When Green Software Engineering (GSE) is approached from a systemic viewpoint, it evolves from a collection of isolated practices into a value-driven framework that fosters enduring environmental, economic, and social advantages.

Viewing Green Software as a Value-Creation and Delivery Mechanism

While traditional software engineering prioritizes the delivery of features, scalability, and quick market entry, systemic GSE places sustainability at the forefront of business objectives. Green software serves not only to cut down emissions but also to create enduring value by boosting brand image, lowering operational expenses, and adhering to new regulations, (Makhloufi, Siddik, & Zhou, 2023).

Recent studies have introduced eco-value stream mapping and green design thinking to identify and prioritize sustainability opportunities throughout the software development lifecycle (SDLC) (Horsthofer-Rauch et al., 2024). These strategies enable teams to transition from reactive efficiency measures to proactive ecological design.

Additionally, cloud-native architectures now incorporate sustainability metrics into orchestration tools, such as Kubernetes with carbon-awareness, integrating green operations into continuous delivery, (Zavieh, Sangaiah, & Javadpour, 2024). Consequently, value creation extends beyond just customers to include ecological stakeholders and societal well-being, (Kelleci, 2021).

The Role of GSE in Long-Term System Sustainability and Performance

Sustainability is fundamentally a long-term attribute. GSE enhances system longevity by reducing technical debt, optimizing energy proportionality, and facilitating adaptive resource scaling in response to workload and environmental factors, (Seo, Yoo, & Lee, 2024).

Systemic GSE practices, including sustainability-focused refactoring, carbon-aware CI/CD, and modular green architectures, have been proven to improve not only the energy efficiency of software but also its maintainability and fault tolerance, (Jalali & Wohlin, 2011). For example, research indicates that well-organized green codebases result in fewer outages and reduced costs for incident recovery, (Abdou et al., 2022).

Moreover, systemic thinking combines ecological sustainability with other software quality aspects like performance, security, and usability (Shah et al., 2021), positioning green software as an enhancer of overall system quality rather than a compromise.

Future Directions: Green Digital Economies and Policy Alignment

Systemic GSE must progress alongside digital policies, sustainable innovation frameworks, and green economic models. Future green software ecosystems will more closely align with carbon credits, green procurement standards, and corporate ESG (Environmental, Social, and Governance) reporting, (Siregar et al., 2024).

Digital economies are starting to view software not merely as infrastructure but as a quantifiable contributor to sustainability goals. Governments are introducing legislation to require carbon disclosures for software operations (Velaoras et al., 2025), and large companies are seeking sustainability certifications from software suppliers, (Abdul Majid et al., 2021).

Emerging interdisciplinary research links GSE with circular economy principles, green AI, eco-informatics, and low-carbon blockchain technologies, paving the way for integrated solutions across policy, economics, and digital innovation, (Hu & Sinniah, 2024; Gao et al., 2024; Hou et al., 2023).

Systemic GSE redefines software not just as a tool but as a dynamic agent in achieving long-term sustainability objectives. By embedding sustainability into value chains, performance metrics, and digital policy, the future of software engineering lies in its capacity to meet both human and planetary needs. A systemic perspective ensures that sustainability is not a peripheral concern but a fundamental design and business imperative.

CONCLUSION AND RECOMMENDATIONS

Summary of Insights from Theory to Practice

Green Software Engineering (GSE) has become an essential framework for integrating digital advancements with global sustainability goals. This chapter's comprehensive analysis delves into the foundational concepts of GSE, including lifecycle impact assessments, sustainability metrics, carbon-conscious programming, and eco-friendly DevOps processes. Practical approaches like designing energy-efficient algorithms, utilizing serverless computing, and incorporating sustainability into agile planning highlight GSE's relevance in business settings, (Bari, Chimhundu, & Chan, 2022).

Case studies from the healthcare sector further reinforce the notion that GSE principles are not only feasible but also effective in cutting energy use, reducing carbon emissions, and enhancing operational efficiency, (Côté-Boileau et al., 2020). These real-world examples emphasize the significant connection between technical design choices and their broader environmental effects, (Pacana et al., 2024).

Strategic Steps for Embedding GSE in Business Project Management

Although GSE holds great potential, its implementation is hindered by obstacles such as the absence of standardized metrics, insufficient stakeholder awareness, and a disconnect between ecological objectives and business motivations, (Jianguo & Solangi, 2023). To bridge these gaps, the following strategic measures are suggested:

- Establish and integrate Environmental KPIs (E-KPIs) into DevOps pipelines, sprint planning, and CI/CD workflows to ensure that sustainability goals are part of everyday development activities, (Alnafessah et al., 2021).
- Employ interdisciplinary frameworks that blend environmental sciences, economics, and system architecture to improve decision-making and balance sustainability considerations, (Mageed, Alsultani, & Abbas, 2024).

- Enhance GSE skills among developers, architects, and project managers through corporate green training initiatives and industry certifications, (Naranjo et al., 2020).
- Encourage sustainability in procurement by prioritizing software vendors that practice carbon-aware design and comply with emerging GSE standards, (Cui, Qi, & Hussain, 2024).
- Align with digital sustainability policies and global frameworks like the UN SDGs, ISO/IEC 30170 (Green ICT), and IEEE 7000 standards to ensure lasting impact and adherence, (Coscieme, Mortensen, & Donohue, 2021).

Call to Action for Developers, Managers, and Sustainability Officers

The pressing issue of climate change demands that software professionals take an active role in creating and implementing systems that bolster ecological resilience. Developers should focus on sustainability by employing energy-efficient coding techniques and utilizing performance profiling tools, (Coscieme, Mortensen, & Donohue, 2021). Project managers need to update their success metrics to encompass environmental impact alongside cost, scope, and timeline, (Pantović et al., 2024). Sustainability officers are tasked with promoting software-related carbon reduction in ESG reports and ensuring the integration of GSE into the organization's digital strategy, (Abinandan et al., 2024). A concerted effort is essential to embed sustainability within the software engineering field. Academia, industry, and policymakers must unite to establish an environment where GSE becomes the norm rather than the exception, (Marijan & Gotlieb, 2020).

ACTIVE RESEARCH PROJECTS IN GREEN SOFTWARE ENGINEERING

Green Software Engineering (GSE) has transitioned from being a theoretical niche to an applied research field, propelled by interdisciplinary partnerships among academia, industry, and regulatory organizations. Globally, institutions are actively engaging in projects that emphasize energy-efficient computing, carbon-aware orchestration, sustainability metrics throughout the lifecycle, and green DevOps frameworks.

Carbon-Aware Scheduling and Execution

The CARBON-AWARE EDGE initiative at Technische Universität Berlin investigates the dynamic coordination between cloud and edge devices by utilizing real-time data on carbon intensity. Their approach involves scheduling tasks to execute when renewable energy is most abundant, thereby minimizing emissions from computational processes, (Ertem, 2024). Similarly, the University of Helsinki is working on incorporating carbon-aware algorithms into fog computing systems designed for smart cities, (Alsadie, 2024).

Green AI and Sustainable Machine Learning

Researchers at the University of California, Berkeley, and ETH Zurich are working on profiling frameworks aimed at training large transformer models while minimizing energy use. Their approach includes hybrid job placement strategies, low-rank adaptation methods, and energy-conscious hyperparameter tuning, (Paulraj et al., 2023). The goal is to develop scalable AI that effectively balances computational needs with carbon limitations.

Green DevOps and CI/CD Integration

The University of São Paulo and TU Dresden are at the forefront of "Green DevOps" by integrating sustainability key performance indicators into continuous integration processes and containerized deployments. Their ECODevOps initiative allows for software artifacts to be labeled, tracked, and optimized for energy efficiency using extensions for GitLab and Jenkins, (Górski, 2021).

Software Sustainability Metrics and Lifecycle Analysis

The University of Applied Sciences Augsburg has created the GREENSOFT Model, a thorough framework for evaluating the sustainability of software products, which is utilized in German industrial projects, (Shawon et al., 2024). Meanwhile, researchers at the University of Melbourne are enhancing lifecycle-based models to incorporate energy forecasting during the requirement and architectural phases, (Jaramillo, Pavón, & Jaramillo, 2024).

Embedded Systems and IoT

Politecnico di Milano and the University of Pisa are collaborating on research into energy optimization at the compiler level for embedded systems used in healthcare and agricultural IoT applications. Their projects emphasize runtime adaptation, voltage scaling, and memory-aware scheduling in devices designed for ultra-low power consumption, (Zhu et al., 2017).

Policy-Aware GSE and Regulatory Alignment

At the Norwegian University of Science and Technology (NTNU) and INRIA France, ongoing projects are investigating the alignment of GSE practices with ESG (Environmental, Social, Governance) compliance and the tracking of SDGs (Sustainable Development Goals). The goal of these initiatives is to ensure that software systems can be audited for their sustainability performance through the use of machine-readable green metrics, (Contini & Peruzzini, 2022).

The current active projects highlight the breadth and advancement of GSE research. From enhancing algorithms to ensuring policy adherence, organizations worldwide are establishing the foundation for digital ecosystems that prioritize scalability and carbon awareness.

FUTURE DIRECTIONS OF GREEN SOFTWARE ENGINEERING

As the world contends with climate change, energy shortages, and the rapid pace of digital transformation, Green Software Engineering (GSE) is set to evolve from a research-focused idea into a fundamental aspect of software system design. Over the next ten years, GSE will transition from being a secondary consideration to becoming a central design principle in system architectures, governance models, and industry standards.

Convergence with Emerging Technologies

One important future direction involves merging GSE with Artificial Intelligence (AI), Quantum Computing, and Blockchain. Although AI models require significant computational resources, they can be made more energy-efficient through techniques like model compression, federated learning, and energy-aware scheduling, (Yuan et al., 2025). Quantum software, which is still in its early stages, offers potential for zero-waste logic operations and extremely low-power computations, (Chauwin et al., 2019). Blockchain systems are being reengineered with consensus mechanisms such as Proof-of-Stake to significantly cut down on energy consumption, (Ahn, Kim, & Yi, 2024).

Automation and Intelligence in Energy-Aware Systems

The emergence of autonomous GSE systems, where AI agents oversee real-time carbon intensity to manage code refactoring, deployment scheduling, and cloud orchestration, is anticipated to transform green computing, (Kuru & Khan, 2020). In the future, CI/CD pipelines are expected to incorporate automated sustainability checkpoints, which will enforce limits on energy use and carbon emissions before software artifacts can advance through the release process, (Lu et al., 2018).

Regulatory and Policy Embedding

Organizations at both national and international levels, including the EU and IEEE, are working on establishing green certification standards for software, which will necessitate formal audits focused on energy use and sustainability. Studies suggest that future software compliance will encompass not just functional accuracy but also environmental performance metrics, (Condori-Fernandez et al., 2020). Governments might require energy transparency in digital infrastructure bids, promoting adherence to Green Software Engineering (GSE) principles.

Expansion of Lifecycle Sustainability Modeling

One of the key theoretical challenges is creating sustainability models that integrate the entire lifecycle within software ecosystems, encompassing supply chains, user interaction patterns, and hardware interdependencies, (Padilla-Rivera et al., 2024). Tools that can simulate the ripple effects across different layers, from code to carbon footprint, will become essential in making decisions about software architecture.

Interdisciplinary Fusion and Green Skills

The evolution of GSE will be characterized by a strong interdisciplinary approach, integrating computer science with fields such as environmental engineering, behavioral science, economics, and systems thinking, (Alenezi & Akour, 2025). Educational programs are already adapting by incorporating sustainability topics into the core curriculum of computing courses, (Arefin et al., 2021). This indicates that the future workforce will be proficient not only in programming but also in assessing, evaluating, and enhancing software for sustainability.

Green Digital Economies

In the future, green digital economies will depend on GSE to guarantee that digital infrastructure, ranging from banking to healthcare, is established on environmentally sustainable principles. Emerging areas of focus include edge-cloud continuum architectures, sustainable software-defined networking, and energy-efficient 6G services, (Apajalahti, Temmes, & Lempiälä, 2017).

Vision for 2030 and Beyond

By the year 2030, GSE is anticipated to transform into a field that is guided by policies, focused on performance, and driven by innovation. Software systems will be evaluated not just on their functionality or scalability, but also based on their environmental impact. Global standards might include "software carbon labels," akin to the energy efficiency ratings found on household appliances.

REFERENCES

Abdou, A. H., Albakhit, A. I., Shehata, H. S., Almakhayitah, M. Y., & Mahmoud, H. M. E. (2022). The Effect of Environmentally Sustainable Practices on Customer Citizenship Behavior in Eco-Friendly Hotels: Does the Green Perceived Value Matter? *Sustainability*, *14*(12), 7167. DOI: 10.3390/su14127167

Abdul Majid, N., Ramli, Z., Awang, A. H., & Md Sum, S. (2021). Sustainable Palm Oil Certification Scheme Frameworks and Impacts: A Systematic Literature Review. *Sustainability*, *13*(6), 3263. DOI: 10.3390/su13063263

Abinandan, S., Praveen, K., Venkateswarlu, K., & Megharaj, M. (2024). Eco-innovation minimizes the carbon footprint of wine production. *Communications Earth & Environment*, *5*(1). Advance online publication. DOI: 10.1038/s43247-024-01766-0

Abujder Ochoa, W. A., Ballesteros-Ballesteros, V., Calabokis, O. P., Vitorio, P. C.Junior, & Iarozinski Neto, A. (2024). The Theory of Complexity and Sustainable Urban Development: A Systematic Literature Review. *Sustainability*, *17*(1), 3. DOI: 10.3390/su17010003

Ahn, J., Kim, M., & Yi, E. (2024). Blockchain Consensus Mechanisms: A Bibliometric Analysis (2014–2024) Using VOSviewer and R Bibliometrix. *Information (Basel)*, *15*(10), 644. DOI: 10.3390/info15100644

Alenezi, M., & Akour, M. (2025). AI-Driven Innovations in Software Engineering: A Review of Current Practices and Future Directions. *Applied Sciences (Basel, Switzerland)*, *15*(3), 1344. DOI: 10.3390/app15031344

Alhosaini, H., Alharbi, S., Wang, X., & Xu, G. (2023). API Recommendation For Mashup Creation: A Comprehensive Survey. *The Computer Journal*, *67*(5), 1920–1940. DOI: 10.1093/comjnl/bxad112

Ali, S., Khan, S., Khan, I., Rehman, A. U., Samuel, O., Albogamy, F. R., Hafeez, G., Murawwat, S., & Wadud, Z. (2022). Demand Response Program for Efficient Demand-Side Management in Smart Grid Considering Renewable Energy Sources. *IEEE Access : Practical Innovations, Open Solutions*, *10*, 53832–53853. DOI: 10.1109/access.2022.3174586

Almusaed, A., Almssad, A., Yitmen, I., & Myhren, J. A. (2024). Assessing the Impact of Recycled Building Materials on Environmental Sustainability and Energy Efficiency: A Comprehensive Framework for Reducing Greenhouse Gas Emissions. *Buildings (Basel, Switzerland)*, *14*(6), 1566. DOI: 10.3390/buildings14061566

Alnafessah, A., Casale, G., Filieri, A., Wang, R., Gias, A. U., & Zhu, L. (2021). Quality-Aware DevOps Research: Where Do We Stand? *IEEE Access : Practical Innovations, Open Solutions*, *9*, 44476–44489. DOI: 10.1109/access.2021.3064867

Alsadie, D. (2024). Advancements in heuristic task scheduling for IoT applications in fog-cloud computing: Challenges and prospects. *PeerJ. Computer Science*, *10*, e2128. DOI: 10.7717/peerj-cs.2128

Alsaleh, A., & Sattler, M. (2019). Comprehensive life cycle assessment of large wind turbines in the US. *Clean Technologies and Environmental Policy*, *21*(4), 887–903. DOI: 10.1007/s10098-019-01678-0

Apajalahti, E.-L., Temmes, A., & Lempiälä, T. (2017). Incumbent organisations shaping emerging technological fields: Cases of solar photovoltaic and electric vehicle charging. *Technology Analysis and Strategic Management*, *30*(1), 44–57. DOI: 10.1080/09537325.2017.1285397

Arefin, M. A., Nabi, M. N., Gudimetla, P., & Sadeque, S. (2021). Incorporating sustainability in engineering curriculum: A study of the Australian universities. *International Journal of Sustainability in Higher Education*, *22*(3), 576–598. DOI: 10.1108/ijshe-07-2020-0271

Ashton, W., Russell, S., & Futch, E. (2017). The adoption of green business practices among small US Midwestern manufacturing enterprises. *Journal of Environmental Planning and Management*, *60*(12), 2133–2149. DOI: 10.1080/09640568.2017.1281107

Bari, N., Chimhundu, R., & Chan, K.-C. (2022). Dynamic Capabilities to Achieve Corporate Sustainability: A Roadmap to Sustained Competitive Advantage. *Sustainability*, *14*(3), 1531. DOI: 10.3390/su14031531

Benzerogue, S., Abdelatif, S., Khamer, L., Merniz, S., & Harous, S. (2024). Multi-Path Transmission Protocol for Video Streaming Over Vehicular Fog Computing Environments. *IEEE Access : Practical Innovations, Open Solutions*, *12*, 87199–87216. DOI: 10.1109/access.2024.3417288

Bibi, U., Mazhar, M., Hassan, A., Abdul, W., Ali Ghazanfar, M., Fasih Uddin Butt, M., Sabir, D., & Ali Khan, A. (2024). Advances in Pruning and Quantization for Natural Language Processing. *IEEE Access : Practical Innovations, Open Solutions*, *12*, 139113–139128. DOI: 10.1109/access.2024.3465631

Cairns, R., Hielscher, S., & Light, A. (2020). Collaboration, creativity, conflict and chaos: Doing interdisciplinary sustainability research. *Sustainability Science*, *15*(6), 1711–1721. DOI: 10.1007/s11625-020-00784-z

Castellanos-Nieves, D., & García-Forte, L. (2024). Strategies of Automated Machine Learning for Energy Sustainability in Green Artificial Intelligence. *Applied Sciences (Basel, Switzerland)*, *14*(14), 6196. DOI: 10.3390/app14146196

Chauwin, M., Garcia-Sanchez, F., Friedman, J. S., Paler, A., Moutafis, C., Hu, X., & Betrabet, N. (2019). Skyrmion Logic System for Large-Scale Reversible Computation. *Physical Review Applied*, *12*(6). Advance online publication. DOI: 10.1103/physrevapplied.12.064053

Chen, T., Kong, L., Gao, X., Chen, G., Wang, Y., & Zhu, Y. (2017). Improving Resource Utilization via Virtual Machine Placement in Data Center Networks. *Mobile Networks and Applications*, *23*(2), 227–238. DOI: 10.1007/s11036-017-0925-7

Chen, X., Lin, B., Min, G., Wolter, K., Zhang, J., & Chen, Z. (2022). Energy-Efficient Offloading for DNN-Based Smart IoT Systems in Cloud-Edge Environments. *IEEE Transactions on Parallel and Distributed Systems*, *33*(3), 683–697. DOI: 10.1109/tpds.2021.3100298

Condori-Fernandez, N., Luaces, M. R., Places, Á. S., & Lago, P. (2020). An Action Research for Improving the Sustainability Assessment Framework Instruments. *Sustainability*, *12*(4), 1682. DOI: 10.3390/su12041682

Contini, G., & Peruzzini, M. (2022). Sustainability and Industry 4.0: Definition of a Set of Key Performance Indicators for Manufacturing Companies. *Sustainability*, *14*(17), 11004. DOI: 10.3390/su141711004

Coscieme, L., Mortensen, L. F., & Donohue, I. (2021). Enhance environmental policy coherence to meet the Sustainable Development Goals. *Journal of Cleaner Production*, *296*, 126502. DOI: 10.1016/j.jclepro.2021.126502

Côté, M.-A., Suryn, W., & Georgiadou, E. (2007). In search for a widely applicable and accepted software quality model for software quality engineering. *Software Quality Journal*, *15*(4), 401–416. DOI: 10.1007/s11219-007-9029-0

Côté-Boileau, É., Denis, J.-L., Breton, M., & Gaboury, I. (2020). Organizational Ethnographic Case Studies: Toward a New Generative In-Depth Qualitative Methodology for Health Care Research? *International Journal of Qualitative Methods*, *19*, 160940692092690. DOI: 10.1177/1609406920926904

Cui, X., Qi, B., & Hussain, M. J. (2024). Vendor sustainability performance and corporate customers' supplier selection. *Corporate Social Responsibility and Environmental Management*, *31*(4), 2910–2928. DOI: 10.1002/csr.2727

Dasallas, L., Jang, S., Jang, S., & Lee, J. (2024). Development and Application of Technical Key Performance Indicators (KPIs) for Smart Water Cities (SWCs) Global Standards and Certification Schemes. *Water (Basel)*, *16*(5), 741. DOI: 10.3390/w16050741

De Almeida Barbosa Franco, J., Bezerra, B. S., Battistelle, R. A. G., & Franco, A. Junior. (2024). Dynamic Capabilities: Unveiling Key Resources for Environmental Sustainability and Economic Sustainability, and Corporate Social Responsibility towards Sustainable Development Goals. *Resources*, *13*(2), 22. DOI: 10.3390/resources13020022

Del Rosario, P., & Traverso, M. (2023). Towards Sustainable Roads: A Systematic Review of Triple-Bottom-Line-Based Assessment Methods. *Sustainability*, *15*(21), 15654. DOI: 10.3390/su152115654

Ertem, M. (2024). Renewable Energy-Aware Machine Scheduling Under Intermittent Energy Supply. *IEEE Access : Practical Innovations, Open Solutions*, *12*, 23613–23625. DOI: 10.1109/access.2024.3365074

. Eshbayev, O., Xursandov, K., Pulatovna, K. U., Jamalova, G., & Sitora, A. (2024). Advancing Green Technology Systems through Digital Economy Innovations: A Study on Sustainable. E3S Web of Conferences, 576, 02009. https://doi.org/DOI: 10.1051/e3sconf/202457602009

Ezzeddine, Z., Khalil, A., Zeddini, B., & Ouslimani, H. H. (2024). A Survey on Green Enablers: A Study on the Energy Efficiency of AI-Based 5G Networks. *Sensors (Basel)*, *24*(14), 4609. DOI: 10.3390/s24144609

Fati, S. M., & Alenezi, M. (2024). Transforming Application Development With Serverless Computing. *International Journal of Cloud Applications and Computing*, *14*(1), 1–16. DOI: 10.4018/ijcac.365288

Gao, J. Q., Li, S. R., Li, D., Gao, H. L., Qiao, G. H., & Jia, Q. R. (2024). Circular economy strategies in supply chains, enhancing resource efficiency and sustainable development goals. *Environmental Science and Pollution Research International*, *31*(6), 8751–8767. DOI: 10.1007/s11356-023-31551-z

Georgiou, K., Kerrison, S., Chamski, Z., & Eder, K. (2017). Energy Transparency for Deeply Embedded Programs. *ACM Transactions on Architecture and Code Optimization*, *14*(1), 1–26. DOI: 10.1145/3046679

Górski, T. (2021). Towards Continuous Deployment for Blockchain. *Applied Sciences (Basel, Switzerland)*, *11*(24), 11745. DOI: 10.3390/app112411745

Guo, C., Ci, S., Yang, Y., & Zhou, Y. (2021). A Survey of Energy Consumption Measurement in Embedded Systems. *IEEE Access : Practical Innovations, Open Solutions*, *9*, 60516–60530. DOI: 10.1109/access.2021.3074070

Guo, Y., Ganti, S., & Wu, Y. (2024). Enhancing Energy Efficiency in Telehealth Internet of Things Systems Through Fog and Cloud Computing Integration: Simulation Study. *JMIR Biomedical Engineering*, *9*(2), e50175. DOI: 10.2196/50175

Han, S., Jeong, Y., In, J., & Lee, K. (2024). Environmental sustainability in health care: An empirical investigation of US hospitals. *Business Strategy and the Environment*, *33*(6), 6045–6065. DOI: 10.1002/bse.3790

Horsthofer-Rauch, J., Guesken, S. R., Weich, J., Rauch, A., Bittner, M., Schulz, J., & Zaeh, M. F. (2024). Sustainability-integrated value stream mapping with process mining. *Production & Manufacturing Research*, *12*(1). Advance online publication. DOI: 10.1080/21693277.2024.2334294

Hou, L., Wu, C., Zhang, Y., & Song, J. (2023). Improving the greenness of enterprise supply chains by designing government subsidy mechanisms: Based on prospect theory and evolutionary games. *Frontiers in Psychology*, *14*. Advance online publication. DOI: 10.3389/fpsyg.2023.1283794

Houf, L., Shepherd, L. A., & Szymkowiak, A. (2024). Promotion of Sustainable Products: Can Sustainability Labels Promote User Selection of Environmentally Friendly Products? *Sustainability*, *16*(13), 5390. DOI: 10.3390/su16135390

Hu, X., & Sinniah, S. (2024). The Role of Green Risk Management Approaches in Promoting Green and Sustainable Supply Chain Management. *Natural and Engineering Sciences*, *9*(2), 33–54. DOI: 10.28978/nesciences.1569144

Jalali, S., & Wohlin, C. (2011). Global software engineering and agile practices: A systematic review. *Journal of Software (Malden, MA)*, *24*(6), 643–659. DOI: 10.1002/smr.561

Jaramillo, M., Pavón, W., & Jaramillo, L. (2024). Adaptive Forecasting in Energy Consumption: A Bibliometric Analysis and Review. *Data*, *9*(1), 13. DOI: 10.3390/data9010013

Jianguo, D., & Solangi, Y. A. (2023). Sustainability in Pakistan's textile industry: Analyzing barriers and strategies for green supply chain management implementation. *Environmental Science and Pollution Research International*, *30*(20), 58109–58127. DOI: 10.1007/s11356-023-26687-x

Kansal, A., & Zhao, F. (2008). Fine-grained energy profiling for power-aware application design. *Performance Evaluation Review*, *36*(2), 26–31. DOI: 10.1145/1453175.1453180

Kelleci, A. (2021). Four-Stage Model of Value Creation for Sustainability-Oriented Marketing: En Route to Participatory Marketing. *Journal of Macromarketing*, *42*(1), 5–11. DOI: 10.1177/02761467211049668

Khan, A. R. (2024). Dynamic Load Balancing in Cloud Computing: Optimized RL-Based Clustering with Multi-Objective Optimized Task Scheduling. *Processes (Basel, Switzerland)*, *12*(3), 519. DOI: 10.3390/pr12030519

Kumar, A., Tyagi, P. K., Tyagi, S., & Ghorbanpour, M. (2024). Integrating green nanotechnology with sustainable development goals: A pathway to sustainable innovation. *Discover Sustainability*, *5*(1). Advance online publication. DOI: 10.1007/s43621-024-00610-x

Kumar, N. M., Chand, A. A., Islam, F. R., Prasad, K. A., Malvoni, M., Mamun, K. A., & Chopra, S. S. (2020). Distributed Energy Resources and the Application of AI, IoT, and Blockchain in Smart Grids. *Energies*, *13*(21), 5739. DOI: 10.3390/en13215739

Kuru, K., & Khan, W. (2020). A Framework for the Synergistic Integration of Fully Autonomous Ground Vehicles With Smart City. *IEEE Access : Practical Innovations, Open Solutions*, *9*, 923–948. DOI: 10.1109/access.2020.3046999

Kutaula, S., Chowdhury, S., Dey, P. K., Gillani, A., & Budhwar, P. S. (2024). Linking HRM with Sustainability Performance Through Sustainability Practices: Unlocking the Black Box. *British Journal of Management*, *36*(2), 615–632. DOI: 10.1111/1467-8551.12861

Lang, C., Michos, O., & Conrad, L. (2018). Mathematical Approaches of Branching Morphogenesis. *Frontiers in Genetics*, *9*(e41643). Advance online publication. DOI: 10.3389/fgene.2018.00673

Li, H., Pang, F., Xu, D., & Dong, L. (2023). New Optimization Framework for Improvement Sustainability of Wastewater Treatment Plants. *Processes (Basel, Switzerland)*, *11*(11), 3156. DOI: 10.3390/pr11113156

Li, M., & Rasiah, R. (2024). Can ESG Disclosure Stimulate Corporations' Sustainable Green Innovation Efforts? Evidence from China. *Sustainability*, *16*(21), 9390. DOI: 10.3390/su16219390

Li, W., Li, W., Zhu, Y., Wang, F., Huang, F., Wang, F., Zhu, Y., Huang, F., Dong, Z., & Zhao, Y. (2024). Research progress in water quality prediction based on deep learning technology: A review. *Environmental Science and Pollution Research International*, *31*(18), 26415–26431. DOI: 10.1007/s11356-024-33058-7

Liang, X., Liu, M., & Huang, Y. (2023). Studying financial development with low-carbon architecture development and green technological innovation: Sustaining SDG-9. *Environmental Science and Pollution Research International*, *31*(2), 2009–2025. DOI: 10.1007/s11356-023-31155-7

Lounis, Z., & Mcallister, T. P. (2016). Risk-Based Decision Making for Sustainable and Resilient Infrastructure Systems. *Journal of Structural Engineering*, *142*(9). Advance online publication. DOI: 10.1061/(asce)st.1943-541x.0001545

Lu, J.-W., Chang, N.-B., & Liao, L. (2013). Environmental Informatics for Solid and Hazardous Waste Management: Advances, Challenges, and Perspectives. *Critical Reviews in Environmental Science and Technology*, *43*(15), 1557–1656. DOI: 10.1080/10643389.2012.671097

Lu, L., Zhu, X., Peters, C. A., Rau, G. H., Ren, Z. J., & Guest, J. S. (2018). Wastewater treatment for carbon capture and utilization. *Nature Sustainability*, *1*(12), 750–758. DOI: 10.1038/s41893-018-0187-9

Luo, Y., Ye, M., Zhou, Y., Su, R., Huang, S., Wang, H., & Dai, X. (2024). Assessing the Environmental Impact of Municipal Waste on Energy Incineration Technology for Power Generation Using Life Cycle Assessment Methodology. *Toxics*, *12*(11), 786. DOI: 10.3390/toxics12110786

Mageed, N. N., Alsultani, R., & Abbas, A. W. N. (2024). The Impact of Using Advanced Technologies in Sustainable Design to Enhance Usability and Achieve Optimal Architectural Design. *International Journal of Sustainable Development and Planning*, *19*(11), 4273–4280. DOI: 10.18280/ijsdp.191116

Makhloufi, L., Siddik, A. B., & Zhou, J. (2023). Why green absorptive capacity and managerial environmental concerns matter for corporate environmental entrepreneurship? *Environmental Science and Pollution Research International*, *30*(46), 102295–102312. DOI: 10.1007/s11356-023-29583-6

Marijan, D., & Gotlieb, A. (2020). Industry-Academia research collaboration in software engineering: The Certus model. *Information and Software Technology*, *132*, 106473. DOI: 10.1016/j.infsof.2020.106473

Moktadir, M. A., Sultana, R., Madaan, J., Dwivedi, A., Rahman, A., Chiappetta Jabbour, C. J., & Paul, S. K. (2020). An investigation of key performance indicators for operational excellence towards sustainability in the leather products industry. *Business Strategy and the Environment*, *29*(8), 3331–3351. DOI: 10.1002/bse.2575

Naranjo, A., Colonia, A., Maury-Ramírez, A., Mesa, J., & Maury, H. (2020). State-of-the-Art Green Roofs: Technical Performance and Certifications for Sustainable Construction. *Coatings*, *10*(1), 69. DOI: 10.3390/coatings10010069

Ngo, T., Ullah, S., Le, T., & Trinh, H. H. (2022). Climate risk disclosures and global sustainability initiatives: A conceptual analysis and agenda for future research. *Business Strategy and the Environment*, *32*(6), 3705–3720. DOI: 10.1002/bse.3323

Pacana, A., Ulewicz, R., Siwiec, D., & Ulewicz, M. (2024). A Novelty Model Employing the Quality Life Cycle Assessment (QLCA) Indicator and Frameworks for Selecting Qualitative and Environmental Aspects for Sustainable Product Development. *Sustainability*, *16*(17), 7821. DOI: 10.3390/su16177821

Padilla-Rivera, A., Güereca-Hernandez, L. P., Morales Brizard, M., & Merveille, N. (2024). Barriers, Challenges, and Opportunities in the Adoption of the Circular Economy in Mexico: An Analysis through Social Perception. *Recycling*, *9*(5), 71. DOI: 10.3390/recycling9050071

Pan, C., Hu, J., & Xie, M. (2018). ENZYME: An Energy-Efficient Transient Computing Paradigm for Ultralow Self-Powered IoT Edge Devices. *IEEE Transactions on Computer-Aided Design of Integrated Circuits and Systems*, *37*(11), 2440–2450. DOI: 10.1109/tcad.2018.2858478

Pantović, V., Jovanović-Milenković, M., Vujičić, S., Vidojević, D., & Sofijanić, S. (2024). Data-Driven Decision Making for Sustainable IT Project Management Excellence. *Sustainability*, *16*(7), 3014. DOI: 10.3390/su16073014

Patros, P., Rana, O., Spillner, J., Varghese, B., Dustdar, S., & Papadopoulos, A. V. (2021). Toward Sustainable Serverless Computing. *IEEE Internet Computing*, *25*(6), 42–50. DOI: 10.1109/mic.2021.3093105

Paulraj, D., Prakash, M., Neelakandan, S., Baburaj, E., & Sethukarasi, T. (2023). An Efficient Hybrid Job Scheduling Optimization (EHJSO) approach to enhance resource search using Cuckoo and Grey Wolf Job Optimization for cloud environment. *PLoS One*, *18*(3), e0282600. DOI: 10.1371/journal.pone.0282600

Quesado, P., Silva, R., & Oliveira, H. C. (2024). Management Control Systems and Sustainability: A Bibliometric Analysis. *Sustainability*, *16*(12), 5067. DOI: 10.3390/su16125067

Radovanović, A., Talukdar, S., Roy, B., Mullen, E., Hung, P., Chen, B., Duarte, A., Care, N., Xiao, D., Schneider, I., Smith, K., Koningstein, R., Cirne, W., Haridasan, M., & Cottman, M. (2023). Carbon-Aware Computing for Datacenters. *IEEE Transactions on Power Systems*, *38*(2), 1270–1280. DOI: 10.1109/tpwrs.2022.3173250

Ramya, K., & Ayothi, S. (2023). Hybrid dingo and whale optimization algorithm-based optimal load balancing for cloud computing environment. *Transactions on Emerging Telecommunications Technologies*, *34*(5). Advance online publication. DOI: 10.1002/ett.4760

Rashid, N., Ilyas, M., Khan, H. U., & Khan, S. U. (2021). Green-Agile Maturity Model: An Evaluation Framework for Global Software Development Vendors. *IEEE Access : Practical Innovations, Open Solutions*, *9*, 71868–71886. DOI: 10.1109/access.2021.3079194

Ruza, C., & Caro-Carretero, R. (2022). The Non-Linear Impact of Financial Development on Environmental Quality and Sustainability: Evidence from G7 Countries. *International Journal of Environmental Research and Public Health*, *19*(14), 8382. DOI: 10.3390/ijerph19148382

Saetang, W., Puttinaovarat, S., Saeliw, A., Chai-Arayalert, S., Kajornkasirat, S., Kongcharoen, J., & Puangsuwan, K. (2024). Eco-Friendly Office Platform: Leveraging Machine Learning and GIS for Carbon Footprint Management and Green Space Analysis. *Sustainability*, *16*(21), 9424. DOI: 10.3390/su16219424

Sani, B., & Jan, S. (2024). Empirical Analysis of Widely Used Website Automated Testing Tools. *EAI Endorsed Transactions on AI and Robotics*, *3*. Advance online publication. DOI: 10.4108/airo.7285

Schoen, J. H., Burdette, J. H., West, T. G., Geer, C. P., Lipford, M. E., & Sachs, J. R. (2024). Savings in CT Net Scan Energy Consumption: Assessment Using Dose Report Metrics and Comparison With Savings in Idle State Energy Consumption. *AJR. American Journal of Roentgenology*, *222*(1). Advance online publication. DOI: 10.2214/ajr.23.30189

Seo, C., Yoo, D., & Lee, Y. (2024). Empowering Sustainable Industrial and Service Systems through AI-Enhanced Cloud Resource Optimization. *Sustainability*, *16*(12), 5095. DOI: 10.3390/su16125095

Shah, S. M. A., Ahmed, Z., Ullah, I., Jiang, Y., Adebayo, T. S., & Wu, H. (2021). Linking Green Human Resource Practices and Environmental Economics Performance: The Role of Green Economic Organizational Culture and Green Psychological Climate. *International Journal of Environmental Research and Public Health*, *18*(20), 10953. DOI: 10.3390/ijerph182010953

Shao, J., Liu, Y. D., Alam, F., Ahmad, H., Butt, A. H., & Shao, H. (2024). Optimizing Sustainable Performance Green Talent Management Strategies Focused on Core Competencies. *Journal of Global Information Management*, *32*(1), 1–24. DOI: 10.4018/jgim.352495

Sharma, V., Chatterjee, P., Kumar, M., & Gonzalez, E. D. R. S. (2023). Modelling of green manufacturing barriers using a survey-integrated decision-making approach. *Reports in Mechanical Engineering*, *4*(1), 256–275. DOI: 10.31181/rme040117112023s

Shawon, A. R., Kottmann, L., Feike, T., Hackauf, B., Uptmoor, R., & Memic, E. (2024). Comprehensive evaluation of the DSSAT-CSM-CERES-Wheat for simulating winter rye against multi-environment data in Germany. *Agronomy Journal*, *116*(4), 1844–1868. DOI: 10.1002/agj2.21590

Siregar, I. F., Soleha, N., Ismail, T., & Taqi, M. (2024). Influence of ESG on Sustainability Reporting: Mediation Rule of Green Innovation and Investor Sentiment. *International Journal of Energy Economics and Policy*, *14*(1), 452–463. DOI: 10.32479/ijeep.14988

Soongpol, B., Rukhiran, M., & Netinant, P. (2024). Practical Sustainable Software Development in Architectural Flexibility for Energy Efficiency Using the Extended Agile Framework. *Sustainability*, *16*(13), 5738. DOI: 10.3390/su16135738

Stojčić, M., Mardani, A., Zavadskas, E. K., Pamučar, D., & Stević, Ž. (2019). Application of MCDM Methods in Sustainability Engineering: A Literature Review 2008–2018. *Symmetry*, *11*(3), 350. DOI: 10.3390/sym11030350

Tehrani, A., Heidar-Zadeh, F., & Richer, M. (2024). CuGBasis: High-performance CUDA/Python library for efficient computation of quantum chemistry density-based descriptors for larger systems. *The Journal of Chemical Physics*, *161*(7). Advance online publication. DOI: 10.1063/5.0216781

Velaoras, K., Polyzos, S., Menegaki, A. N., & Gotzamani, K. (2025). The Role of Environmental Certification in the Hospitality Industry: Assessing Sustainability, Consumer Preferences, and the Economic Impact. *Sustainability*, *17*(2), 650. DOI: 10.3390/su17020650

Vergallo, R., D'Alò, T., Matino, S., Mainetti, L., & Paiano, R. (2024). Evaluating Sustainable Digitalization: A Carbon-Aware Framework for Enhancing Eco-Friendly Business Process Reengineering. *Sustainability*, *16*(17), 7789. DOI: 10.3390/su16177789

Yilmaz, Y., Bandi, V., Mondal, D., Wang, S., Woods, R. A., Chan, T. M., Carey, R., & Thoma, B. (2021). Developing a dashboard for faculty development in competency-based training programs: A design-based research project. *Canadian Medical Education Journal, 12*(4). Advance online publication. DOI: 10.36834/cmej.72067

Yuan, F., Ye, C., Peng, Y., Zuo, Z., Huang, X., Mao, Z., Tian, Z., Shu, W., Gu, S., Yang, J., & Jiang, Y. (2025). AI-Driven Optimization of Blockchain Scalability, Security, and Privacy Protection. *Algorithms, 18*(5), 263. DOI: 10.3390/a18050263

Zanotti, T., Puglisi, F. M., & Pavan, P. (2020). Smart Logic-in-Memory Architecture for Low-Power Non-Von Neumann Computing. *IEEE Journal of the Electron Devices Society, 8*, 757–764. DOI: 10.1109/jeds.2020.2987402

Zavieh, H., Sangaiah, A. K., & Javadpour, A. (2024). Efficient task scheduling in cloud networks using ANN for green computing. *International Journal of Communication Systems, 37*(5). Advance online publication. DOI: 10.1002/dac.5689

Zervakis, G., Soudris, D., Pekmestzi, K., & Xydis, S. (2019). Multi-Level Approximate Accelerator Synthesis Under Voltage Island Constraints. *IEEE Transactions on Circuits and Systems. II, Express Briefs, 66*(4), 607–611. DOI: 10.1109/tcsii.2018.2869025

Zhang, P., Yang, A., Pang, M., Zhang, L., Hao, Y., Wang, C., Xu, M., & Voinov, A. (2024). Food–energy–water nexus optimization brings substantial reduction of urban resource consumption and greenhouse gas emissions. *PNAS Nexus, 3*(2). Advance online publication. DOI: 10.1093/pnasnexus/pgae028

Zhang, Q., Smith, K., Wang, S., Shen, J., Zhao, X., Jin, X., & Ren, Z. J. (2021). Greenhouse gas emissions associated with urban water infrastructure: What we have learnt from China's practice. *WIREs. Water, 8*(4). Advance online publication. DOI: 10.1002/wat2.1529

Zhu, J., Zheng, Z., He, P., & Lyu, M. R. (2017). Online QoS Prediction for Runtime Service Adaptation via Adaptive Matrix Factorization. *IEEE Transactions on Parallel and Distributed Systems, 28*(10), 2911–2924. DOI: 10.1109/tpds.2017.2700796

Zhu, X., Zhao, S., Pang, X., & Jia, Z. (2024). Joint Optimization of Task Caching and Computation Offloading for Multiuser Multitasking in Mobile Edge Computing. *Electronics (Basel), 13*(2), 389. DOI: 10.3390/electronics13020389

Chapter 9
ESG-Aligned Governance in Software-Driven Business Projects:
Strategic Integration of Sustainability, Risk, and Stakeholder Management

M. Irvanni Bahri
https://orcid.org/0000-0002-1213-9427
Institut Teknologi Batam, Indonesia

Ansarullah Lawi
Institut Teknologi Batam, Indonesia

Aulia Agung Dermawan
Institut Teknologi Batam, Indonesia

ABSTRACT

The rapid development of digital technology has made software-driven initiatives crucial for enterprises worldwide. However, traditional project management methods often lack sustainability and responsible governance. This chapter explores project governance in digital projects and software engineering using ESG principles. It emphasizes the importance of energy-efficient systems, transparent development processes, and transparency in project advancements. Baku offers a sustainable governance model, incorporating ESG frameworks, Agile and DevOps method-

DOI: 10.4018/979-8-3373-4652-6.ch009

ologies, and case studies. It also emphasizes the importance of managing human resources, involving stakeholders, and using sustainability performance indicators for green initiatives' success.

INTRODUCTION

The rapid advancement of technology has pushed companies to improve their services and products. Customers, once passive, now actively express their perspectives and expectations. Customer feedback and insights from web platforms provide valuable input. This information helps businesses improve, innovate, and expand their reach (Hans & Khera, 2021; Sauvola et al., 2015). In software application development projects, defining the product scope based on the expectations and views of diverse stakeholders not only directly supports the company's objectives from a software quality perspective but also helps integrate Environmental, Social, and Governance (ESG) factors into the development process. By including ESG considerations, organizations can align their product scope with long-term sustainability goals, ensuring that software projects not only meet user expectations but also contribute positively to environmental and social outcomes (Ignaim & Fernandes, 2025).

This chapter introduces a product scope model based on stakeholder expectations. It formalizes the Project Charter, which can be mathematically expressed using set theory. The Fusynation aspect is derived through meticulous Project Examination, employing Project Mapping Techniques and General Considerations. Adapting the Project Charter's structure enables responsiveness to evolving stakeholder expectations, serving as an initial step toward achieving project quality/control.

Modern software development projects have become foundational to emerging industries and business systems. However, users and developers often hold divergent views and expectations. These complex constraints challenge project managers to consolidate diverse stakeholder inputs and deliver tailored preliminary responses, especially when integrating ESG considerations into the project's scope. This challenge becomes more pronounced as project managers must balance both technical and non-technical perspectives while aligning the product with broader sustainability goals (Udhayakumar & Sivasubramanian, 2024). Project managers must navigate new, formalized processes to synthesize active stakeholder feedback. By integrating ESG considerations into the Project Stakeholder Management process, project managers can ensure that environmental, social, and governance factors are incorporated from the outset, contributing to long-term project success (Silva et al., 2024). This renewed emphasis aims to iteratively refine the Product Scope perspective beyond mere product quality. Environmental, Social, and Governance (ESG) factors are critical to long-term viability (Bahri, Dermawan, et al., 2025; Jannah et al., 2024). Challenges such as environmental protection, carbon neutrality, and efficient energy use have gained global urgency, prompting nations to mitigate economic impacts through policy measures (Wu & Jin, 2022). Amid rapid economic growth, advocating sustainable development is essential to address crises like global warming, resource depletion, and environmental disasters. While international organizations and governments implement policies, desired outcomes remain elusive. As key economic contributors, corporations must adopt sustainable practices. Reducing carbon emissions, promoting disaster preparedness, reforestation, and resource reuse are imperative to ensure human survival. Governance structures must prioritize transparency, ethical audits, and clear roles for boards and committees to prevent corruption (Qing & Jin, 2023). Transparent governance enhances risk management and fosters long-term growth.

The Role of Software-Based Projects in the Context of Sustainability

Sustainable software development has garnered increased attention across both academic and business sectors due to its potential to support broader ESG goals. Environmental sustainability focuses on minimizing carbon footprints and energy usage in software, while social sustainability addresses issues like user privacy, data security, and social equity. Governance in software development ensures transparency, accountability, and adherence to ethical standards, promoting responsible innovation. Collaboration between academia and industry is critical to developing and implementing sustainable software practices, as evidenced by research involving student teams and industry partners (Condori Fernandez & Lago, 2018). Green software is designed to reduce environmental harm by optimizing software energy usage and improving efficiency. It aims to mitigate carbon emissions through techniques such as cloud optimization, energy-efficient coding practices, and better system management. Additionally, the integration of AI and data analytics helps businesses monitor and optimize energy consumption, contributing to long-term sustainability goals (Moshnyaga, 2013). Assessing the energy consumption of systems, applications, and platforms is a software-centric endeavour aimed at reducing carbon emissions. A separate set of software-centric operations concentrates on the creation, distribution, and deployment of reusable and thus more sustainable software modules. The focus on sustainable software is readily explicable. A business need software to meet the demands of its market and clientele, whether it is a small restaurant presenting its menus online or a global fast-food chain creating a centralized software system for procurement management (Pang, 2015; Singhal & Konguvel, 2022). The creation of this software, irrespective of its size and complexity, often depends on a software-driven business initiative or program undertaken by an organization or project team. However, as organizations increasingly adopt ESG-driven principles, the development of such software must go beyond technical specifications to incorporate environmental, social, and governance considerations. Integrating ESG into the project's scope ensures that the software aligns with long-term sustainability objectives, helping organizations meet regulatory standards, reduce environmental impacts, and foster social responsibility.

Software-driven business initiatives often face challenges such as budget overruns, time delays, and resource shortages, especially when the created software fails to meet the expectations of stakeholders. Regardless of size or complexity, successful software development relies on well-managed initiatives that align with organizational objectives (Nadjib et al., 2019). Green software, or sustainable software development, has gained significant attention in both academia and business. This field focuses on creating software solutions that minimize environmental impact through energy-efficient designs, reducing carbon emissions, and promoting long-term sustainability. This increasing focus is matched by a newly developed subject dedicated to enhancing software sustainability or reducing its unsustainability (Ahmad et al., 2018; Oyedeji et al., 2021). Efforts to address sustainability issues in software development have mostly concentrated on the social (S), economic (E), and environmental (G) dimensions, since ESG initiatives have predominated the sustainability research and development landscape for decades (Karita et al., 2022). The appeal of green software is evident, as businesses require software to meet the demands of their market and clientele, whether it be a small restaurant presenting its menu online or a global fast-food chain focused on developing and implementing a software system for managing its procurement. The creation of this software, irrespective of its size and complexity, depends on a software-driven business project or program implemented inside an organization or project team (Rivas-Asanza et al., 2018). A software-centric, business-oriented project often denotes a brief endeavor executed by a team to provide software deliverable or facilitate a product or service. The obsolete or insufficient implementation of software-driven business initiatives may result in issues related to budget, timeline, resources, suitability, benefit realization, and stakeholder satisfaction.

Gaps in Traditional Project Governance Against ESG Dimensions

Sustainability has become one of the biggest trends in the business landscape (Rivas-Asanza et al., 2018). It refers to the ability to maintain certain processes or states for a specified period, ensuring that the organization meets its business objectives without compromising the ability of future generations to meet theirs. In the context of Environmental, Social, and Governance (ESG), sustainability takes on a broader meaning, addressing the need to integrate responsible environmental practices, promote social equity, and ensure strong governance. This approach has become central in guiding businesses toward achieving long-term success and addressing the broader societal challenges of today. In the classic triple bottom line definition, it consists of three dimensions: financial, social, and environmental. In other definitions, however, it is often limited to environmental sustainability. Within this last definition of sustainability, environmental sustainability refers to achieving business development results without threatening the environment and defending the interests of future generations. As is known, there are many approaches today concerning environmental sustainability, among which standards are difficult to use and understand by the general public, such as complex regulations and management systems. However, ESG principles provide a framework that not only simplifies these complex standards but also ensures that businesses can align their operations with broader societal goals. These principles facilitate a holistic approach to sustainability, enabling companies to meet environmental, social, and governance requirements while ensuring compliance with evolving regulatory landscapes. On their own, they act as a problem-reduction mechanism only, which may help organizations proponents of environmental sustainability to face the huge problem of environmental protection(Combs & Curran, 2008).

However, this situation creates an opportunity for organizations to approach alternatives that alleviate these challenges. The need to comply with regulations and reduce environmental impact often requires implementing systems that not only ensure compliance but also align with ESG-driven goals. By embracing ESG principles, businesses can develop innovative solutions that not only mitigate their environmental footprint but also enhance their competitive advantage in a rapidly changing market. help both complying with the former and attaining the latter. Information technology is increasingly being harnessed to define, implement, and enforce compliance and environmental protection systems. If on their own, regulation and standards impose burdens on organizations, by leveraging it with information technology, compliance and protection systems can be boosted to provide organizations with competitive advantages (Jain et al., 2024).

Purpose and Chapter Structure

Software and software-based systems and services have dramatically transformed product and service development as well as business operations. Successful software-driven business endeavors are rapidly developing software innovations in a firm's own organization regardless of ownership, with internal and external marketplaces, and ecosystems for fostering further innovation. Companies are operated as software-driven systems to deliver digital services that generate an ever-increasing mass of data. Artificial intelligence label and train data faster and better than humans and require appropriately structured business services that can be jointly developed and operated by a very large number of cognitively limited but information-based agents (Iyer & K.R, 2020). Software drives the business models of digital platforms to some degree and limits the business scope, further favoring demand-side economies of scale. Therefore, software development and software-driven means of operations are critical for organizational survival and success. This emphasizes the importance of strong and effective software governance to guarantee sustainable value creation in software-driven ecosystems (Septriadi et al., 2019).

The organizations tend to focus only on the software-development life cycles. The finishing product was handed over and maintained. This is not valid when product-oriented sustainability needs to be guaranteed. The other fields of software governance, such as architectures, development processes, and products/service requirement establishment, need to deliver future software investments that are aligned with the business strategy as a whole (Lago et al., 2024; Venters et al., 2018). Software, which structures the creation, development, and use of software, still does not sustain investments to the increasing digitalization evolution (Kismawadi & Irfan, 2025; Volpato et al., 2017). This is not valid, given the emergence of software-driven development in streams of business and operational transformation. Examining such aligned software investments should surely deliver huge benefit potentials. The more general framework for examining and modeling software-driven business projects' governance was developed. More specifically, the ESG concerning aligned software governance was envisioned. Two case studies were conducted with first-hand interviews. An organization was examined regarding its software innovations and concurrent business transformations (Marar, 2024).

BASIC CONCEPTS OF ESG AND ITS RELEVANCE IN SOFTWARE PROJECTS

Definition and Scope of ESG (Environmental, Social, Governance)

Corporate sustainability can be viewed in two essential dimensions: stakeholder management dimensions which include "economic, environmental, and social" domain; and triple bottom line dimensions which involve "people, planet, and profit." Governance can be categorized into internal and external aspects. Internal governance mainly focuses on the firm's internal process to improve integrity (ethics, transparency, accountability, etc.) and business efficiency (incentives, contracts, ownership structure, etc.). On the other hand, external governance mainly deals with market intervention and regulatory control for economic development (Park et al., 2022). Governance is considered "a broad set of processes, policies, laws, and institutions that affect the way a corporation is directed, administered or controlled." In spite of the ambiguity in the definitions of governance, corporate governance is widely used in terms of a system by which companies are directed and controlled. ESG focused on governance in a firm's internal process and conditions under which authority and power are exercised in an organization (Anibal Altamirano & Sloley, 2023; Bahri, Agustina, et al., 2025; Baporikar, 2023). Since the 2001 Enron scandal, corporate governance has been the focus of various debates and discussions among academics and practitioners. Governance literature can be categorized into two essential areas: research toward the anteceding aspects of governance (including governance mechanisms); and research toward the effects of governance (including economic performance) (Cuong, 2011a, 2011b).

ESG Principles in Project Management

In the contemporary landscape, where social and environmental concerns are garnering heightened scrutiny, corporations are anticipated to evaluate the social and environmental ramifications of their operations. The requirement for openness, accountability, and a commitment to sustainability at an elevated level is prompting organizations to transition to financial Implement more proactive strategies and adopt corporate governance that prioritizes social and environmental accountability (Brogi & Lagasio, 2025; Prado Muci de Lima & Costa Fernandes, 2024; Shapsugova, 2023). In this setting, endeavors to establish ESG initiatives are anticipated to integrate with business processes and serve as a pivotal differentiating strategy, fostering innovation through a comprehensive approach. In accordance with this trend, initiatives are underway to formulate ESG governance criteria for projects. As the IT industry experiences fast global growth and software projects of considerable business complexity proliferate across diverse sectors, several companies must concentrate on broadening their outlook and evaluating long-term objectives. Formulated as a framework to address sustainability requirements for systems and incorporate them into software development (Dandapani & Shahrokhi, 2022; Jeong & Choi, 2022). Accordingly, comprehending software as Nonetheless, the complexity of the ordinary project participant renders corporate-level implementation problematic. As the digital landscape swiftly transforms all facets of business and life, and new difficulties emerge, firms must expand their outlook to encompass the magnitude of demands and invest in comprehensive solutions to prepare for the long-term future. Eleven strategies are matched with current business processes. Organizing meeting rooms to accommodate requirements, therefore facilitating group meetings and individual assessments at the start of the day to prevent infringement on working hours and disruption of work morale. It is anticipated that the execution of this analysis and plan development will coincide with the evolution of behavioral patterns and the expansion of company supply(Ba, 2021). The ensuing dangers will propel the formulation of extensive policies and will profoundly influence the intensity of challenges in planning procedures (Brogi & Lagasio, 2025; Tencati, 2016).

Linkages Between Sustainability, Digitalization, and Software-Driven Business

Sustainability, digitalization, and software-driven business have become increasingly important since the advent of the Environmental, Social, and Governance (ESG) paradigm beginning in the early 2000s. From a digital perspective, the rapid advancement in Information Technologies (IT) since the late 2000s has ushered in a fourth technological revolution completely disrupting and transforming nearly every aspect of human life. Given the significance and relevance of the topics at hand, there is an evident need for further research into articulating the interrelationships between these phenomena and their implications on building sustainable software systems (Bibri et al., 2023).

Sustainability is a multi-decadal topic that gained traction in the modern era following the first Earth Summit in Rio de Janeiro, Brazil, in 1992 (Camacho & Cruz, 2022; de Freitas Alves & Santos, 2022). Since then, governments worldwide have enacted a plethora of sustainability rules and regulations. For instance, in the European Union, regulations such as REACH in 2007, the General Data Protection Regulation (GDPR) in 2016, and the EU Taxonomy in 2020 exemplify laws that increase mechanical sustainability. Following suit, various international economic organizations have proposed measures for sustainable development in environmental quality, social welfare, and governance. Companies operating in EU countries are subject to compliance, requiring them to materially increase their sustainability diligence. Nonetheless, societies today shoulder a massive burden of ensuring sustainability, which is unfair and unsustainable in the long run (Awewomom et al., 2024; Ogunkan, 2022).

On the digitalization front, claims of the Third Technological Revolution heralding the formation of an Information Society have been bandied about since the conclusion of the Cold War in the early 1990s. These claims began to be fully realized with the commencement of the Fourth Technological Revolution on January 1, 2000. Digital databases ushered in virtually inexhaustible knowledge and exponentially improving digital productivity (Duc & Leick, 2023; Kranz et al., 2016). This new-found knowledge has revolutionized every aspect of human existence, including education, employment, socialization, entertainment, politics, commerce, investment, research, military action, and creation itself (Rivas-Asanza et al., 2018). Software-driven business is indeed the epitome of such a development. Millions of companies have leveraged software capabilities to utterly disrupt legacy ways of doing business, wielding losses in many billions of dollars. Nevertheless, simultaneously beguiled by the new operative paradigm, societies are woefully unprepared for the ensuing challenge to sustainable development (Bamiduro et al., 2025). In a software-driven economy, it seems impossible to achieve sustainability diligence without fully embracing software capabilities. As it stands, ESG compliance is much too laborious due to the manual and paper-intensive nature of software-driven business processes. Given that digitalization is indeed the answer to the ESG diligence burden, an immediate need arises to incorporate ESG-focused principles into the software systems development process (Yrjönkoski et al., 2019).

Review of Current Literature and Theoretical Framework

Companies today need to promote inclusive and sustainable economic growth. Investment and economic growth will not benefit in the long run if the burden is not borne by future generations. Therefore, companies are slowly required to not only pay attention to short-term profits but also bring positive impacts to the environment and communities where they operate (Bahri, Agustina, et al., 2025; Cahyani & Bahri, 2022). Events such as coal mining that does not pay attention to the environment, resulting in flooding and contamination of land and water, corruption in the management of company funds that harms employees, and the destruction of long-term plots in the control of islands by investors under the pretext of corporate development are also becoming widespread. Due diligence environmental disclosure is the first step for a company to be more sensitive to the issues in which it operates and its policies. Companies that follow the GRI guidelines usually publish a sustainability report that contains qualitative and quantitative disclosures about the policies and applications of the positive and negative impacts generated by the company on the environment and society, such as energy savings or investment in trees as mitigation for handling negative impacts (Latifah & Widiatmoko, 2022). Based on these two principles (Pribadi & Irsyad, 2018), however, what has been adopted and implemented has largely been driven by profit rather than value-based practices. There have been complaints and cases filed regarding activities that damage the environment, destroy people's homes, and bribe officials. Good corporate governance should embrace the principles of sustainability and corporate social responsibility in a comprehensive and firm approach. The principles of corporate governance blend easily with those of corporate sustainability and CSR in a common framework referred to as GCG. It is a company culture of governance, stewardship, and social responsibility where they depend on each other.

ESG-BASED PROJECT GOVERNANCE FRAMEWORK

Key Elements of ESG-Oriented Project Governance

ESG-oriented project governance cannot be separated from the main elements in project governance as in the Project Management Body of Knowledge (PMBOK) 7th Edition. Project governance is a framework that describes organizational structure, individuals, processing, and regulations. Governance concerns important matters in an organization, including the roles and responsibilities of the organization and individuals to have an oversight structure or domain, management systems or processes and procedures, control or oversight mechanisms, standards and regulations, and culture and ethics (Mangutana et al., 2016). In order to achieve project objectives, all of these planning, implementation, and control must be carried out. The person in charge of the project is responsible for planning, implementing, and controlling the project and its reporting. In addition, the person in charge of the project and the team that is appointed to keep in mind the limitations of the project. In terms of cost and time budget constraints, this is the responsibility of the cost budget planning team and the appointed scheduling team.

The following are the main elements of ESG-oriented project management (Bierwolf & Frijns, 2021; Larsen, 2017, 2018), including: 1) Project Objectives, 2) Project Management Plan, 3) Project Governance Management, 4) Project Stakeholder Management, 5) Project Risk Management, 6) Project Change Management, 7) Project Activity Management, 8) Project Quality Management, 9) Project Resource Management, 10) Project Communication Management, 11) Project Commercial Management, and 12) Project Performance Management. These elements refer to the project governance framework proposed by the corporate research team and institutions competent in the field of large-scale project governance and can also be seen in the basic framework found in the 7th edition of PMBOK. In essence, none of these project governance elements are unrelated to ESG aspects. However, in these chapters, three of the twelve key elements are selected and classified as ESG-oriented project governance, namely Project Objectives, Project Stakeholder Management, and Project Change Management.

Environmental: Energy Efficiency Software, Green Cloud, Low-Carbon Design

The environmental dimension of ESG introduces a range of new challenges that software developers must address. These challenges include optimizing energy consumption and reducing carbon emissions while ensuring that the software remains effective and scalable. As businesses and software developers work towards sustainability, it is essential to create applications that are not only energy-efficient but also resilient to future environmental demands. This requires innovative thinking and a proactive approach to integrating ESG principles into the core development process. New computing endeavors can nowistly guarantee at least minimum energy efficiencies if they use known high-performance computing architectures, databases, and design methods. Warnings in graying weather have been unheeded, nonetheless. Data-avenues-management simulations today are throttling massively-cooled computing on the cloud and citizen green computing technologies widely available now. As energy inefficiency becomes a growing concern across all computing applications, there is an urgent need for specialists in energy-efficient computing to collaborate on standardized solutions. While various approaches to improving energy efficiency exist, the absence of unified standards and clear metrics hinders progress. To truly address these issues, the focus must shift to developing comprehensive, standardized solutions that integrate ESG principles, ensuring that energy efficiency is not only optimized but also sustainable in the long term. worry about addressing problems at their roots. Sophisticated design methods that guarantee energy efficiency at the architectural and database levels exist, but coding by blind algorithms and large-language models render such consideration moot. It is here that the first clues may lie. Now that even a small garden-variety computer program can ensconce itself on clouds mitigating difficulty, incorrect floppy source codes might cause programmers to do painstaking and expensive trial-and-error tinkering when they once racked in rewards for judging synthesizing variability (Muralidhar et al., 2022).

Industry practices must prioritize energy-efficient computing solutions, even if they are agile, to mitigate energy inefficiency. Adopting sustainable design principles in software development ensures that the agility of software applications is balanced with energy efficiency, minimizing the environmental impact without compromising on performance. This approach aligns with ESG goals by reducing the carbon footprint of computing applications while maintaining operational effectiveness (Mehra et al., 2022). Today there are off-the-shelf reminder computing methods using read-built databases that can prevent roaming ambitions from running and free radicals from wreaking havoc. All computing applications call on such bases, but information on speed-versus-precision tradeoffs does not circulate and seems virtually unexpunged. Standard prior offline orientation at design sites and information thereafter can allow even novice programmers to run nothing but designs that are clean and weed-free. Avoidance of radical seeking is the first-choice suite. Quasi-motion sweeping or grid-fixed checkers with readiness bumps would do for all critical control paths except in the crushing shapes of iconically symmetric physical systems. For many sums of squares, leaving branches to offer cheap to the best constraint for fractions would be adequate. The programming choices would be entirely prompt excluded or analytically re-aggregated.

Social: data Protection and Privacy, Digital Inclusivity, Social Impact

The emergence of the data era in global life, business, and society also has the potential to generate negative reactions from individuals, institutions, and governments, which must be studied and handled carefully. Consideration must be given to ethically understanding the negative impacts of any existing or implemented content. Data, in this case large-scale data with many attributes, has a positive impact that makes everything easier, more measurable, and faster. Services offered through data-based products or technologies must have an impact that can be exemplified and measured logically. According to Kusumastuti et al. (2021) Such actions are the ultimate goal of social impact. Data and technology can easily lead to social injustice. Interrelated issues of discrimination, such as gender bias in technology, race, and data protection, have recently gained global attention. When data-based technology and big data are used in human decision-making, social impact is inevitable. When the corporate sector discusses data, there is concern that data will reduce individuals to cold, hard numbers. A new perspective introduced in discussions about data is that data is information, and technology is a set of tools for managing information (Bambang, 2018). This means that both information (data) and tools (technology) can be used for many purposes, both for good and for evil.

Misuse of data and data-based technology has the potential to lead to crime and negative social impacts. This report will also provide examples and guidance in understanding data-based content or systems and technology assessments using a data maturity framework. The discussion is classified into two broad categories: the social impacts to be studied and the modelling of data use and technology assessments used for data protection and privacy. To date, there are many unanswered questions outlined in Table 1 below:

Table 1. Mapping issues, critical questions and research directions in social impact evaluation and data technology

Key Issues	Critical Question	Research Needs
Social Impact Methodology	How to choose an accurate and comprehensive method?	Qualitative, quantitative, and mixed-method development
Impact Assessment Technique	Are valid measurement techniques available to assess the social impact of data policies?	Validation of social impact instruments and indicators
New Scales & Measuring Tools	Is the new scale representative enough to assess the effectiveness of data and privacy protection policies?	Need to develop new frameworks based on local data and context
Data Availability	To what extent does the available data support an accurate assessment?	Data quality assurance, data integrity and accessibility

Source: Mapping by author

Governance: Transparency of The Development Process, AI Ethics, Risk Management

Welcoming globalization, the development of information and telecommunications technology, and society's increasing dependence on computer technology, humans utilize computers as tools to complete their activities. The use of computers may prevent such things as death. Meanwhile, incidents occur in artificial intelligence (AI) in the fields of communication technology, etc. These recourse incidences lead to death, even with preventive algorithms set by specialists. Ethically, it holds the developer to moral accountability. This paper focuses on the necessity of transparency in the development process arranged by the vendor developer or software maker (Nurmalasari, 2013).

Consider marketing a number of web applications that produce 3D-presented mushy animation. Generally, the project's basic advertisement, AR and other direct videos are a fraud. Animated video editing is a miscellaneous technique used for reporting that 2D-3D animated videos may risk fraud. In theory, if mathematically prepared by a simple parameter, professional video and assumptions built by top skill are used to prevent fusing, are purchased, library templates are utilized, or the edited cartoon video's detail is set (Koshy & Shyry, 2025; Matsiola et al., 2024). In 1994, the remarkable Sophia was made by Ubtech Jinshan with the same condition. If in Indonesia, this fraud incidence may set forth serious trouble. Marketers take farmers' or other designers intellectual violation input.

A review for consideration regarding risk management in trading. Market risk is a risk of profit or loss on a position stemming from an unfavorable change. This risk can also be due to inflation risk, deflation risk, and interest rate volatility risk (Samuel & Augustine, 2019). It consists of five basic strategies: risk retention or both case losses that are too long, such as an explosion; risk termination; and the price-quality soft policy.

Integration of ESG Principles into Project Methodologies (Agile, DevOps, PM²)

The implementation of ESG principles in software-based organizations and PSBs enables membership, preservation, knowledge transfer, and sustainability of the outcomes during HR replacement. The sustainability of the outcomes provides wider opportunities for multiple parties to capitalize on the investments made and provides the potential for higher software value to the business (Nadjib et al., 2019). Pre-agreed ESG principles should be incorporated into the project methodology when a new software project is undertaken in the organization and into the draft project charter for the project. Organizations that are still using existing, standardized project methodology designs to be more efficient and effective in developing software project methodologies can make use of existing project methodology designs. Agreement/commitment among the stakeholders involved in a software-based PSB is valuable to minimize the occurrence of mid-project changes that can lead to cost overruns, The development of a project charter aims to establish initial guidelines for the implementation of software-based PSB and to provide a common understanding among all stakeholders. In this way, the project charter can be viewed as a contract between all parties involved to commit to each other on the matters expressly mentioned therein. In addition to the activity plans, management and monitoring methods have also been designed, and the proposed organizational structure and HR profile of the project are included (Bahri, Agustina, et al., 2025; Noe et al., 2006).

International Comparisons and Best Practices

Benchmarking and international best practices encompass strategies for information technology governance, including the formulation of a governance framework, the establishment of an organizational structure for IT governance, the identification of policies for IT outsourcing, the alignment of IT with business objectives, and the development of methodologies for IT project governance. Benchmarking and the use of worldwide best practices encompass 24 measures classified into 3 domains and 6 distinct categories (Pribadi & Irsyad, 2018). The metrics are represented by respondents' answers on a five-point Likert scale, which are subsequently averaged to derive a number for each statistic. The acquired values are subsequently contrasted with the intended modifications for each measure. A metric clustering analysis utilizing a cluster test was performed to enhance the comprehension of benchmarking implementation and worldwide best practices. This study's conclusions will offer a thorough examination of the implementation of benchmarking and worldwide best practices at PLN *"Pembangkitan Sumbagsel"*. This research is anticipated to function as a reference for further studies on benchmarking and worldwide best practices (Septriadi et al., 2019). COBA 5 is a framework for the governance and management of business IT, encompassing audit, risk management, and compliance (Oliver & Lainhart, 2012). IT governance illustrates how high-performing businesses administer IT decision-making authority to get exceptional outcomes. Data and information metrics were gathered via interviews, questionnaires, and various data gathering instruments. Measurements and assessments facilitated an examination of the notional accomplishments of benchmarking and worldwide best practice parameters at the Sumbagsel Power Generation Unit (Huygh et al., 2018; Oliver & Lainhart, 2012). Measurements and weightings of indicator accomplishments were obtained by data processing. The attainment of measurement indicators is thereafter contrasted with the assessment of changes and the anticipated outcomes of measurement indicator successes.

THE ROLE OF HR AND ORGANISATIONAL MANAGEMENT IN GREEN PROJECT GOVERNANCE

ESG Value-Based Leadership

Software-driven business initiatives adopt an innovative approach from conception to execution, emphasizing inclusiveness, restitution, traceability, monitoring, responsibility, and transparency. Given the critical role of the software sector in strengthening the global transition towards a more just, equitable, and responsive society across the value chain, at every point, the same questions must arise regarding the operation of software businesses throughout their lifecycle (Edison et al., 2018; Trzeciak et al., 2022). Metrics applicable for sustaining an ESG-oriented cultural environment, including the creation of software goods and services, as well as the deployment of software on this platform. Enhancing ESG awareness across the software user community via software testing centers and community involvement in ESG-oriented software development. Establishing distributed auditors as intermediaries between the user community and software users to enhance knowledge of ESG software utilization (Patil et al., 2020; Surbeck & Tyson, 2024). Promoting the use of ESG software by non-governmental organizations and international entities. Businesses and stakeholders in every value chain confront these concerns as technology-driven democracy is established, with civil society groups anticipating a more favorable global shift towards fairer, more equal, and responsive welfare.

ESG-oriented software is enhanced by a more inclusive and decentralized community throughout the lifecycle of software-driven business projects, facilitated by early community involvement in software architecture, data, and processes, along with collaboratively developed neutral testing software that autonomously regulates software output. Decentralized supervisors and well-maintained digital communities act as intermediaries between user communities and users, safeguarding the platform against software misuse and acknowledging the right to utilize collaboratively developed robust intelligence data and unresolved enquiries beyond accountability mechanisms (Bahri et al., 2021; Bahri, Tambunan, et al., 2025).

Organizational Culture on Sustainability - Alignment

Sustainability is a concept frequently employed yet inadequately comprehended in corporate environments. The word arises in corporate dialogues and deliberations, despite a lack of profound contemplation over its definition and the ways of its attainment. Sustainability generally pertains to a company's capacity to guarantee its long-term viability, contingent upon the restoration and reutilization of natural resources and the environment (Mangutana et al., 2016). Long-term strategies, sustainable development, and intergenerational responsibility are intricately connected to the principles of sustainability. Moreover, a comprehensive examination of corporate stakeholders reveals that corporations exist inside the social institutional framework, which is profoundly and subtly shaped by the thoughts, beliefs, and discussions of its members or workers. Organizational culture provides insight into the internal culture of a company and significantly impacts organizational behavior (Fajri et al., 2004). A culture that venerates and dehumanizes people or groups must be restructured to communicate messages and impacts of enlightenment. The Department of Computer Engineering at the Bandung Institute of Technology is a prominent entity exhibiting traits of a decentralized structure. The department functions as a largely autonomous organizational entity, with the authority to manage resources for the execution of academic programs and activities, including postgraduate programs, with the exception of issues for which it is answerable to the rector. Nonetheless, an issue that must be addressed is the formulation of research programs pertaining to artificial intelligence, sustainable software, and technological advancement, which carry substantial consequences for legislation, management, and oversight concerning effective governance. The two are interconnected, and their influence on the concept of sustainability is substantial.

HR Competence in Ongoing Software Projects

Software development projects have a wide variety of projects and wide scope. On the other hand, Sourcing assurance comes from independently checking the correctness of what has been built within a software development project. The people concerned with the same issue may have very different sets of competences, as seen from one stakeholder's viewpoint to another (Nadjib et al., 2019). The swift gathering of a multitude of individuals who may lack a common understanding may create agglutination rather than cohesion. This makes it essential to share and transmit common knowledge for the growth of teams, the smooth development cooperation, and the formation of an external community. Competence describes a set of introduced capabilities comprising knowledge, skills, and desirable attitudes for operations in a given context. Building, matching and displaying competences is challenging because of their tacit nature, the introduction of situation-specific contextual knowledge, and the needed automatization of competence-aware platforms. For software-driven business projects, a relevant context characterizing these key strings of competences is composed, and this context is anchored in a structured competence model.

Software developers and business experts from the two cooperating organizations join efforts within several roles. The roles are defined in terms of the developmental task at hand, the competence frameworks which the roles are tied to, and the prerequisite soft and hard competences. In up to ten sessions of up to two hours, the requirements for commencing projects, streamlining the progress of projects, and measuring success or failure of projects are interface-deployed. A meta-level competence model is built to lock-in these strings of competences semi-formally to a knowledge-based query engine. Capable software agents are developed to enable paired and un-paired matching of competences. Complementary agents clarify the specifications of competences offered to the competing partners as well as of competences required by seeker companies with whom such partnerships are initiated. The development of the project is executed in a concurrent engineering manner, which allows the various applications to be tried and reflexively adjusted. Domain extensions of the agents ease and enhance their employability and applicability (Asyraf et al., 2022).

Stakeholder Engagement Model

The stakeholder engagement scheme is designed in three tracks, namely information delivery, aspiration collection, and participation. Information delivery is carried out through print media, electronic media, and exposure at the head office, at program implementation locations, and online. Aspiration collection is also carried out through mail mechanisms, complaints and program monitoring events, and online. Meanwhile, participation is carried out through collaborative implementation of activities and/or institutional membership. For each model of information delivery, aspiration collection, and/or participation, the level of involvement that can be pursued is identified in a participation grid with very low, low, medium, high, or very high levels (A. Kusumastuti, 2017).

The existence and characteristics of stakeholders have been identified and classified into two categories, namely primary and secondary stakeholders. Determining which stakeholders are involved has implications for the engagement model that can be implemented for each stakeholder. These engagement models were developed from the IAP2 Model with adjustments from existing practices, namely Screening, Online and Offline Consultation, Embedding into Institutions, TV/Radio Media Interviews/Q&As, Experiential Learning, and Collaborative Implementation of Activities/Press Days. Screening is used in the initial stage for stakeholders with the characteristics of nahi primary stakeholders. Information processing as a result of screening is followed by information delivery to other stakeholders within a scheduled timeframe. Rivas-Asanza et al. (2018) Information delivery is also carried out for stakeholders beyond stakeholders with secondary stakeholder characteristics.

IMPLEMENTATION AND EVALUATION OF ESG IN SOFTWARE PROJECTS

ESG Integration Strategy from Planning Stage to Execution

Sustainable Development Goals—the 2030 Agenda for Sustainable Development of 2015—safeguard people and planet, stressing social, cultural, economic, and environmental sustainability. In this context, sustainable transformation becomes a compliance strategy for citizens, organizations, companies, production sectors, and government policies. The creation of software-based business models that integrate financial, ethical, social, and environmental goals allows organizations to comply with this total transformation in a continuous evolution of the shape and how a business can be executed. The goal is to explore new paths for specific solutions to business problems while focusing on addressing global challenges through software solutions (Jakubczak et al., 2021).

Open-source software enables organizations to design customized applications that meet their business models' specific needs. Hence, organizations may build business models and design software-based products that comply with ESG goals. Software-driven solutions may be designed and created to tackle complex societal problems, allowing transdisciplinary research and cooperation among multiple organizations. The ESG dimension in the context of software-driven business transformation is analyzed in this paper, outlining a transdisciplinary research agenda for the academic community in this emerging field. Strategy on ESG-based business models and software-driven products, compliance with the organizational context of goals, and business transformations are three dimensions addressed in the analysis (Hart et al., 2024).

This article shares some ideas and to guide the academic community in identifying new research paths on ESG-aligned governance in software-driven business projects. The recent boom in business transformation strategies to claim compliance with ESG parameters creates the opportunity to open a new research field. Platforms addressed to generic business needs can also face application domain research holes. In this context, academic community proposals for generic and vertical topics are pertinent. To foster the adoption of accessibility-enabling strategies, compliance requirements, and assurance mechanisms, this open research agenda is designed for collaborative research and knowledge sharing. In addition, the action research strategy can be used as an experimental platform to share insights from revert approaches to academic challenges.

Metrics and Success Indicators (KPIs) for ESG-Based Projects

Software-based project development, as a potentially sensitive process, necessitates the implementation of measurement mechanisms, or KPIs, to provide a comprehensive picture of stakeholder attitudes towards previous stages and ongoing project complexity and future exposure. (Nadjib et al., 2019). The measurements and indicators for KPIs of ESG-based projects can be grouped into six metrics, namely Feasibility Test, Environmental Feasibility, Social Feasibility, Sustainable CSR, Category Appropriate Licensing, and Profit Feasibility. Profit Viability will be adjudicated with 6 measure indicators. At the end of the study, the KPIs offered do not perfect the theoretical validity, but contribute to provide insights on measurement for ESG-based projects.

Supporting Tools

The adoption of all-digital processes has attracted significant interest due to its revolutionary potential in almost all enterprise sectors. Investments in software development initiatives have increased significantly in recent years to drive digital innovation. The increasing focus on achieving sustainable financial goals has made environmentally, socially, and governance (ESG)-aligned governance of software projects a contemporary subject in software studies. This article examines how ESG-aligned governance can enhance digital sustainability in software-based initiatives. Therefore, they utilize a qualitative research methodology that is based on a rigorous literature review. The findings of this research illustrate fundamental ESG concepts and provide an open-source risk management system that incorporates various ESG governance activities by utilizing established financial standards. The proposed project governance framework effectively manages finance-oriented software projects due to its decentralized approach, open governance principles, and panarchical governing principles (Pesqueira & Sousa, 2024).

Digital transformation via entirely digital processes is a contemporary technical evolution that has garnered significant interest across nearly all corporate sectors. It requires enhanced software use and investment in associated software development initiatives. In the past decade, the prevalence of management-focused research on software projects has significantly risen. With the rise of software-driven commercial transactions, the success of software projects has emerged as a prominent study subject. The increasing interest in ESG and sustainable finance has garnered the attention of software researchers. Previous studies have demonstrated that ineffective governance in software projects has resulted in significant failures, causing substantial losses in commercial value for software-driven enterprises. Recently, several sustainable finance rules have been introduced to enhance sustainable investments. Recently, several software researchers have initiated the development of a software project governance framework grounded on established financing standards, aimed at harnessing financial advantages such as enhancing accountability, reducing investment risks, and managing business effects (Aracil & Sancak, 2023; Archer, 2022).

Responding to the promotion of ESG-aligned finance, this study is undertaking to address an important gap in the current literature regarding climate, social, and governance principles and risks in governing software projects. The objectives are to explore how ESG-aligned governance can augment digital sustainability in fund-oriented software-driven business projects by providing ESG project governance principles based on recent sustainable finance standards and implementing a risk management framework for coming up with considerations through its risk dashboard and risk project audit tools. This work is based on the notions that software supports digital transformation in achieving broader sustainability goals. Some ESG principles are provided, and an open-source risk management framework of ESG project governance underlining some software project governance activities that can complement the existing financing standards with regard to non-climate ESG principles and risks is formulated (Dye et al., 2021).

Implementation Case Study

Project management offers standards, rules, and tools to assist project managers in executing projects in alignment with established criteria, so ensuring the quality of the resultant goods or services (Septriadi et al., 2019). Two methodologies can be employed in the execution of project management, with a specific focus on organization. These methodologies are anticipated to yield the creation of project planning programs and documentation. (1) Knowledge and Experience-Based Method; (2) Model-Based Method. The phased implementation of corporate governance, standards, guidelines, and associated formal instruments for the technical and operational governance of online/IT-based courses at UNISA is anticipated to yield beneficial effects and enhance institutional and program accreditation regarding product outcomes, services, and governance implementation achievements. It will also provide governance audit evidence to ensure the availability of personnel, adherence to accounting and reporting practices, accessibility of pre-tendering, tendering, and procurement documentation, technical capabilities of the agency, compliance with project standards, best practices, and processes, fulfilment of output specifications and scope, post-completion practices, and sound corporate governance for managers.

These guidelines and tools will facilitate discipline in governance implementation, risk management, monitoring, review, evaluation, and audit oversight conducted by management alongside managers. Effective project management necessitates the integration of corporate governance at all levels and phases of management, including adherence to governmental regulations and oversight, alongside stakeholder engagement in the procurement and execution of internet/intranet-based application programs for the rental and initiation of online courses. The extensive procedure of a government project encompasses procurement and physical execution, as well as the acquisition and deployment of internet/intranet-based program applications for the rental and initiation of online courses, which also pertain to the faculty accountable for them. Formulating and recording the portfolio of implementation responsibilities, the conceptual framework, and the mapping of potential. The execution plan for the regulation and utilization of online courses is anticipated to be entirely realized within the UNISA Faculty of Physics by the conclusion of the 2012-2013 academic year. On-site supervision is conducted by the project manager, with assistance from the Monitoring, Evaluation, and Audit Unit, which is empowered to do audits on the implementation. The organization of supervision, evaluation, and audit is chiefly intended to assess accomplishments relative to production targets concerning time, cost, and aims for ongoing enhancement and standardization over the 2013-2014 academic year (Widiastuti & Nurhayati, 2019).

CHALLENGES, RISKS AND OPPORTUNITIES

Challenges of ESG Governance Implementation in Software Project-Based Organizations

Sustainable development is a multifaceted notion with three primary dimensions: economic, social, and environmental. In this context, environmental sustainability (ES) refers to the ability to attain corporate growth outcomes without jeopardizing the environment and safeguarding the interests of future generations. Thus, a firm that employs environmentally friendly methods and technology to produce ecologically benign goods is regarded as sustainable (Rivas-Asanza et al., 2018). Furthermore, several risk variables influence company continuity: global recession, volatile competitive landscapes, the necessity to minimize expenses, the imperative to take action, and the enhancement of decision-making processes. This condition creates a favorable climate to explore solutions that alleviate it, such as environmental sustainability (ES) and information technology governance (IT governance or ITG). Both options enable businesses to tackle inherently shared challenges: strategy alignment, value creation, performance enhancement methods, risk management, and resource allocation.

Furthermore, ITG is currently acknowledged as a crucial factor for the success of most enterprises in addressing escalating negative environmental impacts, prompting organizations to implement ITG best practices. Nevertheless, these optimal behaviors are hardly associated with an ES methodology. A gap exists between critical research (ITG) in governance and the regulation of innovative phenomena inside strategic planning and non-market methods. The findings underscore the necessity of broadening the perspective of ITG techniques to incorporate the environmental factor, marking an initial effort in this direction. Criteria for achieving ESG alignment in governance across software-driven business initiatives are established. A comparison of ES alignment variables with those of SDS and other broad non-market hazards is presented below. The environmental dimension of ITG techniques is then studied based on this foundation. Ultimately, first observations are made on the governance problems of ES in information technology (IT) initiatives (Eskantar et al., 2024; Meiden & Silaban, 2023).

ESG Non-Compliance Risk in Software Development

The development of software-based businesses faces the important challenge of complying with many global regulations related to sustainability and social responsibility. That is why many companies are looking for solutions to define and implement governance management systems that are appropriate and integrated with their product differentiation. This study aims to understand the challenges and solutions associated with defining, implementing and managing a governance management system that aligns with software company organizations. This study also aims to validate and refine the solutions proposed above, through a series of test cases, where the described research questions are verified. Finally, more case studies to expand the view to new perspectives and companies and validate broader business decisions in applications within larger and more responsible companies (Putra & Anggreani, 2022).

Software to support ESG control and reporting is in high demand to assist with increasingly complex ESG regulatory compliance processes. Companies also need software to support the management and monitoring of environmental, social, and governance sustainability in their plans and strategies on an ongoing basis (Hardwig et al., 2020). The growing demand for these software solutions presents a significant opportunity for software developers. However, it also brings new challenges for software developers, as they must demonstrate that they use governance and software practices that ensure ESG compromises are positive. Software developers are beginning to face new challenges in meeting ESG and supplier requirements. Since 1994, with the first amendment to Directive 82.328 in Italy, the EMAS Regulation, which is applied across all European Union (EU) member states, has emphasized that everyone has the right to a sustainable environment. Starting in 2022, in its guidelines, the EU MSc, which is required to publish information related to sustainability, has become relevant to the above provisions, demonstrating compliance with a series of proposed LSE criteria. ESG is a new trend in corporate governance, which originated in the Nordic countries but has now spread worldwide, including in EU regulations. These regulations require all companies, excluding SMEs, to comply with ESG measures, not only regarding environmental impact but also related to social impact and impact on sound governance (Rivas-Asanza et al., 2018).

Opportunities For Innovation and Competitive Advantage From Implementing ESG Governance

Recently, the international world has been abuzz with the phrase Environmental, Social, and Governance (ESG). This signifies that contemporary enterprises are encountering novel obstacles in evaluating the repercussions of each economic activity. As social entities, corporations are inevitably influenced by the repercussions of their operations, both beneficial and detrimental, on the environment and society. This scenario poses a distinct challenge for organizations to operate judiciously and ethically about their business effect to ensure sustainability. This possibility may be utilized as a catalyst for corporate innovation, perhaps establishing a competitive edge amid fierce rivalry. Numerous successful firms have achieved digital transformation through the integration of ESG principles. All these instances often start by examining environmental and social dimensions included within a framework of transparent and incorrupt governance. Efficient oversight using cutting-edge digital technology, underpinned by precise and verifiable data, enables firms to substantiate all their business choices and operations, therefore ensuring accountability to all stakeholders. The success of these experiences is undeniably relevant and generally applicable. How can firms implement ESG practices to achieve optimal and sustainable results? The initial step is to identify pertinent and pressing ESG issues, at least in the medium term, for inclusion in an ESG roadmap. Organizations must to engage both internal and external stakeholders in recognizing and articulating these matters. This aims to cultivate a collective commitment, particularly among the most prominent stakeholders. This procedure requires considerable time, sometimes extending over many months, and is generally executed via focus group discussions (FGDs) or pilot studies. Consequently, the endorsement of ESG strategy results is crucial, primarily concentrating on reaching consensus about the substance and committing to the execution of the ESG roadmap (Rivas-Asanza et al., 2018).

CONCLUSIONS AND STRATEGIC RECOMMENDATIONS

This article develops a cohesive method for incorporating Environmental, Social, and Governance (ESG) concepts into software project governance. The suggested conceptual paradigm, ABCDE + G, was created to tackle governance issues stemming from ESG requirements. The model designates Business Governance (BG) as the principal institution responsible for managing and overseeing stakeholder interests in the governance process. This research indicates that ESG-oriented software projects encounter novel hurdles, including intricate decision-making, evolving regulatory compliance, sustainable development planning, and the execution of responsible sourcing and resource management techniques. Moreover, the rapid advancement of technology, especially artificial intelligence (AI), is complicated governance by introducing increasingly critical ethical, social, and agency risk concerns. The incorporation of ESG principles into organizational governance is pertinent not just for technology-driven enterprises but also for the broader socio-technical environment. Consequently, several strategic proposals need consideration. Industry practitioners and project managers are advised to promptly adopt project management methodologies that align with sustainability objectives, modify task assignments in current projects to facilitate the integration of ESG principles, and invest in the advancement of software and technology that fulfil ESG standards.

The creation of specialist tools to facilitate ESG-based decision-making is essential. Simultaneously, it is essential for academics and education to commence the integration of ESG concerns into the curriculum of software engineering and information technology governance. Furthermore, the creation of digital learning environments pertinent to sustainability concerns, along with the adoption of project-based learning frameworks that prioritize cooperation, ethics, and green technology, is essential. Prioritization should be given to the creation of theme databases that facilitate multidisciplinary study on ESG. Policy planners and scholars must further investigate how the decision-making process in information technology governance influences the efficacy of carbon emission reduction. Furthermore, examining the influence of executive-level policy interpretation on ESG implementation is crucial. Additional challenges requiring investigation include the mechanisms for reutilizing software assets within an open-source framework, the dynamics of sustainability in Agile software development, and the degree to which model-based development methodologies can guarantee adherence to sustainable process principles. Despite the existence of several international standards in IT governance, its implementation to promote environmental sustainability remains limited. Consequently, extensive and thorough study is required to bridge the knowledge gap, particularly concerning software sustainability and the use of big data in efficiently facilitating the attainment of Sustainable Development Goals (SDGs).

REFERENCES

Ahmad, R., Hussain, A., & Baharom, F. (2018). Software sustainability characteristic for software development towards long living software. *Wseas Transactions on Business and Economics*, *15*, 55–72.

Anibal Altamirano, M., & Sloley, A. A. (2023). Corporate governance: The role of board of directors in the strategic planning process of organizations. In *Strategic Management and International Business Policies for Maintaining Competitive Advantage*. https://doi.org/DOI: 10.4018/978-1-6684-6845-6.ch001

Aracil, E., & Sancak, I. (2023). Sustainable Finance A Multidimensional and Multi actor Framework. In *Essential Concepts of Sustainable Finance an A Z Guide*. https://doi.org/DOI: 10.4324/9781003310891-1

Archer, M. (2022). The ethics of ESG Sustainable finance and the emergence of the market as an ethical subject. *Focaal: Tijdschrift voor Antropologie*, *2022*(93), 18–31. DOI: 10.3167/fcl.2022.930102

Asyraf, M. Z., Suriani, M. J., Ruzaidi, C. M., Khalina, A., Ilyas, R. A., Asyraf, M. R. M., Syamsir, A., Azmi, A., & Mohamed, A. (2022). Development of Natural Fibre-Reinforced Polymer Composites Ballistic Helmet Using Concurrent Engineering Approach: A Brief Review. In *Sustainability (Switzerland)* (Vol. 14, Issue 12). https://doi.org/DOI: 10.3390/su14127092

Awewomom, J., Dzeble, F., Takyi, Y. D., Ashie, W. B., Ettey, E. N. Y. O., Afua, P. E., Sackey, L. N. A., Opoku, F., & Akoto, O. (2024). Addressing global environmental pollution using environmental control techniques: A focus on environmental policy and preventive environmental management. *Discover Environment*, *2*(1). Advance online publication. DOI: 10.1007/s44274-024-00033-5

Ba, Y. (2021). Corporate-Led Environmental Governance: A Theoretical Model. *Administration & Society*, *53*(1), 97–122. DOI: 10.1177/0095399720918512

Bahri, M. I., Agustina, T. S., & Ridha, A. E. (2025). Human resource management in the digital era: Developing digital-first organizational cultures to drive sustainable competitive advantage. In *Innovative Approaches for International Competitiveness Through Human Resource Management*. https://doi.org/DOI: 10.4018/979-8-3373-1005-3.ch003

Bahri, M. I., Dermawan, A. A., & Tambunan, A. A. (2025). Public-Private Collaborations in Smart Cities: Startup-Driven Innovations in E-Government. In *In Startup-Driven E-Government: Digital Innovation for Sustainable Ecosystems* (pp. 61–86). IGI Global Scientific Publishing.

Bahri, M. I., Sirojuzilam, S. S., Rujiman, R. R., & Kismawadi, E. R. (2021). The Influence of Youth in Regional Development Through the Management of Aceh's Special Autonomy Fund in Langsa City. *E-Mabis: Jurnal Ekonomi Manajemen Dan Bisnis*, *22*(1), 42–53. DOI: 10.29103/e-mabis.v22i1.650

Bahri, M. I., Tambunan, A. A., & Zulfikar. (2025). TRANSFORMATION OF HUMAN RESOURCE MANAGEMENT IN THE ERA OF REGIONAL DECENTRALIZATION AND DIGITAL REVOLUTION: A LITERATURE REVIEW AND ITS IMPLICATIONS. *Jurnal Manajemen Rekayasa Dan Inovasi Bisnis*, *3*(Februari), 92–117. https://doi.org/DOI: 10.62375/jmrib.v3i2.451

Bambang, W. (2018). Data Readiness & Technology Assesment for Indonesian Non Profit Organization Using Data Maturity Framework. *International Journal of Scientific and Engineering Research*, *9*(9). http://www.ijser.org

Bamiduro, M., Fatima, I., Lago, P., & Vos, S. (2025). Challenges in Incorporating Sustainability Practices in the Software Lifecycle. In *Lecture Notes in Business Information Processing* (Vol. 539). LNBIP., DOI: 10.1007/978-3-031-85849-9_23

Baporikar, N. (2023). Governance as a catalyst for public sector sustainability. In *Governance as A Catalyst for Public Sector Sustainability*. https://doi.org/DOI: 10.4018/978-1-6684-6966-8

Bibri, S. E., Alexandre, A., Sharifi, A., & Krogstie, J. (2023). Environmentally sustainable smart cities and their converging AI, IoT, and big data technologies and solutions: an integrated approach to an extensive literature review. In *Energy Informatics* (Vol. 6, Issue 1). https://doi.org/DOI: 10.1186/s42162-023-00259-2

Bierwolf, R., & Frijns, P. (2021). Governance - Structures and Human Perspectives. *IEEE Engineering Management Review*, *49*(2), 172–180. DOI: 10.1109/EMR.2021.3079795

Brogi, M., & Lagasio, V. (2025). Do Corporate Governance Frameworks Affect Sustainability Reporting? *Corporate Social Responsibility and Environmental Management*, *32*(3), 3928–3943. DOI: 10.1002/csr.3159

Cahyani, I. R., & Bahri, M. I. (2022). Change Management and Special Autonomy Paradigm: Opportunities and Challenges of Human Resources in Digital Literacy Implementation in Indonesian Regional Libraries. *Congress of Southeast Asian Librarians (CONSAL) XVIII*.

Camacho, F., & Cruz, C. O. (2022). Toll road sector in Brazil: Regulation by contract and recent innovations. *Competition and Regulation in Network Industries*, *23*(2), 135–152. DOI: 10.1177/17835917221087897

Combs, G., & Curran, M. (2008). What can green do for you? How to develop and use a corporate sustainability program. *NPRA Environmental Conference Papers*, 243–249.

Condori Fernandez, N., & Lago, P. (2018). The influence of green strategies design onto quality requirements prioritization. In *Lecture Notes in Computer Science Including Subseries Lecture Notes in Artificial Intelligence and Lecture Notes in Bioinformatics* (Vol. 10753). LNCS., DOI: 10.1007/978-3-319-77243-1_12

Cuong, N. H. (2011a). Enron fiasco: Business difficulty and the role of enron' directors. *Corporate Ownership and Control, 8*(4 B), 165–168. https://doi.org/DOI: 10.22495/cocv8i4c1p2

Cuong, N. H. (2011b). Factors causing Enron's collapse: An investigation into corporate governance and company culture. *Corporate Ownership and Control, 8*(3 G), 585–593.

Dandapani, K., & Shahrokhi, M. (2022). Guest editorial: Historical perspectives on corporate governance debate and introduction to the special issue on corporate governance and sustainability. *Managerial Finance*, *48*(8), 1117–1122. DOI: 10.1108/MF-05-2022-0237

de Freitas Alves, G., & Santos, C. D. (2022). The diffusion of innovations under normative induction in Brazil. *RAUSP Management Journal*, *57*(2), 149–164. DOI: 10.1108/RAUSP-10-2020-0250

Duc, A. N., & Leick, B. (2023). Digital Technologies and Sustainability Paradoxes – An Empirical Study of a Norwegian Media Group. *Lecture Notes in Information Systems and Organisation, 62 LNISO*, 53–62. https://doi.org/DOI: 10.1007/978-3-031-32436-9_5

Dye, J., McKinnon, M., & Van der Byl, C. (2021). Green Gaps: Firm ESG Disclosure and Financial Institutions' Reporting Requirements. *Journal of Sustainability Research*, *3*(1). Advance online publication. DOI: 10.20900/jsr20210006

Edison, H., Wang, X., Jabangwe, R., & Abrahamsson, P. (2018). Innovation Initiatives in Large Software Companies: A Systematic Mapping Study. *Information and Software Technology*, *95*, 1–14. DOI: 10.1016/j.infsof.2017.12.007

Eskantar, M., Zopounidis, C., Doumpos, M., Galariotis, E., & Guesmi, K. (2024). Navigating ESG complexity: An in-depth analysis of sustainability criteria, frameworks, and impact assessment. *International Review of Financial Analysis, 95*. Advance online publication. DOI: 10.1016/j.irfa.2024.103380

Fajri, L. L., Maarif, S., & Sumarwan, U. (2004). PENDEKATAN BUDAYA KERJA UNTUK MENGURANGI KETIDAKSELARASAN ANTAR DIVISI PADA BATIK BOGOR TRADISIKU. *Jurnal Manajemen Dan Agribisnis, 13*(3). Advance online publication. DOI: 10.17358/jma.13.3.217

Hans, A., & Khera, N. (2021). Extracting Insights from Reviews using Cluster Analysis. *CEUR Workshop Proceedings*, •••, 3080.

Hardwig, T., Klötzer, S., & Boos, M. (2020). Software-supported collaboration in small- and medium-sized enterprises. *Measuring Business Excellence*, *24*(1), 1–23. DOI: 10.1108/MBE-11-2018-0098

Hart, N., Kramer, H., & Duncan, A. (2024). Lawrence Berkeley National Laboratory LBL Publications Title Building Performance Software: Portfolio-Level Capabilities and Applications Permalink https://escholarship.org/uc/item/58p6m0k7 *Publication Date*. https://doi.org/DOI: 10.20357/B78P57

Huygh, T., de Haes, S., Joshi, A., & van Grembergen, W. (2018). Answering key global IT management concerns through IT governance and management processes: A Cobit 5 view. *Proceedings of the Annual Hawaii International Conference on System Sciences, 2018-Janua*, 5335–5344.

Ignaim, K., & Fernandes, J. M. (2025). A Feature-based Process for Effective Stakeholder Management in Software Product Development. *IAENG International Journal of Computer Science*, *52*(1), 171–186.

Iyer, K., & K.R, J. (2020). Buying behaviour model of early adopting organizations of radical software innovations. *Journal of Business and Industrial Marketing*, *36*(6). Advance online publication. DOI: 10.1108/JBIM-12-2019-0533

Jain, V., Balakrishnan, A., Beeram, D., Najana, M., & Chintale, P. (2024). Leveraging Artificial Intelligence for Enhancing Regulatory Compliance in the Financial Sector. *International Journal of Computer Trends and Technology*, *72*(5), 124–140. DOI: 10.14445/22312803/ijctt-v72i5p116

Jakubczak, W., Golebiowska, A., Prokopowicz, D., & Jakubczak, R. (2021). The Key Security Problems Related to the Pro-Environmental Economic Transformation and the Implementation of the Principles of Sustainable Development into the Economy. *EUROPEAN RESEARCH STUDIES JOURNAL, XXIV*(4B). Advance online publication. DOI: 10.35808/ersj/2654

Jannah, N., Bahri, M. I., Kismawadi, E. R., & Handriana, T. (2024). The Effect of Green Brand Image and Green Satisfaction on Green Brand Equity Mediated Green Trust Outpatient's. *Quality - Access to Success*, *25*(198). Advance online publication. DOI: 10.47750/QAS/25.198.40

Jeong, S.-J., & Choi, D.-B. (2022). ESG and Managerial Agency Problems. *Korean Journal of Financial Studies*, *51*(4), 417–445. DOI: 10.26845/KJFS.2022.08.51.4.417

Karita, L., Mourão, B. C., & MacHado, I. (2022). Towards a common understanding of sustainable software development. *ACM International Conference Proceeding Series*, 269–278. https://doi.org/DOI: 10.1145/3555228.3555236

Kismawadi, E. R., & Irfan, M. (2025). Artificial Intelligence as a Catalyst for Innovation in Islamic Entrepreneurship: Balancing Ethics and Efficiency. In *Improving Entrepreneurial Processes Through Advanced AI* (pp. 1–16). IGI Global.

Koshy, L., & Shyry, S. P. (2025). Detection of tampered real time videos using deep neural networks. *Neural Computing & Applications*, *37*(11), 7691–7703. DOI: 10.1007/s00521-024-09988-1

Kranz, J. J., Hanelt, A., & Kolbe, L. M. (2016). Understanding the influence of absorptive capacity and ambidexterity on the process of business model change – the case of on-premise and cloud-computing software. *Information Systems Journal*, *26*(5), 477–517. DOI: 10.1111/isj.12102

Kusumastuti, A. (2017). *MULTI STAKEHOLDER INITIATIVE PRACTICES: PROMOTION OF GOOD GOVERNANCE (A CASE OF COMMUNITY EMPOWERMENT PROJECT IN PESANGGARAHAN VILLAGE, BATU DISTRICT, CITY OF BATU, EAST JAVA, INDONESIA)*.

Kusumastuti, F., Kurnia, N., Astuti, S. I., Birowo, M. A., Hartanti, L. E. P., Amanda, N. M. R., & Kurnia, N. (2021). Modul Etis Bermedia Digital. In *Modul Etis Bermedia Digital*.

Lago, P., Funke, M., & Fatima, I. (2024). Architecting for Sustainability with the SAF Toolkit. *Proceedings IEEE 21st International Conference on Software Architecture Companion Icsa C 2024*, 379–380. https://doi.org/DOI: 10.1109/ICSA-C63560.2024.00070

Larsen, E. R. (2017). The importance of excellent definition of project objectives. *Liaison Functions 2017 Core Programming Area at the 2017 Aiche Annual Meeting, 2017-Octob*, 235–248.

Larsen, E. R. (2018). The importance of excellent definition of project objectives. *Management Division 2018 Core Programming Area at the 2018 Aiche Annual Meeting*, 82–95.

Latifah, F. N., & Widiatmoko, J. (2022). PENGARUH STRUKTUR KEPEMILIKAN TERHADAP CORPORATE SOCIAL RESPONSIBILITY DAN DAMPAKNYA PADA NILAI PERUSAHAAN. In *Jurnal Ilmiah Mahasiswa Akuntansi) Universitas Pendidikan Ganesha* (Vol. 13, Issue 03). www.wbcsd.org

Mangutana, A. Y., Bisnis, P. M., Manajemen, P. S., Petra, U. K., & Siwalankerto, J. (2016). Implementasi Prinsip - Prinsip Good Corporate Governance Untuk Strategi Keberlanjutan Perusahaan Konstruksi Di Sumba. *Ágora*, *4*(1).

Marar, H. W. (2024). Advancements in software engineering using AI. *Computer Software and Media Applications*, *6*(1). Advance online publication. DOI: 10.24294/csma.v6i1.3906

Matsiola, M., Lappas, G., & Yannacopoulou, A. (2024). Generative AI in Education: Assessing Usability, Ethical Implications, and Communication Effectiveness. *Societies (Basel, Switzerland)*, *14*(12). Advance online publication. DOI: 10.3390/soc14120267

Mehra, R., Sharma, V. S., Kaulgud, V., Podder, S., & Burden, A. P. (2022). *Towards a green quotient for software projects*. https://doi.org/DOI: 10.1145/3510457.3513077

Meiden, C., & Silaban, A. (2023). Exploring the Measurement of Environmental Performance in Alignment with Environmental, Social, and Governance (ESG): A Qualitative Study. *Information Sciences Letters*, *12*(9), 2287–2297. DOI: 10.18576/isl/120932

Moshnyaga, V. G. (2013). An assessment of software lifecycle energy. *2013 23rd International Workshop on Power and Timing Modeling Optimization and Simulation Patmos 2013*, 112–119. https://doi.org/DOI: 10.1109/PATMOS.2013.6662163

Muralidhar, R., Borovica-Gajic, R., & Buyya, R. (2022). Energy Efficient Computing Systems: Architectures, Abstractions and Modeling to Techniques and Standards. *ACM Computing Surveys*, *54*(11s). Advance online publication. DOI: 10.1145/3511094

Nadjib, M., Moedjari, S., Nasrullah, H., Hadiputro, A. N., Bonakarta, K., Blok, B., Sa, J., No, T., & Jombang, K. (2019). Penentuan Faktor Kritis Keberhasilan Implementasi ERP di Perusahaan Baja Menggunakan Formulasi Keberhasilan Dari DeLone & McLean. *Jurnal IKRA-ITH Informatika, 3*(3).

Noe, R., Hollenbeck, J., Gerhart, B., & Wright, P. (2006). *Human Resources Management: Gaining a Competitive Advantage, Tenth Global Edition*. kansaigaidai.ac.jp. https://www.kansaigaidai.ac.jp/asp/files/academics/course-syllabi/fall-semester-2019/BUS9F19.pdf

Nurmalasari. (2013). Pengukuran Tingkat Kematangan Tata Kelola Teknologi Informasi Menggunakan Maturity Level Domain Po Dan Ai Framework Cobit 4.1. *Pilar Nusa Mandiri, Vol. IX*(2).

Ogunkan, D. V. (2022). Achieving sustainable environmental governance in Nigeria: A review for policy consideration. In *Urban Governance* (Vol. 2, Issue 1). https://doi.org/DOI: 10.1016/j.ugj.2022.04.004

Oliver, D., & Lainhart, J. (2012). COBIT 5: Adding Value Through Effective Geit. *Edpacs*, *46*(3), 1–12. DOI: 10.1080/07366981.2012.706472

Oyedeji, S., Shamshiri, H., Porras, J., & Lammert, D. (2021). Software Sustainability: Academic Understanding and Industry Perceptions. In *Lecture Notes in Business Information Processing: Vol. 434 LNBIP*. https://doi.org/DOI: 10.1007/978-3-030-91983-2_3

Pang, C.-Y. (2015). A cross-platform architecture with intelligent agents for dynamic processes and services composition. In *Achieving Enterprise Agility Through Innovative Software Development*. https://doi.org/DOI: 10.4018/978-1-4666-8510-9.ch003

Park, J., Choi, W., & Jung, S. U. (2022). Exploring Trends in Environmental, Social, and Governance Themes and Their Sentimental Value Over Time. *Frontiers in Psychology*, *13*. Advance online publication. DOI: 10.3389/fpsyg.2022.890435 PMID: 35837641

Patil, R. A., Ghisellini, P., & Ramakrishna, S. (2020). Towards Sustainable Business Strategies for a Circular Economy: Environmental, Social and Governance (ESG) Performance and Evaluation. In *An Introduction to Circular Economy*. https://doi.org/DOI: 10.1007/978-981-15-8510-4_26

Pesqueira, A., & Sousa, M. J. (2024). Exploring the role of big data analytics and dynamic capabilities in ESG programs within pharmaceuticals. *Software Quality Journal*, *32*(2). Advance online publication. DOI: 10.1007/s11219-024-09666-4

Prado Muci de Lima, I., & Costa Fernandes, D. (2024). ESG 2.0: The New Perspectives for Human Rights Due Diligence. In *Csr Sustainability Ethics and Governance: Vol. Part F3171*. https://doi.org/DOI: 10.1007/978-3-031-56619-6_14

Pribadi, M. R., & Irsyad, H. (2018). Model Konseptual Penerapan Tata Kelola TI PLN Pembangkitan Sumbagsel Berdasarkan COBIT 5. *Jurnal Ilmiah Informatika Global, 9*(1). Advance online publication. DOI: 10.36982/jig.v9i1.440

Putra, K. R., & Anggreani, F. (2022). Perancangan Arsitektur Enterprise Pada Instansi Pemerintahan: Systematic Literature Review. *Computing and Education Technology Journal (CETJ)*. https://ppjp.ulm.ac.id/journals/index.php/cetj

Qing, C., & Jin, S. (2023). Does ESG and Digital Transformation affects Corporate Sustainability? The Moderating role of Green Innovation. *ArXiv.Org, 3*.

Rivas-Asanza, W., Celleri-Pacheco, J., Andrade-Garda, J., García-Vázquez, R., Mato-Abad, V., Rodríguez-Yáñez, S., & Suárez-Garaboa, S. (2018). Environmental sustainability in information technologies governance. *Sustainability (Switzerland), 10*(12). Advance online publication. DOI: 10.3390/su10124792

Samuel, & Augustine, Y. (2019). Competitive Advantage and Corporate Governance in Indonesia with Enterprise Risk Management as Mediating. *Journal of Economics and Sustainable Development*. https://doi.org/DOI: 10.7176/jesd/10-8-05

Sauvola, T., Lwakatare, L. E., Karvonen, T., Kuvaja, P., Olsson, H. H., Bosch, J., & Oivo, M. (2015). Towards customer-centric software development: A multiple-case study. *Proceedings 41st Euromicro Conference on Software Engineering and Advanced Applications Seaa 2015*, 9–17. https://doi.org/DOI: 10.1109/SEAA.2015.63

Septriadi, R., Firdaus, F., & Cholil, W. (2019). Evaluasi Tata Kelola Teknologi Informasi Menggunakan Framework Simcobit, Studi Kasus pada Sekolah Tinggi Ilmu Kesehatan Bina Husada Palembang. *Jurnal Ilmiah Informatika Global, 10*(1). Advance online publication. DOI: 10.36982/jiig.v10i1.747

Shapsugova, M. (2023). ESG principles and social responsibility. *E3s Web of Conferences, 420*. https://doi.org/DOI: 10.1051/e3sconf/202342006040

Silva, A. S., Araujo, A., Palomino, P., Araujo, R., & Dermeval, D. (2024). *Mastering Requirements Volatility: Strategies for Dynamic Environments and Multiple Stakeholders in Government Software Projects*. IEEE., DOI: 10.1109/ACCESS.2024.3510056

Singhal, N., & Konguvel, E. (2022). An Approach for Restaurant Management System during Covid-19. *2022 International Conference on Computer Communication and Informatics Iccci 2022*. https://doi.org/DOI: 10.1109/ICCCI54379.2022.9740862

Surbeck, C. Q., & Tyson, L. (2024). Leveraging Envision and ESG for Improved Sustainability Performance in Projects and Engineering Companies. *World Environmental and Water Resources Congress 2024 Climate Change Impacts on the World We Live in Proceedings of the World Environmental and Water Resources Congress 2024*, 1220–1228. https://doi.org/DOI: 10.1061/9780784485477.108

Tencati, A. (2016). Corporate Reporting Frameworks. In *A Handbook of Corporate Governance and Social Responsibility*. https://doi.org/DOI: 10.4324/9781315564791-27

Trzeciak, M., Sienkiewicz, Ł. D., & Bukłaha, E. (2022). Enablers of Open Innovation in Software Development Micro-Organization. *Journal of Open Innovation*, *8*(4). Advance online publication. DOI: 10.3390/joitmc8040174

Udhayakumar, S. P., & Sivasubramanian, M. (2024). Impact of demographic attributes on requirement elicitation and quality software development. *International Journal of Intelligent Enterprise*, *11*(4), 317–334. DOI: 10.1504/IJIE.2024.141869

Venters, C. C., Capilla, R., Betz, S., Penzenstadler, B., Crick, T., Crouch, S., Nakagawa, E. Y., Becker, C., & Carrillo, C. (2018). Software sustainability: Research and practice from a software architecture viewpoint. *Journal of Systems and Software*, *138*, 174–188. DOI: 10.1016/j.jss.2017.12.026

Volpato, T., Oliveira, B. R. N., Garcés, L., Capilla, R., & Nakagawa, E. Y. (2017). Two perspectives on reference architecture sustainability. *ACM International Conference Proceeding Series, Part F1305*, 188–194. https://doi.org/DOI: 10.1145/3129790.3129815

Widiastuti, A., & Nurhayati, A. S. (2019). *Faktor-Faktor Yang Mempengaruhi Pengembangan Desa Wisata Nganggring Sleman*.

Wu, L., & Jin, S. (2022). Corporate Social Responsibility and Sustainability: From a Corporate Governance Perspective. *Sustainability (Switzerland)*, *14*(22). Advance online publication. DOI: 10.3390/su142215457

Yrjönkoski, K., Jaakkola, H., Systä, K., Mikkonen, T., & Henno, J. (2019). Software business: A short history and trends for the future. *CEUR Workshop Proceedings*, •••, 2508.

Chapter 10
Compliance and Regulation in Green Software Projects

S. Ida Evangeline
https://orcid.org/0000-0003-2997-7897
Government College of Engineering, Tirunelveli, India

ABSTRACT

With the rate of digital transformation speeding up in various industries, environmental concern surrounding software systems is defying closer regulation and organizational consideration. The chapter will analyze the issue of compliance and regulation that play a crucial part in determining the green software development in business project management schemes. It examines the impact that global sustainability requirements, industry standards and regulatory vehicles, including ISO 14001, IEEE 1680, the Green Deal, and ESG disclosure requirements have on software project lifecycles. The chapter can serve as a helpful road map and transfer a practical set of skills to incorporate environmental compliance into projects and Agile, DevOps processes, procurement, quality assurance and reporting. It examines carbon accounting, energy profiling and automated compliance monitoring tools, and presents realistic ways of developing software in line with environmental objectives and legislative requirements.

INTRODUCTION

Sustainability has become one of those breaking frontiers in the ever-changing world of digital shift, not only in physical infrastructure, but also in the software that forms the base of businesses running operations. As companies rush to use

DOI: 10.4018/979-8-3373-4652-6.ch010

digital technologies, the environmental consequences of a software system which is in some instances not prominently included in conventional steps on sustainability have moved to the forefront (Assoratgoon & Kantabutra, 2023). The practice of green software engineering no longer remains on the fringe, as the focus of the field has centered on the design, development and deployment of software systems that have the least environmental impact and footprint. It is also becoming an operating necessity because of global climate goals, evolving consumer demands and a more demanding regulatory environment (Matthew et al. 2024).

The chapter begins with an investigation on how sustainability relates to software development and, in this case, through the prism of compliance and regulation. Although a large part of the ongoing discussion on green software lies in its technical efficiency, optimization, and focused rules concerning ethical coding, the program could not be truly effective until it is framed in a right regulatory framework. Adherence cannot be treated as a simple act of bureaucratic compliance, but rather a tool of achieving a desired software project-scientifically justified environmental alignment, e.g. minimizing greenhouse emissions of greenhouse gases, limiting energy use, and addressing digital waste.

Business enterprises are increasingly taking-on the agenda of sustainability in their corporate operations and are facing an increasingly elaborate ecosystem of laws, policies and standards that influence how software is developed. Whether it is international treaties such as the Paris Climate Accord or regional initiatives such as the European Union Green Deal and regional approaches like those of the United States on energy efficiency in IT, the compliance environment is becoming very complicated and far-reaching in terms of consequences. These directions are increasingly applied directly to software development, or indirectly via procurement policies, environmental reporting practices and calls by stakeholders to improve environmental, social and governance (ESG) performance (Ogutu et al. 2023).

Here, compliance and regulation evolve to be not only two levers in project management but would be a lever creating constraints that the acceptable environmental impact should be based on, as well as a lever that encourages innovation within the constraints. The complex part of this is how the project managers can turn these abstract policy objectives into project deliverables. This will entail inculcating the aspects of sustainability into each of the stages of software lifecycle, including planning and design, implementation, testing, deployment and the after-release monitoring. Importantly, such an integration should adhere to the technical standards, as well as the organizational processes, the procurements procedures, the risk management processes, and the reporting procedures (Gangai et al. 2024).

The chapter sets out regulatory compliance as a non-reactive or standalone activity but one that is also strategic to green software project management. It examines the way compliance is built into different methodologies. Agile, DevOps and traditional waterfall strategies and it demonstrates the tools and measures that allow continuity of monitoring and validation. It also analyzes what an organization can do when ensuring that the minimum of compliance transitions to a voluntary alignment into social regulations, where the policy frameworks are the driving force of sustainable innovation.

This chapter fills the gap between the field of regulation and technology by offering a detailed account of how law, policy, standards inform green software development. It posits that the success of environmental sustainability in software projects does not just lie on the optimization of code or architectural construction but also alignment on the part of the institution towards emerging regulatory expectations. Through this, it sets up the motivation towards a sensitive and operationally applicable methodology of installing compliance as part of the DNA of green software engineering.

GLOBAL AND REGIONAL REGULATORY LANDSCAPE

The drive to make software development greener is becoming encompassed by a multi-strata regulatory environment that incorporates international agreements, national legislation, regional regulations, and business-industry specific standards. All these frameworks impact the design, development, deployment, and management of software as regards to environmental impact as well. Not only is this regulatory landscape critical insight to project managers in understanding how to achieve those sustainability objectives without breaking the law, but also to software engineers embarking on development with a need to ensure operational and legal compliance (Kempe & Massey, 2021).

Global climate and sustainability goals, the macro-level climate and sustainability goals in global environmental governance are provided by the United Nations Sustainable Development Goals regarded as SDGs and the Paris Agreement. Though these tools do not purposefully regulate computer software, they can have substantial downstream effect on country-level policies and corporate disclosures in the field of ESG. As an example, the focus of the Paris agreement on carbon reduction has seen governments and regulators enforce carbon accounting across all sectors including the digital and software processes (Neogi et al. 2022).

First, the European Union, regionally has led in pursuing regulatory approaches that have a direct and indirect impact on green software. The European Green Deal, which is a broad strategy on how EU can achieve climate-neutrality by 2050, also prohibits several clauses that affect the environmental impact of digital technologies. Such an initiative is the Digital Product Passport that is likely to contain the details of energy efficiency and the lifecycle of digital services and software parts. The EU

Taxonomy Regulation also categories sustainable economic activities and requires companies to report on their activities including software, and their environmental alignment (Gu et al. 2021).

The most influential of all standards globally is ISO 14001 which is an international standard of environmental management systems. Although ISO 14001 is not intentional to software, it creates an organizational achievement which companies may incorporate in order to control their environmental dimensions of software engineering. The standard promotes a culture of unending enhancement, lifecycle thinking and compliance with regulations, which do not contradict green software initiatives. Designing software products in organizations that have been ISO 14001 certified has increased chances where sustainability can be implanted into the product (Fang & Shao, 2022).

Within the technology industry, industry specifications (like the IEEE 1680 (Environmental Assessment of Electronic Products) standard, as well as the IEEE 1680 related ePEAT (Electronic Product Environmental Assessment Tool) criteria) were developed very much hardware based but are now being expanded to encompass software energy consumption and resource costs. These criteria continue to consider the impact of software in accelerating hardware energy usage and data centers functions thus making software a hub in the estimation of sustainability (Ozili, 2022).

Environmental Protection Agency (EPA) and Department of Energy (DOE) of the United States have provided recommendations on sustainable computing—especially as regards cloud services, data centers, and software- facilitate optimization of hardware. Although, traditionally, U.S. regulations have tended to be more disjointed than at the EU level, recent changes, including proposed federal climate disclosure rules by the Securities and Exchange Commission (SEC) have seen an acceleration of expectations there when it comes to environmental reporting, and this must extend to the emissions wrought by digital operations (Verdecchia et al. 2021).

Corporate governance mechanisms, in particular ESG (Environmental, Social, Governance) protocols today perform a quasi-regulatory role and establish a level of expectations which goes beyond what the environment law commands. Investors, procurement organizations as well as regulatory agencies have a tendency to use ESG measurements to find out how sustainable the organization is. New areas that were not previously covered in ESG assessments are now being examined as items which refine software development and digital infrastructure such as their carbon footprint, efficiency of data uses and energy requirements (Yang et al. 2024).

This changing quilt of international and local rules means a compliance requirement to project managers. Those projects which do not consider the impacts on the environment may suffer not only legal and financial punishment but also lose reputation and business opportunities. Conversely, the ones that actively become aligned to these regulatory frameworks will be able to access green funding, increase the level of stakeholder trust, as well as become leaders in sustainability innovation (Mishra, et al. 2025).

The point that becomes evident out of this regulatory setting is two-fold; on the one hand, enforcement regulations tend to predispose a burden of compliance; on the other hand, they provide a more organized framework of operationalizing green software principles. Organizations can meet such externally declared mandates by translating them into internal project requirements so that any software programs that they implement are part of overall climate and sustainability goals.

INTEGRATION OF COMPLIANCE INTO PROJECT MANAGEMENT FRAMEWORKS

One of the most important--and difficult--parts of green software engineering involve translating environmental regulations and sustainability standards into the kind of action that can take place on a project. To the project manager compliance is no longer downstream of legal teams or audit of post deployment. Rather, it has to be an indispensible part of the project planning, execution and delivery and incorporated wholly in the methodologies that serve as guides to software development. Regardless of an Agile, DevOps, or compliance with the traditional Waterfall approaches, adjusting the project to green compliance would imply revisiting the way of work, delivering and allocating roles and responsibilities (Ahmad Ibrahim et al. 2022).

The iterative and incremental development of Agile environments gives a special chance to introduce environmental check points at frequent intervals. It is possible to add user stories or acceptance criteria as sustainability-related tasks such as energy profiling, carbon accounting, or eco-efficiency testing to the backlog. Sprint reviews can be used as a point of measuring the adherence to the environmental standards, whereas a retrospective can be used as a time when sustainability gaps can be considered and further solutions can be implemented. Agile artifacts like the Definition of Done can be extended to cover environmental compliance status indicators to make sure that the approach to sustainability does not become an after-thought towards the end of the project but moves with it as a quality attribute (Rashid et al. 2021).

DevOps, with its preferred focus on automation, continuous integration/continuous deployment (CI/CD), and infrastructure as code introduces not only possibilities, but also challenges to integrating regulatory compliance. What automated pipelines can do on the one hand is to include checks on sustainability like ensuring that building processes were not too power-intensive or raising alerts about code that causes wasteful use of resources. Conversely, visibility on compliance risks can be impeded by the lightning-fast deployment of DevOps as well as decentralized decision-making. To counter this, companies should implement the use of tools that offer instantaneous responses on the performance of the environmental state, include the metrics of green in the CI/CD dashboards, and implement governance guidelines which enforce the maintenance of the sustainability standards across disparate groups (Leong et al. 2023).

Conventional project management methodology like PMBOK or PRINCE2-based will adopt a more systematic and documentation-intense design and may be beneficial in incorporating finer grain compliance frameworks. Such practices assist formal risk registries, baselines of the required actions, and change management mechanisms that may directly deal with the regulatory and sustainability issues. The entire requirements of environmental compliance can be charted directly to project scope document, quality assurance strategy, the procurement plan and the communication strategy towards the stakeholders. Moreover, the environmental performance measures may be considered as one of the decision-making criteria in favor of structured gate reviews and milestones approvals (Almusawi & Khalefa, 2021).

Irrespective of the adopted approach, compliance with project management requires mental, as well as practical, transformation. It obliges project teams to make sustainability a non-functional requirement like security or performance that will need to be acknowledged through the software lifecycle. This entails early detection of any pertinent regulatory structures, legal interpretation of law language into technical specifications and continuous interaction with the compliance officers, lawyer and sustainability professionals (Feng, 2022).

The documentation is a major component in such a process of integration. Keeping a close document of the enviro-checks, design choices, testing and mitigation strategies not only makes it easier to keep each other accountable but also makes them ready to face the external audits and external verification process. These records can further be used to facilitate ESG reporting, which enables organisations to report issues related to their sustainability to shareholders, customers and regulators.

Team culture and leadership equally matter. The sponsors of the project and the product owners are obliged to focus on the environment compliance at early stages, and the development teams should be trained and assisted so that they could comprehend all the aspects of sustainability conditions. This could be facilitated by forming cross-functional sustainability committees or putting in place a compliance champion who will assist in making sure that regulatory considerations are always taken care of at all levels of a project (Wen & Qiang, 2022).

However, the bottom line is that compliance should not be a piece ministered in project management practice but an ongoing process which will change with the changes in regulation, technological trends, and corporate emphasis. It affects the notion of environmental responsibility, which till now is more of a peripheral concern, but rather, makes it a matter of central project success so that software teams can come up with solutions that are not just useful and easy to use, but also environmentally sound and legally legal.

TOOLS, METRICS, AND MONITORING MECHANISMS

To ensure that the green software projects meet environmental standards and internal sustainability targets, powerful tool, precise metrics, and credible monitoring processes are needed. Although the stage has been set with respect to intent and structure, there is a more tangible need in the realm of instrumentation which involves quantitative analysis, performance monitoring, and feedback loops, through which compliance will transpire as a measurable endpoint that can be managed and advanced over time. This section goes into the operations and technology framework that can support the translation of compliance mandates to measurable outcomes (Freed et al. 2023).

The bedrock of the green software compliance is carbon accounting also known as greenhouse gas (GHG) counting the emissions of greenhouse that are related to software development and use. The main causes of software carbon footprints include compute energy, data transmission, storage and end-user device. Systems like the Green Software Foundation Software Carbon Intensity (SCI) specification offer frameworks of finding the emissions at the software level. These frameworks provide unit of work-normalized metrics (e.g. per API call, user session or transaction level) so that cross-project and cross-platform comparisons can be made fairly (Bolón-Canedo et al. 2024).

A number of carbon profiling and energy analysis platforms have come up to assist in this. Application and service energy tracking can be done with tools such as Cloud Carbon Footprint, Scaphandre and GreenFrame which enable teams to track and compare the energy usage of applications that are deployed on the cloud infrastructure or locally. These tools also give breakdowns of power consumption on CPU, memory, and storage giving engineers an opportunity to optimize their code on energy usage and discover operations consuming a lot of resources. By making the metrics open to CI/CD pipelines they can be monitored and displayed continually allowing sustainability data to become as available as performance or security metrics (Katal et al. 2023).

Other services that cloud providers have started to offer include sustainability dashboard, through which emissions and resource utilization can be monitored. As an example, Microsoft Azure has an Emissions Impact Dashboard, AWS an Customer Carbon Footprint Tool, and Google Cloud an Carbon Footprint Reporting offering providing transparency on the environmental impact of cloud service providers which are now part and parcel of most software systems. These dashboards do more than just provide compliance perspectives, as they contribute to internalized sustainability reporting and alignment to ESG goals (Ahmed et al. 2023).

In addition to energy use, other resource efficiency benchmarks, including memory footprint, storage requirements, network bandwidth, and compute cycles are also being used as the proxy measures of environmental performance. These indicators are of interest especially to serverless and microservices, in which distributed functions can dynamically scale to meet user demand. Monitoring tools such as Prometheus, Grafana and Datadog can be used to visualize these metrics and signal to teams working on projects that these parameters are being monitored so that teams not only manage overall system health but are able to manage environmental impact as well.

To make the compliance procedures less time-consuming, other companies operate them using automated policy engines that enforce sustainability regulations across the development lifecycle. Such tools as the Open Policy Agent (OPA), or homegrown engines that utilize rules may be set up to prohibit the deployment of environments that meet either energy limits or non-conformance to environmental regulations. These systems with the help of automated testing have the side effects of non-compliant builds being caught early and can be fixed before shipping (Raza & Khan, 2022).

The other requirement is to monitor the manner in which the environmental decision is made and put in practice using audit trail and traceability logs. These records contribute to internal governance and external audit and are transparent and accountable. They also guide the fulfillment of disclosure requirements like those under frameworks like the EU Corporate Sustainability Reporting Directive (CSRD) or Task Force on Climate-related Financial Disclosures (TCFD).

Measures do not mean anything unless they instruct decisions. Hence, in successful green software projects, the feedback mechanisms are integrated such that compliance information are connected to planning, design and prioritize. The dashboards can be used during the sprint reviews, quantify sustainability parameters in Key Performance Indicators (KPIs) or carry out retrospective analysis to get acquainted with the trade-offs between the performance and energy consumption. Contextualizing and making compliance measurable makes metrics actionable so it can become part of a continuous improvement process as opposed to something that is a burden of the bureaucracy (Irani et al. 2022).

Nevertheless, there still exist difficulties. Most of the tools are not uniform, interoperable or validated with respect to regulatory standards. Furthermore, green metrics may differ based on the use patterns, sources of the energy and/or system boundaries, thereby making cross-comparison to be a challenging task. Consequently, to meet the regulatory requirements, organizations need to integrate the quantitative analysis with the application of expert judgment so that the process of sustainability assessment would be rigorous, open, and compliant with all regulatory requirements.

To conclude, green software compliance relies on tools and metrics that will serve as the basis of its operations. They allow companies to convert their theoretical sustainability objectives into quantifiable results and come up with informed decisions that will have to weigh functionality, cost, and environmental responsibility. These tools ensure there is a culture of data-driven sustainability when integrated with day-to-day operations to facilitate not only compliance but also innovation.

RISKS, AUDITS, AND REGULATORY ACCOUNTABILITY

With maturation of the regulatory frameworks surrounding the concept of sustainability in software development, an organization can expect more scrutiny on to its environmental claims and practices. Green software projects are no longer being sheltered by the legal, financial and reputation perils. Violation of environmental policy, or rather, lack of evidence that they sustain what they claim, may lead to court cases, penalties, disturbances in operation and loss of brand trust. This, therefore, means there is a need to organize effective accountability systems and conduct readiness on environmental audit to aid risk management and regulatory compliance on the green software projects (De Almeida et al. 2021).

Regulatory non-compliance is one of the main risks in the field that can be related to the inability to achieve certain standards of environmental compliance, poor disclosure, or the false claiming of a given product regarding sustainability performance. To give an example, when a company sells its software as either being an eco-efficient or a carbon-neutral enterprise without strict verifiable data, it may attract criticism of greenwashing which is the act of creating a false impression about its environmental impression. Truth-in-advertising laws, environmental labeling regulations, and ESG reporting requirements are some of the ways in which regulatory authorities in places like the European Union and the United States are getting stricter in cracking down on greenwashing (Zhao & Gómez Fariñas, 2023).

Simultaneously, the third-party audits are on the rise and these are acquiring the required necessity of defining environmental compliance within the projects of software. These audits can be done by an authority body, investigation agencies or ESG investment firms. Audits determine the suitability with which an organization has implemented right mechanisms to monitor, record and control the effects of its electronic infrastructural systems on the environment. Using the example of ISO 14001-certified entities, these firms are required to be audited periodically whereby their environmental management systems are checked to ensure that they are still effective, current, and in concurrence with the changing trend of regulatory expectations.

The preparation of green software projects under audit has various levels. The first of them is documentation integrity: organizations have to keep sufficient records about the decisions made related to sustainability, environmental indicators, lifecycle analysis, and risk mitigation strategies. These recordings will show not only compliance but also can be used in situations of legal challenges or investigations by the investors. Second is that of transparency in processes, which require teams to demonstrate the manner in which the environmental concerns are integrated within modules of software lifecycle including requirements engineering, system design, development, testing, and deployment (Liu et al. 2021).

Further, the compliance matrix and risk registers may be utilized to detect sustainability-associated risks in advance and deal with them. These tools assist teams in predicting change relating to regulations, identifying possible areas of non-compliance, and recording mitigation responses. To give an example, a project may document the potential risk in the project of breaching carbon intensity budgets at deployment in a cloud environment and offer in turn mitigating actions, like regional workload-optimization or refactoring of the code base, to reduce processing overheads (Zetzsche & Anker-Sørensen, 2022).

Legal liability in this situation will not be just a liability in terms of the environmental damage but will also be failure to comply with the contractual sustainability requirements e.g. the requirements stipulated in government tenders or ESG commitments as made by corporates. Particularly, the focus of clauses in contracts by the public sector is on addition of requirements of either carbon transparency or green software principles. Failure to perform to these terms may lead to cancellation of contracts, fines or lead to future business prospects being cut out (Ahlström & Monciardini, 2022).

Regulatory accountability in addition to complying looks at the accountability of the stakeholders. Heat on digital product environmental impacts It is an increasing demand by investors, customers, employees, and advocacy groups to see more transparency in the way that digital products affect the environment. Sustainability charters and public environmental dashboards are now becoming the norm in open-source projects and platforms, and help build not only credibility, but also ensure readiness in formal regulatory frequency. Companies which exhibit transparency in their sustainability strategy tend to have a competitive edge especially when dealing with ESG driven procurement and investment worlds (Ren & Ji, 2021).

New technologies therefore present a viable future towards achieving accountability. Automated verification and tamper-proof record-based analytics As a potential solution to automate verification and create tamper-proof compliance records, blockchain-based audit trails, artificial intelligence-based compliance analytics, and smart contracts are being considered. Although the technologies discussed below are early inventions within the sustainability compliance platform, they should give us a picture of what the future would hold as far as environmental responsibility is concerned- a real-time change that cannot be changed (Hermawan et al. 2024).

To conclude, the nature of risks of green software compliance is multi-dimensional in the sense it falls into legal, financial, operational, and reputational categories. These risks cannot just be dealt with through technical perfection but also institutional preparedness towards audit and scrutiny. Organizations can not only meet expectations of regulators in terms of compliance but also can take the lead of excellence in transparency, verifiability and perpetual amelioration in the emerging green software environment by constructing their own systems with such priorities.

CASE STUDIES AND BEST PRACTICES

Transcending the theory/practice divide, real-life case studies provide critical information on the way organizations are wading through this difficult landscape towards compliance with green software. These indicators describe the potentiality of regulatory consistency, tactical project organization and technological creation accomplishing to generate computer software solutions together with functional and ecological aims. Significantly, they do not only present technical reforms undertaken but also changes in organization that must be instantiated in an organizational attempt to make sustainability part and parcel of the software development processes.

Case Study 1: Enterprise SaaS Platform Embedding Carbon-Aware Architecture

Due to its commitment to minimise the carbon footprint of its cloud-hosted services, a large enterprise SaaS provider wanted to improve on performance and scalability. The company is working under mounting pressure by investors to enhance its ESG performance and took a green transformation initiative that uses the guidelines of the Green Software foundation involving software carbon intensity (SCI) (Gupta & Gupta, 2024).

Increasing the carbon intensity data to real-time levels was incorporated into the deployment strategy of the project by dynamically scheduling workloads when the grid carbon intensity was lower utilising regional emissions profiles to enable flexibility. As an example, batch processes and analytics jobs have been stopped or moved to different geographies with renewable energy. Such move not only cut the SCI of the major services but allowed the company to signal its actual practice in its annual sustainability reporting, which contributes to ESG ratings increase (Rao, 2025).

The Agile process had compliance in it. Carbon benchmarks were established as acceptance criteria, energy profiling was included into CI/CD pipelines in terms of open-source solutions, and environmental impact reporting was surfaced on internal dashboards. Notably, these practices were not considered as the value addition, they made such practices as a mandatory practice with internal policies and executive sponsorship.

Case Study 2: Public Sector IT Platform and the EU Green Deal

A national digital government agency in one European country reacting to the European Commission green deal and circular economy action plan, started a program to green its digital infrastructure both catering to citizens, web facing services, and internally used administrative tools. The agency has harmonized its focus with EU regulations like the idea of Digital Product Passport initiative and ISO 14001 standards (Santarius et al. 2023).

The top-down strategy of the project was to approach compliance, where the requirements of sustainability were clearly incorporated into the project charters and procurement contracts. The vendors should have shown that they fitted the green-design guidelines and software vendors were judged on their energy consumption and data transfer rate and flexible-reuse features (Sharma et al. 2022).

In the development process, the agency used life cycle assessment (LCA) tools to calculate the estimate of the environmental impact of various architectural decisions, such as the use of monolithic or microservices architectures and deployment of the system into the clouds or on-premises hosting. Such observations were used to formulate design choices that substantially reduced the amount of energy consumed by the platform by 22%, as part of the environmentally-friendly pledges made by the agency.

Independent evaluators performed the audits, both in terms of technicalities and in terms of adherence to available sustainability policies. The acquired knowledge was stored and shared with other EU member states making the agency a role model of regulatory-based digital sustainability (Hainsch et al. 2022).

Best Practices Emerging Across Projects

As a result of these and other projects, a number of best practices have appeared:

- Compliance-as-Code: Enabling policies and rules associated with sustainability in an infrastructure code and CI/CD configurations enable compliance to occur in an automated and mass-scale manner. This will involve threshold alerts, deployment blocking of those deployments that do not meet KPIs in the environments, and automated logging toward auditing.

- Cross-functional Governance: Cross functional governance is necessary to make green software compliant, including software engineers, legal teams, sustainability officers, and heads of procurement. The effective projects have established teamwork called the green compliance task forces, which leads to the convergence of the silos.
- Carbon-Aware Design Thinking Carbon-aware design thinking projects that manage to succeed in minimizing the environmental footprint have adopted carbon-aware design principles in its initial stages of conceptualizing. These incorporate information decreasing, proficient algorithms, information center localization and deliberate overloading.
- Stakeholder Transparency: Posting environmental dashboard, open APIs of sustainability data, third party audit reports increases trust and makes organizations sustainability leaders.
- Iterative Improvement: Most organizations will view compliance as a destination, when in reality it is a dynamic and changing destination, requiring active adjust regulators and best practices evolve. Such an attitude helps in flexibility when reacting to emerging disclosures, standards and enforcement regimes.

When combined with the practices, these case studies offer a more practical guide to any project manager and organizations that want regulatory compliance integrated into the genes of their green software efforts. They highlight the fact that environmental responsibility, when unscrupulously handled, can go hand in hand with innovation, performance and competitive edge.

FUTURE DIRECTIONS

The legal context defining the development of green software is always changing as it adapts to the climate policy, pace of innovation and pressure on companies to assume greater responsibility towards their environment. As that critical infrastructure and emissions reduction plans across the world rely more heavily on software systems, future regulation trends will alter how compliance is attained, tracked, and even conceived. This part summarizes some of the major trends that will most probably characterize the next stage of compliance in green software initiatives and provides a glimpse of new problems and opportunities to be able to adapt proactively.

Carbon-Aware Computing as a Regulatory Norm

Carbon-aware computing, in which systems are dynamically adaptive to the carbon content of the energy grid, is becoming not only a technical innovation idea but potentially a regulatory demand. Policies in the future might stipulate that software systems, especially in energy-intensive areas (AI, Data Analytics and video streaming systems) must have the ability to perform their workloads in the most carbon-efficient way possible and to be able to update their continuous workload execution according to real-time emissions (Wiesner et al. 2025).

This is consistent with wider decarbonization targets and perhaps endorsed by the upcoming legislation in the form of national programs such as the European Digital Decade or legislation limited to a certain sector such as cloud services. Dynamic scheduling, energy-aware workload assignment and carbon labeling will be aspects which must be built into project teams in terms of architecture, workflows, and reporting (Patel et al. 2024).

Mandatory Climate Disclosures for Digital Operations

The scope of climate disclosure requirements is increasing, and this will require an increasing focus on digital operations, so far regarded as low impact or hard to quantify. Examples of this broader emissions reporting include the U.S. Securities and Exchange Commission (SEC) and the EU under its Corporate Sustainability Reporting Directive (CSRD) as well as at the international level via the Task Force on Climate-related Financial Disclosures (TCFD), all of which are expanding their emissions scope to include Scope 3 emissions, which in many cases include software use and IT services (Amel-Zadeh & Tang, 2025).

The transition will make organizations evaluate and report the carbon footprint of software products, services, and supply chain. Software development teams will be closely interacting with the sustainability and the finance departments to make sure that accurate, auditable, and timely reporting is provided. Further, procurement strategies are likely to prefer the vendors capable of providing carbon validated accounting and life cycle evaluation of theirs digital products (Hsu & Schletz, 2024).

AI-Powered Compliance Automation

With the increase in the number and complexity of sustainability compliance requirements, artificial intelligence and machine learning are likely to take center-stage in handling regulatory workflows. Automated monitoring of codebases, infrastructure and runtime settings against deviations to green standards can be achieved with AI systems. They are also able to forecast or predict compliance risk out of historical data, recommend remediation actions, and create documentation ready to submit to audit (Yadav et al. 2024).

New tools are starting to allow natural language processing (NLP) and environmental knowledge graphs to be used together to construe the text of a regulatory document, discover requirements applicable to the software, and trace those requirements to software characteristics. These functions will be invaluable particularly in multinational developments where different jurisdictions have various regulations to contend with. Dependability and predictability of the AI-driven compliance systems will however become matter of regulatory interest themselves opening up a demand that requires governance approaches to the application of AI in compliance automation (Kotte et al. 2025).

Standardization of Green Software Benchmarks

The measures of software sustainability e.g. energy consumption, the amount of carbon emitted, and resource use, are not internationalized and, thus, inconsistent in reporting and comparison. Governments, standards organizations and industry organizations are actively pursuing harmonizing benchmarks, certification procedures and lifecycle assessment (LCA) processes to software systems (Cruz et al. 2025).

As it develops soon, compliance can follow a standardization of sustainability labels on software- similar to energy ratings on appliances or LEED certification on buildings. Such labels may develop into pre-conditions of public procurement, entry into ESG investments or joining state-financed innovation initiatives. In doing so, project managers will be required to make sure that software projects are not only performance optimized, but also environmentally certified (Rajput & Sharma, 2024).

Regulatory Innovation in Cloud and Edge Computing

With the rise of cloud and edge compute infrastructures, the hardware that underpins them, and its environmental effects, are getting increasing attention- and so is the underlying software. Regulations scheduled in the future are likely to set limits on infrastructure level data replication, energy usage, and cooling needs with software itself having to answer to how efficiently it is using the available resources (Rancea et al. 2024).

New compliance issues will face us such as how to measure distributed energy foot-prints, merging emissions reporting across hybrid architectures, and how to facilitate data locality to minimize transmission energy that is not necessary. On the other hand, regulation incentives can incentivize software that can be used to execute efficient edge computing, energy demand prediction, or smarter load shifting in energy networks (Sun, 2025).

In the projections, there is going to be more proactive, automated, and incorporated regulatory compliance in green software engineering, which makes up ones project success. Companies that make early investments into studying and adapting to such future directions will not only reduce risks but will also place themselves in leadership positions concerning green digital change. As far as project managers are concerned, it implies taking compliance as a force of innovation, not limitation, one that opens new avenues to deliver software that is efficient, ethical, and environmentally responsible (Kolevski & Michael, 2024).

CONCLUSION AND STRATEGIC RECOMMENDATIONS

The need to marry environmental sustainability with software engineering is transforming the way organisations do their project designing, production, and delivery. It is not an extraneous detail, as this chapter has shown, but a pillar of green software projects regulatory compliance. It acts as an orientation restriction and a source of innovation, so that activating digital systems fit into the global climate agenda and the changing legal requirements.

Environmental compliance needs to be factored in software project management and this needs a paradigm shift in strategies and tools, roles and culture. Whether it is in Agile and DevOps or traditional project governance, sustainability has to be factored-in across the entire life cycle, beginning with gathering the requirements to deployment and maintenance. The most effective organizations integrate compliance into their day to day business processes using automation, interdepartmental collaboration, transparent reporting, and the process of iterative improvement.

Due to the ever-changing regulatory environment resulting from the government policy and market demands, project managers and software teams should be in touch with new tendencies. The technologies through which carbon-aware computing, digital climate disclosures, AI-powered compliance tools and quantifiable green benchmarks will help to create truly sustainable software are not still some years into the future: they are right here, around the corner of reality, and will mean a new era in the meaning of what it will be possible to build into sustainable software.

In order to make this landscape, the following strategic suggestions are vital:

- Make compliance operational: Weave the environmental requirements into project charter and the sprint plan not an after the development solution.
- Automate where possible: In a large organization, compliance-as-code, monitoring dashboards, and energy profiling tracking in real-time can be used to scale sustainability.

- Multidisciplinary teams: Include compliance officers, legal attorney, and sustainability professionals early in the process to have the proper alignment to the technical and regulatory domain.
- Treat sustainability as a design objective: Code, data and infrastructure should be optimized with environmental performance as a reality, not necessarily on a cost basis or on speed.
- Pace regulation: Keep pace with developments around the world and regionally and pre-empt any regulatory changes and future legislation where your software products might be concerned.

With regulatory compliance viewed as a strategic resource and not just an obstacle, organizations are bound to future-proof their software projects, manage risk less likely to happen and make significant contributions toward global sustainability goals. It is necessary to align legal, technical, and ethical aspects to develop digital systems that are innovative, responsible, and resilient in the climate-conscious world.

REFERENCES

Ahlström, H., & Monciardini, D. (2022). The regulatory dynamics of sustainable finance: Paradoxical success and limitations of EU reforms. *Journal of Business Ethics*, *177*(1), 193–212. PMID: 33642657

Ahmad Ibrahim, S. R., Yahaya, J., & Sallehudin, H. (2022). Green software process factors: A qualitative study. *Sustainability*, *14*(18), 11180.

Ahmed, I., Irshad, A., Zafar, S., Khan, B. A., Raza, M., & Ali, P. R. (2023). The role of environmental initiatives and green value co-creation as mediators: Promoting corporate entrepreneurship and green innovation. *SN Business & Economics*, *3*(4), 85.

Almusawi, S. M., & Khalefa, M. S. (2021, June). Study of knowledge management framework to enhance Enterprise Resource Planning system in Green software development process. In *2021 International Conference on Communication & Information Technology (ICICT)* (pp. 1-6). IEEE.

Amel-Zadeh, A., & Tang, Q. (2025). Managing the shift from voluntary to mandatory climate disclosure: The role of carbon accounting. *The British Accounting Review*, *57*(2), 101594.

Assoratgoon, W., & Kantabutra, S. (2023). Toward a sustainability organizational culture model. *Journal of Cleaner Production*, *400*, 136666.

Bolón-Canedo, V., Morán-Fernández, L., Cancela, B., & Alonso-Betanzos, A. (2024). A review of green artificial intelligence: Towards a more sustainable future. *Neurocomputing*, *599*, 128096.

Cruz, L., Fernandes, J. P., Kirkeby, M. H., Martínez-Fernández, S., Sallou, J., Anwar, H., & Yamshchikov, I. P. (2025). Greening ai-enabled systems with software engineering: A research agenda for environmentally sustainable ai practices. *Software Engineering Notes*, *50*(3), 14–23.

De Almeida, P. G. R., Dos Santos, C. D., & Farias, J. S. (2021). Artificial intelligence regulation: A framework for governance. *Ethics and Information Technology*, *23*(3), 505–525.

Fang, Y., & Shao, Z. (2022). Whether green finance can effectively moderate the green technology innovation effect of heterogeneous environmental regulation. *International Journal of Environmental Research and Public Health*, *19*(6), 3646. PMID: 35329333

Feng, N. (2022). [Retracted] The Influence Mechanism of BIM on Green Building Engineering Project Management under the Background of Big Data. *Applied Bionics and Biomechanics*, *2022*(1), 8227930. PMID: 36263254

Freed, M., Bielinska, S., Buckley, C., Coptu, A., Yilmaz, M., Messnarz, R., & Clarke, P. M. (2023, August). An investigation of green software engineering. In *European conference on software process improvement* (pp. 124-137). Cham: Springer Nature Switzerland.

Gangai, K. N., Joshi, D., Murali, M., & Verma, A., TK, B., & Dash, S. R. (2024, November). Strategic Approach for Integrating Legal Compliance into Engineering Project Management. In *2024 International Conference on Intelligent & Innovative Practices in Engineering & Management (IIPEM)* (pp. 1-6). IEEE.

Gu, B., Chen, F., & Zhang, K. (2021). The policy effect of green finance in promoting industrial transformation and upgrading efficiency in China: Analysis from the perspective of government regulation and public environmental demands. *Environmental Science and Pollution Research International*, *28*(34), 47474–47491. PMID: 33895949

Gupta, S., & Gupta, A. (2024, June). Optimising the Carbon Footprint for Cloud Resources in a Cloud Environment. In *2024 IEEE 21st International Conference on Software Architecture Companion (ICSA-C)* (pp. 215-221). IEEE.

Hainsch, K., Löffler, K., Burandt, T., Auer, H., Del Granado, P. C., Pisciella, P., & Zwickl-Bernhard, S. (2022). Energy transition scenarios: What policies, societal attitudes, and technology developments will realize the EU Green Deal? *Energy*, *239*, 122067.

Hermawan, A. N., Masudin, I., Zulfikarijah, F., Restuputri, D. P., & Shariff, S. S. R. (2024). The effect of sustainable manufacturing on environmental performance through government regulation and eco-innovation. *International Journal of Industrial Engineering and Operations Management*, *6*(4), 299–325.

Hsu, A., & Schletz, M. (2024). Digital technologies–the missing link between climate action transparency and accountability? *Climate Policy*, *24*(2), 193–210.

Irani, F., Kiliç, H., & Adeshola, I. (2022). Impact of green human resource management practices on the environmental performance of green hotels. *Journal of Hospitality Marketing & Management*, *31*(5), 570–600.

Katal, A., Dahiya, S., & Choudhury, T. (2023). Energy efficiency in cloud computing data centers: A survey on software technologies. *Cluster Computing*, *26*(3), 1845–1875. PMID: 36060618

Kempe, E., & Massey, A. (2021, September). Perspectives on regulatory compliance in software engineering. In *2021 IEEE 29th International Requirements Engineering Conference (RE)* (pp. 46-57). IEEE.

Kolevski, D., & Michael, K. (2024). Edge computing and iot data breaches: Security, privacy, trust, and regulation. *IEEE Technology and Society Magazine, 43*(1), 22–32.

Kotte, K. R., Thammareddi, L., Kodi, D., Anumolu, V. R., Kumar, A., & Joshi, S. (2025, February). Integration of Process Optimization and Automation: A Way to AI Powered Digital Transformation. In *2025 First International Conference on Advances in Computer Science, Electrical, Electronics, and Communication Technologies (CE2CT)* (pp. 1133-1138). IEEE.

Leong, J., May Yee, K., Baitsegi, O., Palanisamy, L., & Ramasamy, R. K. (2023). Hybrid project management between traditional software development lifecycle and agile based product development for future sustainability. *Sustainability, 15*(2), 1121.

Liu, Y., Lei, J., & Zhang, Y. (2021). A study on the sustainable relationship among the green finance, environment regulation and green-total-factor productivity in China. *Sustainability, 13*(21), 11926.

Matthew, U. O., Asuni, O., & Fatai, L. O. (2024). Green Software Engineering Development Paradigm: An Approach to a Sustainable Renewable Energy Future. In *Advancing Software Engineering Through AI, Federated Learning, and Large Language Models* (pp. 281-294). IGI Global.

Mishra, N. K., Mishra, N., & Sharma, P. P. (2025). Unraveling the relationship between corporate governance and green innovation: A systematic literature review. *Management Research Review, 48*(5), 825–845.

Neogi, S., Sharma, V., Khan, N., Chaurasia, D., Ahmad, A., Chauhan, S., & Bhargava, P. C. (2022). Sustainable biochar: A facile strategy for soil and environmental restoration, energy generation, mitigation of global climate change and circular bioeconomy. *Chemosphere, 293*, 133474. PMID: 34979200

Ogutu, H., Adol, G. F. C., Bujdosó, Z., Andrea, B., Fekete-Farkas, M., & Dávid, L. D. (2023). Theoretical nexus of knowledge management and tourism business enterprise competitiveness: An integrated overview. *Sustainability, 15*(3), 1948.

Ozili, P. K. (2022). Green finance research around the world: A review of literature. *International Journal of Green Economics, 16*(1), 56–75.

Patel, P., Gregersen, T., & Anderson, T. (2024). An agile pathway towards carbon-aware clouds. *ACM SIGENERGY Energy Informatics Review, 4*(3), 10–17.

Rajput, S., & Sharma, T. (2024, June). Benchmarking emerging deep learning quantization methods for energy efficiency. In *2024 IEEE 21st International Conference on Software Architecture Companion (ICSA-C)* (pp. 238-242). IEEE.

Rancea, A., Anghel, I., & Cioara, T. (2024). Edge computing in healthcare: Innovations, opportunities, and challenges. *Future Internet, 16*(9), 329.

Rao, N. R. (2025). Optimizing Enterprise Application Deployment Strategies for Package Distribution and Installation With a Focus on Sustainability and Education. In *Integrating AI and Sustainability in Technical and Vocational Education and Training (TVET)* (pp. 279-298). IGI Global Scientific Publishing.

Rashid, N., Khan, S. U., Khan, H. U., & Ilyas, M. (2021). Green-agile maturity model: An evaluation framework for global software development vendors. *IEEE Access : Practical Innovations, Open Solutions*, *9*, 71868–71886.

Raza, S. A., & Khan, K. A. (2022). Impact of green human resource practices on hotel environmental performance: The moderating effect of environmental knowledge and individual green values. *International Journal of Contemporary Hospitality Management*, *34*(6), 2154–2175.

Ren, W., & Ji, J. (2021). How do environmental regulation and technological innovation affect the sustainable development of marine economy: New evidence from China's coastal provinces and cities. *Marine Policy*, *128*, 104468.

Santarius, T., Dencik, L., Diez, T., Ferreboeuf, H., Jankowski, P., Hankey, S., & Staab, P. (2023). Digitalization and sustainability: A call for a digital green deal. *Environmental Science & Policy*, *147*, 11–14.

Sharma, R., Lopes de Sousa Jabbour, A. B., Jain, V., & Shishodia, A. (2022). The role of digital technologies to unleash a green recovery: Pathways and pitfalls to achieve the European Green Deal. *Journal of Enterprise Information Management*, *35*(1), 266–294.

Sun, Y. (2025). Cloud and Edge Computing as Effective Trends in Business Model Innovation: A Bibliometric Review. *Journal of Software (Malden, MA)*, *37*(1), e2754.

Verdecchia, R., Lago, P., Ebert, C., & De Vries, C. (2021). Green IT and green software. *IEEE Software*, *38*(6), 7–15.

Wen, S., & Qiang, G. (2022). Managing stakeholder concerns in green building projects with a view towards achieving social sustainability: A Bayesian-network model. *Frontiers in Environmental Science*, *10*, 874367.

Wiesner, P., Grinwald, D., Weiß, P., Wilhelm, P., Khalili, R., & Kao, O. (2025, June). Carbon-Aware Quality Adaptation for Energy-Intensive Services. In *Proceedings of the 16th ACM International Conference on Future and Sustainable Energy Systems* (pp. 415-422).

Yadav, N., Gupta, V., & Garg, A. (2024). Industrial automation through ai-powered intelligent machines—enabling real-time decision-making. In *Recent Trends in Artificial Intelligence Towards a Smart World: Applications in Industries and Sectors* (pp. 145–178). Springer Nature Singapore.

Yang, Z., Na, J., & Dong, X. (2024). Corporate governance for sustainable development: A study on mechanism configuration. *Journal of Cleaner Production*, *458*, 142509.

Zetzsche, D. A., & Anker-Sørensen, L. (2022). Regulating sustainable finance in the dark. *European Business Organization Law Review*, *23*(1), 47–85.

Zhao, J., & Gómez Fariñas, B. (2023). Artificial intelligence and sustainable decisions. *European Business Organization Law Review*, *24*(1), 1–39.

KEY TERMS AND DEFINITIONS

Agile Practices of Sustainability: Agile could be more specifically integrated with environmental objectives and checkpoints associated with those objectives will be built in; such that, the aspects of sustainability will be re-visited during the development process iteratively.

Carbon-Aware Computing: A software design and operating strategy to dynamically optimize the behaviour of the system (e.g. the timing of work loads or geographical location) through real-time carbon intensity information of energy grids.

Compliance-as-Code: The act of automating regulatory and policy rules as automated scripts or configurations applied within CI/CD pipelines requiring zero-hour compliance across the development lifecycle.

Digital Product Passport: A policy instrument being prepared in the EU will mandate digital products, such as software, to disclose lifecycle sustainability information about their product to be more transparent and meet regulatory obligations.

Environmental Audit: An organised survey on the environmental performance, procedures and records of an organization, which are applied to check compliance with regulations and standards of software or other digital activities.

Environmental, social and governance reporting (ESG Reporting): A reporting mechanism employed by firms to report their environmental, social and governance performance to stakeholders, which may contain figures to assess digital and software emissions.

Green Software Engineering: A style of software development that focuses on minimizing environmental opportunities throughout the software life-cycle, such as energy efficiency, carbon footprint, consumption of resources, and optimization of data centers.

Greenwashing: The process of making false or overstated claims of the environmental benefits of any product including software or service that may often result in legal, financial and reputation risks.

ISO 14001: A standard covering the environment management systems, which is internationally recognized and assists interested organizations to manage, identify, monitor, as well as control their environmental degrading problems in a systematic manner.

Life Cycle Assessment (LCA): A practice of evaluating the environmental costs involved with all phases of a product life cycle (including the original product design and its eventual discarding) potentially adapted to software in order to measure the complete ecological impact of software.

Regulatory Framework: The way in which governments or institutions have provided standard patterns of legal, policy, or procedural provision to assure and influence environmental conduct that characterizes the software development and deployment.

Scope 3 Emissions: Emissions that are caused indirectly in the value chain of a company and also those made by customers, and the end users, when they use the software products or the digital services.

Software Carbon Intensity (SCI): A measure that gives the amount of carbon emissions produced given a unit of work done by the software which is the standardized method of measuring and benchmarking the sustainability of any software.

Sustainability Compliance: The method or activity of fulfilling the software systems and development practices within the local, national of international rules, regulations and also sustainably.

Task Force on Climate-related Financial Disclosures (TCFD): A global program that offers climate-related disclosure suggestions on risk management systems, including those of the digital environment and emissions related to software programs and IT-structures.

Chapter 11
Geospatial Tools for Corporate Sustainability Reporting and ESG Compliance

Munir Ahmad
https://orcid.org/0000-0003-4836-6151
Survey of Pakistan, Pakistan

ABSTRACT

This chapter explores the transformative role of geospatial tools in corporate sustainability reporting and ESG compliance. GIS, remote sensing, and IoT-enabled spatial data enable organizations to visualize environmental footprints, assess social impacts, and verify regulatory adherence across geographic scales. Applications in environmental monitoring, risk assessment, supply chain analysis, and community engagement demonstrate how spatial intelligence enhances transparency, accountability, and operational efficiency. The chapter also examines challenges in data quality, technical capacity, and integration, and highlights emerging trends such as AI-driven analytics and real-time ESG dashboards, offering pathways for dynamic, spatially informed sustainability management.

INTRODUCTION

Over the last few years, the issue of corporate sustainability and the need to adhere to Environmental, Social, and Governance (ESG) have become the key tenets of responsible business practices (Barbosa et al., 2024; de Souza Barbosa et al., 2023; Dicuonzo et al., 2022). Stakeholders, such as investors, regulators, consum-

DOI: 10.4018/979-8-3373-4652-6.ch011

ers, and communities, are making more and more demands, seeking transparency in the manner in which organizations conduct their operations in regard to their environmental footprint, their social impact, and their governance mechanisms. The increasing realization that long-term financial performance is closely linked to sustainability and socially responsible operations has accelerated this shift (Audi & Yu, 2024; Coelho et al., 2023; Sarfraz et al., 2023). Thus, organizations are feeling increased pressure to measure, report, and reduce their effects in a manner that is both accurate and verifiable.

Although the focus on ESG compliance grows over time, effectively capturing and reporting environmental and social impacts presents a major challenge to companies. The use of traditional reporting methods tends to be based on aggregated, non-granular, or self-reporting data that can be neither spatially specific nor time-granular, and contextually relevant. Indicatively, greenhouse gas emissions reporting at the facility or corporate level can hide localized environmental risk, such as being near a protected area, water-stressed area, or climate-vulnerable communities (Wang, 2023). Similarly, social impact evaluations often overlook geographic labor allocation, community participation, and environmental resource availability, thereby limiting their ability to inform decision-making and demonstrate accountability.

Geospatial applications such as Geographic Information Systems (GIS), satellite and aerial images, and spatial data powered by the Internet of Things (IoT) can provide a strong set of tools to solve these problems. With the combination of location-based intelligence and conventional corporate data, organizations are in a position to visualize environmental footprints, evaluate risk exposure, create social impacts, and confirm regulatory framework compliance across various geographic levels (Chen et al., 2022; Soares et al., 2025; Zhang et al., 2021). Actionable insights are delivered by real-time dashboards, predictive analytics, and spatial modeling to allow a broader, more transparent, and evidence-based approach to sustainability reporting.

This chapter explores how geospatial technologies can enhance corporate sustainability reporting, making it more sustainable and ESG-compliant. It begins by examining how spatial tools have been utilized to support ESG metrics, and then proceeds to describe some of the most significant technologies and data sources. Applications in environmental monitoring, risk assessment, social impact assessment, and compliance checks are then presented in the chapter. The application of geospatial intelligence in the sustainability of corporate operations is bound to present both practical advantages and challenges, as shown by real-life case studies in the energy, agricultural, and manufacturing sectors. Lastly, the chapter concludes with a discussion of emerging opportunities, ongoing challenges, and future directions for integrating geospatial tools with ESG reporting and decision-making frameworks.

GEOSPATIAL TOOLS IN ESG AND SUSTAINABILITY REPORTING

Corporate sustainability reporting and ESG compliance are based on systematic frameworks according to which organizations monitor, report, and control their environmental, social, and governance impacts. Such frameworks as the Global Reporting Initiative (GRI) (Mougenot & Doussoulin, 2024), Sustainability Accounting Standards Board (SASB) (Eng et al., 2022; Parfitt, 2024), and the Task Force on Climate-related Financial Disclosures (TCFD) (Chua et al., 2022) offer standardized indicators and reporting requirements that compare and make practices comparable and transparent across the industry. Although these frameworks are focused on data quality, risk assessment, and accountability to stakeholders, they tend not to explicitly give spatial representations of the ESG-related processes. Integrating geospatial intelligence, however, can greatly augment these reporting frameworks by providing geographic detail and spatial context to allow organizations to see and report more about where and how their operations have effects on the environment and society.

Geospatial applications - GIS, remote sensing tools, and IoT-based spatial data platforms can provide unrivaled mapping, analysis, and visualization of ESG-related data at a wide geographical range. These technologies enable organizations to go beyond more traditional, aggregate reporting and integrate spatial context to allow a more subtle view of how operations, supply chains, and resource use affect environmental, social, and governance outcomes. An ability to combine various data layers, starting with the satellite imagery and aerial survey and continuing with real-time IoT sensor data, can help companies to have a multidimensional view of their own operations, enabling them to make evidence-based decisions and manage sustainability proactively. Table 1 compares three prominent frameworks with the additional value that geospatial tools bring to enhance ESG reporting.

Table 1. ESG reporting frameworks and the added value of geospatial intelligence

Framework	Primary Focus Areas	Limitation	Added Value of Geospatial Tools
GRI (Global Reporting Initiative)	Broad sustainability disclosures across E, S, and G dimensions	Provides aggregate, non-spatial indicators	GIS maps environmental/social impacts at precise locations for greater accountability
SASB (Sustainability Accounting Standards Board)	Industry-specific ESG metrics and financial materiality	Limited integration of spatial risk assessment	Enables industry-specific spatial risk modeling (e.g., pollution hotspots in manufacturing)
TCFD (Task Force on Climate-related Financial Disclosures)	Climate risk disclosure (physical & transitional)	Focuses on risk assessment without geospatial layers	Incorporates climate hazard maps, predictive spatial modeling for future risk scenarios

Environmental Dimension

Environmentally, geospatial tools offer important capabilities in the tracking and control of resource use and environmental effects. GIS systems, such as, can be used to produce finer maps that indicate the positions of the industrial plants and their closeness to delicate ecosystems, water catchments, or even living quarters (Rai et al., 2022). These kinds of mapping can allow the organizations to find the hotspots of localized air or water pollution, to estimate the spatial distribution of greenhouse gas emissions, and to strategize what interventions can be done to mitigate the environmental pollution. Moreover, remote sensing methods, such as satellite images and surveys by drones, enable full-time tracking of the alterations in land-use, deforestation processes, urban sprawl, and natural resource extraction. Temporal analysis of these data allows information on environmental impacts changing over time to be obtained to support retrospective reporting and predictive modeling. As an example, a company dealing in energy can use satellite images to identify illegal logging in its supply chain or to trace the variations in vegetative cover in and around its places of operation. On the same note, multispectral satellite data can be utilized by agricultural firms to determine crop health, soil erosion, or irrigation effectiveness and relate environmental surveillance to sustainability performance indicators. Using predictive models and GIS analytics, organizations become capable of predicting possible environmental risks, maximizing the use of resources, and minimizing their ecological impact.

Social Dimension

Geospatial technologies allow organizations to know and have a clear picture of the social implications of their activities on human beings and communities on the social aspect (Kent & Specht, 2023). As an example, labor mapping enables businesses to understand where workers, contractors, and other stakeholders are located on the map and in which areas there is a greater risk of occupational health because of the environmental conditions, lack of health care access, or occupational hazards. The planning and assessment of community engagement programs, such as education programs, healthcare outreach, and infrastructure development, can be supported with the help of spatial analytics. They can use the visualization of the closeness of operations with vulnerable communities, schools, hospitals, or cultural heritage sites to guarantee that their social interventions are focused on being effective and not creating an increase in the risks within the local communities. Geospatial understanding can help with stakeholder engagement, offering intuitive, visually map-based data that can be used to communicate social impact in a transparent way, enabling regulators, investors, and community members to evaluate efforts in corporate responsibility. As an illustration, a mining firm would like to show how it is able to alleviate social disturbance through the location of workforce housing and community facilities without encroaching on ecologically or socially sensitive areas, and at the same time monitor the success of local employment programs.

Governance Dimension

Geospatial intelligence is very important in governance, checking compliance, and management. Spatial information can enable organizations to follow compliance with environmental and land-use laws, including the presence of buffer areas around parks or other places of ecological interest, emission levels within ecologically sensitive areas, or zoning ordinances in urban settings (Das et al., 2022; Eshetie et al., 2024). In addition to compliance, geospatial analytics enable the evaluation of risk, as they can reveal possible exposure to climate hazards, natural disasters, etc., or to regulatory changes. Spatial intelligence, when combined with corporate dashboards and reporting systems, helps track operational performance and ESG indicators in real-time, generating verifiable evidence-based documentation that is shareable with auditors, regulators, and investors. An example of this is when a manufacturing company superimposes factory points with flood risk areas to determine the probability of operations being interrupted, and at the same time checks the adherence to the environmental regulations in the area. Equally, logistics businesses are in a position to trace transport paths with regard to environmental conservation zones to achieve sustainable and ethically acceptable supply chains. Organizations can be made more transparent, accountable, and strategic in the decisions they take by integrating geospatial insights into their governance structures, following regulatory obligations, and voluntary ESG standards. Table 2 summarizes the applications of geospatial tools across the three ESG dimensions, highlighting their role in enhancing environmental monitoring, social responsibility, and governance compliance.

Table 2. Applications of geospatial tools in ESG dimensions

ESG Dimension	Geospatial Applications	Example Use Case
Environmental	Pollution mapping, deforestation monitoring, land-use change detection, predictive ecological modeling	An energy company uses satellite imagery to detect illegal logging in the supply chain
Social	Labor distribution analysis, community proximity mapping, social impact visualization	Mining firm locates housing and services away from sensitive community zones
Governance	Regulatory compliance mapping, climate hazard overlay, and real-time performance dashboards	Manufacturing firm overlays factory sites with flood-prone zones for compliance and risk management

The strategic, operational, and reputational benefits of using geospatial tools to support ESG reporting go way beyond regulatory compliance to give organizations strategic, operational, and reputational benefits. Improved decision-making is by far one of the greatest advantages. The conventional ESG reporting may use aggregated and high-level data, which may be used to hide localized effects or operational inefficiencies. Geospatial intelligence, in its turn, offers location-specific information at a granular level and helps organizations to determine the exact location of environmental/social impacts. The spatial granularity enables managers to make sensible operational choices, e.g., optimize energy or water consumption at particular facilities, where pollution is at the highest risk, or to intervene in sustainability with the highest impact. An example is that a multinational agricultural company may be able to utilize GIS and satellite images in order to determine areas where crop management activities may be causing soil degradation or overuse of water, then change the management practices. Equally, logistics companies can use spatial analysis to redirect transportation systems and minimize carbon emissions and travel to climate-sensitive areas.

Increased transparency is another important benefit. Investors, regulators, and civil society organizations are growing increasingly critical of ESG reporting, and they seek evidence-based information on corporate effects clearly. The visualization of ESG data in space enables organizations to represent the complex data in an intuitive and easily explainable manner. To give an example, interactive maps of emissions hotspots, the environmental impact of the supply chain, or community outreach programs simplify the process for stakeholders to learn and validate corporate claims. With the presence of a visual story and using conventional metrics, companies can prove their belief in transparency and accountability, which can build trust and credibility. Moreover, such visualization has made it easier to compare across locations and time horizons, enabling decision-makers and external stakeholders to monitor the progress against sustainability goals and regulations more easily.

Geospatial tools can enhance stakeholder engagement. By mapping environmental and social impacts against communities, workforce locations, and natural resources, organizations are able to communicate complex issues in a manner that traverses the divide between the technical data and the stakeholder comprehension. As a case in point, a mining company may demonstrate the ways in which mitigation practices lessen environmental and social risks within the surrounding communities, or a power company may demonstrate how renewable facilities are located and, at the same time, cause the least harm to sensitive ecosystems and communities. Converting abstract ESG data into actionable, visual insights, geospatial intelligence can provide more substantive dialogue with the local communities, regulators, investors, and NGOs, arriving at a consensus to solve problems and form stronger and more-trust-based relations.

In addition to communication and engagement, geospatial intelligence turns the ESG reporting into a dynamic system of decision support. Rather than being a retrospective compliance exercise, spatially informed reporting enables organizations to foresee risks, model the future, and align sustainability strategies with the realities of operations. As an example, predictive spatial analytics can be used to determine areas that face an increased risk of flooding, drought, or deforestation, so companies would take the initiative to reduce risks and to better allocate and use their resources. The IoT sensor data and GIS platforms provide real-time dashboards that allow continuous monitoring of environmental performance to alert and provide insights to support rapid response and continuous improvement.

KEY GEOSPATIAL TECHNOLOGIES AND DATA SOURCES

The efficient use of geospatial intelligence in corporate sustainability reporting depends on a wide range of technologies and data sources that make it possible to gather, combine, visualize, and analyze geographically oriented data. Such technologies are the basis for accurate, timely, and geographically relevant insights that enable organizations to monitor environmental impacts, social outcomes, and governance compliance at diverse geographic scales. Table 3 provides an overview of the major geospatial technologies and data sources that underpin corporate sustainability reporting, summarizing their functions and key applications across ESG dimensions.

Table 3. Key geospatial technologies and their applications in ESG reporting

Technology/Data Source	Core Function	Example Applications
GIS	Visualization, analysis, and integration of spatial datasets	Facility mapping, scenario modeling, compliance monitoring
Remote Sensing & Satellite Imagery	Monitoring land, vegetation, water, and atmospheric changes	Deforestation tracking, soil health assessment, habitat monitoring
IoT Sensors & Location Data	Real-time environmental and operational monitoring	Air/water quality sensing, energy/water use tracking, fleet emissions monitoring
Integrated Dashboards	Synthesizing multi-source data for decision-making	ESG performance dashboards, stakeholder reporting, risk modeling

Geographic Information Systems (GIS)

Spatial analysis is based on GIS, which is a critical part of corporate sustainability reporting and environmental, social, and governance (ESG) compliance

(Dimmelmeier, 2024; Gopal & Pitts, 2024a; Rossi et al., 2024). These systems grant organizations the ability to store, manage, integrate, and analyze complex geospatial data by converting raw data into actionable information that can be used in strategic, operational, and compliance decision-making processes. Compared to conventional forms of reporting that are mainly based on aggregate quantitative information, GIS allows visualization of the spatial relationships, trends, and patterns that remain latent in tabular data.

GIS platforms are used to develop a broad range of visualizations, such as thematic maps, heatmaps, layered spatial models, and interactive dashboards. These devices enable companies to superimpose various data sets, including the locations of facilities, natural resource boundaries, population distributions, and regulatory zones, which creates a multidimensional perspective of ESG performance. To illustrate: an industrial firm can map the position of its manufacturing facilities relative to reserves, stressed water zones, flood-prone zones, or vulnerable populations and find out where there may be a risk to the environment or society. Such visualization of these relationships allows the decision-makers to rank interventions, allocate resources efficiently, and prevent any negative effects on the local populations as well as the ecosystems.

In addition to fixed visualization, the GIS promotes progressive spatial analysis and the modeling of scenarios. Organizations are able to model the impact of operating change, policy interference, or environmental conditions on sustainability results. As an example, a utility company dealing with renewable energy source development may model the suitability of land sites by using GIS to consider solar irradiance, wind patterns, access to the transmission line, ecological sensitivity, and local community effects, which greatly reduces environmental risks and helps to concentrate projects. In like manner, in agriculture, GIS may be used to model the effects of various irrigation treatments or crop rotation on water requirement, soil conditions, and yield potential in order to support more environmentally friendly land management. Table 4 highlights how GIS supports corporate sustainability by enabling both visualization and advanced analysis across environmental, social, and governance domains.

Table 4. Applications of GIS in ESG dimensions

ESG Dimension	GIS Applications	Example Use Case
Environmental	Overlay of facilities with natural resource boundaries; modeling land suitability for renewables	Energy firm assesses solar farm sites based on irradiance and ecological sensitivity
Social	Mapping communities near industrial zones; analyzing labor distribution and service access	Mining company maps proximity of operations to vulnerable communities
Governance	Compliance verification with buffer zones, discharge limits, and regulatory zones	Manufacturing facility checks effluent discharge compliance in water-stressed areas

GIS can support the risk evaluation and regulatory oversight by ensuring that they are able to monitor operational activities spatially (Contini et al., 2000; Efraimidou & Spiliotis, 2024). By overlaying real-time or historical data points like emissions measurements, water use, and waste production on spatial layers, organizations can evaluate the compliance of operations with local environmental rules or voluntary ESG requirements. An example is that a manufacturing plant can use GIS to determine that its effluent output does not exceed permissible levels in water-stressed basins, and a mining firm can observe its closeness to ecologically sensitive habitats and make sure it follows the rules of the buffer zones.

More than that, the integration of other spatial and non-spatial data, including remote sensing imagery, IoT sensor data, or socioeconomic indicators, is enabled through GIS to provide a holistic tool for sustainability reporting. This integration allows organizations to monitor environmental performance as well as social performance on a variety of scales, beginning with site-level operations all the way up to a whole supply chain or regional landscape. Such decision-makers can determine the problematic areas of environmental impact, predict risks, and assess the efficiency of mitigation actions over time, which can support a proactive approach to ESG management.

Remote Sensing and Satellite Imagery

Satellite imaging, aerial photography, and drone-based sensors known as remote sensing technologies play a pivotal role in checking the environmental conditions on various spatial and time scales. These technologies enable organizations to gather multi-dimensional, high-resolution data across wide geographic scales and, therefore, monitor hard-to-monitor or impossible-to-monitor areas using ground-based surveys alone. Remote sensing enables companies to monitor the changes in vegetation, land cover, water resources, and atmospheric conditions due to the ability to capture visual, infrared, thermal, and multispectral data, which is the foundation of evidence-based sustainability reporting (Gopal & Pitts, 2024b; Gu et al., 2023; Rapach et al., 2024).

Satellite images and aerial surveys enable organizations to identify and measure changes in the environment over a period, including deforestation, degraded land, urban sprawl, lost wetlands, and the movement of biodiversity habitats. Indicatively, multispectral satellite images allow a multinational agricultural company to scan thousands of hectares of soil and crops to detect where there is erosion, nutrients, or water wastage processes. Likewise, energy and extractive industries can monitor vegetation clearing and habitat disaggregation to make sure that activities are in accordance with environmental policy and sustainability pledges. Time series monitoring, as it is sometimes called, time monitoring allows organizations to notice trends, assess the efficiency of mitigation efforts, and notice new environmental threats before they can develop into major impacts.

Remote sensing can be especially useful in terms of overseeing the supply chain and geographically dispersed operations. Businesses that have their operations distributed in various locations, like forests, mining, or agricultural supply chains, can utilise satellite imagery to monitor activities in inaccessible or remote regions. An example is that a palm oil company could use satellite-based surveillance to identify any illegal clearing of land in supplier plantations so that they comply with zero-deforestation pledges. Similarly, aero images can help water companies observe catchments and their sources of contamination or overexploitation to exercise sustainable water management.

Remote sensing compliance and ESG reporting are other important uses of the technology. Satellite data can assist organizations in verifying information that is self-reported or in documenting regulatory and voluntary disclosures. As an illustration, it is possible to identify any illegal mining, unauthorized construction, or encroachment into the protected areas and implement corrective measures ahead of time, or show that the companies act under the environmental laws. Another application of remote sensing is that it allows organizations to indirectly quantify the amount of greenhouse gas emissions, including measuring forest loss or wetland area change, to supplement on-site measurements with a more comprehensive account of environmental impact.

Also, remote sensing data can be incorporated with GIS and IoT systems to increase analytical functions. Advanced spatial modeling and scenario analysis can be accomplished by combining satellite imagery with additional geospatial layers like corporate facilities, infrastructure, and areas of protection, as well as community locations. The ability to make decisions early and manage risks is supported by the ability to model the consequences of land-use change, climate phenomena, or operational development on environmental and social outcomes in organizations. A case in point is the ability of predictive models based on satellite observations of vegetation and rainfall to predict locations that are subject to soil erosion or drought, which can be used by agricultural firms to optimize planting plans and water to prevent water wastage.

IoT Sensors and Location-Based Data

The swift spread of Internet of Things (IoT) devices has transformed the manner in which organizations watch over on environmental, social, and operational parameters in real time. IoT devices, consisting of sensors to measure energy and water, air quality, temperature, and emissions, create continuous, high-frequency sets of data that log the dynamic performance of corporate operations. Combining these devices with geolocation data can yield spatially resolved insights via which organizations can track ESG metrics with a granularity and timeliness never before seen (Ateeq et al., 2025; Saxena et al., 2022).

Among the main advantages of monitoring with the help of IoT is the possibility of monitoring the use of resources and emissions in the environment at the facility level. As an example, smart meters in producing facilities can be used to track real-time electricity and water consumption, with use patterns tied to particular areas within a facility or several sites. This can allow organizations to determine hotspots where consumption is high, and the efficiency of various production lines and interventions may be implemented as an upgrade of equipment, optimization of a certain process, or behavioral changes. Through the spatial visualization of this information, companies are able to learn more about the inefficiencies of their operations and focus sustainability efforts in areas where the company can make the most difference.

IoT sensors are also important in monitoring the quality of air and water. Industrial or energy facilities can use sensors placed inside and outside of the facility to constantly monitor pollutants, particulate matter, greenhouse gas emissions, and effluent discharge. As an illustration, an industrial facility such as a chemical plant could have IoT-powered air quality sensors to measure emissions of volatile organic compounds (VOCs) and automatically initiate mitigation steps should the limits be surpassed. Likewise, water quality sensors used in the aquaculture, agricultural, or manufacturing processes can monitor the pH level, turbidity, or chemical pollution, and send early alerts before environmental destruction and regulatory issues occur.

IoT devices, with GPS, can be used in logistics and supply chain operations to enable organizations to track vehicle location, fuel consumption, route efficiency, and emissions in real-time. This is a spatially explicit monitoring that aids carbon accounting and allows companies to streamline transportation networks to minimize environmental impacts. To illustrate, those involved in logistics can calculate the delivery path and change the timetables or redirect the vehicles to prevent congestion, fuel inefficiency, as well as the emission of greenhouse gases. These kinds of insights can aid in the adherence to environmental policies and voluntary ESG reporting frameworks, giving verifiable evidence of sustainable operations.

Besides, IoT devices may be linked to GIS platforms and centralized ESG dashboards to ensure that the combined tools enable a decision-maker to visualize and analyze real-time data within a spatial framework. Adding IoT sensor data to other spatial data, including facility boundaries, land use maps, or community locations, enables organizations to perform more advanced analysis, such as where environmental or social risks are in overlap with operational activity. Such integration can make predictive analytics and modeling scenarios possible and can enable intervention before problems get out of control. To take an example, real-time data on emissions can be combined with meteorological and topographical data to allow an energy company to predict patterns of dispersion of air pollution and take action to prevent it at the appropriate time.

Spatial monitoring based on IoT can improve stakeholder interaction and transparency of reporting. Real-time dashboards and map-based visualizations enable regulators, investors, and community members to have access to current information on the use of resources, emissions, and environmental performance. Such visibility in real-time encourages trust and accountability and makes it easier to respond to operational anomalies or compliance issues on time. Table 5 compares the strengths of GIS, remote sensing, and IoT sensors, showing how each technology contributes distinct but complementary capabilities to ESG monitoring.

Table 5. Comparative strengths of core geospatial technologies

Technology	Spatial Scale	Temporal Resolution	Key Strengths	Typical Limitations
GIS	Local to global (flexible)	Periodic (depends on input data)	Data integration, visualization, scenario modeling	Relies on availability of accurate input data
Remote Sensing	Regional to global	Days to weeks (depending on satellite)	Broad coverage, time-series analysis, ecosystem monitoring	Cloud cover, cost of high-res imagery, interpretation complexity
IoT Sensors	Site-specific, local	Real-time to continuous	High-frequency monitoring, granular facility-level data	Infrastructure cost, maintenance, and connectivity challenges

Integration of Multi-Source Spatial Data

Geospatial intelligence is powerful not only in the collection of data but also in the synthesis and integration of the data. There is growing dependence on modern sustainability reporting on platforms that integrate GIS, remote sensing, IoT, and other location-based data into coherent dashboards. These dashboards enable decision-makers to visualize multi-dimensional ESG metrics in real-time, evaluate performance against regulatory and internal benchmarks, and effectively communicate impacts to stakeholders. To allow the cross-referencing of heterogeneous datasets, such as the clustering of emissions data available due to IoT sensors and land-use maps available due to satellite imagery, integration can be used to generate a holistic risk analysis and aid evidence-based sustainability approaches. With the help of these geospatial technologies and data sources, organizations are no longer limited to the past, retrospective reporting nature; they are now able to engage in the dynamic, spatially informed management of ESG. Such integration increases transparency, operational efficiency, and accountability, and hence, geospatial tools are essential in current corporate sustainability practices. Figure 1 illustrates how different geospatial technologies—GIS, remote sensing, IoT sensors, and integrated dashboards—interact to create a dynamic ESG reporting ecosystem.

Figure 1. Integration of geospatial technologies for ESG reporting

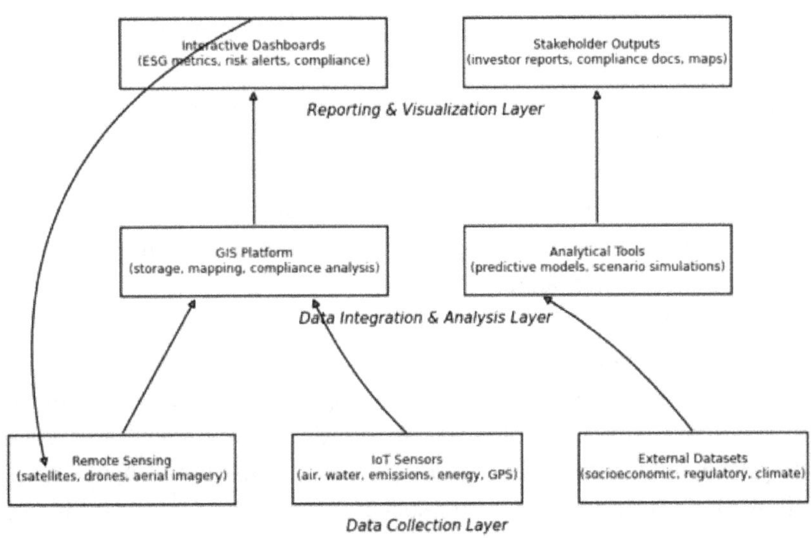

APPLICATIONS IN CORPORATE SUSTAINABILITY

Geospatial solutions are now essential in bringing corporate sustainability and ESG compliance to life. Through location-specific information, organizations are able to chart their environmental and social footprint, determine risks, and improve transparency and accountability in the various sectors. This segment is a discussion on the significant uses of geospatial intelligence within corporate sustainability.

Environmental Footprint Mapping

A key use of geospatial tools is mapping environmental footprint, which helps organizations in quantifying, visualizing, and managing their effects on natural resources and ecosystems over a variety of geographic levels. Footprint mapping, in contrast to more traditional approaches to reporting, which tend to present more aggregated and facility-level data, introduces a spatial aspect to the information, enabling organizations to see where the pressure on the environment is the most significant and how their actions touch upon vulnerable ecosystems, waterways, and human settlements (Fang et al., 2021; Franco et al., 2021).

With the help of GIS and remote sensing data, firms can map the emissions of greenhouse gases (GHG), energy, and water usage, changes in land-use, and other environmental indicators at the levels of facilities, regions, and entire supply chains. Indicatively, ecosystem maps can be stacked on industrial facilities to determine where emissions are likely to have a disproportionate impact on air quality or water bodies, or where waste discharge may endanger biodiversity. In this way, organizations can be able to identify the areas with the greatest impact and focus on the specific mitigation practices, including the replacement of equipment with newer clean sources of energy or changing schedules of production schedules to reduce stress on the environment.

One major benefit of environmental footprint mapping is the temporal analysis. Combined with remote sensing and satellite imagery, GIS enables organizations to monitor land-cover changes, deforestation, or urban development over a certain period and give insights into the long-term environmental trends. Such a historical outlook allows the companies to assess the success of sustainability efforts, including reforestation programs, water-saving efforts, or emission-cutting strategies. As an example, an energy company can trace the impact of introducing renewable energy projects on the carbon emissions in the region, or a mining enterprise may trace the success of reclamation projects at decommissioned sites. Beyond static assessment, environmental footprint mapping supports predictive and scenario-based analyses. Through modeling possible effects of operational change, policy intervention, or climate events, organizations can anticipate future resource requirements, recognize new environmental risks, and build proactive management. As a case in point, an agricultural business can model the potential impacts of various irrigation methods on water supply in drought-prone areas, or a manufacturing company can model the potential impacts of facility increase on the local air quality or land-use patterns.

When footprint data is integrated with corporate sustainability dashboards, accessibility and usefulness increase. Spatial visualizations. The complexity of environmental information, including heatmaps, density maps, and layered GIS models, can be communicated in an intuitive way to internal teams, regulators, investors, and other stakeholders. As organizations report their ESG, they not only enhance transparency and credibility but also go further to stimulate engagement because data are presented in a spatial manner that enables stakeholders to comprehend the extent and place of corporate impacts. Along with first-hand operational information, environmental footprint mapping is also being brought to bear on supply chain analysis. Businesses whose suppliers are distributed geographically can trace resource utilization, emissions, and deforestation at multiple locations, and ensure their sustainability pledges are not limited to their premises. As a case in point, a consumer goods company can utilize footprint mapping to track water usage and emissions within the upstream agricultural suppliers, showing where action is required to ensure that the ESG requirements are met.

Risk Assessment and Supply Chain Analysis

Supply chain analysis and risk assessment represent an important part of corporate ESG management, and geospatial technologies can offer effective tools in the identification, analysis, and mitigation of environmental, social, and regulatory risks in complex operational networks. Contemporary corporations are typically multi-regional and multi-national, and their supply chains are usually long with a rich array of ecosystems, regulations, and socio-economic contexts. Spatially mapping these operations enables organizations to see possible risk exposure and take proactive and data-driven decisions to protect sustainability and operational continuity (Baryannis et al., 2019; Choudhary et al., 2023; Wong et al., 2024).

Geospatial applications allow organizations to superimpose a combination of spatial data, such as locations of facilities, suppliers, transportation networks, and distribution hubs, with environmental and social markers of risk. Such indicators can be climate-vulnerable areas, flood plains, drought-prone areas, deforestation hot spots, or other areas of protection or of increased regulatory attention. With such overlaps analyzed, companies are able to determine where they are at maximum risk of operations disruption or environmental impact or social concern with regard to their suppliers. An illustration is that a multinational agricultural company can overlay satellite-based deforestation information with its plantations to determine that its suppliers are upholding zero deforestation pledges. On the same note, an energy firm can superimpose the locations of facilities on flood or wildfire risk maps to assess the exposure to climate risks and institute mitigation measures.

A significant advantage of the geospatially informed analysis is proactive risk reduction. The knowledge of companies in the geographical areas helped by the spatial overlays can be utilized to redirect the supply chains, reshape sourcing policies, or identify new operations locations with a low rate of environmental and social effects. An example of this is a logistics company that can optimize its transportation system to circumvent ecologically sensitive zones so that it can reduce emissions and reduce the risk of regulation. Likewise, manufacturers can choose expansion locations in areas where they are less vulnerable to natural hazards or have better regulatory frameworks to enhance resilience and improve sustainability performance. The possible disruptions (extreme weather events, geopolitical risks, or social unrest) can be simulated and modeled with scenario modeling to enable organizations to prepare contingency plans and ensure continuity of business. The geospatial technologies can be used to improve monitoring and controlling supplier compliance. With the incorporation of GIS, remote sensing, and IoT data, businesses can be able to monitor environmental and labor performance and compliance with the regulations in suppliers that are located elsewhere geographically. As an example, satellite images can identify illegal ground clearing or water misuse within supplier activities, whereas tracking of transportation systems with a location can emphasize carbon-intensive transportation or delivery chain inefficiency. This is a more responsible sourcing with the help of spatially informed oversight, which enhances ESG compliance and decreases reputational and operational risk.

Besides that, geospatial analysis enhances ESG reporting and stakeholder transparency. Risk exposure mapping and mitigation strategy offer physical, visual stress that organizations are undertaking due diligence and managing the environment and social consequences proactively. Indicatively, a corporation can generate interactive maps of where suppliers are placed around the regions that are considered to be under protection and the efforts involved to reduce environmental interference. Equally, a heatmap can convey areas of intense climate or social hazard along supply chains that show proactive governance to investors, regulators, and civil society organizations. Such visualizations are useful in ensuring that ESG reporting is no longer in the form of a firm, statistical disclosure, but rather, an evidence-based story that clearly demonstrates the responsibility and accountability of corporations.

Lastly, strategic decision-making and resilience planning can be assisted with geospatial risk assessment. Based on spatially determined vulnerabilities, organizations are able to focus their investments in risk mitigation (e.g., resilient infrastructure, the integration of renewable energies, or neighborhood development projects). Companies can be able to foresee the emerging risks with the addition of time and predictive analysis, like climate projections, deforestation trends, or urban expansion models, among others, which can enable a company to make adaptive choices to align operational goals and sustainability goals.

Community Engagement and Social Impact Mapping

Although environmental monitoring is arguably the most popular focus of corporate ESG efforts, the social aspect is also key to long-term sustainability and trust within the community. Geospatial technologies are not just for ecological analysis; they can allow organizations to determine, map, and report on the social consequences of their activities. This involves assessing the way corporate operations affect the local communities, visualizing the balance of benefits and risks, and enhancing stakeholder involvement by means of open and fair information exchange (Anthony, 2024; Chilvers et al., 2021).

The mapping offered by GIS gives a distinct advantage in terms of examining the impact that corporate operations have on communities. As an illustration, organisations can be able to monitor the movement of the labour force and where the employees and contractors are located with respect to the operational places. This aids in pointing out the interdependence between corporate facilities and local livelihoods, as well as determining the possible vulnerabilities in the case of disruptions. More than that, businesses may determine how near the activities are to marginalized or vulnerable populations, including low-income communities, indigenous people, or low access to medical care, education, or clean water. These kinds of insights are critical to aligning operations to social responsibility and equity principles.

In addition to risk identification, geospatial technologies are also potent tools to measure the extent and effectiveness of the corporate social initiatives. Some of the areas that many organizations spend their resources on projects in an effort to achieve their ESG or Corporate Social Responsibility (CSR) programs are health, education, housing, infrastructure development, and water security. Through mapping the geographic location of these projects, companies should be able to assess whether the benefits are fairly allocated and point out underserved locations. As an example, the distribution of mapping schools or health clinics created as a part of corporate programs can help illustrate gaps in how some specific communities are missed, allowing more comprehensive and focused interventions. One of the applications is especially relevant in terms of mapping water access within the community in the areas impacted by industrial activities. Mining, energy, or agricultural firms usually depend greatly on the water in their area, leading to water scarcity among the locals. Through the combination of remote sensing information, hydrological models, and community surveys, the organizations can map the intersection of corporate water use and community access points. This enables proactive mitigation measures

- like putting alternative water supply systems in place, investing in clean water infrastructure, or more efficient water management practices - that ease tensions and reinforce corporate-community relationships.

Geospatial tools can enhance stakeholder engagement and communication. Communities can be able to visualize the social impacts of corporate projects through interactive maps, dashboards, and participatory GIS platforms in an accessible and transparent manner. As an illustration, a company may come up with a publicly available dashboard that displays the geographic extent of its social investments, infrastructure development advancement, or live air and water quality data around the operational locations. Organizations can be able to establish trust, enhance conversation, and develop a sense of collective responsibility with the local stakeholders by offering them spatially-grounded evidence. Moreover, spatial analysis facilitates social impact assessment (SIA) procedures that most regulatory systems and global standards demand. By integrating demographic information, census data, and field surveys with corporate spatial footprints, the corporations can predict the impact of new initiatives that may be implemented on the local communities. This involves modeling population displacement, or alterations in land use, or effects on cultural heritage sites. This foresight allows organizations to take mitigation or compensatory action when conflicts begin to grow, minimizing the reputational risk and meeting global ESG requirements.

Lastly, social impact mapping is a part of corporate sustainability and the resilience of communities in the long term. By constantly controlling and updating the spatial information, the companies can be able to notice the changing needs of the community, demographic changes, and the results of their social programs after periods of time. It is a continuous cycle that assists organizations in converting one-time CSR initiatives to strategic and data-driven community development initiatives that fit corporate interests and community interests at the same time.

Compliance Verification

Responsible corporate governance is one of the factors that entail ensuring that environmental regulations, zoning laws, and sustainability standards are adhered to. Failure to comply not only puts organizations at the risk of incurring legal liability but also compromises their reputation and investor and community confidence. In this regard, geospatial technologies have become an essential part of compliance verification, providing evidence-based ways of keeping track and auditing compliance with mandatory laws as well as optional ESG pledges.

On its simplest level, spatial audits can offer organizations the capability to map and compare operational footprints with regulatory requirements. As an example, the geographic boundaries of their facilities, extraction sites, or transport routes can be overlaid with official zoning maps, land-use classifications, or protected ecological areas by the companies. This would allow confirmation on whether the activities are trespassing in restricted areas, like national parks, biodiversity reserves, or indigenous areas. Through these spatial comparisons, organizations are in a position to spot non-compliant activities rapidly and implement corrective action prior to escalation of violations into legal battles or fines.

Geospatial technologies are also critical in compliance with environmental standards. By using satellite imagery, drones, and remote sensing, land degradation, deforestation, or illegal resource extraction can be identified. As an example, mining or forestry industries can be sure that they do not engage in excessive mining by using high-resolution satellite images, and agriculture companies can be sure that they do not expand their crops in the zones of deforestation. On the same note, geospatial data like atmospheric records by satellite sensors can be incorporated in the GIS platforms to determine the extent to which air quality levels in the vicinity of the operating sites do not surpass the legal standards.

The other important use is in examining whether there is a level of adherence to water use and sustainability pledges. With water withdrawal mapping, wastewater discharge sources, and hydrological trends, companies can benchmark their operations against regulatory constraints on water extraction or pollution. This is especially significant in arid regions where commercial, agricultural, and social demands are on. Geospatial analysis enables companies to show, through clear evidence, that their water management activities comply with the law and more extensive ESG objectives regarding resource stewardship. In addition to regulatory requirements, geospatial tools can support compliance with various voluntary ESG reporting, like the Global Reporting Initiative (GRI), the Task Force on Climate-Related Financial Disclosures (TCFD), or the Sustainability Accounting Standards Board (SASB). These frameworks are also more and more embracing or demanding organizations to evidence spatially the claims of their sustainability. As an illustration, the company can report on biodiversity protection activities, and this can be explained by providing a map of the GIS area being maintained around the sensitive ecosystems. On the same note, carbon offset projects can be checked by mapping afforestation or the process of reforestation through satellite images in order to make the disclosures in climate issues transparent.

Critically, a geospatial compliance check is also able to enhance stakeholder trust and credibility. There is certainly a need to show regulators, investors, NGOs, and local communities that corporate activities are in line with sustainability pledges. Compared to self-reported or anecdotal evidence, spatial data gives objective, verifiable, and often publicly available data. As an example, a firm dealing with renewable energy can post dynamic maps that indicate the location of wind or solar facilities and exclusion areas that keep migration routes of birds or cultural heritage sites untouched. Through transparency of such information, companies not only lessen suspicion but also enhance their relationship with other stakeholders.

Also, real-time monitoring systems that incorporate compliance verification make organizations more responsive. Satellite constellations, Internet of Things (IoT) sensing technologies, and cloud-based GIS systems enable compliance indicators to be monitored in near real time. As an illustration, a pipeline firm may observe the land-use patterns along the pipeline routes to identify illicit intrusion, and energy firms may observe the satellite-detected methane gas emissions to ensure that they do not exceed the allowable limits. This shift from periodic audits to continuous monitoring reduces compliance risks and enables rapid corrective action. Last but not least, long-term strategic governance is assisted by geospatial compliance checking. By storing historical spatial data, organizations are able to show compliance trends over time, where there is progressive growth in sustainability performance. Such a historical view is priceless in terms of regulatory inspections, as well as corporate sustainability reports, ESG ratings, and communications to investors. This, in the long term, builds a demonstrable history of responsible practices and increases resilience to reputational or legal issues.

CHALLENGES, OPPORTUNITIES, AND FUTURE DIRECTIONS

Although geospatial tools could be transformative in corporate sustainability reporting and ESG compliance, organizations are experiencing some challenges in making the most out of them. Meanwhile, new technologies and best practices offer new possibilities in the field of improving spatial intelligence in making sustainability decisions.

Data Quality, Availability, and Standardization Issues

Another key issue in using geospatial for ESG reporting is that the quality, completeness, and availability of data vary. The nature of corporate operations often extends over many regions, countries, and supply chains, leading to disjointed datasets with varying formats, magnitudes, spatial resolution, or time coverage. As an example, a multinational energy company can have fine-resolution emissions data in facilities in one country, but only coarse satellite-based estimates in remote operations. On the same note, the agricultural supply chains tend to use the suppliers' third-party data that might not be standardized to a single standard, which introduces inconsistency that makes integration and analysis complex.

Remote sensing, IoT sensor reading, and other third-party spatial information can be of differing accuracy, reliability, or frequency of updates. The disjointed nature of data over time may restrict the possibility of monitoring changes through time or identifying new risks, whereas the differences in resolution or coordinate surface may reduce overlay and spatial analysis. In addition, ESG measurements themselves are not universally agreed upon in terms of geospatial indicators, which would enable the comparison of environmental footprints, social impacts, or regulatory compliance across organizations or industries. In the absence of strict data validation, harmonization, and standardization guidelines, spatial analyses can generate a misleading or incomplete understanding of the data, negating the validity of sustainability reporting and decision-making.

Data governance approaches capable of handling these problems include data collection, data cleaning, data validation, and data documentation protocols, the use of common geospatial formats, and ESG indicators. It is also necessary that organizations assess data sources on their accuracy, resolution, and timeliness in order to balance access and reliability to meaningful and comparable analysis. Table 6 summarizes the major data-related challenges that organizations encounter when integrating geospatial tools into ESG reporting, along with their implications for sustainability practices.

Table 6. Data-related challenges in geospatial ESG reporting

Challenge	Description	Implications for ESG Reporting
Data Quality Variability	Inconsistent accuracy and reliability across datasets (e.g., satellite vs. sensor data).	May lead to misleading insights or inaccurate reporting.
Data Availability Gaps	Missing or incomplete data in certain regions or supply chains.	Limits the ability to monitor global operations consistently.
Resolution & Scale Differences	Variations in spatial/temporal resolution and coordinate systems.	Hinders integration, overlay, and comparability.
Lack of Standard Indicators	Absence of universal geospatial ESG metrics.	Makes cross-company and cross-sector comparisons difficult.
Fragmented Sources	Reliance on third-party or supplier data with no uniform standards.	Creates inconsistencies that undermine credibility.

Technical and Organizational Barriers

Technological and organizational barriers may prevent integration of geospatial intelligence with ESG reporting in organizations, even when high-quality spatial data is available. Companies could technically not possess enough GIS infrastructure, cloud storage, high-performance computing, or analytics infrastructure to process large, complex spatial data. Employees might lack knowledge of geospatial analysis, interpretation of remote sensing, or visualization, and therefore, the capabilities to convert raw spatial information into actionable information.

Barriers in organizations are also important. The departments can be run in silo, where roles and responsibilities are not well defined, and this poses a challenge to cross-functional interactions. It can be slower to implement spatial intelligence into ESG reporting processes because it is difficult to embrace new technologies or alter the traditional workflows. In one example, integrating GIS analysis into corporate dashboards or regulatory filings might involve redesigning process flows across operations, environmental management, and reporting departments, and training personnel to read and respond to spatial insights.

All these barriers must be dealt with by a strategic organization-wide approach that integrates technical capacity building with managing change. Creating defined ownership of geospatial programs, developing cooperation among departments, and conducting continuous training can promote the effective incorporation of geospatial intelligence into ESG reporting. Table 7 highlights the technical and organizational barriers that limit effective use of geospatial intelligence, alongside potential solutions to overcome these constraints.

Table 7. Technical and organizational barriers to geospatial ESG integration

Barrier	Description	Potential Solutions
Technical Infrastructure Gaps	Lack of GIS platforms, cloud storage, or high-performance computing.	Invest in scalable cloud-based platforms and computing resources.
Limited Expertise	Insufficient skills in GIS, remote sensing, or data visualization.	Provide training, hire geospatial specialists, and build internal capacity.
Departmental Silos	Lack of coordination across ESG, operations, and IT teams.	Foster cross-departmental collaboration and data-sharing protocols.
Resistance to Change	Reluctance to adopt new workflows or tools.	Apply change management strategies and leadership support.
Workflow Integration Issues	Difficulty embedding geospatial insights into dashboards and reports.	Redesign workflows and establish clear ownership of geospatial initiatives.

Geospatial ESG Analytics Trends

Nevertheless, several emerging trends influence the future of geospatial-enabled ESG reporting:

Algorithms based on artificial intelligence and machine learning are being used more and more frequently on large spatial data to identify patterns, predict risks, and maximize resource allocation. As an example, AI could be used to classify land-use on satellite images, locate emissions hotspots along supply chains, or detect deforestation in near real time. It is also possible to combine different datasets with machine learning models, including weather, land use, and operational data, to forecast the effects on the environment or exposure to social risks.

Real-time visualization of ESG performance can be achieved through the integration of IoT sensors, GIS platforms, and cloud computing, and it will be dynamic. Emissions, energy usage, watering, and the footprints of operations can be observed at all times by organizations, and decision-makers can react quickly to arising risks or non-meeting sustainability goals. Real-time dashboards are also useful in making the reporting to regulators, investors, and communities more transparent. Environmental, social, and regulatory risks scenario modelling is supported by spatial data and predictive analytics. The organizations can be able to model possible results of climate events, disruption of the supply chain, or change of policies, and thus implement mitigation in advance. As an example, predictive models can predict impacts of floods or wildfires on facilities, so companies can implement adaptation steps ahead of time.

These patterns reflect a movement toward active, data-driven ESG management, in which geospatial intelligence is used to support sustained enhancement, strategic decision making, and operational resiliency.

Recommendations for Leveraging Geospatial Intelligence

Best practices that can be embraced by organizations to maximize the potential of geospatial tools in sustainability reporting include the following:

- Establish robust protocols for data collection, validation, standardization, and integration. Be consistent in more than one region, supplier, and site of operation to improve reliability and comparability of ESG insights.
- Build in-house GIS and analytics expertise or collaborate with external geospatial specialists. Educating employees in the use of spatial analysis, remote sensing interpretation, and dashboards enhances the capacity of the organizations.
- Embed geospatial insights into corporate decision-making, supply chain management, risk assessment, and stakeholder communication processes. Cross-functional cooperation can guarantee that spatial intelligence is used in operational reporting, strategy, and ESG reporting.
- Make use of AI, machine learning, IoT, and cloud platforms to make predictive analytics, automated monitoring, and real-time reporting. The technologies also advance efficiency, improve accuracy, and promote proactive ESG risk management.

- Apply spatial visualization and interactive dashboards to convey ESG performance effectively to regulators and investors, as well as communities. This enhances accountability, trust, and stakeholder buy-in as well as enhances the visibility of sustainability initiatives.
- Data and organizational issues, and the adoption of new technologies, can allow companies to turn the process of ESG reporting into an evidence-based process with a spatial perspective. Geospatial intelligence enhances compliance and transparency as well as strategic sustainability efforts, risk mitigation, and long-term resilience and value creation.

CONCLUSION

Geospatial solutions are also transforming the reality of corporate sustainability reporting and ESG compliance to offer place-specific knowledge, increase transparency, and facilitate evidence-based decision-making. Traditional reporting techniques are often not enough as organizations come under increasing pressure from regulators, investors, and other stakeholders to prove a responsible approach to the environment and social responsibility. Spatial data powered by GIS, remote sensing, and the IoT offer the essential ability to visualize environmental footprints, evaluate the social impact, and check regulatory and ESG standards adherence along several geographic levels.

As noted in this chapter, geospatial technologies have a multifaceted role to play in supporting ESG goals. Environmental footprint mapping and supply chain risk assessment, to community engagement and compliance verification, can be done using spatial intelligence to convert complex data on operations in the organization to actionable information. Energy, agriculture, and manufacturing are examples of sector-specific applications where geospatial tools can be used to maximize activities, reduce risks, and enable sustainable activities at the same time, increasing stakeholder trust and accountability.

Regardless of their potential, organizations have to overcome the issues concerning data quality, standardization, technical expertise, and organizational integration. New opportunities to address these barriers and improve sustainability performance include the use of emerging trend AI-enabled spatial analytics, real-time ESG dashboards, and predictive modeling. Organizations can use geospatial intelligence to not only meet ESG standards but also promote long-term strategic sustainability efforts and value creation by following best practices in data governance, cross-functional integration, and technological adoption.

Conclusively, adoption of geospatial tools in corporate sustainability practices is a paradigm shift, a shift in corporate sustainability activities, which were historically marked by fixed, retrospective reporting, to a dynamic, spatially informed ESG management. Those companies that adopt this strategy are in a better position to gain insights into how they are affecting the environment and society around them, involve the stakeholders, and contribute positively towards achieving sustainability in the world at large. With the evolving geospatial technologies, they will become very important in ensuring corporate sustainability to ensure that the organizations can be firm, transparent, and accountable in a more complex and interconnected world.

REFERENCES

Anthony, B. (2024). The Role of Community Engagement in Urban Innovation Towards the Co-Creation of Smart Sustainable Cities. *Journal of the Knowledge Economy*, *15*(1). Advance online publication. DOI: 10.1007/s13132-023-01176-1

Ateeq, M., Zhang, N., Zhao, W., Gu, Y., Wen, Z., Zheng, C., & Hao, J. (2025). Enhancing Construction Waste Transportation Management Using Internet of Things (IoT): An Evaluation Framework Based on AHP–FCE Method. *Buildings 2025, Vol. 15, Page 1381*, *15*(8), 1381. https://doi.org/DOI: 10.3390/BUILDINGS15081381

Audi, M., & Yu, H. (2024). Strategic value creation through corporate social responsibility adoption for sustainable financial performance. *Journal of Policy Options*, *7*(4), 14–21.

Barbosa, A. de S., Crispim, M. C., da Silva, L. B., da Silva, J. M. N., Barbosa, A. M., & Morioka, S. N. (2024). How can organizations measure the integration of environmental, social, and governance (ESG) criteria? Validation of an instrument using item response theory to capture workers' perception. *Business Strategy and the Environment*, *33*(4). Advance online publication. DOI: 10.1002/bse.3675

Baryannis, G., Validi, S., Dani, S., & Antoniou, G. (2019). Supply chain risk management and artificial intelligence: state of the art and future research directions. In *International Journal of Production Research* (Vol. 57, Issue 7). https://doi.org/DOI: 10.1080/00207543.2018.1530476

Chen, J., Chen, S., Fu, R., Li, D., Jiang, H., Wang, C., Peng, Y., Jia, K., & Hicks, B. J. (2022). Remote Sensing Big Data for Water Environment Monitoring: Current Status, Challenges, and Future Prospects. In *Earth's Future* (Vol. 10, Issue 2). https://doi.org/DOI: 10.1029/2021EF002289

Chilvers, J., Bellamy, R., Pallett, H., & Hargreaves, T. (2021). A systemic approach to mapping participation with low-carbon energy transitions. *Nature Energy*, *6*(3). Advance online publication. DOI: 10.1038/s41560-020-00762-w

Choudhary, N. A., Singh, S., Schoenherr, T., & Ramkumar, M. (2023). Risk assessment in supply chains: A state-of-the-art review of methodologies and their applications. *Annals of Operations Research*, *322*(2). Advance online publication. DOI: 10.1007/s10479-022-04700-9 PMID: 35531565

Chua, W. F., James, R., King, A., Lee, E., & Soderstrom, N. (2022). Task Force on Climate-related Financial Disclosures (TCFD) Implementation: An Overview and Insights from the Australian Accounting Standards Board Dialogue Series. *Australian Accounting Review*, *32*(3). Advance online publication. DOI: 10.1111/auar.12388

Coelho, R., Jayantilal, S., & Ferreira, J. J. (2023). The impact of social responsibility on corporate financial performance: A systematic literature review. In *Corporate Social Responsibility and Environmental Management* (Vol. 30, Issue 4). https://doi.org/DOI: 10.1002/csr.2446

Contini, S., Bellezza, F., Christou, M. D., & Kirchsteiger, C. (2000). The use of geographic information systems in major accident risk assessment and management. *Journal of Hazardous Materials*, *78*(1–3). Advance online publication. DOI: 10.1016/S0304-3894(00)00224-7 PMID: 10978568

Das, S. N., Sreenivasan, G., Srinivasa Rao, S., Joshi, A. K., Varghese, A. O., Prakasa Rao, D. S., Chandrasekar, K., & Jha, C. S. (2022). *Geospatial Technologies for Development of Cadastral Information System and its Applications for Developmental Planning and e-Governance*. https://doi.org/DOI: 10.1007/978-3-030-98981-1_21

de Souza Barbosa, A., da Silva, M. C. B. C., da Silva, L. B., Morioka, S. N., & de Souza, V. F. (2023). Integration of Environmental, Social, and Governance (ESG) criteria: their impacts on corporate sustainability performance. In *Humanities and Social Sciences Communications* (Vol. 10, Issue 1). https://doi.org/DOI: 10.1057/s41599-023-01919-0

Dicuonzo, G., Donofrio, F., Iannuzzi, A. P., & Dell'Atti, V. (2022). The integration of sustainability in corporate governance systems: An innovative framework applied to the European systematically important banks. *International Journal of Disclosure and Governance*, *19*(3). Advance online publication. DOI: 10.1057/s41310-021-00140-2

Dimmelmeier, A. (2024). The financial geography of sustainability data: A mapping exercise of the spatial dimension of the ESG information industry. *Finance and Space*, *1*(1), 76–79. DOI: 10.1080/2833115X.2023.2296980

Efraimidou, E., & Spiliotis, M. (2024). A GIS-Based Flood Risk Assessment Using the Decision-Making Trial and Evaluation Laboratory Approach at a Regional Scale. *Environmental Processes*, *11*(1). Advance online publication. DOI: 10.1007/s40710-024-00683-w

Eng, L. L., Fikru, M., & Vichitsarawong, T. (2022). Comparing the informativeness of sustainability disclosures versus ESG disclosure ratings. *Sustainability Accounting. Management and Policy Journal*, *13*(2). Advance online publication. DOI: 10.1108/SAMPJ-03-2021-0095

Eshetie, G. G., Alemie, B. K., & Wubie, A. M. (2024). Geospatial technologies in support of responsible land tenure governance: A systematic review. *Geomatica*, *76*(2), 100014.

Fang, K., Wang, S., He, J., Song, J., Fang, C., & Jia, X. (2021). Mapping the environmental footprints of nations partnering the Belt and Road Initiative. *Resources, Conservation and Recycling, 164*. Advance online publication. DOI: 10.1016/j.resconrec.2020.105068

Franco, S., Pancino, B., & Martella, A. (2021). Mapping national environmental sustainability distribution by ecological footprint: The case of Italy. *Sustainability (Switzerland), 13*(15). Advance online publication. DOI: 10.3390/su13158671

Gopal, S., & Pitts, J. (2024a). *Geospatial Finance: Foundations and Applications*. 225–273. https://doi.org/DOI: 10.1007/978-3-031-74418-1_6

Gopal, S., & Pitts, J. (2024b). *Satellite Remote Sensing: Pioneering Tools for Environmental Insight and Sustainable Investment*. 275–315. https://doi.org/DOI: 10.1007/978-3-031-74418-1_7

Gu, Y., Dai, J., & Vasarhelyi, M. A. (2023). Audit 4.0-based ESG assurance: An example of using satellite images on GHG emissions. *International Journal of Accounting Information Systems, 50*, 100625. DOI: 10.1016/J.ACCINF.2023.100625

Kent, A. J., & Specht, D. (2023). The Routledge Handbook of Geospatial Technologies and Society. In *The Routledge Handbook of Geospatial Technologies and Society*. https://doi.org/DOI: 10.4324/9780367855765

Mougenot, B., & Doussoulin, J. P. (2024). A bibliometric analysis of the Global Reporting Initiative (GRI): Global trends in developed and developing countries. *Environment, Development and Sustainability, 26*(3). Advance online publication. DOI: 10.1007/s10668-023-02974-y PMID: 36788933

Parfitt, C. (2024). A foundation for 'ethical capital': The Sustainability Accounting Standards Board and Integrated Reporting. *Critical Perspectives on Accounting, 98*. Advance online publication. DOI: 10.1016/j.cpa.2022.102477

Rai, P. K., Mishra, V. N., & Singh, P. (2022). *Geospatial technology for landscape and environmental management: sustainable assessment and planning*. Springer.

Rapach, S., Riccardi, A., Liu, B., & Bowden, J. (2024). A taxonomy of earth observation data for sustainable finance. *Journal of Climate Finance, 6*, 100029. DOI: 10.1016/J.JCLIMF.2023.100029

Rossi, C., Byrne, J. G., & Christiaen, C. (2024). Breaking the ESG rating divergence: An open geospatial framework for environmental scores. *Journal of Environmental Management, 349*. Advance online publication. DOI: 10.1016/j.jenvman.2023.119477 PMID: 37944316

Sarfraz, M., Ozturk, I., Yoo, S., Raza, M. A., & Han, H. (2023). Toward a new understanding of environmental and financial performance through corporate social responsibility, green innovation, and sustainable development. *Humanities & Social Sciences Communications, 10*(1). Advance online publication. DOI: 10.1057/s41599-023-01799-4

Saxena, A., Singh, R., Gehlot, A., Akram, S. V., Twala, B., Singh, A., Montero, E. C., & Priyadarshi, N. (2022). Technologies Empowered Environmental, Social, and Governance (ESG): An Industry 4.0 Landscape. *Sustainability 2023, Vol. 15, Page 309, 15*(1), 309. https://doi.org/DOI: 10.3390/SU15010309

Soares, I. V., Yarime, M., & Klemun, M. M. (2025). Estimating GHG emissions from cloud computing: Sources of inaccuracy, opportunities and challenges in location-based and use-based approaches. *Climate Policy*. Advance online publication. DOI: 10.1080/14693062.2025.2450054;SUBPAGE:STRING:ABSTRACT;REQUESTEDJOURNAL:JOURNAL:TCPO20;WGROUP:STRING:PUBLICATION

Wang, C. (2023). *The effect of mandatory GHG Disclosure regulation on GHG disclosure quality, corporate financial and environmental performance: a UK study*. Doctoral dissertation.

Wong, L. W., Tan, G. W. H., Ooi, K. B., Lin, B., & Dwivedi, Y. K. (2024). Artificial intelligence-driven risk management for enhancing supply chain agility: A deep-learning-based dual-stage PLS-SEM-ANN analysis. *International Journal of Production Research, 62*(15). Advance online publication. DOI: 10.1080/00207543.2022.2063089

Zhang, X., Geng, Y., Tong, Y. W., Kua, H. W., Tian, X., Wu, R., Zhao, X., & Chiu, A. S. F. (2021). Spatial characteristics and its driving factors of low-carbon energy technology innovation in China: A gravity movement and exploratory spatial data analysis. *Journal of Cleaner Production, 295*. Advance online publication. DOI: 10.1016/j.jclepro.2021.126481

Chapter 12
AI and Sustainability: Combining Ethics With Environmental Impact Assessment

Usharani Bhimavarapu
https://orcid.org/0000-0001-5050-0415
Department of Computer Science and Engineering, Koneru Lakshmaiah Education Foundation, Vaddeswaram, India

ABSTRACT

The broad scope of applications of artificial intelligence (AI) in many fields has also raised important issues concerning responsible practice and sustainability of the environment. In the current research, designing ethical AI systems and their impact on the environment are argued with a deliberate effort at embracing responsible and sustainable technology. Information were collected from the site under construction via a preprocessed systematic investigation for validity and processed later using Particle Swarm Optimization (PSO) with feature selection in mind. Bi-stacked Gated Recurrent Unit (GRU) has been utilized to feature extract of temporal patterns within ethics and environmental features to facilitate predictive analysis and identify possible biases. The conclusion highlights the need to reconcile fairness, transparency, and accountability of AI systems with their carbon footprint.

INTRODUCTION

Morality-based development of AI is the designing and development of AI systems based on justice, morality, and the betterment of society. Since AI is being used extensively in day-to-day life, choices made by these machines have far-reaching effects on a group or an individual of individuals. Such bias in AI systems can lead to greater discrimination if unchecked. Transparency in decision-making

DOI: 10.4018/979-8-3373-4652-6.ch012

is extremely important in keeping it trustworthy and accountable. Ethical AI is a matter of respect for privacy and data protection. Ethical standards keep discrimination out of recruitment, the police force, and the healthcare system. Ethical AI ensures inclusivity and diversity of thought. Ethical standards are required so that the weaker sections of the citizenry are not inadvertently harmed by AI. Developers, policymakers, and researchers need to collaborate to formulate transparent ethical standards. Ethically AI is a social responsibility and not one prescribed by policymakers. Data-driven AI depend on data, which can be itself inherently historically biased or unrepresentational.

Bias will get amplified if not contained appropriately and result in discriminatory outcomes. One example is that hiring software would be biased towards others if skewed historical employment statistics. Fairness methods must be used in accountable AI development, such as bias detection and correction tools. Programmers must vet frequently for unseen effects on AI systems. Data sets must have varied populations to offset bias. AI bias affects not only individuals but also unity and trust in technology. Transparent visibility of AI decision-making allows stakeholders to accept possible bias. Ethically designed training for AI helps engineers identify and reduce biased patterns. Avoidance of bias is actually a key objective of ethical AI. Accountability makes developers and organizations responsible for the effects of AI systems. Transparent AI systems allow stakeholders to view the rationale behind automated decisions.

This prevents abuse or unintended harm caused by black-box algorithms. Logically documenting AI decision-making helps in reproducing and credence. Ethical AI systems are typically tested on a regular basis and for compliance. Clear consent and public education are possible by transparency, especially in such sensitive applications as in the healthcare industry. Through AI-decision-transparency, organizations can just rectify mistake or injustice. Accountability mechanisms are improving the ethical landscape in tech companies. Transparency can be harnessed by policymakers to facilitate rules and ethical behavior. Finally, transparency and accountability protect people and society. Human-oriented AI centers on human flourishing, using technology for social and ethical purposes. The intent is to augment human capability, not replace it.

AI must facilitate decision-making without concession in autonomy or human judgment. Ethical AI starts human-machine interaction with safe ethical stewardship in human hands. Human-centered design also centers on accessibility to enable all with technology. Engage stakeholders, including end-users, in attempting to understand needs and issues. Ethical AI avoids manipulation or exploitation, especially social and behavior applications. Human-centered practices help guarantee that AI promotes human-centered development and well-being. Social and long-term effects of AI application should be considered by developers. Human-centered ethical AI requires trust and social value. AI deployment and design have broad environmental effects primarily through computationally intensive processes that use energy. Large amounts of electricity are used when training deep AI models, producing carbon.

Ethically accountable AI design today includes environmental sustainability among its moral imperatives. Energy spending is reduced by efficiency algorithms without compromising performance. Data storage and cloud computing tech can be designed to operate on renewable power. Green AI also explores evaluating the green footprint of hardware and e-waste. Companies employing green AI practices demonstrate corporate responsibility. Reduced environmental impact aligns with global climate goals and reduces environmental devastation. Open transparency of the carbon footprint of AI promotes corporate responsibility. Ethical AI thus integrates environment conservation and innovation. Ethical AI aligns innovation towards beneficial social impacts. Innovators are encouraged to foresee possible harms in the future prior to implementing systems.

Foresight for anticipation reduces risks of AI misuse or unintended consequences. Careful innovation entails the combination of AI innovation and ethics, law, and human rights. Interdisciplinary work ensures that varied approaches inform design choices. Ethical AI preserves public confidence, and it becomes less challenging for novel technologies to be accepted. Ethics integration within R&D reduces reputational and legal threats. Responsible and sustainable AI guarantees long-term sustainability of AI solutions. Ethical compliance at all levels of the life cycle is ensured through regular monitoring and auditing. Ethical AI, thus, balances innovation and social as well as ethical responsibility. Regulatory agencies from around the globe are demanding frameworks to regulate AI development and deployment. Compliancy guarantees that AI systems are secure, fair, and respect individuals' privacy.

Dealing with ethical AI is easy to stay in line with these regulations. Ethically behaving companies demonstrate how much they care about social and global norms. Compliancy also reduces the likelihood of lawsuits and penalties. Standards provide interoperability, security, and accountability in AI systems. Ethical AI frameworks enable organizations to enhance documentation of process and decision-making process. The process is needed for certification and auditing. Compliance-based ethical AI fosters integrity culture in technology. On the whole, ethical AI widens the divide between tech progress and lawful accountability. Ethical AI is accessible to all for equal access to technology and technology benefits. By minimizing discrimination, encouraging participation, and eliminating bias, AI delivers social justice.

Equal treatment under labor practices is also guaranteed through AI by ethical standards. Economically, ethical AI brings benefits to disadvantaged societies. Open AI reduces the risk of exploitation by dominant market forces. Ethical AI has the potential to empower start-ups and small enterprises with equal access. Encouraging equality in the use of AI across global digital differences removes global digital differences. Equality on the social side allows user trust and acceptability towards AI technology. Ethical AI therefore becomes possible for fair and equitable societies. Mass use of AI technology requires trust. The users will utilize the AI systems as ethical, equitable, and open. Ethical AI is concerned with the security, privacy, and social accountability of users. Abuse, bias, or vagueness in AI systems causes public distrust. Empowerment based on ethical principles resolves such instances and creates trust. Public engagement in AI development enhances public debate and learning from each other. Trust is fostered among the private sector, governments, and civil society through collaboration. A trusted AI system creates investment and innovation. Ethical AI practice also develops company reputation and brand credibility. The total public trust is the passport to the success and sustainability of AI technologies. As technology becomes more advanced, and AI continues to expand, ethics and the environment become more urgent. Prudence guarantees long-term social benefit and sustainability.

Ethics-led AI designs lead to ethical innovation of new-generation technologies such as autonomous systems and generative AI. Planetary conscience renders AI development sustainable to planetary health. Ethics embedded at early stages avoids retrofitting costs and reduces risk. Awareness programs and education enlighten developers, policymakers, and society regarding the implications of AI. Redefining on an ongoing basis based on society, ethics, and ecologic necessities future-proofs AI technologies. Compatibility with human values re-construction makes AI pertinent and acceptable. Moral AI excludes its misuse, makes it sustainable, and allows society to benefit. Above all, it provides an AI road map for responsibly and sustainably serving humankind. Marx and Engels (2004) provide philosophical guidance but are in real life not present in existing technology ethics. Nietsche (1989) presents a philosophical deconstruction of morality and truth, but pragmatic application in AI ethics is dismissed by the general philosophical atmosphere.

Sartre et al. (2004) provide humanist and existentialism models but no empirical basis for ethical application in contemporary systems. Muguerza (2004) bases itself on dialogical reason but its theoretic character limits actionable use in AI regulation. Jobin et al. (2019) provide comprehensive global comparison of guidelines for AI ethics but do not assess operational effectiveness of guidelines. Vinuesa et al. (2020) provide benefit of AI to Sustainable Development Goals but in their study emphatically replicate the future effect without testing in actual world. Rahwan et al. (2019) suggest machine behavior norms but say very little on regulation or enforcement on an ethics basis. Barocas and Selbst (2016) discuss conflicting impacts with big data but frame the argument based on legal issues instead of technical limitation. Sachs (2012) discusses MDG to SDG transition but does not highlight short discussion on use of new technology at the time of implementation. Griggs et al. (2013) discuss SDG targets for people and planet but do not discuss practical application processes at organizational levels. Pastor-Escuredo et al. (2014) employ mobile phone data to analyze disasters, which could be scalability-limited and privacy-risky. Zufiria et al. (2018) predict seasonality patterns in mobility from anonymized data but might hide variance at the individual level by resorting to pooled data. Khamis et al. (2019) have termed AI as the enabler of SDGs, but controversy is only in the descriptive stage in the absence of empirical evidence of performance. Damjanović et al. (2022) give an integrated reinforcement learning approach to autonomous power flow control but the paper is marred by simulated topology operations without any empirical data. Wang et al. (2023) give an energy management approach based on GM to hydrogen fuel cell buses but simulation performance under various weather scenarios is not presented.

Fayyazi et al. (2023) give a review of AI/ML applications for hydrogen fuel cell vehicle management but the paper merely gives literature without any original empirical results. El Jery et al. (2023) integrate thermodynamic simulation and ANN-based prediction for solar thermochemical power plants and where predictions are constrained by model assumptions in the electrolyzer. Zhang et al. (2023) offer half-power fuel cell bus energy management prediction but are not scalable to different bus fleets and situations. Shoeibi et al. (2021) suggest deep learning approaches to seizure detection in epileptic seizures, but clinical utility is limited because of heterogeneity of data and lack of standardization. VoPham et al. (2018) detail geoAI applications to environmental epidemiology and not real-world deployment limitations or data privacy. Alafif et al. (2021) overview deep and machine learning in treatment and diagnosis of COVID-19 but have different approaches with limited clinical data. Lee and Lee (2018) improve predictions of harmful algal bloom with deep learning but are limited to river-exclusive data and therefore require non-generalizability. Cirillo et al. (2020) note sex and gender discrimination in biomedical AI but primarily recognize issues without specifying successful mitigation techniques. Campero-Jurado et al. (2020) apply an industrial IoT smart helmet through AI, but industrial reliability and real-time scalability are concerns. Akçay et al. (2020) apply AI to robot bird population enumeration, but geography and seasonality will likely compromise accuracy. Wang and Ye (2022) search for spatial-temporal imbalance trends of tourism development, but outcomes will be descriptive and very likely not total representations of causation. Seuring and Müller (2008) formulate a conceptual framework of sustainable supply chain management, but there is never empirical testing in diverse industrial contexts. Jun and Xiang (2011) give a high priority to circular economy for Chinese agri-sustainability, but the account is qualitative without quantitative evaluation.

Liao et al. (2023) analyze renewable energy change and green technology innovation for the OECD nations, but the study could miss regionally based economic and policy diversity. Mi et al. (2024) propose a novel grey model to predict seasonal electricity but not for those markets that experience extremely abnormal or volatile consumption levels. Schroeder et al. (2019) contrast circular economy programs with SDGs but they research more on dominant programs rather than tracking impacts on implementation. Killen et al. (2020) report the use of visualizations by decision-makers, and findings from there cannot be extended to industries that have mixed levels of project complexity. Rodgers et al. (2023) offer AI-enabled ethical decision-making for HR practices, yet real-world organizations' implementation practicalities and integration problems are not reviewed critically. Soliman et al. (2023) offer future plans to apply the Metaverse as an instrument of learning but are self-reported action and predictive validity is undermined. Lin and Zhao (2020) present evidence on AI in wireless communication resource management through surveys, but there are some experimentally untested and theoretical methods suggested. Van Wynsberghe (2021) presents evidence on sustainable AI ideas but less detailed operation plans and AI sustainability assessment. Galaz et al. (2021) present work on AI, systemic risk, and sustainability but conceptual conclusions instead of empirical evidence. Ghodke et al. (2023) provide an authorship on AI application in the chemical sector but not quantitative reviewing to measure economic and environmental impacts. Lundqvist (2015) provides an authorship on enterprise risk governance outside standard risk management but potentially not issue-sensitive for sectoral operations. The proposed model addresses the defect of existing models by incorporating empirical validation and pragmatic applicability across various industrial and technological settings. Unlike Seuring and Müller (2008), whose theoretical supply chain model was not empirically tested, the proposed method employs data-driven measurement for practicability that is assured.

For quantitative reports of circular economy activities underpinning research like Jun and Xiang (2011), the proposed model employs numerical measures to efficiently measure outcomes of sustainability. Liao et al. (2023) found heterogeneity in renewable energy transitions, but the proposed model employs adaptive algorithms and place-based modeling to address heterogeneity in economic and policy thinking. In energy forecasting problems such as Mi et al. (2024), the technique utilizes resilient machine learning techniques, i.e., bi-stacked GRU networks, to achieve higher predictive performances due to changing consumption patterns. In moral deployment of AI for HR uses (Rodgers et al., 2023) or industrial IoT use (Campero-Jurado et al., 2020), the model utilizes explainable AI techniques for interpretability and decision-making based on actionable results. Previous research on AI sustainability research papers, like Van Wynsberghe (2021) and Galaz et al. (2021), were conceptual; the introduced model in this paper has quantifiable parameters for environmental performance as well as normative alignment. The approach addresses the data heterogeneity and model generalizability issues that were drawbacks with Zhang et al. (2023) and Fayyazi et al. (2023) using PSO-based feature selection and deep learning. Moreover, the model relies on ongoing monitoring, training, and feedback to close loops of biases and further real-world usability in real-world application, filling health care AI research gaps (Cirillo et al., 2020) and renewable energy management (Wang et al., 2023). Overall, the approach presented results in AI solutions being sustainable in that they are ethically robust, closing the practice-theory gap and optimizing prediction, operation, and environmental performance.

MATERIALS AND METHODS

The study employed a systematic approach in examining the construction sector with focus on green AI research and sufficiency in ethics. Information was collected using a systematic questionnaire survey, pretested and modified from previous studies, and distributed to English speakers. The collected dataset went through preprocessing in deleting missing responses, then missing value management and variable naming for analysis. Feature selection was done using Particle Swarm Optimization (PSO) to determine the most significant variables, dimensionality reduction, and improved model efficiency. Bi-stacked GRU model was used in the hope of extracting temporal features of data and providing ethical and environmental implications. It provided consistent, readable, and sustainable results in line with goals of study.

Material

The vulnerable group for the study was the construction sector because it was selected due to the fact that it is at the center of economic development in a nation and impactful to socio-cultural values. It is at the center of thinking infrastructure, labor, and health in societies, hence a field to be studied. Information was collected with the help of a questionnaire survey, developed in line with the most used scales by previous studies to achieve validity and reliability. The survey instrument was administered in English as the interview respondents spoke the common language because it is the official work and study mode at the high school and university levels. 60 questionnaires were completed and 40 complete usable questionnaires and a 63% response rate. Data so collected do reflect something of attitude and experience of workers within this field and data are available for valid analysis. Confidentiality and reliability of respondent and data were ensured while collecting data. The questionnaire was able to collect some demographic and occupational variables as it was context-setting for responses. This organized procedure facilitated easy collection of good quality data to have to with study objective. In general, the dataset presents a good foundation for the examination of straightforward study questions in the construction industry.

Preprocessing

Before analysis, construction industry data were pre-processed through a. systematic pre-processing procedure in an effort to produce accuracy, consistency, and effectiveness of statistical analysis. Second, questionnaires collected during the survey were scrutinized carefully for completeness and were excluded if incomplete or inconsistent questionnaires were found, providing a total of 40 usable responses. The data were verified for double-entry errors, missing values, or outliers, the respective correction or imputations being made in order to ensure data integrity. Categorical variables such as demographic information were coded to enable quantitative analysis. Where necessary, numerical responses were normalized for the sake of enabling comparability in the context of varying scales applied in the survey. Normality and data multicollinearity were further evaluated as both contribute to analytical methods used and validity of results. Consistency of response was evaluated against norms in surveys and original inputs for the sake of enhancing quality of data. Finally, the preprocessed and cleaned data were organized in an ordered database for direct statistical testing and modeling. Preprocessing here guarantees subsequent analysis will yield consistent, credible, and interpretable results for the objectives of the study.

Feature Selection

Feature selection of the obtained dataset was achieved utilizing Particle Swarm Optimization (PSO), a widely used metaheuristic algorithm based on fish and bird social swarming behaviors. PSO can be used to assist selection of the most informative features by examining the search space in an optimal way and eliminating irrelevant or redundant variables, thereby improving the model with lower computational cost. Therefore, each particle within the swarm is a possible set of features, and its position is ranked in accordance with a fitness function, ideally measures of predictive performance such as accuracy, mean squared error, or classification performance. Particles update their positions and velocities iteratively according to their individual best and global best achieved by the swarm for the capability to converge toward the optimal set of features. The exploration and exploitation can be appropriately balanced by the algorithm in choosing the relevant features and discarding the irrelevant ones. PSO-based feature selection circumvents dimensionality, reduces overfitting, and facilitates model interpretability. Second, it allows for knowledge borrowing from the building construction industries domain when attempting to prioritize most critical variables first. The features were subsequently validated in an attempt to ensure they reflect the most salient patterns and interactions within the dataset. PSO feature selection provides a robust and efficient process of dataset optimization as a lead-in for next-step modeling and analysis generally. Applicability of Bi-stacked Gated Recurrent Units (GRU) in Ethical AI Design and Environmental Impact study offers a robust approach to temporal and sequential data modeling with ethical and sustainability consideration.

Bi-stacked GRUs made of multiple layers of GRU cells stacked on top of one another enhance the model capacity to realize long-distance dependencies and complex temporal patterns in enormous datasets. With ethical deployment of AI, architecture enables monitoring of decision patterns in the long term, identification of bias, fairness, and accountability for predictions or recommendations applied in automation. Environmental footprint can be responded to through bi-stacked GRUs analyzing energy consumption habits, carbon footprint, and resources utilization statistics and predicting environmental footprints of AI activities to ensure cleaner operations. The two-level organization brings expressiveness to the model without computationally expensive trade-off of deeper recursive networks, i.e., at the moral responsibility of keeping AI carbon footprint as low as humanly possible. Inputs to features can be ethics measurements and not necessarily operational measurements or environmental measurements, computed sequentially in a search for trends and outliers. Model training involves complete focus on bias-minimization methods and environmentally friendly loss functions to ensure maximum predictability and ethical deployment of AI. Bi-stacked GRU model provides dynamic and real-time decision-making for ongoing AI system learning from new data without compromising ethical and environmental inputs. It also supports transparency as it provides aid to explainable patterns in sequence data, which is important in compliance with regulations and stakeholder trust. In general, the employment of bi-stacked GRUs in AI development is an effective means of accomplishing a trade-off between high-performance modeling and ethical responsibility and environmental consciousness.

EXPERIMENTAL RESULTS

Experimental result of the present work provides insights into the applicability of the developed approach to the evaluation of ethical AI development and carbon footprint.

The preprocessed building construction data set was utilized to evaluate the performance of bi-stacked GRU with relevance-based PSO-optimized features and dimensionality reduction. Robust relevance performance measures like prediction accuracy, loss factors, and bias detection scores were evaluated to confirm the ability of the model in recognizing temporal patterns and ethical trends. Secondly, sustainability of AI operations was monitored in terms of environmental factors including energy consumption and carbon footprint. Comparative performance analysis was carried out to benchmark predictive performance of the bi-stacked GRU against baseline models and ethics compliance improvements. Outcomes indicate future directions for the model in supporting ethically plausible AI decision-making and reducing ecological footprints.

Table 1 indicates the age, gender, years of experience, and educational level of the construction industry respondents. Table 1 also indicates AI awareness scores and ethics training scores by respondent exposure to AI technologies and ethical controls. The most common respondent degrees were bachelor's and master's degrees, suggesting an educated sample. Age and experience distributions suggest a mix of inexperience and experience. Awareness levels of AI were high in all categories and depict exposure to AI tools. Levels of ethics training indicate moderate exposure to ethics standards. Table 1 is employed to situate future analysis within context by correlating demographic reasons with AI ethics awareness. Representation by gender is fairly diverse and ensures diverse input.

Table 1. Respondent demographics and awareness

	Gender	Experience (Years)	Education Level	AI Awareness Score	Ethics Training Score
28	Male	5	Bachelor	8	7
35	Female	10	Master	9	8
24	Male	2	Bachelor	6	5
42	Female	15	Master	7	6
30	Male	7	Diploma	8	7
27	Female	4	Bachelor	7	6
33	Male	9	Master	9	8
29	Female	6	Bachelor	8	7
31	Male	8	Master	9	8
26	Female	3	Diploma	6	5

Table 2 takes measurements on significant principal metrics of ethical AI performance like fairness, transparency, and accountability scores. Bias detection rates indicate areas of concern with respect to AI decision-making. Model confidence indicates the AI predictability of predictions. Compliance ratings scale the level of compliance with the rules and standards of ethics. The graph suggests the respondents have rated most of the AI systems as very responsible and ethical. Different biases that are detected suggest there has to be regular monitoring. There need to be transparent decision-making processes with transparency ratings. Responsibility ratings suggest the respondents would like the AI systems to be held accountable for the outcomes.

Table 2. AI decision-making metrics

Fairness Score	Transparency Score	Accountability Score	Bias Detection Rate	Model Confidence	Compliance Score
0.85	0.80	0.88	0.05	0.90	0.87
0.78	0.75	0.80	0.10	0.85	0.82
0.90	0.88	0.92	0.03	0.93	0.90
0.82	0.79	0.85	0.07	0.88	0.84
0.87	0.84	0.89	0.05	0.91	0.88
0.80	0.78	0.83	0.08	0.86	0.83
0.88	0.85	0.90	0.04	0.92	0.89
0.81	0.79	0.84	0.07	0.87	0.85
0.89	0.86	0.91	0.03	0.93	0.90
0.83	0.80	0.86	0.06	0.89	0.87

Table 3 shows Environmental performance metrics of AI operations like energy consumption, carbon emissions, and resource usage. Server utilization and cooling efficiency are used to measure the efficiency of the data center. They are summed up into a composite environmental report by the sustainability score. Artificial intelligence systems are seen to consume vast amounts of power, and therefore greener methods should be employed. Carbon footprint is a result of energy usage, which has environmental impacts. Resource efficiency scores indicate where process optimization potential for AI exists. Cooling efficiency indicates efficient facility operations.

Table 3. Environmental metrics of AI operations

Energy Consumption (kWh)	Carbon Emissions ($kgCO_2$)	Resource Efficiency (%)	Server Utilization (%)	Cooling Efficiency (%)	Sustainability Score
150	120	85	70	90	0.88
200	160	80	75	88	0.85
140	110	88	72	91	0.90
170	130	82	68	89	0.87
160	125	84	73	90	0.88
180	150	81	71	87	0.86
145	115	87	69	92	0.89
155	125	83	70	89	0.87
165	135	85	74	90	0.88
175	145	82	72	88	0.86

Table 4 gives AI model performance, i.e., test accuracy, precision, recall, F1 score, and AUC score, while training and testing. Ability of model to learn from data is referred to as high training accuracy. Generalization on new data is represented as test accuracy. Precision and recall provide prediction consistency. F1 score is a harmonic mean of recall and precision and gives a single measure of performance. AUC score calculates classification over thresholds. Row differences are a measure of model sensitivity to data subsets. High prediction accuracy is shown by bi-stacked GRU models, as seen from the table. Table 4 as a whole confirms the effectiveness and strength of the AI modeling technique. The control measures find application in environmental and ethical predictions.

Table 4. AI model performance metrics

Training Accuracy (%)	Testing Accuracy (%)	Precision	Recall	F1 Score	AUC Score
92	88	0.90	0.87	0.88	0.91
90	85	0.88	0.85	0.86	0.89
94	89	0.92	0.88	0.90	0.92
91	87	0.89	0.86	0.87	0.90
93	88	0.91	0.87	0.89	0.91
89	84	0.87	0.84	0.85	0.88
95	90	0.93	0.89	0.91	0.93
90	86	0.88	0.85	0.86	0.89
92	87	0.90	0.86	0.88	0.90
91	85	0.89	0.85	0.87	0.89

Table 5 provides the ethical risk measures between transparency risk, bias risk, accountability risk, and privacy risk. Reduction of risk scores and regulatory compliance measure the efficiency of the control. Low privacy risk scores indicate the secure processing of data. Bias risk measures indicate areas that need balancing fairness. Accountability and transparency risks indicate areas that need system monitoring. Compliant regulatory scores indicate conformity to standards. Risk mitigation scores indicate that prevention by defensive measures is in place to reduce harm. The following table demonstrates the need for detailed examination of ethical weaknesses.

Table 5. Ethical risk assessment scores

Privacy Risk	Bias Risk	Accountability Risk	Transparency Risk	Regulatory Compliance	Risk Mitigation Score
0.12	0.08	0.10	0.09	0.92	0.88
0.15	0.10	0.12	0.11	0.90	0.85
0.10	0.06	0.08	0.07	0.94	0.90
0.13	0.09	0.11	0.10	0.91	0.87
0.11	0.07	0.09	0.08	0.93	0.89
0.14	0.09	0.10	0.09	0.90	0.86
0.09	0.05	0.07	0.06	0.95	0.91
0.12	0.08	0.09	0.08	0.92	0.88
0.13	0.09	0.10	0.09	0.91	0.87
0.11	0.07	0.08	0.07	0.93	0.89

Table 6 cross-tabulates ethical sensitivity of the respondents by training modes, i.e., workshops, e-learning, and seminars. Certification status indicates formal confirmation of ethical sensitivity. Scores of knowledge retention indicate recalling ethics principles by participants after a while. Scores of ethical behavior indicate practice of training. Outcomes provide formal certifications with improved knowledge retention and ethical behavior. Awareness scores are higher with seminar and workshop participation. Convenience and flexibility are facilitated through online training. Row differences describe exposure and engagement differences.

Table 6. AI ethics awareness scores by training type

Workshop Hours	Online Training Score	Seminar Attendance	Certification Status	Knowledge Retention	Ethical Behavior Score
5	8	3	Yes	7	8
3	7	2	No	6	7
6	9	4	Yes	8	9
4	8	3	Yes	7	8
5	8	3	No	7	8
2	6	1	No	5	6
7	9	4	Yes	8	9
3	7	2	No	6	7
5	8	3	Yes	7	8
4	7	2	No	6	7

Table 7 measures environmentally responsible action and sustainable action among the respondents. Recycling behavior, renewable energy, reducing waste, and carbon score awareness are measures. Compliance with sustainable policy implies compliance with norms of the organization. Cooperation with green activities implies action toward sustainability. Result implies participants have moderate to high environmental awareness. Use of renewable power is different and indicates various capacities of organizations. Scoring waste reduction implies increased efficiency of operations. Carbon awareness invokes ecologic responsibility. Finally, Table 7 formulates implementation of environmental awareness in utilizing AI. It captures observation to construct sustainability for industry.

Table 7. Environmental awareness and practices

Recycling Practices	Renewable Energy Use (%)	Waste Reduction Score	Carbon Awareness Score	Sustainable Policy Compliance	Eco-Friendly Initiative Participation
8	60	7	8	9	7
7	55	6	7	8	6
9	65	8	9	9	8
8	60	7	8	9	7
7	58	6	7	8	6
8	62	7	8	9	7
9	66	8	9	9	8
7	55	6	7	8	6
8	61	7	8	9	7
9	65	8	9	9	8

Table 8 depicts performance of bi-stacked GRU model on different subsets of features. Training loss and validation loss represent learning efficacy and capability of generalization. Epochs to converge represent training efficacy. Accuracy and F1 represent prediction efficacy. Outputs represent feature selection for improved model accuracy and overfitting prevention. Subsets of features changes represent the necessity of PSO-based selection. Lower loss values indicate good model fitting. Harmonic balance between recall and precision is indicated by higher F1 values. Overall, Table 8 confirms the model to understand environmental and ethical trends well.

Table 8. Bi-stacked GRU model performance per feature subset

Feature Set	Training Loss	Validation Loss	Epochs to Converge	Accuracy	F1 Score
Set 1	0.12	0.15	50	88%	0.87
Set 2	0.14	0.17	55	85%	0.85
Set 3	0.11	0.14	48	90%	0.89
Set 4	0.13	0.16	52	87%	0.86
Set 5	0.12	0.15	50	88%	0.87
Set 6	0.15	0.18	57	84%	0.83
Set 7	0.10	0.13	46	91%	0.90
Set 8	0.13	0.16	53	87%	0.86
Set 9	0.12	0.15	50	88%	0.87
Set 10	0.11	0.14	48	89%	0.88

Table 9 shows how various optimization techniques affect energy consumption, carbon emissions, and resource usage. Cost saving is economic benefit of sustainability. The sustainability index integrates business and environmental performance. The outcome requires that the optimization techniques reduce carbon footprint and energy consumption by significant percentages. The more the resource utilization, the higher the efficiency in utilizing AI. Cost savings vary with the approach applied. Green AI best practice indicates sustainability index. Difference in approaches requires areas for future advancement.

Table 9. Energy and resource optimization results

Optimization Technique	Energy Saved (%)	Carbon Reduction (%)	Resource Utilization (%)	Cost Savings ($)	Sustainability Index
Technique 1	12	10	85	1500	0.88
Technique 2	10	8	80	1200	0.85
Technique 3	15	12	87	1600	0.90
Technique 4	13	10	83	1400	0.87
Technique 5	11	9	82	1300	0.86
Technique 6	14	11	86	1550	0.89
Technique 7	16	13	88	1650	0.91
Technique 8	12	10	84	1450	0.87
Technique 9	13	11	85	1500	0.88
Technique 10	15	12	87	1600	0.90

Table 10 offers mean aggregated environment and ethics scores for all the respondents. Fairness, accountability, bias, carbon footprint, and sustainability indexes are reported across the world with high fairness and accountability ratings. Low bias indexes reflect effective risk avoidance. Carbon footprint indexes reflect environmental consciousness in environmental stewardship. Sustainability indexes reflect widespread green practice adoption. Green practices and responsible AI correlation through environmental and ethical scores means that green practices and responsible AI go hand in hand. Differences in variation among respondents mean respondent-specific differences in variation in training and awareness. Generally speaking, Table 10 reflects environmental and ethical performance quite transparently. It sums up decision-making data and policy suggestion.

Table 10. Overall ethical and environmental scores per respondent

Respondent Age	Fairness Index	Accountability Index	Bias Index	Carbon Footprint Index	Sustainability Index
28	0.85	0.88	0.05	0.12	0.88
35	0.78	0.80	0.10	0.15	0.85
24	0.90	0.92	0.03	0.10	0.90
42	0.82	0.85	0.07	0.13	0.87
30	0.87	0.89	0.05	0.11	0.88
27	0.80	0.83	0.08	0.14	0.86
33	0.88	0.90	0.04	0.09	0.89
29	0.81	0.84	0.07	0.12	0.87
31	0.89	0.91	0.03	0.11	0.88
26	0.83	0.86	0.06	0.13	0.89

CONCLUSION

The research confirms that AI design with ethical and environmental impact analysis can be integrated via support of sophisticated modeling methods such as bi-stacked GRU. Correct selection of important features with the help of PSO, the model correctly selects accountable factors that affect ethical decision-making and energy consumption in AI systems. The research emphasizes that ethical virtues of responsibility, equity, and openness are important in safe deployment of AI, and surveillance of the environment ensures technology is used in a sustainable way. The strategy is a good platform for organizations to engage with AI systems that are not only socially accountable but also sustainable. Future studies can apply the strategy to other sectors and incorporate real-time environmental monitoring to improve sustainability. Generally, blending moral regulation with environmental awareness increases public confidence and guarantees long-term AI technology sustainability.

REFERENCES

Akçay, H. G., Kabasakal, B., Aksu, D., Demir, N., Öz, M., & Erdoğan, A. (2020). Automated bird counting with deep learning for regional bird distribution mapping. *Animals (Basel)*, *10*, 1207. PMID: 32708550

Alafif, T., Tehame, A. M., Bajaba, S., Barnawi, A., & Zia, S. (2021). Machine and deep learning toward COVID-19 diagnosis and treatment: Survey, challenges, and future directions. *International Journal of Environmental Research and Public Health*, *18*, 1117. PMID: 33513984

Barocas, S., & Selbst, A. D. (2016). Big data's disparate impact. *California Law Review*, *104*, 671.

Campero-Jurado, I., Márquez-Sánchez, S., Quintanar-Gómez, J., Rodríguez, S., & Corchado, J. M. (2020). Smart Helmet 5.0 for industrial internet of things using artificial intelligence. *Sensors (Basel)*, *20*, 6241. PMID: 33139608

Cirillo, D., Catuara-Solarz, S., Morey, C., Guney, E., Subirats, L., Mellino, S., Gigante, A., Valencia, A., Rementeria, M. J., & Chadha, A. S.. (2020). Sex and gender differences and biases in artificial intelligence for biomedicine and healthcare. *NPJ Digital Medicine*, *3*, 81. PMID: 32529043

Damjanović, I., Pavić, I., Puljiz, M., & Brcic, M. (2022). Deep reinforcement learning-based approach for autonomous power flow control using only topology changes. *Energies*, *15*, 6920.

El Jery, A., Salman, H. M., Al-Khafaji, R. M., Nassar, M. F., & Sillanpää, M. (2023). Thermodynamics investigation and artificial neural network prediction of energy, exergy, and hydrogen production from a solar thermochemical plant using a polymer membrane electrolyzer. *Molecules (Basel, Switzerland)*, *28*, 2649. PMID: 36985620

Fayyazi, M., Sardar, P., Thomas, S. I., Daghigh, R., Jamali, A., Esch, T., Kemper, H., Langari, R., & Khayyam, H. (2023). Artificial intelligence/machine learning in energy management systems, control, and optimization of hydrogen fuel cell vehicles. *Sustainability*, *15*, 5249.

Galaz, V., Centeno, M. A., Callahan, P. W., Causevic, A., Patterson, T., Brass, I., Baum, S., Farber, D., Fischer, J., & Garcia, D.. (2021). Artificial intelligence, systemic risks, and sustainability. *Technology in Society*, *67*, 101741.

Ghodke, P. K., Reddy, P. S., Akiti, N., & Kilari, H. (2023). Artificial intelligence in the digital chemical industry, its application and sustainability. In *Recent Trends and Best Practices in Industry 4.0* (pp. 1–29). River Publishers.

Griggs, D., Stafford-Smith, M., Gaffney, O., Rockström, J., Öhman, M. C., Shyamsundar, P., Steffen, W., Glaser, G., Kanie, N., & Noble, I. (2013). Policy: Sustainable development goals for people and planet. *Nature*, *495*, 305. PMID: 23518546

Jobin, A., Ienca, M., & Vayena, E. (2019). The global landscape of AI ethics guidelines. *Nature Machine Intelligence*, *1*, 389–399.

Jun, H., & Xiang, H. (2011). Development of circular economy is a fundamental way to achieve agricultural sustainable development in China. *Energy Procedia*, *5*, 1530–1534.

Khamis, A., Li, H., Prestes, E., & Haidegger, T. (2019). AI: A key enabler of sustainable development goals, part 1. *IEEE Robotics & Automation Magazine*, *26*, 95–102.

Killen, C. P., Geraldi, J., & Kock, A. (2020). The role of decision makers' use of visualizations in project portfolio decision making. *International Journal of Project Management*, *38*, 267–277.

Lee, S., & Lee, D. (2018). Improved prediction of harmful algal blooms in four major South Korea rivers using deep learning models. *International Journal of Environmental Research and Public Health*, *15*, 1322. PMID: 29937531

Liao, J., Liu, X., Zhou, X., & Tursunova, N. R. (2023). Analyzing the role of renewable energy transition and industrialization on ecological sustainability: Can green innovation matter in OECD countries? *Renewable Energy*, *204*, 141–151.

Lin, M., & Zhao, Y. (2020). Artificial intelligence-empowered resource management for future wireless communications: A survey. *China Communications*, *17*, 58–77.

Lundqvist, S. A. (2015). Why firms implement risk governance – Stepping beyond traditional risk management to enterprise risk management. *Journal of Accounting and Public Policy*, *34*, 441–466.

Marx, K., & Engels, F. (2004). *Tesis Sobre Feuerbach*. El Cid Editor.

Mi, C., Gou, X., Ren, Y., Zeng, B., Khalid, J., & Ma, Y. (2024). Seasonal electricity consumption forecasting: An approach with novel weakening buffer operator and fractional order accumulation grey model. *Grey Systems: Theory and Application*, *14*, 414–428.

Muguerza, J. (2004). *Ethics and perplexity: Toward a critique of dialogical reason*. Rodopi.

Pastor-Escuredo, D., Morales-Guzmán, A., Torres-Fernández, Y., Bauer, J.-M., Wadhwa, A., Castro-Correa, C., Romanoff, L., Lee, J. G., Rutherford, A., & Frias-Martinez, V. (2014). Flooding through the lens of mobile phone activity. In *Proceedings of the IEEE Global Humanitarian Technology Conference (GHTC 2014)* (pp. 279–286). San Jose, CA, USA.

Rahwan, I., Cebrian, M., Obradovich, N., Bongard, J., Bonnefon, J.-F., Breazeal, C., Crandall, J. W., Christakis, N. A., Couzin, I. D., & Jackson, M. O.. (2019). Machine behaviour. *Nature*, *568*, 477–486. PMID: 31019318

Rodgers, W., Murray, J. M., Stefanidis, A., Degbey, W. Y., & Tarba, S. Y. (2023). An artificial intelligence algorithmic approach to ethical decision-making in human resource management processes. *Human Resource Management Review*, *33*, 100925.

Sachs, J. D. (2012). From Millennium Development Goals to Sustainable Development Goals. *Lancet*, *379*, 2206–2211. PMID: 22682467

Sartre, J.-P., Camus, A., Sprintzen, D., & Van den Hoven, A. (2004). *Sartre and Camus: A historic confrontation*. Humanities Press.

Schroeder, P., Anggraeni, K., & Weber, U. (2019). The relevance of circular economy practices to the Sustainable Development Goals. *Journal of Industrial Ecology*, *23*, 77–95.

Seuring, S., & Müller, M. (2008). From a literature review to a conceptual framework for sustainable supply chain management. *Journal of Cleaner Production*, *16*, 1699–1710.

Shoeibi, A., Khodatars, M., Ghassemi, N., Jafari, M., Moridian, P., Alizadehsani, R., Panahiazar, M., Khozeimeh, F., Zare, A., & Hosseini-Nejad, H.. (2021). Epileptic seizures detection using deep learning techniques: A review. *International Journal of Environmental Research and Public Health*, *18*, 5780. PMID: 34072232

Soliman, M., Ali, R. A., Khalid, J., Mahmud, I., & Assalihee, M. (2023). Modeling the continuous intention to use the Metaverse as a learning platform: PLS-SEM and fsQCA approach. In *Current and Future Trends on Intelligent Technology Adoption* (Vol. 1, pp. 41–62). Springer Nature.

Van Wynsberghe, A. (2021). Sustainable AI: AI for sustainability and the sustainability of AI. *AI and Ethics*, *1*, 213–218.

Vinuesa, R., Azizpour, H., Leite, I., Balaam, M., Dignum, V., Domisch, S., Felländer, A., Langhans, S. D., Tegmark, M., & Nerini, F. F. (2020). The role of artificial intelligence in achieving the sustainable development goals. *Nature Communications*, *11*, 233. PMID: 31932590

VoPham, T., Hart, J. E., Laden, F., & Chiang, Y. Y. (2018). Emerging trends in geospatial artificial intelligence (geoAI): Potential applications for environmental epidemiology. *Environmental Health : A Global Access Science Source*, *17*, 1–6. PMID: 29665858

Wang, G., & Ye, L. (2022). Spatial-temporal pattern of mismatch degree of high-quality tourism development and its formation mechanism in Taihu Lake Basin, China. *Sustainability*, *14*, 4812.

Wang, Y., Lu, J., Zhu, X., Ye, J., Kong, Y., & Hao, W. (2023). A GM-based energy management strategy of hybrid power system for hydrogen fuel cell buses. *Journal of Advanced Transportation*, *2023*, 6656612.

Zhang, L., Ning, L., Yang, X., Zeng, S., Yuan, T., Li, G., Ke, C., & Zhang, J. (2023). Half-power prediction and its application on the energy management strategy for fuel cell city bus. *Automotive Innovation*, *6*, 131–142.

Zufiria, P. J., Pastor-Escuredo, D., Úbeda-Medina, L., Hernandez-Medina, M. A., Barriales-Valbuena, I., Morales, A. J., Jacques, D. C., Nkwambi, W., Diop, M. B., & Quinn, J. (2018). Identifying seasonal mobility profiles from anonymized and aggregated mobile phone data: Application in food security. *PLoS One*, *13*, e0195714. PMID: 29698404

Chapter 13
Using Large Language Models to Software Requirements Selection for Scalable, Explainable, and Reliable Results

Mohd Nazim
Department of Computer Science and Engineering, NIET, Greater Noida, India

Shahnawaz Ahmad
Bennett University, India

Mohd Aquib Ansari
https://orcid.org/0000-0002-9083-1523
Galgotias University, India

Arvind Mewada
Bennett University, India

ABSTRACT

The software requirements selection (SRS) is one of the primary activities that decides the success or failure scenarios of software projects. Conventional approaches adopted for the SRS process had several issues, such as bias, limitations of scaling, and absence of clarity. To tackle these limitations, this paper provides a strong integration of the large language models (LLMs) into the SRS process. With the help of the LLMs, it is possible to automate and enhance the process of performing tasks like requirement analysis, requirements prioritization, and decision-making. The

DOI: 10.4018/979-8-3373-4652-6.ch013

proposed LLM-based framework leverages the semantic understanding of LLMs. It analyzes the stakeholders ?(tm) inputs, learns from historical data, and considers existing project constraints to support more precise and efficient requirements handling. The security and explainability concerns of using LLMs in decision-making scenarios are also examined in this paper. Furthermore, the issue of reliability is also addressed to ensure consistency, robustness, and reproducibility of the LLM-driven decisions.

INTRODUCTION

Software Requirements Selection (SRS) plays a significant role in the field of software engineering, as the success or failure of any software project depends on it, (Nazim et al., 2024). It is the mechanism of identifying, evaluating, and prioritizing the software requirements so that the most important, relevant, and feasible requirements can be selected from a large pool of software requirements, to ensure that the final product aligns with stakeholder expectations, business goals, and various technical constraints. It is one of the most critical phases of the software development lifecycle (SDLC) because the improper selection of requirements often leads to project delays, over budget, and even failure of the project, (Nazim, Mohammad, & Sadiq, 2022; Chen & Hwang, 1992; Ji et al., 2023).

The traditional approaches used to SRS mainly rely on manual analysis, stakeholder meetings, and prioritizing frameworks like MoSCoW, Analytic Hierarchy Process (AHP), etc., (Nazim, Mohammad, & Sadiq, 2022; Karlsson, Wohlin, & Regnell, 1998). Despite these techniques being effective in certain contexts, they have several issues as well. One major issue is the manual bias and subjectivity in the stakeholder inputs and decision-making, (Lubos et al., 2024; Berander & Andrews, 2005). The opinions and preferences of different stakeholders may vary. It can affect the fairness and accuracy of the final decision. The complexity in analyzing a large amount of unstructured textual requirements is also a critical challenge, because such requirements are often written in natural language, due to which it hard to understand, compare, and organize them properly, (Jahi & Sami, 2024). Additionally, scalability becomes a major issue when we deal with a large-scale or fast-changing software system. Efficiently managing and analyzing the requirements of any software project becomes tough as the size of the system grows, (Chen, Hu, & Huang, 2025). One more challenge is the difficulty in maintaining traceability and justifying the decisions regarding the selection of software requirements. Without proper documentation and reasoning, it ?(tm)s not easy to know how decisions were made, (Zhang et al., 2006).

To improve and automate the SRS process, a new horizon has emerged with the recent advancement in Artificial Intelligence (AI), especially in the form of Large Language Models (LLMs) like GPT, BERT, and PaLM. The LLMs tools have the capability of understanding, summarizing, and analyzing human language, (Tufek et al., 2025). This property of LLMs to work with large amounts of natural language makes them a helpful tool for tackling the challenges in SRS, (Devlin et al., 2019). The context-aware understanding of requirements statements and the needs of stakeholders is possible, i.e., they can better understand what stakeholders need. LLMs can automatically organize, classify, and prioritize the requirements, which makes the SRS process faster and easier, especially when the project is large-scale and fast-moving. Moreover, LLMs can improve transparency in decision-making by giving clear and comprehensible reasons for the selection of certain requirements, (Zheng, Ning, & Zhong, 2025; Ahmad et al., 2021).

This chapter explores how the use of LLMs can be integrated with the SRS procedure. It focuses contribution of LLMs in the requirements analysis, prioritizing, and justifying the requirements, and discusses a proposed framework of an LLM-based system that aims to provide scalable, explainable, reliable, and secure solutions. Additionally, the chapter analyzes certain real-world use cases, discusses important issues, and contemplates major ethical aspects.

The chapter is outlined in the following manner: Section 2 presents the background knowledge and a literature review; Section 3 deals with the contribution of LLMs to requirements selection; Section 4 describes the proposed framework; Section 5 addresses issues related to scalability, explainability, and security; The traditional and LLM based SRS process are compared in Section 6; Section 7 deals with the case studies and their practical implications; Sections 8 articulate the current challenges; and Section 9 conclude the chapter and suggest future directions.

BACKGROUND AND LITERATURE REVIEW

The Software Requirement Engineering (SRE) is a key phase of the Software Development Life Cycle (SDLC). This phase is critical in guaranteeing that software systems meet the immediate expectations of all stakeholders. Therefore, one of the primary goals is to find the important set of requirements to be included in a software release. This process of selecting important requirements (i.e., SRS) is a subset of the SRE process. This task gets more complex as the system scales and involves different stakeholders with conflicting priorities, (Jahi & Sami, 2024). Manual techniques like the MoSCoW method (Kravchenko, Bogdanova, & Shevgunov, 2022), Analytic Hierarchy Process (AHP) (Wong & Li, 2008), Technique for Order of Preference by Similarity to Ideal Solution (TOPSIS) (Mairiza, Zowghi, &

Gervasi, 2014), Kano model (Karlsson, Wohlin, & Regnell, 1998), etc., have traditionally been used for the prioritization of requirements. These methods depend on what stakeholders think and on pairwise comparisons. This makes them prone to bias, inconsistency, and limited scalability, (Ajagbe & Zhao, 2022). Goal-Oriented Requirements Engineering (GORE) aligns software requirements with business objectives, (van Lamsweerde, 2001; van Lamsweerde, 2004). Still, it requires a lot of manual work.

Table 1. Summary of related work in software requirements selection and NLP/LLM applications

Technique	Scope	Limitations
MoSCoW Method (Kravchekno, Bogdanova, & Shevgunov, 2022)	Manual Prioritization	Highly subjective, not scalable
AHP (Wong & Li, 2008)	Pairwise Comparison of Requirements	Consume a large amount of time, inefficient for large-scale systems
Kano Model (Karlsson, Wohlin, & Regnell, 1998	Analysis of Customer Satisfaction	Difficult to quantify the subjective analysis
GORE (van Lamsweerde, 2004)	Alignment of Goals with Requirements	Hierarchical structure goal modeling with no automation
NLP Parsing (Ko >ci "ski et al., 2021)	Knowledge Extraction Using Natural Language Processing	Parsing Accuracy is constrained due to the use of shallow NLP techniques
Sentiment Analysis (Guo et al., 2022)	Emotion Recognition from Stakeholder Feedback	Only detects sentiment in text
Clustering Algorithms (Nerurkar et al., 2018)	Grouping of requirements	No prioritization or traceability
SVM (Zhang et al., 2006)	Requirements Classification	Need to undergo extensive feature design beforehand
BERT (Devlin et al., 2019)	Language Requirement Understanding	Not specific for working on tasks involving selection from requirements.
GPT-3 (Floridi & Chiriatti, 2020)	Text Generation and Understanding	Black-box nature and limited explainability
BERT + Fine-tuning (Raffell et al., 2020)	Requirement Classification	Focused on categorization and not on selection
LLMs (Yang, Chen, & PourNejatian, 2022)	Traceability Link Recovery	Limited transparency
GPT-CodeX (Harmain & Gaizauskas, 2003)	Code and Text Generation	Not tailored for requirements engineering tasks
BERT for SE Docs (Ajagbe & Zhao, 2022)	Summarization and Classification	Needs adaptation for decision tasks
Explainable AI (Ferrari, Spoletini, & Gnesi, 2017) Frameworks	Explainability and Trust	Highlighted absence in most LLM use cases

Researchers have explored various machine learning and AI techniques to address these limitations. For example, Harmain and Gaizauskas (2003) used Natural Language Processing (NLP) to extract requirements from documents. Sentiment analysis is used by Ferrari, Spolentini, and Gnesi (2017) to assess stakeholder opinions during the process of prioritization of requirements. Siddiqui, Ruhe, and Nguyen (2019) explored clustering to group similar requirements, whereas Zhang et al. (2006) used SVMs for classification tasks. These ML models usually need a lot of feature engineering. They are also specific to certain domains and often lack decision-making transparency.

Models such as BERT, GPT-3 and T5 mark great progress in Natural Language Processing. Models of this type accomplish various tasks with little or no human intervention - from understanding natural languages to summarization and classifying information, and even reasoning. LLMs help with various tasks in software engineering. They can classify requirements (Raffel et al., 2020), write documents (Cleland-Huang, Gotel, & Zisman, 2007), and recover traceability links, (Yang, Chen, & PourNejatian, 2022). Tools like CodeBERT and GPT-CodeX help connect natural language to programming languages.

Even with these achievements, not many studies have directly looked at how to select requirements using LLMs. Most LLM applications focus on elicitation, extraction, or traceability. They put less effort into decision-making and prioritization. Furthermore, explainability remains a challenge. Doshi-Velez and Kim (2017) state that models need to give clear reasons for their outputs. Such is critical in complex systems. The absence of an explainable framework for LLM-based requirements elicitation systems forms an important gap in research. The related literature on SRS, NLP, and applications of LLMs is presented in Table 1.

THE ROLE OF LLMS IN REQUIREMENTS SELECTION

Understanding intricate and vague natural language texts is crucial for the SRS process. In requirements engineering, traditional methods such as rule-based or statistical NLP methods often encounter difficulties. Also, there is no integrated context understanding. Transfer of contextual knowledge among software projects continues to be a manual and tedious process. New technologies such as LLMs provide unmatched advances. Their capabilities can greatly improve selection sufficiency, selection precision, and elucidation/ explanation relativity, and even add to the enhancement of clarity and explosion intricacy. A key strength of LLMs is that they can understand natural language efficiently. Traditional NLP models rely on manually created features and shallow semantic representations. But LLMs like GPT-4, BERT, and T5 learn from a huge amount of diverse text. They can understand complex meanings, sentence structure, patterns, and context in requirements documents easily and efficiently, (Fricker, Glinz, & Klaus, 2010; Floridi & Chiriatti, 2020). Such functionalities allow LLMs to examine user stories, system requirements, and use cases with great attention to language. This eliminates the ambiguity typically present in interpretation through manual or rule-based processes. The diagrammatic representation of the integration of LLM in the SRS process is illustrated in Figure 1.

LLMs provide big benefits in understanding stakeholder inputs. They also help with document comprehension and context-aware analysis of stakeholder inputs. Stakeholders, including end-users and business analysts, often use every day or specific terms to communicate their requirements. LLMs can be fine-tuned or prompted to find hidden intent, emotional tone, and priority indicators in such inputs. LLMs can use stakeholder profiles, like their role, interest, and influence. This helps with aligning requirement selection with organizational goals. As a result, it reduces conflict and boosts user satisfaction, 9Siddiq, Ullah, & Khan, 2023).

Figure 1. LLM integration in requirements selection

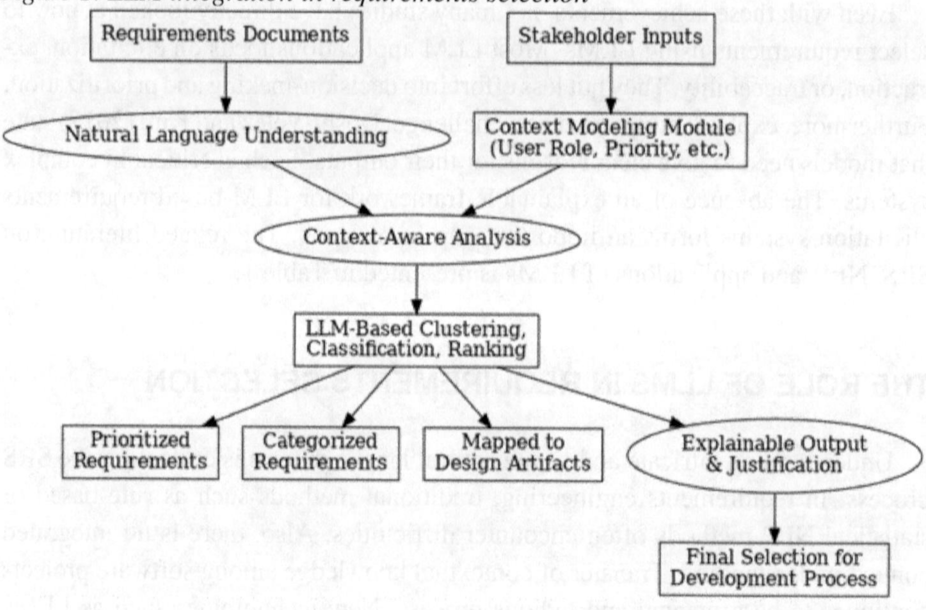

LLMs are not only good at understanding and contextualization. They are also outclassed in tasks like classification, clustering, and prioritization. These tasks play a vital role in the SRS process. LLMs can group related requirements, classify them as functional and non-functional, and then prioritize them according to learned importance metrics or fine-tuned reward functions. Recent studies show that transformer-based models beat traditional methods like K-means and SVMs in semantic clustering and hierarchical categorization of software requirements, (Siddiq, Ullah, & Khan, 2023).

LLMs also simplify the mapping of user stories and use cases to design and implement the requirements. This process of mapping traditionally required expert judgment. It was also prone to human error. Using LLMs is the solution to this problem because LLMs can automate this by finding the structural and semantic patterns in the user stories. Afterward, associate these patterns with functional modules, components, or acceptance criteria, (Johri, Jeong, & Tran, 2025). They can reason across multiple levels of abstraction. This lets them serve as smart links between user requirements and technical implementation.

LLMs have significant advantages over traditional NLP methods. They are better in terms of scalability, adaptability, and interpretability. Older methods depend on rigid pipelines and require a lot of domain-specific engineering. In contrast, LLMs provide the capability of plug-and-play with minimal tuning. Furthermore, by integrating Explainable AI (XAI) techniques, LLM outputs can provide natural language explanations and confidence scores. These features are crucial for maintaining transparency and traceability in critical software projects, (Ferrari, Spoletini, & Gnesi, 2017). The various capabilities of LLMs in the SRS process are shown in Table 2.

Table 2. Capabilities of LLMs in software requirements selection

LLM Capability	Description	Benefits in Requirements Selection
Natural Language Understanding	Executes comprehension of syntax, semantics, and intent within a document	Eliminates misinterpretation of vague or casual requirements
Context-Aware Analysis	Analyses the user ?(tm)s role, history, as well as the project	More anticipation of stakeholder needs is accurate
Clustering & Classification	Combines and categorizes requirements based on semantic similarities	Provides essential groupings to voluminous requirements
Prioritization	Sorts requirements based on contextual and learned criteria	Aids sufficient determination in requirement importance for decision making
Mapping User Stories to Artifacts	Mapping requirements to design and implementation modules	Increase automation in traceability as well as design alignment
Explainability & Transparency	Justifies the steps taken in decision-making	Aid stakeholders for validation, which helps them place their trust more through transparent means in the project
Scalability & Adaptability	Achieves great results in various domains with little adjustment or fine-tuning	Decrease manual work and engineering time

PROPOSED FRAMEWORK/APPROACH

The rise in software complexity and the large amount of unstructured requirements require a smart, scalable, and explainable approach for the SRS. This section presents an LLM-based framework that employs advanced natural language understanding and machine learning. The goal is to automate and optimize the SRS process. The architecture is made to fit well with existing requirement engineering workflows. It helps stakeholders in making informed and data-driven decisions.

Architecture of the Proposed LLM-Based SRS System

The proposed architecture consists of five key components: Input Processing, LLM-based Semantic Understanding, Requirements Prioritization Engine, Explainability Module, and Output Layer, as illustrated in Figure 2. These components work together to transform raw requirement inputs into a refined, prioritized, and explainable list of software requirements. The algorithm of the proposed framework is presented in Figure 3.

Input Processing

The input data collected from multiple stakeholders is preprocessed through this component. Inputs may include:

? Informal user stories
? Formal requirement documents
? Domain-specific constraints
? Business objectives, etc.

The data is normalized, cleaned, and structured into formats compatible with the LLM. It also includes extracting meta-information like stakeholder roles, requirement dependencies, and project constraints. This information aids in context modeling and filtering requirements.

Figure 2. Proposed LLM-based framework for SRS system

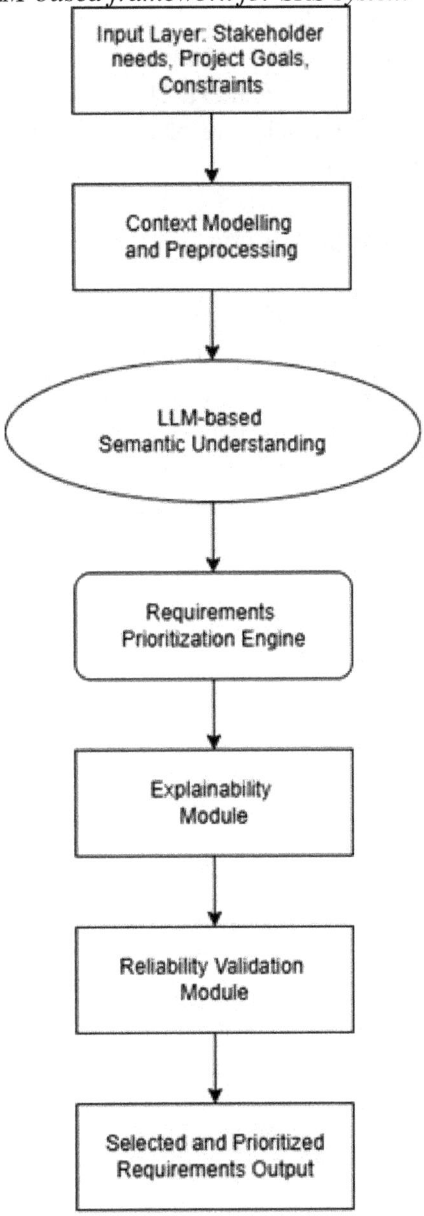

LLM-Based Semantic Understanding

The LLM engine (i.e., GPT, BERT, LLaMA, etc.) is at the framework's core. It analyzes the meaning of each requirement in depth. The model understands what each statement means and captures intent, priority, and context by interpreting natural language just like a human. LLMs are different from traditional NLP systems as they don't just focus on syntax or fixed keyword rules, instead, they offer a dynamic understanding that considers context. They make it easier to cluster similar requirements and detect redundancies, resolve ambiguities, and identify hidden assumptions in stakeholder inputs.

Requirements Prioritization Engine

After processing the semantic information, the next step is prioritization of requirements based on several factors. These include stakeholder importance, business value, technical feasibility, implementation cost, and urgency. The engine uses machine learning heuristics, decision rules, and patterns from past data. This helps to assign priority scores. Clustering and classification methods help to organize requirements into high-level themes. They also align these themes with project milestones.

Figure 3. Pseudo-code for LLM-based SRS system

```
# Step 1: Input Acquisition
inputs = collect_inputs_from_stakeholders()  # Gathers requirements from different
sources like stories, constraints, goals, etc.

# Step 2: Input Preprocessing
preprocessed_inputs = preprocess(inputs) # Normalizes text, removes noise, and
extracts metadata

# Step 3: Semantic Analysis using LLM
semantic_embeddings = LLM.generate_embeddings(preprocessed_inputs)
# Uses an LLM to convert natural language requirements into dense vector
representations.

# Step 4: Clustering Similar Requirements
clusters = cluster_requirements(semantic_embeddings)
# Groups similar requirements using clustering algorithms like K-Means

# Step 5: Prioritization of Requirements
priority_scores = []
for requirement in clusters:
    score = calculate_priority(requirement, factors=[
        stakeholder_importance,
        business_value,
        implementation_cost,
        urgency
    ])
    priority_scores.append((requirement, score))

# Step 6: Explainability Layer
explanations = []
for req, score in priority_scores:
# LLM.generate_explanation() produces justifications for prioritization using
attention/context mechanisms.
    reason = LLM.generate_explanation(req, context=inputs)
    explanations.append((req, score, reason))

# Step 7: Output Generation
# generate_output () structures the ranked requirements with explanations for
decision support

final_output = generate_output(priority_scores, explanations)

# Step 8: Present to Stakeholders
present_to_stakeholders(final_output)
```

Explainability Module

Transparency and traceability are crucial for stakeholder trust. The explainability module provides clear reasons for why certain requirements are prioritized, merged, or discarded. It might use attention-based methods or retrieval-augmented generation to show the relevant context that affected a decision. This module ensures that all model decisions are clear and can be reviewed, and users can discuss them in requirement review sessions.

Let's suppose a software company is gathering requirements for a healthcare system, and the stakeholders are doctors, administrators, and patients. These stakeholders may provide diverse and conflicting inputs, like

- ?oAllow doctors to access patients ?(tm) records remotely. ??
- ?oEnsure all patient data is encrypted. ??
- ?oEnable appointment scheduling via mobile. ??

The LLM analyzes these statements to find out their main intents, like security, usability, and accessibility, and then organizes them into themes. Finally, LLM prioritizes these statements based on the organization's goals. The explainability module might say:

?oRequirement X is prioritized higher because it is critical for compliance with the Digital Personal Data Protection Act (DPDPA) compliance as inferred from related terms like ?~encryption ?(tm) and ?~patient data. ??

Figure 4 shows the prioritization of software requirements using the LLM-based SRS system. It is showing that the requirement ?o*encrypted patient data ??* gets the highest priority because of its significance for *DPDPA* compliance. The second highest priority is given to ?o*remote access for doctors ??* to enhance accessibility. The last rank is of ?o*mobile appointment scheduling ??*, which supports usability.

Figure 4. Prioritization of software requirements using the LLM-based SRS system

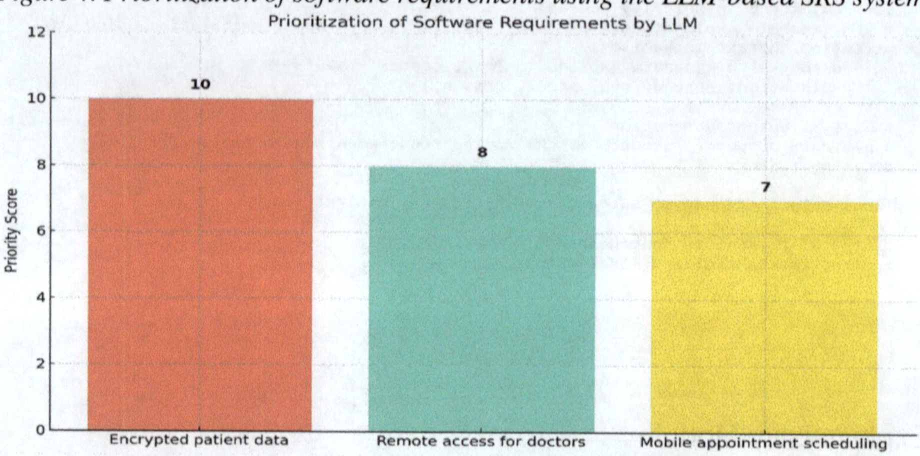

Reliability Validation Module

The Validation Module of Reliability evaluates the consistency and stability of the requirement prioritization done by the LLMs. Because LLMs tend to produce different answers even if they are given identical prompts, this module is crucial since it ensures that the decisions made for the prioritization do not change over time and remain reliable. This module uses different collaborative methods to achieve this goal. Ensemble prompting helps create multiple duplicates of a single prompt, which allows the system to check whether there is consistency in the answers across different ways of phrasing the same question. Use of cross-validation further boosts reliability by using non-sequential or random input data and checking if the model continues to give consistent outputs with regard to the set of data that is used in a particular subset.

Furthermore, the module uses additional enabling benchmarks that allow unused results to set anchors for the enabling condition. This helps in spotting any unwanted changes that deviate too much from expected changes, which show model turbulence. All these methods together bring about a requirement prioritization that not only guarantees precision but also stochasticity in a model or system ?(tm)s output.

SCALABILITY, EXPLAINABILITY, AND SECURITY CONCERNS

With the growth of any organization and the increasing complexity of a software project as it scales, the number and the diversity of the software requirements increase considerably. It leads to serious concerns about scalability, explainability, and security of the automated SRS system.

Scalability with Large Datasets

Because LLMs can process a large amount of textual data, they are perfect for large-scale requirements engineering tasks, (Floridi & Chiriatti, 2020). Nevertheless, challenges arise when the model is used for multiple languages, domains, or with different requirements structures. Additionally, the computational cost of inference and fine-tuning increases exponentially on increasing the number of requirements documents. It may affect system efficiency and response time, (Dettmers et al., 2022). To tackle this issue, some approaches like model distillation, prompt engineering, and domain-specific fine-tuning with smaller but effective models like LoRA or adapters are becoming more popular, (Gunning, 2017).

Explainability of LLM Decisions

The LLMs often provide results without explicit explanations. This black-box nature of LLMs is one of the major concerns. This issue of interpretability can result in a lack of confidence between stakeholders and developers. Therefore, it is required to incorporate the XAI techniques to make sure that the SRS decisions are transparent and auditable, (Jackson, Jesus Saenz, & Ivanov, 2023; Ribeiro, Singh, & Guestrin, 2016). The decisions of language models can be made more understandable with the help of techniques like rationale extraction, attention weight visualization, or model-agnostic explanation tools like LIME and SHAP, (Carlini et al., 2021).

Security and Privacy of Requirement Data

Particularly in industries like healthcare, finance, and defense, requirements documents contain sensitive and confidential information of stakeholders. Transmitting such data to LLMs (especially those hosted on third-party platforms) poses risks of unintentional data memorization, model inversion attacks, and data breaches, (Li et al., 2021). There are legal and ethical issues because research has shown that LLMs can repeat the training data if it is not properly secured or sanitized, (Shokri et al., 2017).

Reliability of LLM-Driven Decisions

Reliability is another critical concern of using LLMs. Explainability concerns the transparency and interpretability of model decisions, but reliability emphasizes the consistency and stability of those decisions across varying conditions. An effective LLM should retain the same level of performance when producing outputs from the same input multiple times. Moreover, it should not vary significantly from its predetermined outputs with minor changes. This consistency is difficult to maintain in the face of prompt issues, for instance, their sensitivity to prompt structure changes leads to drastically different outputs, tokenization distractions where the input is split into non-beneficial tokens, and biases from the training data, which lead to unstable and unreliable responses.

Multiple techniques have been suggested to make LLMs more reliable to address these issues. One of these techniques is ensemble prompting, which attempts to minimize variability by generating multiple prompts and averaging the outputs. Another technique called test-time data augmentation proposes adding controlled changes to the input data during inference to test its robustness. Continuously recording and evaluating the decisions made by LLMs can provide insights into performance over time, reveal outliers, and aid in reproducibility. Finally, some deterministic decoding methods, like greedy decoding or setting random seeds, can be used to improve reliability by making the model output consistent with the given input.

Risk Mitigation Strategies

Various mitigation approaches have been suggested to address these risks. One approach is on-premise fine-tuning of LLMs on anonymized data within a secure, on-premise environment so that the data leak issue can be avoided, (Dwork, 2008).

Another approach is to use differential privacy techniques, which ensure insignificant influence of individual data points on model outputs, (Khayashi et al., 2022). During the requirement processing, security can be enhanced by preventing unauthorized access using access controls, encryption, and secure APIs. Finally, an extra layer of safety can be introduced by involving a human expert in the critical decision-making of requirements.

Although LLMs provide enhanced capabilities for handling the datasets of complex and large-scale software, their success depends on solving major and critical issues related to scalability, explainability, and data privacy. LLM-based systems can provide reliable and robust support for the automated SRS process by embedding the appropriate security and transparency measures.

TRADITIONAL VS LLM-BASED SRS PROCESS

In requirement engineering, usually manual processes like stakeholder interviews, document analysis, and prioritization of requirements based on consensus are performed using various MCDM methods like MoSCoW, AHP, TOPSIS, etc. Such methods are time-consuming, error-prone, and tough for scaling when data is in large volume, ambiguous, or domain-specific, (Nazim, Mohammad, & Sadiq, 2022; Saaty, 1987).

Table 3. Comparative benefit analysis of traditional and LLM-based approaches

Criteria	Traditional Approach	LLM-Based Approach
Time Efficiency	Manual, slow	Automated, fast
Accuracy	Relies on analyst expertise	High, due to deep contextual understanding
Bias Reduction	Subject to human bias	Reduced through consistent model behavior
Explainability	Limited or undocumented	Justified via LLM-generated rationale
Scalability	Poor scalability	Easily scalable with large or multilingual datasets
Reliability	High human variation in repeated decisions	Reliable with validation and controlled inference
Domain Adaptability	Requires human domain knowledge	Adaptable through pretraining and fine-tuning

An LLM-based approach provides the intelligent automation that replaces manual effort. Unlike traditional systems, LLM-based systems provide scalability, accuracy, and consistent reliability. Maintaining reproducible decisions is critical for trust from stakeholders in various regulatory frameworks. In an LLM-based SRS process, the first step is to understand the meaning and context of the requirement. The intent of a requirement can be grasped by using powerful language models like transformers, (Devlin et al., 2019). It makes the system able to process the information much like human experts can. Next, it groups related requirements. It makes it easier to find out the common themes like security, performance, or accessibility, (Fricker, Glinz, & Klaus, 2010). Through this step, the duplication of requirements can be avoided. After categorization of software requirements, the system ranks them based on their importance. Various factors are considered for it, like how critical a requirement is, how it aligns with business goals, how frequently stakeholders mention it, it is legally necessary or not. The most important features are considered first. It helps teams to focus on what matters. Finally, a clear explanation is provided by the system for its choices that make the decision-making process more transparent. For example, suppose it prioritizes a feature related to security. In that case, it might say: ?oThe higher priority was given to this requirement because it guarantees compliance with *DPDPA* regulations and is often mentioned by stakeholders. ?? This type of reasoning is beneficial for teams to trust the system ?(tm)s recommendations and to understand why certain criteria are more important than others. A comparative benefit analysis is illustrated in Table 3. A graphical representation of the comparison between traditional SRS and LLM-based SRS is given in Figure 5.

Figure 5. Comparison between traditional SRS and LLM-based SRS

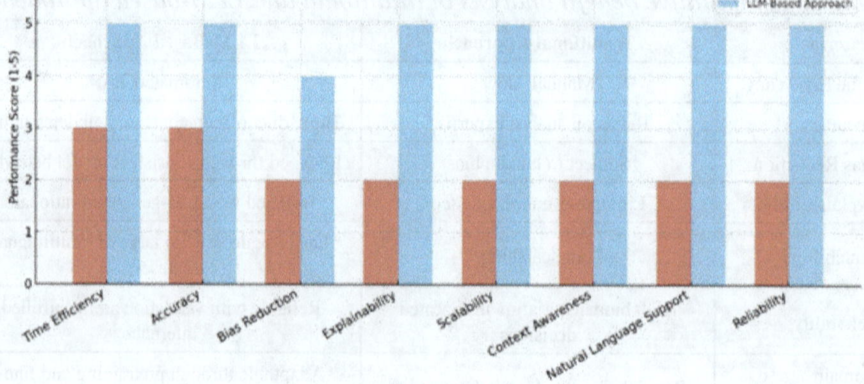

CASE STUDIES

We considered three hypothetical case studies to demonstrate the practical benefits of using LLMs for SRS. The first case study concerns a hospital management system (HMS), the second an E-commerce platform, and the third is a finance application.

Case Study 1: Hospital Management System

Based on industry reports and healthcare studies, it is analyzed that the large hospitals faced inefficiencies in managing patient records, scheduling appointments, and billing processes. Traditional systems rely on manual data inputs, paper-based records, and disjointed software, that leads to many serious issues like high error rates in patient records (~15-20%), appointment conflicts (25% appointment overlaps), slow verification of insurance (average processing time = 48 hours), and security vulnerabilities in handling sensitive health data. To overcome these issues, the hospital collaborated with an AI solution provider to integrate LLMs into its HMS. The goal was to automate the patient record analysis based on medical history, prescriptions, and allergies; optimization of doctor schedules, minimize billing errors, and improve data security.

Analysis of Appointment Conflict Reduction

An effective appointment scheduling is important in the healthcare sector. It is also crucial in other service-based industries. Because of many factors like double booking (overlapping appointments), no shows (missing appointments without any information), and manual scheduling errors (mistakes by humans in handling reschedules or cancellations), there may be a chance of high conflict rates in traditional appointment systems. These conflicts may be minimized significantly by integrating LLMs in appointment management. The percentage reduction in appointment conflicts can be calculated using the following formula:

The percentage reduction in the appointment conflicts can be computed using eq. 1.

$$Conflict\text{A}Reduction$$

$$= \left(\frac{Traditional\text{A}Conflict\text{A}Rate - LLM\text{A}Conflict\text{A}Rate}{Traditional\text{A}Conflict\text{A}Rate}\right)\text{A-100} \quad (1)$$

By substituting the given values:

$$ConflictAReduction = \left(\frac{25-7}{25}\right)\text{A-}100$$

$$= \left(\frac{18}{25}\right)\text{A-}100$$

$$= 72\%$$

Figure 6 shows the 72% of conflict reduction in LLM based appointment scheduling.

Figure 6. Conflict reduction in LLM based appointment scheduling

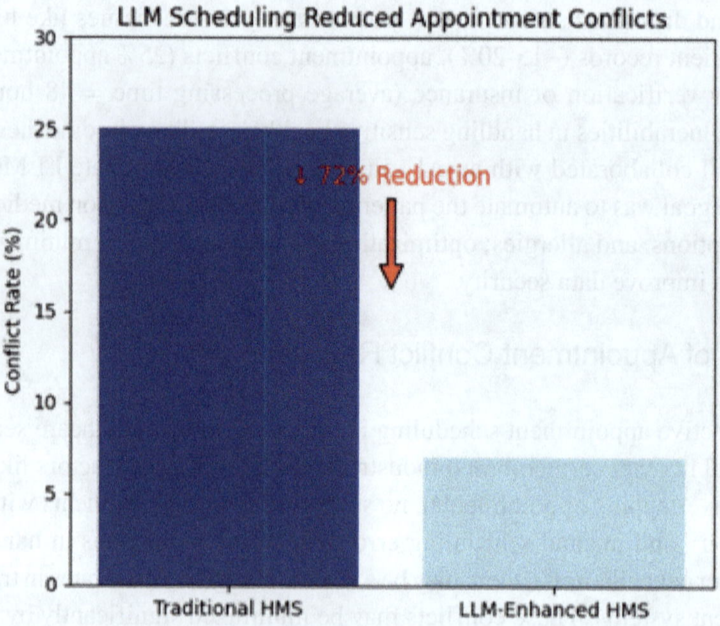

Patient Record Retrieval Time

There are many reasons for delaying patient records retrieval through any traditional HMS. For example, storage of records in paper files or digital formats like PDF, Word, etc., or from any digital systems, staff search on multiple platforms, physically accessing files, and unstructured data format, leads to emergency room bottlenecks (during emergencies, clinicians wasted up to 4 minutes assembling a full patient history), clinical frustration (68% of nurses reported spending >1 hour/day on record retrieval), and a ~5% risk of mismatched records. An LLM-based system has the capabilities of unified semantic search and summarization. It drops retrieval time by 5 seconds, i.e., ~83% improvement, as illustrated in Fig. 7. It is achieved by an LLM-based system by making a centralized vector database that can understand NLP queries, can handle variations in the medical terminologies, and other means of related data. The improvement in average retrieval time can be calculated using the eq. 2.

$$timeAsaved = \left(\frac{TraditionalATime - LLMAPoweredATime}{TraditionalATime}\right)\text{A-100} \quad (2)$$

As the traditional retrieval time (manual search in paper files/digital records) is 30 Seconds, and LLM-powered retrieval time (semantic search + auto-summarization) is 5 seconds. Therefore, time improvement will be:

$$timeAsaved = \left(\frac{30-5}{30}\right)\text{A-100} = \left(\frac{25}{30}\right)\text{A-100} = 83.33\%$$

This improvement not only speeds Emergency Room (ER) throughput by ~22%, but also minimizes the misidentification errors by ~94%. Consequently, save the hospital ?(tm)s annual staff overtime cost. A comparison of quantitative results produced by the traditional method and LLM LLM-based method is illustrated in Table 6.

Figure 7. Average retrieval time

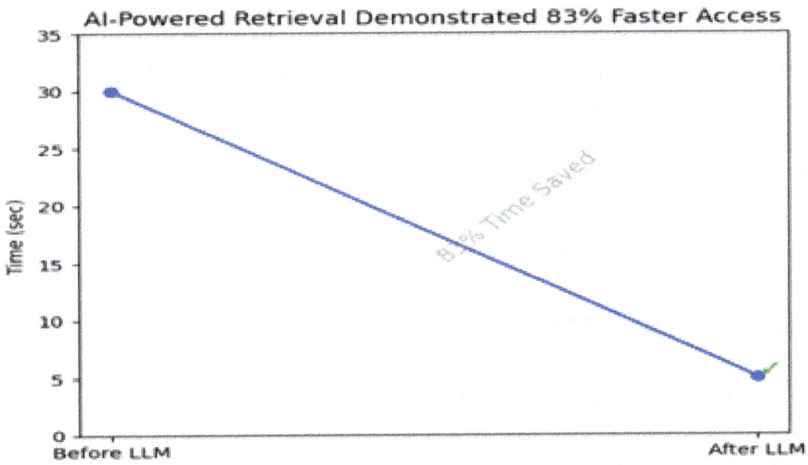

Table 6. Quantitative results produced by the traditional method and LLM-based method

Metric	Before LLM	After LLM	Improvement
Avg. Retrieval Time	30 sec	5 sec	**83%** +"
ER Record Assembly Time	4 mins	45 sec	**81%** +"
Daily Time Saved per Nurse	65 mins	12 mins	**82%** +"
Misidentification Errors	5%	0.3%	**94%** +"

Billing Error Reduction

In healthcare and even in other sectors, billing errors lead to financial losses, inefficiencies at the administrative level, and delays in payments. The traditional billing process (i.e., manual process) has a 12% error rate because of many reasons, like incorrect medical codes, missing documents, and misinterpretations of insurance policies, which lead to claim denials and revenue loss. The error rate can be reduced up to 2% with the help of LLMs and an AI-driven verification system. LLMs improve the accuracy of billing by automating code verification, flagging issues, and ensuring that the documentation is complete. It reduces the manual mistakes and increases the chances of claim approval. This billing error reduction is very significant for financial purposes because lowering billing error from 12% to 2% can save ~$250,000 annually. AI-driven billing also speeds up payments, enhances compliance, and improves overall operational efficiency. Suppose there are 50,000 claims processed per year, and the average cost per denied claim is $500. As the traditional error rate is 12% and the LLM-verified error rate is 2%, therefore traditional billing error cost will be:

50,000A-12% = 6,000 (erroneous claims)

6,000A-500 = 3,000,000 (total loss due to billing errors)

Erroneous claims after AI implementation will be:

50,000A-2% = 1,000 (erroneous claims)

6,000A-500 = 3,000,000 (total loss due to billing errors)

The total cost of errors after AI will be:

1,000A-500 = 500,000

To find the annual cost savings, we have calculated the reduction in billing errors, total savings from fewer denials, and administrative cost savings as well.

Reduction in billing errors: 6,000 – 1,000 = 5000

Total savings from fewer denials: 5,000A-500 = 2,500,000

Since artificial intelligence lowers human effort spent on reprocessing claims, additional administrative cost savings can be computed using the estimated value of about 10% of the overall savings.

Additional administrative cost savings: 2,500,000A-10% = 250,000

Therefore, the final cost savings per year is $250,000 as shown in Figure 8.

Figure 8. Final cost saving per year

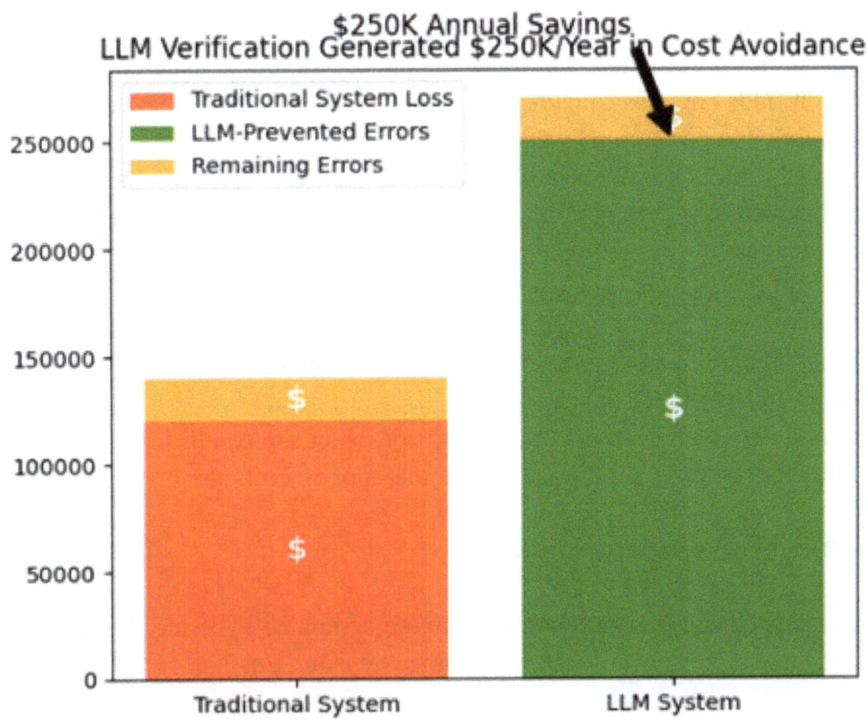

Case Study 2: Optimizing E-Commerce Platforms with LLMs

Mid-sized e-commerce platforms have encountered many key challenges before using LLM. The clients' conversion rate was only 5.5% because of generic product recommendations. Due to the slow response time of customer support, the cart abandonment was very high (~68%). Another major concern was fraudulent transactions. It cost the company ~$159,000/month in chargebacks. Moreover, orders were processed manually. It caused delays in average fulfilment time and results in inefficiencies and frustrated customers. These problems ?,together undercut growth, raise expenses, and erode customer satisfaction.

The company implemented LLM-powered solutions throughout several critical business areas to overcome the challenges. For personalized product recommendations, a real-time behavioral analysis system was produced. This system provides the dynamic adjustment of the suggestions based on various things like browsing history, session activity, and past purchases. An AI-based chatbot was created to provide automatic customer support, reduce cart abandonment, and respond to common queries immediately. For fraud detection, NLP-based pattern recognition was used. It finds out the suspicious transactions, and NLP-based pattern recognition is used. It was performed by analyzing the various inconsistencies in purchase behavior, billing details, and other red flags. Finally, order processing was simplified by making processing automate, reducing human errors, and speeding up the order fulfillment times.

The results were revolutionary as conversion rates nearly doubled, increasing from 5.5% to 9.8%. Due to the real-time support provided by the AI chatbot, the cart abandonment fell from 68% to 42%. The fraud-related losses fell by 65%. It saves the company tens of thousands of dollars per month. The time taken for fulfillment of orders was reduced from 4 hours to 1.2 hours. It results in improvement of operational efficiency. Additionally, customer support costs also dropped by 30%.

Conversion Rate Improvement

The improvement in conversion rate can be computed by using the pre-LLM conversion rate and the post-LLM conversion rate using Eq. 3.

$$Conversion\text{A}increament = \frac{postLLM\text{A}conversion\text{A}rate - preLLM\text{A}conversion\text{A}rate}{preLLM\text{A}conversion\text{A}rate}\text{A-}100 \quad (3)$$

As the pre-LLM conversion rate is 5.5% and the post-LLM conversion rate is 7.4%, therefore increment in conversion will be:

$$ConversionAincreament = \frac{7.4 - 5.5}{5.5} \text{A-}100 = 34.5\%$$

The final result is depicted in Figure 9.

Figure 9. Conversion rate improvement

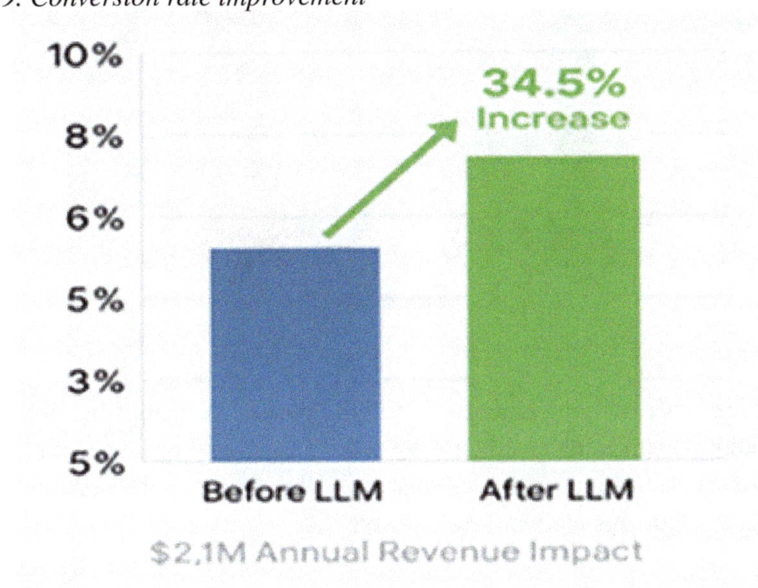

Customer Query Resolution Time

Earlier, it took 15 minutes per query in manual customer support. It leads to cart abandonment. The LLM-powered chatbot makes the system faster by reducing resolution time to just 3 minutes, i.e., an efficiency gain of 80%. The time reduction is calculated using Eq. 4.

$$TimeAReduction = \frac{TraditionalASupportATime - LLMAChatbotATime}{TraditionalASupportATime} \text{A-}100 \quad (4)$$

As the traditional support time is 15 minutes and LLM chatbot time is 3 minutes, therefore reduction in customer query resolution time will be:

$$TimeAReduction = \frac{15 - 3}{15} \text{A-}100 = 80\%$$

The result is shown in Figure 10.

Figure 10. Customer query resolution time

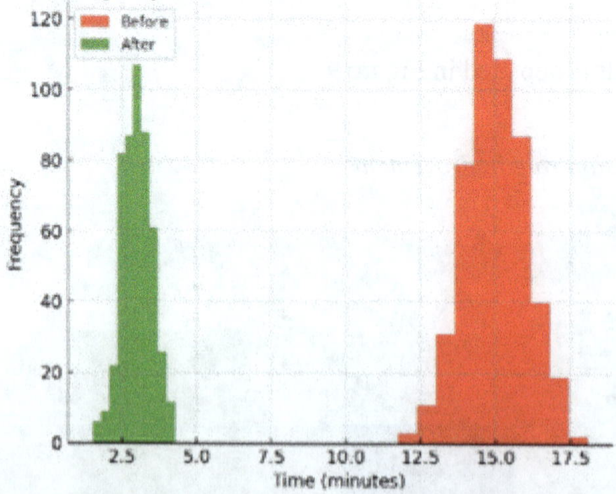

There are several improvements seen in the post-LLM platforms, like reduced query resolution time, enhanced customer satisfaction and operational efficiency, improved fraud detection, etc. A comparative illustration of the performances of both types of platforms is illustrated in Table 7.

Table 7. Performance comparison of pre-LLM and post-LLM platforms

Metric	Pre-LLM	Post-LLM	Improvement
Conversion Rate (%)	5.5	7.4	34.5% +'
Query Resolution Time (min)	15	3	80% +"
Fraud Detection Rate (%)	72	94	30.5% +'
Order Processing Time (hr)	4	0.5	87.5% +"
Cart Abandonment Rate (%)	68	49	28% +"

Figure 11. Pre-LLM and post-LLM fraud detection analysis

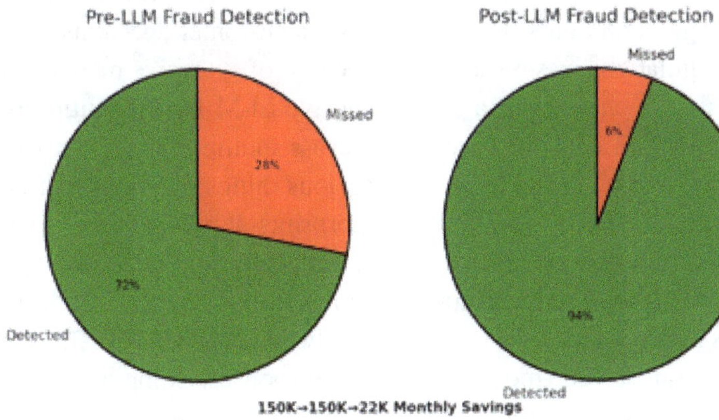

Figure 12. Pre-LLM and post-LLM cart abandonment reduction analysis

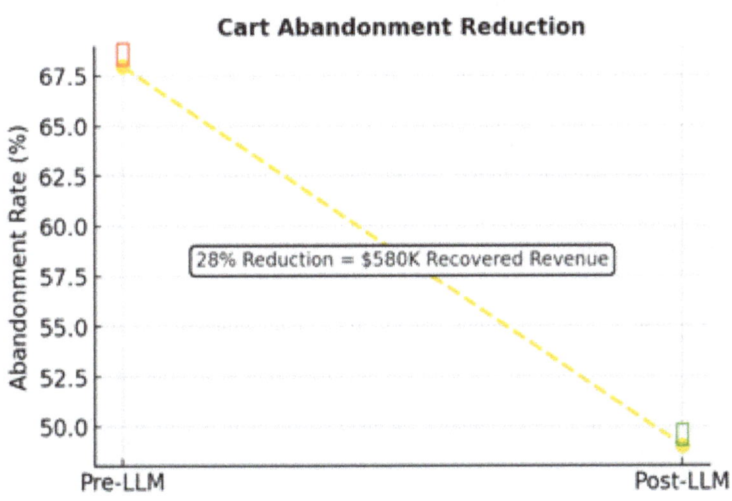

Case Study 3: Enhancing Financial Applications with LLMs

Multinational banking institutions faced various significant operational challenges like fraud detection, customer experience, loan approvals, and compliance monitoring. These challenges affect both efficiency and customer satisfaction. The fraud detection systems of banks had a 22% false positive rate that led to a legitimate transaction being flagged as fraudulent. The traditional loan approval processing was taking an average of 48 hours. It caused delays in customer decisions. Compliance with various regulations was burdensome because of extensive manual auditing.

To address these challenges, a comprehensive LLM-based solution is used by banks. It led to significant improvements across multiple areas. An LLM-based fraud detection system is used to identify various things like customer behavioral patterns, transaction history, and device fingerprints. It reduces false positives and enhances fraud detection accuracy by 95%. For loans, an automated system now makes faster decisions. It reduced approval times from 48 hours to 10 hours. LLM-based systems improve customer service by analyzing emotions in calls, emails, and chat. It results in quicker and more personalized responses. Compliance also became easier with the use AI AI-based systems because these systems can automatically create accurate audit reports to meet regulations.

Fraud Detection Accuracy

The accuracy gain by traditional systems of fraud detection is ~78%, with a 22% false positive rate. On the other hand, the accuracy of the LLM-based system is higher, i.e., ~95%, and it reduces false positives to 5%. The accuracy gain can be calculated as:

$$\textbf{\textit{Accuracy}}\mathrm{A}\textbf{\textit{Gain}} = \frac{(95-78)}{78}\mathrm{A\text{-}100} = 21.8\%$$

The LLM-based system provides 21.8% of accuracy gain, as illustrated in Figure 13.

Figure 13. Fraud detection accuracy

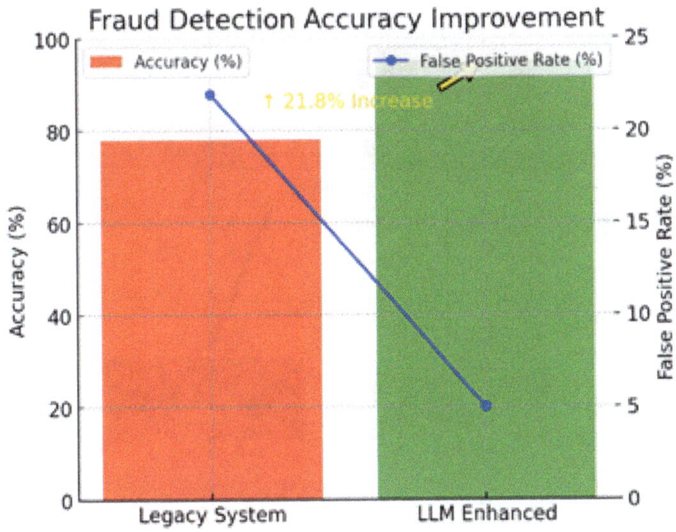

Loan Processing Efficiency

The manual load processing system needs ~48 hours per application. This time has been reduced to ~10 hours with the help of an LLM-based system. Such an efficiency gain can be calculated as:

$$\textbf{\textit{Efficiency}}\text{A}\textbf{\textit{Gain}} = \frac{(48-10)}{48}\text{A-}100 = 79\%$$

The result shows that the LLM system provides a 79% reduction in processing time, as illustrated in Figure 14.

Figure 14. Fraud detection accuracy

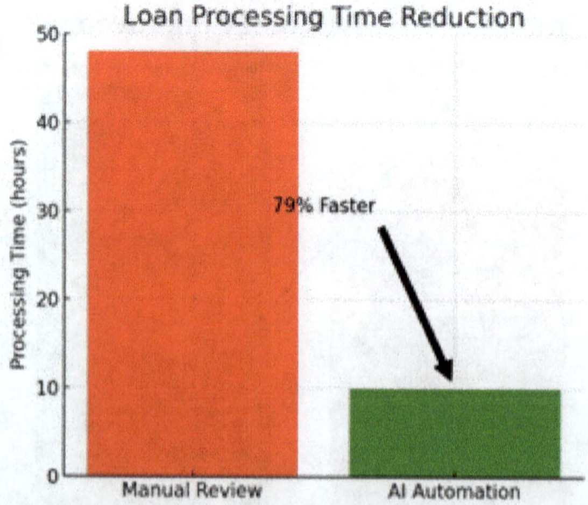

Cost and Compliance Impact

The use of LLMs in business operations has made a significant difference in minimizing costs, enhancing compliance, and increasing customer satisfaction. The pre-LLM and post-LLM performance of the key business areas is presented in Table 8.

Table 8. Comparative performance of pre-LLM and post-LLM systems in some areas

Area	Before LLM	After LLM	Improvement
Fraud Detection Accuracy	78%	95%	21.8% better
Loan Processing Time	48 hours	10 hours	79% faster
False Positive Rate	22%	5%	77% lower
Compliance Audit Time	14 days	2 days	86% faster
Customer Retention Rate	73%	89%	22% more customers stayed

A comparative analysis of all three case studies discussed above, summarizing key points across the domains (Healthcare, E-commerce, and Finance), is given in Table 9.

Table 9. A comparative analysis of all three case studies

Aspect	Healthcare	E-commerce	Finance
Primary Stakeholders	Doctors, Admins, Patients	Sellers, Inventory Managers, Logistics	Investors, Advisors, Compliance Officers
Key Themes	Security, Usability, Accessibility	Inventory, pricing, and UX	Compliance, Risk, Personalization
Top Priority Requirement	Patient data encryption	Multi-language checkout	SEBI regulation compliance
LLM benefit highlighted	Regulatory compliance via semantic clustering	Market expansion insights from usage patterns	Legal risk mitigation from inferred policies

CHALLENGES AND LIMITATIONS

LLMs can automate and improve the process of SRS. But there are still various challenges and limitations that must be addressed to make effective real-world projects. Interpretability of deep learning models is one of the prime concerns. It is difficult for developers, analysts, and stakeholders to understand the reasoning behind a decision or prioritization. It is because of the black box nature of the LLM's functionality. Compared to conventional rule-based systems, explainability modules and attention mechanisms still fall short in providing comprehensive interpretability. Even though they provide partial transparency, (Ferrari, Spoletini, & Gnesi, 2017).

Another important issue is the availability of domain-specific datasets and the data dependency. A significant amount of labeled and context-rich requirements data of the specific software domain is required so that the LLMs can be trained for requirements engineering tasks. Unfortunately, such datasets are either limited, unstructured, or private. This restricts how well the model can generalize across projects or industries, (Ji et al., 2023).

Some other limitations are computational cost and the need for model fine-tuning. Modern LLMs like GPT, PaLM, or LLaMA need a huge amount of processing power and memory from their hardware. Deploying and maintaining such models at scale may be challenging for organizations with limited infrastructure. Furthermore, domain experts, NLP engineers, and annotated data are required for fine-tuning or adapting models so that the specific project contexts can be handled, (Floridi & Chiriatti, 2020).

The risk of hallucinations is another significant limitation. It is a condition in which LLMs produce plausible but inaccurate or deceptive information. This might result in the inclusion of the fabricated or unnecessary requirements in the context of requirements engineering. It may compromise the integrity and quality of the final project. Hallucination mitigation is still an active research area. It is essential for reliable and trustworthy use in sensitive domains like healthcare and finance, (Ji et al., 2023).

CONCLUSION AND FUTURE DIRECTIONS

The software requirements selection problem is more complicated than ever due to the increasing complexity of modern software systems and the diverse growth in stakeholder expectations. The traditional techniques, without dealing with subjectivity or scalability, tend to provide incomplete answers when unstructured stakeholder information is blended with dynamically changing priorities.

This chapter demonstrated how powerful natural language understanding capabilities of LLMs can revolutionize the process of software requirements selection. From explainability and prioritization at the semantic level to cross-domain adaptation, LLMs outperform conventional approaches based on NLP or human effort on numerous fronts. We designed and described an LLM selection system and showcased its functionality in three case studies, i.e., healthcare, e-commerce, and finance, using charts, pseudocode, and other visual aids. We also compared their performances to the existing solutions.

We also discussed critical considerations such as scalability, explainability, and data privacy, as well as challenges like interpretability, domain data scarcity, and hallucination risks. Finally, we outlined future research avenues, including the integration of domain specific LLMs, agile tool interoperability, reinforcement learning feedback loops, and ethical governance.

The field of software requirements engineering is evolving continuously, therefore, the integration of LLM opens several exciting future directions to overcome the present limitations and to unlock new opportunities. Some major future directions may be:

? to develop and deploy the domain specific LLMs for specific domains like healthcare, defense, finance, education, etc.

? to integrate an LLM-based system with agile management project tools like JIRA, Asana, or Trello.

? to use reinforcement learning in LLM-based systems so that models will be able to learn from previous decisions to enhance the relevance, quality, and ranking of the selected software requirements.

AUTHOR CONTRIBUTION

[Mohd. Nazim, Shahnawaz Ahmad, Mohd Aquib Ansari] Conceptualization, Methodology, Software, Investigation, Data curation, Writing ?" original draft. **[Mohd. Nazim, Shahnawaz Ahmad, Mohd Aquib Ansari]** Visualization, Validation, Formal analysis, Writing ?" review & editing.

REFERENCES

Ahmad, W. U., Chakraborty, S., Ray, B., & Chang, K.-W. (2021). Unified pre-training for program understanding and generation. *arXiv preprint arXiv:2103.06333.*

Ajagbe, M., & Zhao, L. (2022). Retraining a BERT model for transfer learning in requirements engineering: A preliminary study. In *2022 IEEE 30th International Requirements Engineering Conference (RE)* (pp. 309-315). IEEE. https://doi.org/ DOI: 10.1109/RE54965.2022.00046

Berander, P., & Andrews, A. (2005). Requirements prioritization. In Aurum, A., & Wohlin, C. (Eds.), *Engineering and Managing Software Requirements*. Springer., DOI: 10.1007/3-540-28244-0_4

Carlini, N.. (2021). Extracting training data from large language models. *USENIX Security Symposium.*

Chen, S. J., & Hwang, C. L. (1992). Fuzzy multiple attribute decision making methods. In *Fuzzy Multiple Attribute Decision Making* (Lecture Notes in Economics and Mathematical Systems, Vol. 375)*. Springer, Berlin, Heidelberg. https://doi.org/ DOI: 10.1007/978-3-642-46768-4_5

Chen, X., Hu, X., & Huang, Y.. (2025). Deep learning-based software engineering: Progress, challenges, and opportunities. *Science China. Information Sciences*, *68*, 111102. DOI: 10.1007/s11432-023-4127-5

Cleland-Huang, J., Gotel, O., & Zisman, A. (2007). *Software traceability: Trends and future directions*. ICSE.

Dettmers, E.. (2022). Efficient fine-tuning of language models with parameter-efficient adapters. *Proceedings of the ICML.*

Devlin, J., Chang, M. W., Lee, K., & Toutanova, K. (2019). BERT: Pre-training of deep bidirectional transformers for language understanding. In *Proceedings of NAACL-HLT.*

Doshi-Velez, F., & Kim, B. (2017). Towards a rigorous science of interpretable machine learning. *arXiv preprint arXiv:1702.08608.*

Dwork, C. (2008). Differential privacy: A survey of results. In *Theory and Applications of Models of Computation* (pp. xx ?"xx). Springer.

Ferrari, A., Spoletini, P., & Gnesi, S. (2017). Ambiguity and vagueness in natural language requirements engineering. *ACM Transactions on Software Engineering and Methodology*.

Floridi, L., & Chiriatti, M. (2020). GPT-3: Its nature, scope, limits, and consequences. *Minds and Machines*, *30*, 681 ?"694. DOI: 10.1007/s11023-020-09548-1

Fricker, S. A., Glinz, M., & Klaus, P. (2010). *Requirements engineering: Best practices*. Springer.

Gunning, D. (2017). *Explainable artificial intelligence*. XAI. [DARPA Program Briefing]

Guo, J., Li, J., Sun, Y., & Wang, H. (2022). Deep learning for software traceability: A survey. *Journal of Systems and Software*.

Harmain, H., & Gaizauskas, R. (2003). CM-Builder: A natural language-based CASE tool for object-oriented analysis. *Automated Software Engineering*, *10*, 157 ?"181.

Jackson, I., Jesus Saenz, M., & Ivanov, D. (2023). From natural language to simulations: Applying AI to automate simulation modelling of logistics systems. *International Journal of Production Research*, *62*(4), 1434 ?"1457. DOI: 10.1080/00207543.2023.2276811

Jahi , J., & Sami, A. (2024). State of practice: LLMs in software engineering and software architecture. In *2024 IEEE 21st International Conference on Software Architecture Companion (ICSA-C)* (pp. 311-318). IEEE. https://doi.org/DOI: 10.1109/ICSA-C63560.2024.00059

Ji, Z., Lee, N., Frieske, R., Yu, T., Su, D., Xu, Y., Ishii, E., Bang, Y. J., Madotto, A., & Fung, P. (2023). Survey of hallucination in natural language generation. *ACM Computing Surveys*, *55*(12), 1 ?"38. DOI: 10.1145/357173

Johri, S., Jeong, J., & Tran, B. A. (2025). An evaluation framework for clinical use of large language models in patient interaction tasks. *Nature Medicine*, *31*, 77 ?"86. DOI: 10.1038/s41591-024-03328-5 PMID: 39747685

Karlsson, J., Wohlin, C., & Regnell, B. (1998). An evaluation of methods for prioritizing software requirements. *Information and Software Technology*, *39*(14 ?"15), 939 ?"947.

Khayashi, F., Jamasb, B., Akbari, R., & Shamsinejadbabaki, P. (2022). Deep learning methods for software requirement classification: A performance study on the PURE dataset. [Space Frontiers]. *Information and Software Technology, 147*, 106877. Advance online publication. DOI: 10.1016/j.infsof.2022.106877

Ko >ci "ski, V., Gambardella, C., Gerstner, E., Zappavigna, M., Cassetti, J., & Mirakhorli, M. (2021). A natural language processing technique for formalization of systems requirement specifications. In *2021 IEEE 29th International Requirements Engineering Conference Workshops (REW)* (pp. 350-356). IEEE. https://doi.org/DOI: 10.1109/REW53955.2021.00062

Kravchenko, T., Bogdanova, T., & Shevgunov, T. (2022). Ranking requirements using MoSCoW methodology in practice. In Silhavy, R. (Ed.), *Cybernetics Perspectives in Systems. CSOC 2022. Lecture Notes in Networks and Systems, 503*. Springer., DOI: 10.1007/978-3-031-09073-8_18

Li, L., ... (2021). Membership inference attacks against language models. *arXiv preprint arXiv:2102.06514.*

Lubos, S., ... (2024). Leveraging LLMs for the quality assurance of software requirements. In *2024 IEEE 32nd International Requirements Engineering Conference (RE)* (pp. 389-397). IEEE. https://doi.org/DOI: 10.1109/RE59067.2024.00046

Mairiza, D., Zowghi, D., & Gervasi, V. (2014). Utilizing TOPSIS: A multi-criteria decision analysis technique for non-functional requirements conflicts. In Zowghi, D., & Jin, Z. (Eds.), *Requirements Engineering. Communications in Computer and Information Science, 432*. Springer., DOI: 10.1007/978-3-662-43610-3_3

Nazim, M., Ahmad, S., Arif, M., Mishra, V., & Ahmad, J. (2024, Moradabad, India). Optimizing software requirements selection: A hybrid K-means and intuitionistic fuzzy TOPSIS approach. In *2024 13th International Conference on System Modeling & Advancement in Research Trends (SMART)* (pp. 750-755). IEEE. https://doi.org/DOI: 10.1109/SMART63812.2024.10882593

Nazim, M., Mohammad, C. W., & Sadiq, M. (2022). Analysis of fuzzy AHP and fuzzy TOPSIS methods for the prioritization of the software requirements. In Kulkarni, A. J. (Ed.), *Multiple Criteria Decision Making. Studies in Systems, Decision and Control, 407*. Springer., DOI: 10.1007/978-981-16-7414-3_4

Nazim, M., Mohammad, C. W., & Sadiq, M. (2022). Fuzzy-based methods for the selection and prioritization of software requirements: A systematic literature review. In Bhateja, V., Tang, J., Satapathy, S. C., Peer, P., & Das, R. (Eds.), *Evolution in Computational Intelligence. Smart Innovation, Systems and Technologies, 267*. Springer., DOI: 10.1007/978-981-16-6616-2_11

Nerurkar, P., Shirke, A., Chandane, M., & Bhirud, S. (2018). Empirical analysis of data clustering algorithms. *Procedia Computer Science*, *125*, 770 ?"779. DOI: 10.1016/j.procs.2017.12.099

Raffel, C.. (2020). Exploring the limits of transfer learning with a unified text-to-text transformer. *Journal of Machine Learning Research*.

Ribeiro, M., Singh, S., & Guestrin, C. (2016, August). ?oWhy should I trust you? ?? Explaining the predictions of any classifier. In *Proceedings of the 22nd ACM SIGKDD International Conference on Knowledge Discovery and Data Mining (KDD ?(tm)16)*.

Saaty, R. W. (1987). The analytic hierarchy process ?" What it is and how it is used. *Mathematical Modelling*, *9*(3-5), 161 ?"176. DOI: 10.1016/0270-0255(87)90473-8

Shokri, R.. (2017). Membership inference attacks against machine learning models. In *Proceedings of IEEE Symposium on Security and Privacy*.

Siddiq, M., Ullah, I., & Khan, M. I. (2023). Clustering software requirements using transformer-based models. *IEEE Access : Practical Innovations, Open Solutions*.

Siddiqui, M. S., Ruhe, G., & Nguyen, T. N. (2019). Decision support for requirements reprioritization in software release planning. *Automated Software Engineering*.

Tufek, N.. (2025). Validating semantic artifacts with large language models. In MeroA o PeA uela, A. (Eds.), Lecture Notes in Computer Science: Vol. 15344. *The Semantic Web: ESWC 2024 Satellite Events*. Springer., DOI: 10.1007/978-3-031-78952-6_9

van Lamsweerde, A. (2001). Goal-oriented requirements engineering: A guided tour. In *Proceedings of the Fifth IEEE International Symposium on Requirements Engineering* (pp. 249-262). IEEE. https://doi.org/DOI: 10.1109/ISRE.2001.948567

van Lamsweerde, A. (2004). Goal-oriented requirements engineering: A roundtrip from research to practice. In *Proceedings of the 12th IEEE International Requirements Engineering Conference* (pp. 4-7). IEEE. https://doi.org/DOI: 10.1109/ICRE.2004.1335648

Wong, J. K. W., & Li, H. (2008). Application of the analytic hierarchy process (AHP) in multi-criteria analysis of the selection of intelligent building systems. *Building and Environment*, *43*(1), 108 ?"125. DOI: 10.1016/j.buildenv.2006.11.019

Yang, X., Chen, A., & PourNejatian, N.. (2022). A large language model for electronic health records. *NPJ Digital Medicine*, *5*, 194. DOI: 10.1038/s41746-022-00742-2 PMID: 36572766

Zhang, H., Berg, A. C., Maire, M., & Malik, J. (2006). SVM-KNN: Discriminative nearest neighbor classification for visual category recognition. In *2006 IEEE Computer Society Conference on Computer Vision and Pattern Recognition (CVPR ?(tm)06).*

Zheng, Z., Ning, K., & Zhong, Q.. (2025). Towards an understanding of large language models in software engineering tasks. *Empirical Software Engineering*, *30*, 50. Advance online publication. DOI: 10.1007/s10664-024-10602-0

Compilation of References

Abdou, A. H., Albakhit, A. I., Shehata, H. S., Almakhayitah, M. Y., & Mahmoud, H. M. E. (2022). The Effect of Environmentally Sustainable Practices on Customer Citizenship Behavior in Eco-Friendly Hotels: Does the Green Perceived Value Matter? *Sustainability*, *14*(12), 7167. DOI: 10.3390/su14127167

Abdul Majid, N., Ramli, Z., Awang, A. H., & Md Sum, S. (2021). Sustainable Palm Oil Certification Scheme Frameworks and Impacts: A Systematic Literature Review. *Sustainability*, *13*(6), 3263. DOI: 10.3390/su13063263

Abdul-Hamid, A.-Q., Ali, M. H., Tseng, M.-L., Lan, S., & Kumar, M. (2020). Impeding challenges on Industry 4.0 in circular economy: Palm oil industry in Malaysia. *Computers & Operations Research*, *123*, 105052.

Abinandan, S., Praveen, K., Venkateswarlu, K., & Megharaj, M. (2024). Eco-innovation minimizes the carbon footprint of wine production. *Communications Earth & Environment*, *5*(1). Advance online publication. DOI: 10.1038/s43247-024-01766-0

Abujder Ochoa, W. A., Ballesteros-Ballesteros, V., Calabokis, O. P., Vitorio, P. C.Junior, & Iarozinski Neto, A. (2024). The Theory of Complexity and Sustainable Urban Development: A Systematic Literature Review. *Sustainability*, *17*(1), 3. DOI: 10.3390/su17010003

Ahlström, H., & Monciardini, D. (2022). The regulatory dynamics of sustainable finance: Paradoxical success and limitations of EU reforms. *Journal of Business Ethics*, *177*(1), 193–212. PMID: 33642657

Ahmad Ibrahim, S. R., Yahaya, J., & Sallehudin, H. (2022). Green software process factors: A qualitative study. *Sustainability*, *14*(18), 11180.

Ahmad, W. U., Chakraborty, S., Ray, B., & Chang, K.-W. (2021). Unified pre-training for program understanding and generation. *arXiv preprint arXiv:2103.06333*.

Ahmad, R., Hussain, A., & Baharom, F. (2018). Software sustainability characteristic for software development towards long living software. *Wseas Transactions on Business and Economics, 15*, 55–72.

Ahmed, I., Irshad, A., Zafar, S., Khan, B. A., Raza, M., & Ali, P. R. (2023). The role of environmental initiatives and green value co-creation as mediators: Promoting corporate entrepreneurship and green innovation. *SN Business & Economics, 3*(4), 85.

Ahmed, R. R., Streimikiene, D., & Zheng, X. (2021). The Impact of Proactive Environmental Strategy on Competitive and Sustainable Development of Organizations. *Journal of Competitiveness, 13*(4), 5–24. DOI: 10.7441/joc.2021.04.01

Ahn, J., Kim, M., & Yi, E. (2024). Blockchain Consensus Mechanisms: A Bibliometric Analysis (2014–2024) Using VOSviewer and R Bibliometrix. *Information (Basel), 15*(10), 644. DOI: 10.3390/info15100644

Ajagbe, M., & Zhao, L. (2022). Retraining a BERT model for transfer learning in requirements engineering: A preliminary study. In *2022 IEEE 30th International Requirements Engineering Conference (RE)* (pp. 309-315). IEEE. https://doi.org/DOI: 10.1109/RE54965.2022.00046

Akçay, H. G., Kabasakal, B., Aksu, D., Demir, N., Öz, M., & Erdoğan, A. (2020). Automated bird counting with deep learning for regional bird distribution mapping. *Animals (Basel), 10*, 1207. PMID: 32708550

Akinade, O., & Oyedele, L. (2019). Integrating construction supply chains within a circular economy: An ANFIS-based waste analytics system (A-WAS). *Journal of Cleaner Production, 229*, 863–873.

Alafif, T., Tehame, A. M., Bajaba, S., Barnawi, A., & Zia, S. (2021). Machine and deep learning toward COVID-19 diagnosis and treatment: Survey, challenges, and future directions. *International Journal of Environmental Research and Public Health, 18*, 1117. PMID: 33513984

Alberti, M. (1996). Measuring urban sustainability. *Environmental Impact Assessment Review, 16*, 381–424.

Alcayaga, A., & Hansen, E. G. (2019). Smart products as enabler for circular business models: The case of B2B textile washing services. In *Proceedings of the 3rd PLATE 2019 Conference* (pp. 18–20). Berlin, Germany.

Alcayaga, A., Wiener, M., & Hansen, E. G. (2019). Towards a framework of smart-circular systems: An integrative literature review. *Journal of Cleaner Production, 221*, 622–634.

Alenezi, M., & Akour, M. (2025). AI-Driven Innovations in Software Engineering: A Review of Current Practices and Future Directions. *Applied Sciences (Basel, Switzerland), 15*(3), 1344. DOI: 10.3390/app15031344

Alhosaini, H., Alharbi, S., Wang, X., & Xu, G. (2023). API Recommendation For Mashup Creation: A Comprehensive Survey. *The Computer Journal, 67*(5), 1920–1940. DOI: 10.1093/comjnl/bxad112

Ali, S., Khan, S., Khan, I., Rehman, A. U., Samuel, O., Albogamy, F. R., Hafeez, G., Murawwat, S., & Wadud, Z. (2022). Demand Response Program for Efficient Demand-Side Management in Smart Grid Considering Renewable Energy Sources. *IEEE Access : Practical Innovations, Open Solutions, 10*, 53832–53853. DOI: 10.1109/access.2022.3174586

Almusaed, A., Almssad, A., Yitmen, I., & Myhren, J. A. (2024). Assessing the Impact of Recycled Building Materials on Environmental Sustainability and Energy Efficiency: A Comprehensive Framework for Reducing Greenhouse Gas Emissions. *Buildings (Basel, Switzerland), 14*(6), 1566. DOI: 10.3390/buildings14061566

Almusawi, S. M., & Khalefa, M. S. (2021, June). Study of knowledge management framework to enhance Enterprise Resource Planning system in Green software development process. In *2021 International Conference on Communication & Information Technology (ICICT)* (pp. 1-6). IEEE.

Alnafessah, A., Casale, G., Filieri, A., Wang, R., Gias, A. U., & Zhu, L. (2021). Quality-Aware DevOps Research: Where Do We Stand? *IEEE Access : Practical Innovations, Open Solutions, 9*, 44476–44489. DOI: 10.1109/access.2021.3064867

Alsadie, D. (2024). Advancements in heuristic task scheduling for IoT applications in fog-cloud computing: Challenges and prospects. *PeerJ. Computer Science, 10*, e2128. DOI: 10.7717/peerj-cs.2128

Alsaleh, A., & Sattler, M. (2019). Comprehensive life cycle assessment of large wind turbines in the US. *Clean Technologies and Environmental Policy, 21*(4), 887–903. DOI: 10.1007/s10098-019-01678-0

Amel-Zadeh, A., & Tang, Q. (2025). Managing the shift from voluntary to mandatory climate disclosure: The role of carbon accounting. *The British Accounting Review, 57*(2), 101594.

Ampatzidis, P., & Kershaw, T. (2020). A review of the impact of blue space on the urban microclimate. *The Science of the Total Environment, 730*, 139068. PMID: 32422454

Anand, G., Chandrasekaran, A., & Sharma, L. (2020). Sustainable process improvements: Evidence from intervention-based research. *Journal of Operations Management*, *67*(2), 212–236. DOI: 10.1002/joom.1119

Anderl, R., Haag, S., Schützer, K., & Zancul, E. (2018). Digital twin technology – an approach for Industrie 4.0 vertical and horizontal lifecycle integration. *IT Inf. Technol.*, *60*(3), 125–132.

Andersen, S. C., Birgisdottir, H., & Birkved, M. (2022). Life cycle assessments of circular economy in the built environment—A scoping review. *Sustainability*, *14*(11), 6887.

Andersen, T., & Jæger, B. (2021). Circularity for electric and electronic equipment (EEE), the edge and distributed ledger (Edge & DL) model. *Sustainability*, *13*, 9924.

Andersson, E., Langemeyer, J., Borgström, S., McPhearson, T., Haase, D., Kronenberg, J., Barton, D., Davis, M., Naumann, S., & Röschel, L.. (2019). Enabling green and blue infrastructure to improve contributions to human well-being and equity in urban systems. *Bioscience*, *69*, 566–574. PMID: 31308573

Andrae, A. S. G., & Edler, T. (2015). On global electricity usage of communication technology: Trends to 2030. *Challenges*, *6*(1), 117–157. DOI: 10.3390/challe6010117

Anibal Altamirano, M., & Sloley, A. A. (2023). Corporate governance: The role of board of directors in the strategic planning process of organizations. In *Strategic Management and International Business Policies for Maintaining Competitive Advantage*. https://doi.org/DOI: 10.4018/978-1-6684-6845-6.ch001

Anthony, B. (2024). The Role of Community Engagement in Urban Innovation Towards the Co-Creation of Smart Sustainable Cities. *Journal of the Knowledge Economy*, *15*(1). Advance online publication. DOI: 10.1007/s13132-023-01176-1

Apajalahti, E.-L., Temmes, A., & Lempiälä, T. (2017). Incumbent organisations shaping emerging technological fields: Cases of solar photovoltaic and electric vehicle charging. *Technology Analysis and Strategic Management*, *30*(1), 44–57. DOI: 10.1080/09537325.2017.1285397

Aracil, E., & Sancak, I. (2023). Sustainable Finance A Multidimensional and Multi actor Framework. In *Essential Concepts of Sustainable Finance an A Z Guide*. https://doi.org/DOI: 10.4324/9781003310891-1

Archer, M. (2022). The ethics of ESG Sustainable finance and the emergence of the market as an ethical subject. *Focaal: Tijdschrift voor Antropologie*, *2022*(93), 18–31. DOI: 10.3167/fcl.2022.930102

Arefin, M. A., Nabi, M. N., Gudimetla, P., & Sadeque, S. (2021). Incorporating sustainability in engineering curriculum: A study of the Australian universities. *International Journal of Sustainability in Higher Education*, *22*(3), 576–598. DOI: 10.1108/ijshe-07-2020-0271

Arnemann, L., Winter, S., Quernheim, N., Grieser, P., Anderl, R., & Schleich, B. (2023). Information model to return data of digital twins into product design. *Procedia CIRP*, *116*, 173–178.

Arruda, T. de L., da Costa, F. P., Diniz, R. C., Rodrigues, A. M., Menezes, R. R., & Neves, G. de A. (2023). Statistical Design of Eco-Friendly Mortar Mixtures Containing Scheelite Tailings and Quartzite Sand: Evaluation of Resistance to Alkali-Aggregate Reaction. *Sustainability (Switzerland)*, *15*(15). Advance online publication. DOI: 10.3390/su151511544

Ashton, W., Russell, S., & Futch, E. (2017). The adoption of green business practices among small US Midwestern manufacturing enterprises. *Journal of Environmental Planning and Management*, *60*(12), 2133–2149. DOI: 10.1080/09640568.2017.1281107

Assoratgoon, W., & Kantabutra, S. (2023). Toward a sustainability organizational culture model. *Journal of Cleaner Production*, *400*, 136666.

Asyraf, M. Z., Suriani, M. J., Ruzaidi, C. M., Khalina, A., Ilyas, R. A., Asyraf, M. R. M., Syamsir, A., Azmi, A., & Mohamed, A. (2022). Development of Natural Fibre-Reinforced Polymer Composites Ballistic Helmet Using Concurrent Engineering Approach: A Brief Review. In *Sustainability (Switzerland)* (Vol. 14, Issue 12). https://doi.org/DOI: 10.3390/su14127092

Atadoga, A., Lottu, O., Sodiya, E., & Umoga, U. (2024). Advancing green computing: Practices, strategies, and impact in modern software development for environmental sustainability. *World Journal of Advanced Engineering Technology and Sciences*, *11*(1), 220–230. DOI: 10.30574/wjaets.2024.11.1.0052

Ateeq, M., Zhang, N., Zhao, W., Gu, Y., Wen, Z., Zheng, C., & Hao, J. (2025). Enhancing Construction Waste Transportation Management Using Internet of Things (IoT): An Evaluation Framework Based on AHP–FCE Method. *Buildings 2025, Vol. 15, Page 1381, 15*(8), 1381. https://doi.org/DOI: 10.3390/BUILDINGS15081381

Audi, M., & Yu, H. (2024). Strategic value creation through corporate social responsibility adoption for sustainable financial performance. *Journal of Policy Options*, *7*(4), 14–21.

Awan, U., Shamim, S., Khan, Z., Zia, N. U., Shariq, S. M., & Khan, M. N. (2021). Big data analytics capability and decision-making: The role of data-driven insight on circular economy performance. *Technological Forecasting and Social Change, 168*, 120766.

Awewomom, J., Dzeble, F., Takyi, Y. D., Ashie, W. B., Ettey, E. N. Y. O., Afua, P. E., Sackey, L. N. A., Opoku, F., & Akoto, O. (2024). Addressing global environmental pollution using environmental control techniques: A focus on environmental policy and preventive environmental management. *Discover Environment, 2*(1). Advance online publication. DOI: 10.1007/s44274-024-00033-5

Azanha, A., Antoniolli, P. D., Argoud, A. R. T. T., & Camargo, J. B. D.Junior. (2017). Agile project management with Scrum. *International Journal of Managing Projects in Business, 10*(1), 121–142. DOI: 10.1108/ijmpb-06-2016-0054

Bahri, M. I., Agustina, T. S., & Ridha, A. E. (2025). Human resource management in the digital era: Developing digital-first organizational cultures to drive sustainable competitive advantage. In *Innovative Approaches for International Competitiveness Through Human Resource Management*. https://doi.org/DOI: 10.4018/979-8-3373-1005-3.ch003

Bahri, M. I., Dermawan, A. A., & Tambunan, A. A. (2025). Public-Private Collaborations in Smart Cities: Startup-Driven Innovations in E-Government. In *In Startup-Driven E-Government: Digital Innovation for Sustainable Ecosystems* (pp. 61–86). IGI Global Scientific Publishing.

Bahri, M. I., Tambunan, A. A., & Zulfikar. (2025). TRANSFORMATION OF HUMAN RESOURCE MANAGEMENT IN THE ERA OF REGIONAL DECENTRALIZATION AND DIGITAL REVOLUTION: A LITERATURE REVIEW AND ITS IMPLICATIONS. *Jurnal Manajemen Rekayasa Dan Inovasi Bisnis, 3*(Februari), 92–117. https://doi.org/DOI: 10.62375/jmrib.v3i2.451

Bahri, M. I., Sirojuzilam, S. S., Rujiman, R. R., & Kismawadi, E. R. (2021). The Influence of Youth in Regional Development Through the Management of Aceh's Special Autonomy Fund in Langsa City. *E-Mabis: Jurnal Ekonomi Manajemen Dan Bisnis, 22*(1), 42–53. DOI: 10.29103/e-mabis.v22i1.650

Bambang, W. (2018). Data Readiness & Technology Assesment for Indonesian Non Profit Organization Using Data Maturity Framework. *International Journal of Scientific and Engineering Research, 9*(9). http://www.ijser.org

Bamiduro, M., Fatima, I., Lago, P., & Vos, S. (2025). Challenges in Incorporating Sustainability Practices in the Software Lifecycle. In *Lecture Notes in Business Information Processing* (Vol. 539). LNBIP., DOI: 10.1007/978-3-031-85849-9_23

Baporikar, N. (2023). Governance as a catalyst for public sector sustainability. In *Governance as A Catalyst for Public Sector Sustainability*. https://doi.org/DOI: 10.4018/978-1-6684-6966-8

Barakat, B., Alzoraiki, M., Abro, Z., Ateeq, A., Muda, H. B., Milhem, M., & Naji, G. M. A. (2023). Assessing the impact of green training on sustainable business advantage: Exploring the mediating role of green supply chain practices. *Sustainability, 15*(19), 14144. DOI: 10.3390/su151914144

Barbosa, A. de S., Crispim, M. C., da Silva, L. B., da Silva, J. M. N., Barbosa, A. M., & Morioka, S. N. (2024). How can organizations measure the integration of environmental, social, and governance (ESG) criteria? Validation of an instrument using item response theory to capture workers' perception. *Business Strategy and the Environment, 33*(4). Advance online publication. DOI: 10.1002/bse.3675

Barclay, C. (2008). Towards an integrated measurement of IS project performance: The project performance scorecard. *Information Systems Frontiers, 10*(3), 331–345. DOI: 10.1007/s10796-008-9083-6

Bari, N., Chimhundu, R., & Chan, K.-C. (2022). Dynamic Capabilities to Achieve Corporate Sustainability: A Roadmap to Sustained Competitive Advantage. *Sustainability, 14*(3), 1531. DOI: 10.3390/su14031531

Barni, A., Fontana, A., Menato, S., Sorlini, M., & Canetta, L. (2018). Exploiting the digital twin in the assessment and optimization of sustainability performances. In Harriott, S. (Ed.), *2018 International Conference on Intelligent Systems (IS)*. Funchal - Madeira, Portugal.

Barocas, S., & Selbst, A. D. (2016). Big data's disparate impact. *California Law Review, 104*, 671.

Baryannis, G., Validi, S., Dani, S., & Antoniou, G. (2019). Supply chain risk management and artificial intelligence: state of the art and future research directions. In *International Journal of Production Research* (Vol. 57, Issue 7). https://doi.org/DOI: 10.1080/00207543.2018.1530476

Bausch, P., Weyand, A., Weigold, M., & Metternich, J. (2023). Design model for traceability-supported assessment of product carbon footprint. In Herberger, D., Hübner, M., & Stich, V. (Eds.), *Technische Informationsbibliothek (TIB)*. Publish-Ing.

Ba, Y. (2021). Corporate-Led Environmental Governance: A Theoretical Model. *Administration & Society, 53*(1), 97–122. DOI: 10.1177/0095399720918512

Becker, C., Chitchyan, R., Duboc, L., Easterbrook, S., Penzenstadler, B., Seyff, N., & Venters, C. C. (2021). Requirements: The key to sustainability. *IEEE Software, 38*(1), 56–65. DOI: 10.1109/MS.2020.3025071

Behzadan, A., Dong, S., & Kamat, V. (2015). Augmented reality visualization: A review of civil infrastructure system applications. *Advanced Engineering Informatics, 29*, 252–267.

Belkhir, L., & Elmeligi, A. (2018). Assessing ICT global emissions footprint: Trends to 2040 & recommendations. *Journal of Cleaner Production, 177*, 448–463. DOI: 10.1016/j.jclepro.2017.12.239

Beltrami, M., Orzes, G., Sarkis, J., & Sartor, M. (2021). Industry 4.0 and sustainability: Towards conceptualization and theory. *Journal of Cleaner Production, 312*, 127733.

Benzerogue, S., Abdelatif, S., Khamer, L., Merniz, S., & Harous, S. (2024). Multi-Path Transmission Protocol for Video Streaming Over Vehicular Fog Computing Environments. *IEEE Access : Practical Innovations, Open Solutions, 12*, 87199–87216. DOI: 10.1109/access.2024.3417288

Berander, P., & Andrews, A. (2005). Requirements prioritization. In Aurum, A., & Wohlin, C. (Eds.), *Engineering and Managing Software Requirements*. Springer., DOI: 10.1007/3-540-28244-0_4

Bergs, T., Brecher, C., Schmitt, R., & Schuh, G. (2021). Internet of production – turning data into sustainability. Aachen: apprimus verlag.

Bibi, U., Mazhar, M., Hassan, A., Abdul, W., Ali Ghazanfar, M., Fasih Uddin Butt, M., Sabir, D., & Ali Khan, A. (2024). Advances in Pruning and Quantization for Natural Language Processing. *IEEE Access : Practical Innovations, Open Solutions, 12*, 139113–139128. DOI: 10.1109/access.2024.3465631

Bibri, S. E., Alexandre, A., Sharifi, A., & Krogstie, J. (2023). Environmentally sustainable smart cities and their converging AI, IoT, and big data technologies and solutions: an integrated approach to an extensive literature review. In *Energy Informatics* (Vol. 6, Issue 1). https://doi.org/DOI: 10.1186/s42162-023-00259-2

Bierwolf, R., & Frijns, P. (2021). Governance - Structures and Human Perspectives. *IEEE Engineering Management Review, 49*(2), 172–180. DOI: 10.1109/EMR.2021.3079795

Blessing, L. T. M. (2009). *DRM, a design research methodology. With Assistance of Amaresh Chakrabarti*. Springer.

Bloemhof, J. M., Van Der Vorst, J. G. A. J., Bastl, M., & Allaoui, H. (2015). Sustainability assessment of food chain logistics. *International Journal of Logistics Research and Applications*, *18*(2), 101–117. DOI: 10.1080/13675567.2015.1015508

Bocken, N. M., Mugge, R., Bom, C. A., & Lemstra, H. J. (2018). Pay-per-use business models as a driver for sustainable consumption: Evidence from the case of HOMIE. *Journal of Cleaner Production*, *198*, 498–510.

Bolón-Canedo, V., Morán-Fernández, L., Cancela, B., & Alonso-Betanzos, A. (2024). A review of green artificial intelligence: Towards a more sustainable future. *Neurocomputing*, *599*, 128096.

Bordeleau, F., Combemale, B., Eramo, R., van den Brand, M., & Wimmer, M. (2020). Towards model-driven digital twin engineering: current opportunities and future challenges. In Harriott, S. (Ed.), *Systems Modelling and Management, 1262* (pp. 43–54). Springer International Publishing.

Boz, Z., & Martin-Ryals, A. (2023). The role of digitalization in facilitating circular economy. *Journal of the ASABE*, *66*(2), 479–496.

Bremer, C., Rylander Eklund, A., & Elmquist, M. (2025). Scaling or growing agile? Proposing a manifesto for agile organization development. *Journal of Organization Design*, *14*(1), 23–34. DOI: 10.1007/s41469-024-00179-9

Brenner, B., & Hartl, B. (2021). The perceived relationship between digitalization and ecological, economic, and social sustainability. *Journal of Cleaner Production*, *315*, 128128.

Bressanelli, G., Adrodegari, F., Pigosso, D. C. A., & Parida, V. (2022). Towards the smart circular economy paradigm: A definition, conceptualization, and research agenda. *Sustainability*, *14*, 4960.

Bressanelli, G., Adrodegari, F., Pigosso, D. C., & Parida, V. (2022). Circular economy in the digital age. *Sustainability*, *14*(9), 5565.

Brogi, M., & Lagasio, V. (2025). Do Corporate Governance Frameworks Affect Sustainability Reporting? *Corporate Social Responsibility and Environmental Management*, *32*(3), 3928–3943. DOI: 10.1002/csr.3159

Bushuyev, S., Bushuyeva, N., Bushuiev, D., & Bushuieva, V. (2023, September). Implementing Project Management Principles Aligned with the Circular Economy. In *2023 IEEE 12th International Conference on Intelligent Data Acquisition and Advanced Computing Systems: Technology and Applications (IDAACS)* (Vol. 1, pp. 331-335). IEEE.

Cagno, E., Neri, A., Negri, M., Bassani, C. A., & Lampertico, T. (2021). The role of digital technologies in operationalizing the circular economy transition: A systematic literature review. *Applied Sciences (Basel, Switzerland)*, *11*, 3328.

Cahyani, I. R., & Bahri, M. I. (2022). Change Management and Special Autonomy Paradigm: Opportunities and Challenges of Human Resources in Digital Literacy Implementation in Indonesian Regional Libraries. *Congress of Southeast Asian Librarians (CONSAL) XVIII*.

Cairns, R., Hielscher, S., & Light, A. (2020). Collaboration, creativity, conflict and chaos: Doing interdisciplinary sustainability research. *Sustainability Science*, *15*(6), 1711–1721. DOI: 10.1007/s11625-020-00784-z

Calero, C., & Piattini, M. (2015). *Introduction to green in software engineering*. Springer International Publishing., DOI: 10.1007/978-3-319-08581-9

Camacho, F., & Cruz, C. O. (2022). Toll road sector in Brazil: Regulation by contract and recent innovations. *Competition and Regulation in Network Industries*, *23*(2), 135–152. DOI: 10.1177/17835917221087897

Camarinha-Matos, L. M., Rocha, A. D., & Graça, P. (2022). Collaborative approaches in sustainable and resilient manufacturing. *Journal of Intelligent Manufacturing*, *35*(2), 1–21. PMID: 36532704

Campero-Jurado, I., Márquez-Sánchez, S., Quintanar-Gómez, J., Rodríguez, S., & Corchado, J. M. (2020). Smart Helmet 5.0 for industrial internet of things using artificial intelligence. *Sensors (Basel)*, *20*, 6241. PMID: 33139608

Carlini, N.. (2021). Extracting training data from large language models. *USENIX Security Symposium*.

Carvalho, J., Nascimento, L., Soares, M., Valério, N., Ribeiro, A., Faria, L., & Vilarinho, C. (2022). Life cycle assessment (LCA) of biochar production from a circular economy perspective. *Processes (Basel, Switzerland)*, *10*(12), 2684.

Castellanos-Nieves, D., & García-Forte, L. (2024). Strategies of Automated Machine Learning for Energy Sustainability in Green Artificial Intelligence. *Applied Sciences (Basel, Switzerland)*, *14*(14), 6196. DOI: 10.3390/app14146196

Cegielska, K., Noszczyk, T., Kukulska, A., Szylar, M., Hernik, J., Dixon-Gough, R., Jombach, S., Valánszki, I., & Filepné Kovács, K. (2018). Land use and land cover changes in post-socialist countries: Some observations from Hungary and Poland. *Land Use Policy*, *78*, 1–18.

Çetin, S., De Wolf, C., & Bocken, N. (2021). Circular digital built environment: An emerging framework. *Sustainability*, *13*, 6348.

Chandrasekaran, S., & Pollachi, S. (2023). Greening the digital frontier: A sustainable approach to software solutions. *International Journal of Scientific Research*. Advance online publication. DOI: 10.21275/sr24304114256

Chang, C. R., Li, M. H., & Chang, S. D. (2007). A preliminary study on the local cool-island intensity of Taipei city parks. *Landscape and Urban Planning*, *80*, 386–395.

Charef, R., & Emmitt, S. (2021). Uses of building information modelling for overcoming barriers to a circular economy. *Journal of Cleaner Production*, *285*, 124854.

Chauwin, M., Garcia-Sanchez, F., Friedman, J. S., Paler, A., Moutafis, C., Hu, X., & Betrabet, N. (2019). Skyrmion Logic System for Large-Scale Reversible Computation. *Physical Review Applied*, *12*(6). Advance online publication. DOI: 10.1103/physrevapplied.12.064053

Chen, J., Chen, S., Fu, R., Li, D., Jiang, H., Wang, C., Peng, Y., Jia, K., & Hicks, B. J. (2022). Remote Sensing Big Data for Water Environment Monitoring: Current Status, Challenges, and Future Prospects. In *Earth's Future* (Vol. 10, Issue 2). https://doi.org/DOI: 10.1029/2021EF002289

Chen, S. J., & Hwang, C. L. (1992). Fuzzy multiple attribute decision making methods. In *Fuzzy Multiple Attribute Decision Making* (Lecture Notes in Economics and Mathematical Systems, Vol. 375)*. Springer, Berlin, Heidelberg. https://doi.org/DOI: 10.1007/978-3-642-46768-4_5

Chen, C., Zhao, Z., Xiao, J., & Tiong, R. (2021). A conceptual framework for estimating building embodied carbon based on digital twin technology and life cycle assessment. *Sustainability*, *13*(24), 13875.

Chen, S., Qiu, H., Xiao, H., He, W., Mou, J., & Siponen, M. (2021). Consumption behavior of eco-friendly products and applications of ICT innovation. *Journal of Cleaner Production*, *287*. Advance online publication. DOI: 10.1016/j.jclepro.2020.125436

Chen, T., Kong, L., Gao, X., Chen, G., Wang, Y., & Zhu, Y. (2017). Improving Resource Utilization via Virtual Machine Placement in Data Center Networks. *Mobile Networks and Applications*, *23*(2), 227–238. DOI: 10.1007/s11036-017-0925-7

Chen, X., Despeisse, M., & Johansson, B. (2020). Environmental sustainability of digitalization in manufacturing: A review. *Sustainability*, *12*(24), 10298.

Chen, X., Hu, X., & Huang, Y.. (2025). Deep learning-based software engineering: Progress, challenges, and opportunities. *Science China. Information Sciences*, *68*, 111102. DOI: 10.1007/s11432-023-4127-5

Chen, X., Lin, B., Min, G., Wolter, K., Zhang, J., & Chen, Z. (2022). Energy-Efficient Offloading for DNN-Based Smart IoT Systems in Cloud-Edge Environments. *IEEE Transactions on Parallel and Distributed Systems*, *33*(3), 683–697. DOI: 10.1109/tpds.2021.3100298

Chen, Z., & Huang, L. (2019). Application review of LCA (Life Cycle Assessment) in circular economy: From the perspective of PSS (Product Service System). *Procedia CIRP*, *83*, 210–217.

Chib, S., Mehta, A. K., Selvakumar, P., Saravanan, A., Mishra, B. R., & Manjunath, T. C. (2025). Mental Health Challenges and Solutions in High-Pressure Work Environments. In Harriott, S. (Ed.), *Innovative Approaches to Managing Conflict and Change in Diverse Work Environments* (pp. 247–272). IGI Global Scientific Publishing.

Chilvers, J., Bellamy, R., Pallett, H., & Hargreaves, T. (2021). A systemic approach to mapping participation with low-carbon energy transitions. *Nature Energy*, *6*(3). Advance online publication. DOI: 10.1038/s41560-020-00762-w

Cholewa, M., & Minh, L. H. B. (2021). PLM solutions in the process of supporting the implementation and maintenance of the circular economy concept in manufacturing companies. *Sustainability*, *13*(19), 10589.

Chong, C. T., Van Fan, Y., Lee, C. T., & Klemeš, J. J. (2022). Post COVID-19 ENERGY sustainability and carbon emissions neutrality. *Energy*, *241*, 122801. DOI: 10.1016/j.energy.2021.12280136570560

Choudhary, N. A., Singh, S., Schoenherr, T., & Ramkumar, M. (2023). Risk assessment in supply chains: A state-of-the-art review of methodologies and their applications. *Annals of Operations Research*, *322*(2). Advance online publication. DOI: 10.1007/s10479-022-04700-9 PMID: 35531565

Chua, W. F., James, R., King, A., Lee, E., & Soderstrom, N. (2022). Task Force on Climate-related Financial Disclosures (TCFD) Implementation: An Overview and Insights from the Australian Accounting Standards Board Dialogue Series. *Australian Accounting Review*, *32*(3). Advance online publication. DOI: 10.1111/auar.12388

Cirillo, D., Catuara-Solarz, S., Morey, C., Guney, E., Subirats, L., Mellino, S., Gigante, A., Valencia, A., Rementeria, M. J., & Chadha, A. S.. (2020). Sex and gender differences and biases in artificial intelligence for biomedicine and healthcare. *NPJ Digital Medicine*, *3*, 81. PMID: 32529043

Cleland-Huang, J., Gotel, O., & Zisman, A. (2007). *Software traceability: Trends and future directions*. ICSE.

Coelho, R., Jayantilal, S., & Ferreira, J. J. (2023). The impact of social responsibility on corporate financial performance: A systematic literature review. In *Corporate Social Responsibility and Environmental Management* (Vol. 30, Issue 4). https://doi.org/DOI: 10.1002/csr.2446

Colding, J. (2011). The role of ecosystem services in contemporary urban planning. In Niemelä, J., Breuste, J. H., Guntenspergen, G., McIntyre, N. E., Elmqvist, T., & James, P. (Eds.), *Urban Ecology: Patterns, Processes, and Applications* (pp. 228–237). Oxford University Press.

Combs, G., & Curran, M. (2008). What can green do for you? How to develop and use a corporate sustainability program. *NPRA Environmental Conference Papers*, 243–249.

Condori Fernandez, N., & Lago, P. (2018). The influence of green strategies design onto quality requirements prioritization. In *Lecture Notes in Computer Science Including Subseries Lecture Notes in Artificial Intelligence and Lecture Notes in Bioinformatics* (Vol. 10753). LNCS., DOI: 10.1007/978-3-319-77243-1_12

Condori-Fernandez, N., Luaces, M. R., Places, Á. S., & Lago, P. (2020). An Action Research for Improving the Sustainability Assessment Framework Instruments. *Sustainability*, *12*(4), 1682. DOI: 10.3390/su12041682

Connop, S., Vandergert, P., Eisenberg, B., Collier, M. J., Nash, C., Clough, J., & Newport, D. (2016). Renaturing cities using a regionally-focused biodiversity-led multifunctional benefits approach to urban green infrastructure. *Environmental Science & Policy*, *62*, 99–111.

Contini, G., & Peruzzini, M. (2022). Sustainability and Industry 4.0: Definition of a Set of Key Performance Indicators for Manufacturing Companies. *Sustainability*, *14*(17), 11004. DOI: 10.3390/su141711004

Contini, S., Bellezza, F., Christou, M. D., & Kirchsteiger, C. (2000). The use of geographic information systems in major accident risk assessment and management. *Journal of Hazardous Materials*, *78*(1–3). Advance online publication. DOI: 10.1016/S0304-3894(00)00224-7 PMID: 10978568

Cornago, S., Tan, Y. S., Brondi, C., Ramakrishna, S., & Low, J. S. C. (2022). Systematic literature review on dynamic life cycle inventory: Towards industry 4.0 applications. *Sustainability*, *14*(11), 6464.

Coscieme, L., Mortensen, L. F., & Donohue, I. (2021). Enhance environmental policy coherence to meet the Sustainable Development Goals. *Journal of Cleaner Production*, *296*, 126502. DOI: 10.1016/j.jclepro.2021.126502

Côté-Boileau, É., Denis, J.-L., Breton, M., & Gaboury, I. (2020). Organizational Ethnographic Case Studies: Toward a New Generative In-Depth Qualitative Methodology for Health Care Research? *International Journal of Qualitative Methods*, *19*, 160940692092690. DOI: 10.1177/1609406920926904

Côté, M.-A., Suryn, W., & Georgiadou, E. (2007). In search for a widely applicable and accepted software quality model for software quality engineering. *Software Quality Journal*, *15*(4), 401–416. DOI: 10.1007/s11219-007-9029-0

Coutinho, V., Videira, N., Painho, M., Walker, R. M., Domingues, A. R., Antunes, P., Santos, R., Ramos, T. B., Huisingh, D., & Caeiro, S. (2017). Employee-driven sustainability performance assessment in public organisations. *Corporate Social Responsibility and Environmental Management*, *25*(1), 29–46. DOI: 10.1002/csr.1438

Cruz, L., Fernandes, J. P., Kirkeby, M. H., Martínez-Fernández, S., Sallou, J., Anwar, H., & Yamshchikov, I. P. (2025). Greening ai-enabled systems with software engineering: A research agenda for environmentally sustainable ai practices. *Software Engineering Notes*, *50*(3), 14–23.

Cui, X., Qi, B., & Hussain, M. J. (2024). Vendor sustainability performance and corporate customers' supplier selection. *Corporate Social Responsibility and Environmental Management*, *31*(4), 2910–2928. DOI: 10.1002/csr.2727

Cuong, N. H. (2011a). Enron fiasco: Business difficulty and the role of enron' directors. *Corporate Ownership and Control, 8*(4 B), 165–168. https://doi.org/DOI: 10.22495/cocv8i4c1p2

Cuong, N. H. (2011b). Factors causing Enron's collapse: An investigation into corporate governance and company culture. *Corporate Ownership and Control, 8*(3 G), 585–593.

Dąbrowska, J., Bawiec, A., Pawęska, K., Kamińska, J., & Stodolak, R. (2017). Assessing the impact of wastewater effluent diversion on water quality. *Polish Journal of Environmental Studies*, *26*, 9–16.

Dahiya, R., & Selvakumar, P. Vidyadhara, & Manjunath, T. C. (2025). Design and aerodynamics: Principles and advances. In M. Mellal (Ed.), Innovations and developments in unmanned aerial vehicles (pp. 145-170). IGI Global Scientific Publishing.

Dahiya, R., & Selvakumar, P. Vidyadhara, & Manjunath, T. C. (2025). Design and Aerodynamics: Principles and Advances. In M. Mellal (Ed.), *Innovations and Developments in Unmanned Aerial Vehicles* (pp. 145-170). IGI Global Scientific Publishing.

Dahiya, S., Katakojwala, R., Ramakrishna, S., & Mohan, S. V. (2020). Biobased products and life cycle assessment in the context of circular economy and sustainability. *Materials Circular Economy*, *2*, 1–28.

Damjanović, I., Pavić, I., Puljiz, M., & Brcic, M. (2022). Deep reinforcement learning-based approach for autonomous power flow control using only topology changes. *Energies*, *15*, 6920.

Dandapani, K., & Shahrokhi, M. (2022). Guest editorial: Historical perspectives on corporate governance debate and introduction to the special issue on corporate governance and sustainability. *Managerial Finance*, *48*(8), 1117–1122. DOI: 10.1108/MF-05-2022-0237

Daraojimba, E., Nwasike, C., Gidiagba, J., Ezeigweneme, C., & Adegbite, A. (2024). Comprehensive review of agile methodologies in project management. *Computer Science & IT Research Journal*, *5*(1), 190–218. DOI: 10.51594/csitrj.v5i1.717

Das, S. N., Sreenivasan, G., Srinivasa Rao, S., Joshi, A. K., Varghese, A. O., Prakasa Rao, D. S., Chandrasekar, K., & Jha, C. S. (2022). *Geospatial Technologies for Development of Cadastral Information System and its Applications for Developmental Planning and e-Governance*. https://doi.org/DOI: 10.1007/978-3-030-98981-1_21

Dasallas, L., Jang, S., Jang, S., & Lee, J. (2024). Development and Application of Technical Key Performance Indicators (KPIs) for Smart Water Cities (SWCs) Global Standards and Certification Schemes. *Water (Basel)*, *16*(5), 741. DOI: 10.3390/w16050741

Datapad. (2022). KPIs vs metrics: What's the difference? *Datapad*. https://www.datapad.io/blog/kpis-vs-metrics

De Almeida Barbosa Franco, J., Bezerra, B. S., Battistelle, R. A. G., & Franco, A. Junior. (2024). Dynamic Capabilities: Unveiling Key Resources for Environmental Sustainability and Economic Sustainability, and Corporate Social Responsibility towards Sustainable Development Goals. *Resources*, *13*(2), 22. DOI: 10.3390/resources13020022

De Almeida, P. G. R., Dos Santos, C. D., & Farias, J. S. (2021). Artificial intelligence regulation: A framework for governance. *Ethics and Information Technology*, *23*(3), 505–525.

De Felice, F., & Petrillo, A. (2021). Green transition: The frontier of the digicircular economy evidenced from a systematic literature review. *Sustainability*, *13*, 11068.

de Freitas Alves, G., & Santos, C. D. (2022). The diffusion of innovations under normative induction in Brazil. *RAUSP Management Journal*, *57*(2), 149–164. DOI: 10.1108/RAUSP-10-2020-0250

de Oliveira, S. F., & Soares, A. L. (2017). A PLM vision for circular economy. In *Collaboration in a Data-Rich World: 18th IFIP WG 5.5 Working Conference on Virtual Enterprises, PRO-VE 2017, Vicenza, Italy, September 18-20, 2017* [Springer International Publishing.]. *Proceedings*, *18*, 591–602.

de Souza Barbosa, A., da Silva, M. C. B. C., da Silva, L. B., Morioka, S. N., & de Souza, V. F. (2023). Integration of Environmental, Social, and Governance (ESG) criteria: their impacts on corporate sustainability performance. In *Humanities and Social Sciences Communications* (Vol. 10, Issue 1). https://doi.org/DOI: 10.1057/s41599-023-01919-0

Del Rosario, P., & Traverso, M. (2023). Towards Sustainable Roads: A Systematic Review of Triple-Bottom-Line-Based Assessment Methods. *Sustainability*, *15*(21), 15654. DOI: 10.3390/su152115654

Demestichas, K., & Daskalakis, E. (2020). Information and communication technology solutions for the circular economy. *Sustainability*, *12*(18), 7272.

Dennis, M., Barlow, D., Cavan, G., Cook, P. A., Gilchrist, A., Handley, J., James, P., Thompson, J., Tzoulas, K., & Wheater, C. P.. (2018). Mapping urban green infrastructure: A novel landscape-based approach to incorporating land use and land cover in the mapping of human-dominated systems. *Land (Basel)*, *7*, 17.

Dettmers, E.. (2022). Efficient fine-tuning of language models with parameter-efficient adapters. *Proceedings of the ICML.*

Devlin, J., Chang, M. W., Lee, K., & Toutanova, K. (2019). BERT: Pre-training of deep bidirectional transformers for language understanding. In *Proceedings of NAACL-HLT*.

Díaz, J., Garbajosa, J., Pérez, J., & Almaraz, R. (2018). *DevOps in practice*. ACM., DOI: 10.1145/3234152.3234199

Dicuonzo, G., Donofrio, F., Iannuzzi, A. P., & Dell'Atti, V. (2022). The integration of sustainability in corporate governance systems: An innovative framework applied to the European systematically important banks. *International Journal of Disclosure and Governance, 19*(3). Advance online publication. DOI: 10.1057/s41310-021-00140-2

Dimmelmeier, A. (2024). The financial geography of sustainability data: A mapping exercise of the spatial dimension of the ESG information industry. *Finance and Space, 1*(1), 76–79. DOI: 10.1080/2833115X.2023.2296980

Doshi-Velez, F., & Kim, B. (2017). Towards a rigorous science of interpretable machine learning. *arXiv preprint arXiv:1702.08608.*

Duc, A. N., & Leick, B. (2023). Digital Technologies and Sustainability Paradoxes – An Empirical Study of a Norwegian Media Group. *Lecture Notes in Information Systems and Organisation, 62 LNISO*, 53–62. https://doi.org/DOI: 10.1007/978-3-031-32436-9_5

Dwork, C. (2008). Differential privacy: A survey of results. In *Theory and Applications of Models of Computation* (pp. xx ?"xx). Springer.

Dye, J., McKinnon, M., & Van der Byl, C. (2021). Green Gaps: Firm ESG Disclosure and Financial Institutions' Reporting Requirements. *Journal of Sustainability Research, 3*(1). Advance online publication. DOI: 10.20900/jsr20210006

Edison, H., Wang, X., Jabangwe, R., & Abrahamsson, P. (2018). Innovation Initiatives in Large Software Companies: A Systematic Mapping Study. *Information and Software Technology, 95*, 1–14. DOI: 10.1016/j.infsof.2017.12.007

Efraimidou, E., & Spiliotis, M. (2024). A GIS-Based Flood Risk Assessment Using the Decision-Making Trial and Evaluation Laboratory Approach at a Regional Scale. *Environmental Processes, 11*(1). Advance online publication. DOI: 10.1007/s40710-024-00683-w

El Jery, A., Salman, H. M., Al-Khafaji, R. M., Nassar, M. F., & Sillanpää, M. (2023). Thermodynamics investigation and artificial neural network prediction of energy, exergy, and hydrogen production from a solar thermochemical plant using a polymer membrane electrolyzer. *Molecules (Basel, Switzerland), 28*, 2649. PMID: 36985620

Elia, V., Gnoni, M. G., & Tornese, F. (2017). Measuring circular economy strategies through index methods: A critical analysis. *Journal of Cleaner Production, 142*, 2741–2751.

Eng, L. L., Fikru, M., & Vichitsarawong, T. (2022). Comparing the informativeness of sustainability disclosures versus ESG disclosure ratings. *Sustainability Accounting. Management and Policy Journal*, *13*(2). Advance online publication. DOI: 10.1108/SAMPJ-03-2021-0095

Ertem, M. (2024). Renewable Energy-Aware Machine Scheduling Under Intermittent Energy Supply. *IEEE Access : Practical Innovations, Open Solutions*, *12*, 23613–23625. DOI: 10.1109/access.2024.3365074

Eshetie, G. G., Alemie, B. K., & Wubie, A. M. (2024). Geospatial technologies in support of responsible land tenure governance: A systematic review. *Geomatica*, *76*(2), 100014.

Eskantar, M., Zopounidis, C., Doumpos, M., Galariotis, E., & Guesmi, K. (2024). Navigating ESG complexity: An in-depth analysis of sustainability criteria, frameworks, and impact assessment. *International Review of Financial Analysis*, *95*. Advance online publication. DOI: 10.1016/j.irfa.2024.103380

European Commission. (2020). *The European Green Deal*. https://ec.europa.eu/info/strategy/priorities-2019-2024/european-green-deal_en

European Commission. (2021). *Forging a climate-resilient Europe—The new EU strategy on adaptation to climate change* (COM/2021/82 Final). Brussels, Belgium: Author.

European Commission. (2021). *PM² Project Management Methodology Guide*. https://ec.europa.eu

European Environment Agency. (2012). *Urban adaptation to climate change in Europe: Challenges and opportunities for cities together with supportive national and European policies*. Office for Official Publications of the European Union.

European Environment Agency. (2016). *Urban adaptation to climate change in Europe 2016: Transforming cities in a changing climate*. Publications Office of the European Union.

European Environmental Agency. (2014). *Spatial analysis of green infrastructure in Europe* (EEA Technical Report No. 2). Copenhagen, Denmark: European Environmental Agency.

Ezzeddine, Z., Khalil, A., Zeddini, B., & Ouslimani, H. H. (2024). A Survey on Green Enablers: A Study on the Energy Efficiency of AI-Based 5G Networks. *Sensors (Basel)*, *24*(14), 4609. DOI: 10.3390/s24144609

Fagarasan, C., Cristea, C., Popa, O., Cristea, M., & Pisla, A. (2023). Integrating sustainability metrics into project and portfolio performance assessment in agile software development: A data-driven scoring model. *Sustainability*, *15*(17), 13139. DOI: 10.3390/su151713139

Fajri, L. L., Maarif, S., & Sumarwan, U. (2004). PENDEKATAN BUDAYA KERJA UNTUK MENGURANGI KETIDAKSELARASAN ANTAR DIVISI PADA BATIK BOGOR TRADISIKU. *Jurnal Manajemen Dan Agribisnis*, *13*(3). Advance online publication. DOI: 10.17358/jma.13.3.217

Fang, K., Wang, S., He, J., Song, J., Fang, C., & Jia, X. (2021). Mapping the environmental footprints of nations partnering the Belt and Road Initiative. *Resources, Conservation and Recycling*, *164*. Advance online publication. DOI: 10.1016/j.resconrec.2020.105068

Fang, Y., & Shao, Z. (2022). Whether green finance can effectively moderate the green technology innovation effect of heterogeneous environmental regulation. *International Journal of Environmental Research and Public Health*, *19*(6), 3646. PMID: 35329333

Faruk, M., Rahman, M., & Hasan, S. (2021). How digital marketing evolved over time: A bibliometric analysis on scopus database. In *Heliyon* (Vol. 7, Issue 12). Elsevier Ltd. https://doi.org/DOI: 10.1016/j.heliyon.2021.e08603

Fati, S. M., & Alenezi, M. (2024). Transforming Application Development With Serverless Computing. *International Journal of Cloud Applications and Computing*, *14*(1), 1–16. DOI: 10.4018/ijcac.365288

Fayyazi, M., Sardar, P., Thomas, S. I., Daghigh, R., Jamali, A., Esch, T., Kemper, H., Langari, R., & Khayyam, H. (2023). Artificial intelligence/machine learning in energy management systems, control, and optimization of hydrogen fuel cell vehicles. *Sustainability*, *15*, 5249.

Feng, N. (2022). [Retracted] The Influence Mechanism of BIM on Green Building Engineering Project Management under the Background of Big Data. *Applied Bionics and Biomechanics*, *2022*(1), 8227930. PMID: 36263254

Ferrari, A., Spoletini, P., & Gnesi, S. (2017). Ambiguity and vagueness in natural language requirements engineering. *ACM Transactions on Software Engineering and Methodology*.

Flaherty, T., Domegan, C., & Anand, M. (2021). The use of digital technologies in social marketing: A systematic review. *Journal of Social Marketing*, *11*, 378–405.

Floridi, L., & Chiriatti, M. (2020). GPT-3: Its nature, scope, limits, and consequences. *Minds and Machines*, *30*, 681 ?"694. DOI: 10.1007/s11023-020-09548-1

Fontana, A., Barni, A., Leone, D., Spirito, M., Tringale, A., Ferraris, M., & Goncalves, G. (2021). Circular economy strategies for equipment lifetime extension: A systematic review. *Sustainability*, *13*(3), 1117.

Forman, R. T. (1995). *Land mosaics: The ecology of landscapes and regions*. Cambridge University Press.

Franco, S., Pancino, B., & Martella, A. (2021). Mapping national environmental sustainability distribution by ecological footprint: The case of Italy. *Sustainability (Switzerland)*, *13*(15). Advance online publication. DOI: 10.3390/su13158671

Freed, M., Bielinska, S., Buckley, C., Coptu, A., Yilmaz, M., Messnarz, R., & Clarke, P. M. (2023, August). An investigation of green software engineering. In *European conference on software process improvement* (pp. 124-137). Cham: Springer Nature Switzerland.

Freed, M., Bielinska, S., Buckley, C., Coptu, A., Yilmaz, M., Messnarz, R., & Clarke, P. M. (2023, August). An investigation of green software engineering. In *European Conference on Software Process Improvement* (pp. 124–137). Springer. https://doi.org/DOI: 10.1007/978-3-031-42307-9_10

Fricker, S. A., Glinz, M., & Klaus, P. (2010). *Requirements engineering: Best practices*. Springer.

Galaz, V., Centeno, M. A., Callahan, P. W., Causevic, A., Patterson, T., Brass, I., Baum, S., Farber, D., Fischer, J., & Garcia, D.. (2021). Artificial intelligence, systemic risks, and sustainability. *Technology in Society*, *67*, 101741.

Gangai, K. N., Joshi, D., Murali, M., & Verma, A., TK, B., & Dash, S. R. (2024, November). Strategic Approach for Integrating Legal Compliance into Engineering Project Management. In *2024 International Conference on Intelligent & Innovative Practices in Engineering & Management (IIPEM)* (pp. 1-6). IEEE.

Gao, J. Q., Li, S. R., Li, D., Gao, H. L., Qiao, G. H., & Jia, Q. R. (2024). Circular economy strategies in supply chains, enhancing resource efficiency and sustainable development goals. *Environmental Science and Pollution Research International*, *31*(6), 8751–8767. DOI: 10.1007/s11356-023-31551-z

Gatzioura, A., Sànchez-Marrè, M., & Gibert, K. (2019). A hybrid recommender system to improve circular economy in industrial symbiotic networks. *Energies*, *12*, 3546.

Georgiou, K., Kerrison, S., Chamski, Z., & Eder, K. (2017). Energy Transparency for Deeply Embedded Programs. *ACM Transactions on Architecture and Code Optimization, 14*(1), 1–26. DOI: 10.1145/3046679

Ghodke, P. K., Reddy, P. S., Akiti, N., & Kilari, H. (2023). Artificial intelligence in the digital chemical industry, its application and sustainability. In *Recent Trends and Best Practices in Industry 4.0* (pp. 1–29). River Publishers.

Goldberg, D. E., & Holland, J. H. (1988). Genetic algorithms and machine learning. *Machine Learning, 3*, 95–99.

Gopal, S., & Pitts, J. (2024a). *Geospatial Finance: Foundations and Applications*. 225–273. https://doi.org/DOI: 10.1007/978-3-031-74418-1_6

Gopal, S., & Pitts, J. (2024b). *Satellite Remote Sensing: Pioneering Tools for Environmental Insight and Sustainable Investment*. 275–315. https://doi.org/DOI: 10.1007/978-3-031-74418-1_7

Górski, T. (2021). Towards Continuous Deployment for Blockchain. *Applied Sciences (Basel, Switzerland), 11*(24), 11745. DOI: 10.3390/app112411745

Grafström, J., & Aasma, S. (2021). Breaking circular economy barriers. *Journal of Cleaner Production, 292*, 126002.

Griggs, D., Stafford-Smith, M., Gaffney, O., Rockström, J., Öhman, M. C., Shyamsundar, P., Steffen, W., Glaser, G., Kanie, N., & Noble, I. (2013). Policy: Sustainable development goals for people and planet. *Nature, 495*, 305. PMID: 23518546

Groß, J., & Ouhbi, S. (2024). Clearing the path for software sustainability. *arXiv*. https://doi.org//arxiv.2405.15637DOI: 10.48550

Grzywna, H., Dąbek, P. B., & Olszewska, B. (2018). Analysis of moisture conditions in the lowland areas using high-resolution spectral data from the Sentinel-2 satellite and GIS tools. *E3S Web of Conferences, 44*, 00048.

Gu, B., Chen, F., & Zhang, K. (2021). The policy effect of green finance in promoting industrial transformation and upgrading efficiency in China: Analysis from the perspective of government regulation and public environmental demands. *Environmental Science and Pollution Research International, 28*(34), 47474–47491. PMID: 33895949

Gunning, D. (2017). *Explainable artificial intelligence*. XAI. [DARPA Program Briefing]

Guo, C., Ci, S., Yang, Y., & Zhou, Y. (2021). A Survey of Energy Consumption Measurement in Embedded Systems. *IEEE Access : Practical Innovations, Open Solutions*, *9*, 60516–60530. DOI: 10.1109/access.2021.3074070

Guo, J., Li, J., Sun, Y., & Wang, H. (2022). Deep learning for software traceability: A survey. *Journal of Systems and Software*.

Guo, Y., Ganti, S., & Wu, Y. (2024). Enhancing Energy Efficiency in Telehealth Internet of Things Systems Through Fog and Cloud Computing Integration: Simulation Study. *JMIR Biomedical Engineering*, *9*(2), e50175. DOI: 10.2196/50175

Gupta, S., & Gupta, A. (2024, June). Optimising the Carbon Footprint for Cloud Resources in a Cloud Environment. In *2024 IEEE 21st International Conference on Software Architecture Companion (ICSA-C)* (pp. 215-221). IEEE.

Gu, Y., Dai, J., & Vasarhelyi, M. A. (2023). Audit 4.0-based ESG assurance: An example of using satellite images on GHG emissions. *International Journal of Accounting Information Systems*, *50*, 100625. DOI: 10.1016/J.ACCINF.2023.100625

Guzzo, D., Trevisan, A. H., Echeveste, M., & Costa, J. M. H. (2019). Circular innovation framework: Verifying conceptual to practical decisions in sustainability-oriented product–service system cases. *Sustainability*, *11*, 3248.

Hainsch, K., Löffler, K., Burandt, T., Auer, H., Del Granado, P. C., Pisciella, P., & Zwickl-Bernhard, S. (2022). Energy transition scenarios: What policies, societal attitudes, and technology developments will realize the EU Green Deal? *Energy*, *239*, 122067.

Halstenberg, F. A., Lindow, K., & Stark, R. (2019). Leveraging circular economy through a methodology for smart service systems engineering. *Sustainability*, *11*(13), 3517.

Han, S., Jeong, Y., In, J., & Lee, K. (2024). Environmental sustainability in health care: An empirical investigation of US hospitals. *Business Strategy and the Environment*, *33*(6), 6045–6065. DOI: 10.1002/bse.3790

Hans, A., & Khera, N. (2021). Extracting Insights from Reviews using Cluster Analysis. *CEUR Workshop Proceedings*, •••, 3080.

Hansen, R., & Pauleit, S. (2014). From multifunctionality to multiple ecosystem services? A conceptual framework for multifunctionality in green infrastructure planning for urban areas. *Ambio*, *43*, 516–529. PMID: 24740622

Han, Y., Shevchenko, T., Yannou, B., Ranjbari, M., Shams Esfandabadi, Z., Saidani, M., & Li, G. (2023). Exploring how digital technologies enable a circular economy of products. *Sustainability*, *15*(3), 2067.

Hao, C., & Yue, Y. (2016). Optimization on combination of transport routes and modes on dynamic programming for a container multimodal transport system. *Procedia Engineering*, *137*, 382–390.

Hardwig, T., Klötzer, S., & Boos, M. (2020). Software-supported collaboration in small- and medium-sized enterprises. *Measuring Business Excellence*, *24*(1), 1–23. DOI: 10.1108/MBE-11-2018-0098

Hariyani, D., Hariyani, P., Mishra, S., & Sharma, M. K. (2024). *Leveraging digital technologies for advancing circular economy practices and enhancing life cycle analysis: A systematic literature review*. Waste Management Bulletin.

Harmain, H., & Gaizauskas, R. (2003). CM-Builder: A natural language-based CASE tool for object-oriented analysis. *Automated Software Engineering*, *10*, 157 ?"181.

Hart, N., Kramer, H., & Duncan, A. (2024). Lawrence Berkeley National Laboratory LBL Publications Title Building Performance Software: Portfolio-Level Capabilities and Applications Permalink https://escholarship.org/uc/item/58p6m0k7 *Publication Date*. https://doi.org/DOI: 10.20357/B78P57

Hermawan, A. N., Masudin, I., Zulfikarijah, F., Restuputri, D. P., & Shariff, S. S. R. (2024). The effect of sustainable manufacturing on environmental performance through government regulation and eco-innovation. *International Journal of Industrial Engineering and Operations Management*, *6*(4), 299–325.

Hernández-barco, M., Sánchez-martín, J., Corbacho-cuello, I., & Cañada-cañada, F. (2021). Emotional performance of a low-cost eco-friendly project based learning methodology for science education: An approach in prospective teachers. *Sustainability (Switzerland)*, *13*(6). Advance online publication. DOI: 10.3390/su13063385

Hidalgo, E. S. (2019). Adapting the Scrum framework for agile project management in science: Case study of a distributed research initiative. *Heliyon*, *5*(3), e01447. DOI: 10.1016/j.heliyon.2019.e01447

Hilty, L. M., & Aebischer, B. (2015). *ICT innovations for sustainability*. Springer., DOI: 10.1007/978-3-319-09228-2

Hintemann, R., & Hinterholzer, S. (2020). *Energy consumption of data centers worldwide*. Borderstep Institute. https://www.borderstep.org/publications

Hirve, S. A., Kunjir, A., Shaikh, B., & Shah, K. (2017). An approach towards data visualization based on AR principles. In *Proceedings of the International Conference on Big Data Analytics and Computational Intelligence (ICBDAC)* (pp. 128–133). Chirala, India.

Horsthofer-Rauch, J., Guesken, S. R., Weich, J., Rauch, A., Bittner, M., Schulz, J., & Zaeh, M. F. (2024). Sustainability-integrated value stream mapping with process mining. *Production & Manufacturing Research, 12*(1). Advance online publication. DOI: 10.1080/21693277.2024.2334294

Houf, L., Shepherd, L. A., & Szymkowiak, A. (2024). Promotion of Sustainable Products: Can Sustainability Labels Promote User Selection of Environmentally Friendly Products? *Sustainability, 16*(13), 5390. DOI: 10.3390/su16135390

Hou, L., Wu, C., Zhang, Y., & Song, J. (2023). Improving the greenness of enterprise supply chains by designing government subsidy mechanisms: Based on prospect theory and evolutionary games. *Frontiers in Psychology, 14*. Advance online publication. DOI: 10.3389/fpsyg.2023.1283794

Hsu, A., & Schletz, M. (2024). Digital technologies–the missing link between climate action transparency and accountability? *Climate Policy, 24*(2), 193–210.

Hu, X., & Sinniah, S. (2024). The Role of Green Risk Management Approaches in Promoting Green and Sustainable Supply Chain Management. *Natural and Engineering Sciences, 9*(2), 33–54. DOI: 10.28978/nesciences.1569144

Huygh, T., de Haes, S., Joshi, A., & van Grembergen, W. (2018). Answering key global IT management concerns through IT governance and management processes: A Cobit 5 view. *Proceedings of the Annual Hawaii International Conference on System Sciences, 2018-Janua*, 5335–5344.

Ignaim, K., & Fernandes, J. M. (2025). A Feature-based Process for Effective Stakeholder Management in Software Product Development. *IAENG International Journal of Computer Science, 52*(1), 171–186.

Ingemarsdotter, E., Jamsin, E., Kortuem, G., & Balkenende, R. (2019). Circular strategies enabled by the Internet of Things—A framework and analysis of current practice. *Sustainability, 11*, 5689.

Irani, F., Kiliç, H., & Adeshola, I. (2022). Impact of green human resource management practices on the environmental performance of green hotels. *Journal of Hospitality Marketing & Management, 31*(5), 570–600.

Issa, M., Ilinca, A., & Martini, F. (2022). Ship energy efficiency and maritime sector initiatives to reduce carbon emissions. *Energies, 15*(21), 7910. DOI: 10.3390/en15217910

Iyer, K., & K.R, J. (2020). Buying behaviour model of early adopting organizations of radical software innovations. *Journal of Business and Industrial Marketing, 36*(6). Advance online publication. DOI: 10.1108/JBIM-12-2019-0533

İzmirli, D., Ekren, B. Y., Kumar, V., & Pongsakornrungsilp, S. (2021). Omni-channel network design towards circular economy under inventory share policies. *Sustainability, 13*, 2875.

Jabbour, C., Jabbour, A., Sarkis, J., & Filho, M. (2019). Unlocking the circular economy through new business models based on large-scale data: An integrative framework and research agenda. *Technological Forecasting and Social Change, 144*, 546–552.

Jackson, I., Jesus Saenz, M., & Ivanov, D. (2023). From natural language to simulations: Applying AI to automate simulation modelling of logistics systems. *International Journal of Production Research, 62*(4), 1434 ?"1457. DOI: 10.1080/00207543.2023.2276811

Jacob, J. (2024). A background history of the sustainable development goals. *Sustainable Development*. Advance online publication. DOI: 10.1002/sd.3317

Jahan, I., Zhang, G., Bhuiyan, M., & Navaratnam, S. (2022). Circular economy of construction and demolition wood waste—A theoretical framework approach. *Sustainability, 14*(17), 10478.

Jahi , J., & Sami, A. (2024). State of practice: LLMs in software engineering and software architecture. In *2024 IEEE 21st International Conference on Software Architecture Companion (ICSA-C)* (pp. 311-318). IEEE. https://doi.org/DOI: 10.1109/ICSA-C63560.2024.00059

Jain, V., Balakrishnan, A., Beeram, D., Najana, M., & Chintale, P. (2024). Leveraging Artificial Intelligence for Enhancing Regulatory Compliance in the Financial Sector. *International Journal of Computer Trends and Technology, 72*(5), 124–140. DOI: 10.14445/22312803/ijctt-v72i5p116

Jakubczak, W., Golebiowska, A., Prokopowicz, D., & Jakubczak, R. (2021). The Key Security Problems Related to the Pro-Environmental Economic Transformation and the Implementation of the Principles of Sustainable Development into the Economy. *EUROPEAN RESEARCH STUDIES JOURNAL, XXIV*(4B). Advance online publication. DOI: 10.35808/ersj/2654

Jalali, S., & Wohlin, C. (2011). Global software engineering and agile practices: A systematic review. *Journal of Software (Malden, MA)*, *24*(6), 643–659. DOI: 10.1002/smr.561

Jannah, N., Bahri, M. I., Kismawadi, E. R., & Handriana, T. (2024). The Effect of Green Brand Image and Green Satisfaction on Green Brand Equity Mediated Green Trust Outpatient's. *Quality - Access to Success*, *25*(198). Advance online publication. DOI: 10.47750/QAS/25.198.40

Jaramillo, M., Pavón, W., & Jaramillo, L. (2024). Adaptive Forecasting in Energy Consumption: A Bibliometric Analysis and Review. *Data*, *9*(1), 13. DOI: 10.3390/data9010013

Jatsch, A. S., Jacobs, S., Wommer, K., & Wanieck, K. (2023). Biomimetics for Sustainable Developments—A Literature Overview of Trends. *Biomimetics*, *8*(3). Advance online publication. DOI: 10.3390/biomimetics8030304 PMID: 37504192

Jeong, S.-J., & Choi, D.-B. (2022). ESG and Managerial Agency Problems. *Korean Journal of Financial Studies*, *51*(4), 417–445. DOI: 10.26845/KJFS.2022.08.51.4.417

Jia, B. Q., & Qiu, K. B. (2017). The cooling effect of plain afforestation in the Beijing project and its remote sensing-based valuation. *Acta Ecologica Sinica*, *37*, 726–735.

Jianguo, D., & Solangi, Y. A. (2023). Sustainability in Pakistan's textile industry: Analyzing barriers and strategies for green supply chain management implementation. *Environmental Science and Pollution Research International*, *30*(20), 58109–58127. DOI: 10.1007/s11356-023-26687-x

Ji, Z., Lee, N., Frieske, R., Yu, T., Su, D., Xu, Y., Ishii, E., Bang, Y. J., Madotto, A., & Fung, P. (2023). Survey of hallucination in natural language generation. *ACM Computing Surveys*, *55*(12), 1 ?"38. DOI: 10.1145/357173

Jobin, A., Ienca, M., & Vayena, E. (2019). The global landscape of AI ethics guidelines. *Nature Machine Intelligence*, *1*, 389–399.

Johri, S., Jeong, J., & Tran, B. A. (2025). An evaluation framework for clinical use of large language models in patient interaction tasks. *Nature Medicine*, *31*, 77 ?"86. DOI: 10.1038/s41591-024-03328-5 PMID: 39747685

Jones, N. (2018). How to stop data centres from gobbling up the world's electricity. *Nature*, *561*(7722), 163–166. DOI: 10.1038/d41586-018-06610-y

Jun, H., & Xiang, H. (2011). Development of circular economy is a fundamental way to achieve agricultural sustainable development in China. *Energy Procedia*, *5*, 1530–1534.

Kamińska, J. A. (2018). Residuals in the modelling of pollution concentration depending on meteorological conditions and traffic flow, employing decision trees. *XLVIII Seminarium Applied Mathematics*, 00016.

Kang, J. R., Liu, Z. B., & Yang, R. B. (2010). Fuzzy comprehensive evaluation of ecological suitability of land based on GIS. *Systems Engineering*, *9*, X826.

Kannan, P. (2019). *Bibliometric Analysis of Library Philosophy and Practice: A study based on Scopus Database*. https://digitalcommons.unl.edu/libphilprac

Kansal, A., & Zhao, F. (2008). Fine-grained energy profiling for power-aware application design. *Performance Evaluation Review*, *36*(2), 26–31. DOI: 10.1145/1453175.1453180

Karita, L., Mourão, B. C., & MacHado, I. (2022). Towards a common understanding of sustainable software development. *ACM International Conference Proceeding Series*, 269–278. https://doi.org/DOI: 10.1145/3555228.3555236

Karlsson, J., Wohlin, C., & Regnell, B. (1998). An evaluation of methods for prioritizing software requirements. *Information and Software Technology*, *39*(14 ?"15), 939 ?"947.

Kashyap, S., & Kumar, P. (2024). Benefits and relevance of agile principle and sustainable practise to modern organisation. In *Advances in Logistics* (pp. 403–422). Operations, and Management Science Book Series., DOI: 10.4018/979-8-3693-6274-7.ch021

Katal, A., Dahiya, S., & Choudhury, T. (2023). Energy efficiency in cloud computing data centers: A survey on software technologies. *Cluster Computing*, *26*(3), 1845–1875. PMID: 36060618

Kaur, M., Selvakumar, P., & Dinesh, N. Mohit, Chandel, P. S., & Manjunath, T. C. (2025). Reconstruction and preservation strategies for cultural heritage. In S. Oflazoğlu & M. Dora (Eds.), Preserving cultural heritage in post-disaster urban renewal (pp. 385-412). IGI Global Scientific Publishing.

Kaur, M., Selvakumar, P., & Dinesh, N. Mohit, Chandel, P. S., & Manjunath, T. C. (2025). Reconstruction and Preservation Strategies for Cultural Heritage. In S. Oflazoğlu & M. Dora (Eds.), *Preserving Cultural Heritage in Post-Disaster Urban Renewal* (pp. 385-412). IGI Global Scientific Publishing.

Kaur, R., & Gupta, K. (2022). Blue-green infrastructure (BGI) network in urban areas for sustainable storm water management: A geospatial approach. *City and Environment Interactions*, *16*, 100087.

Kelleci, A. (2021). Four-Stage Model of Value Creation for Sustainability-Oriented Marketing: En Route to Participatory Marketing. *Journal of Macromarketing*, *42*(1), 5–11. DOI: 10.1177/02761467211049668

Kempe, E., & Massey, A. (2021, September). Perspectives on regulatory compliance in software engineering. In *2021 IEEE 29th International Requirements Engineering Conference (RE)* (pp. 46-57). IEEE.

Kent, A. J., & Specht, D. (2023). The Routledge Handbook of Geospatial Technologies and Society. In *The Routledge Handbook of Geospatial Technologies and Society*. https://doi.org/DOI: 10.4324/9780367855765

Kerr, J. T., & Ostrovsky, M. (2003). From space to species: Ecological applications for remote sensing. *Trends in Ecology & Evolution*, *18*, 299–305.

Khamis, A., Li, H., Prestes, E., & Haidegger, T. (2019). AI: A key enabler of sustainable development goals, part 1. *IEEE Robotics & Automation Magazine*, *26*, 95–102.

Khan, A. R. (2024). Dynamic Load Balancing in Cloud Computing: Optimized RL-Based Clustering with Multi-Objective Optimized Task Scheduling. *Processes (Basel, Switzerland)*, *12*(3), 519. DOI: 10.3390/pr12030519

Khan, M. H., & Muktar, S. N. (2020). A bibliometric analysis of green human resource management based on scopus platform. *Cogent Business & Management*, *7*(1). Advance online publication. DOI: 10.1080/23311975.2020.1831165

Khan, W. A., & Hussain, A. (2014). Automatic object-oriented coding facility for product life cycle management of discrete products. *International Journal of Computer Integrated Manufacturing*, *27*(1), 60–84.

Khayashi, F., Jamasb, B., Akbari, R., & Shamsinejadbabaki, P. (2022). Deep learning methods for software requirement classification: A performance study on the PURE dataset. [Space Frontiers]. *Information and Software Technology*, *147*, 106877. Advance online publication. DOI: 10.1016/j.infsof.2022.106877

Kiełkowska, J., Tokarczyk-Dorociak, K., Kazak, J., Szewrański, S., & van Hoof, J. (2018). Urban adaptation to climate change plans and policies – The conceptual framework of a methodological approach. *Journal of Ecological Engineering*, *19*, 50–62.

Kifor, C. V., & Grigore, N. A. (2023). Circular economy approaches for electrical and conventional vehicles. *Sustainability*, *15*(7), 6140.

Killen, C. P., Geraldi, J., & Kock, A. (2020). The role of decision makers' use of visualizations in project portfolio decision making. *International Journal of Project Management, 38*, 267–277.

Kim, S., Laschi, C., & Trimmer, B. (2013). Soft robotics: A bioinspired evolution in robotics. *Trends in Biotechnology, 31*(5), 287–294. PMID: 23582470

Kim, Y., Yuk, H., Zhao, R., Chester, S. A., & Zhao, X. (2018). Printing ferromagnetic domains for untethered fast-transforming soft materials. *Nature, 558*(7709), 274–279. PMID: 29899476

Kintscher, L., Lawrenz, S., & Poschmann, H. (2021). A life cycle-oriented data-driven architecture for an advanced circular economy. *Procedia CIRP, 98*, 318–323.

Kismawadi, E. R., & Irfan, M. (2025). Artificial Intelligence as a Catalyst for Innovation in Islamic Entrepreneurship: Balancing Ethics and Efficiency. In *Improving Entrepreneurial Processes Through Advanced AI* (pp. 1–16). IGI Global.

Klapa, P., Mitka, B., & Zygmunt, M. (2017). Application of integrated photogrammetric and terrestrial laser scanning data to cultural heritage surveying. *IOP Conference Series. Earth and Environmental Science, 95*, 032007.

Ko >ci "ski, V., Gambardella, C., Gerstner, E., Zappavigna, M., Cassetti, J., & Mirakhorli, M. (2021). A natural language processing technique for formalization of systems requirement specifications. In *2021 IEEE 29th International Requirements Engineering Conference Workshops (REW)* (pp. 350-356). IEEE. https://doi.org/ DOI: 10.1109/REW53955.2021.00062

Kokkhangplu, A., Onlamai, W., Chokpreedapanich, T., & Phikul, K. (2023). What Predicts Behavioral Intention in Eco-Friendly Hotels? The Roles of Tourist's Perceived Value and Satisfaction: A Case Study of Thailand. *Sustainability (Switzerland), 15*(4). Advance online publication. DOI: 10.3390/su15043219

Kolevski, D., & Michael, K. (2024). Edge computing and iot data breaches: Security, privacy, trust, and regulation. *IEEE Technology and Society Magazine, 43*(1), 22–32.

Kolodner, J. (2014). *Case-based reasoning*. Morgan Kaufmann.

Kommineni, M., Chundru, S., Maroju, P. K., & Selvakumar, P. (2025). Ethical implications of AI in sustainable development pedagogy. In Chinedu, C., Mafarja, N., Hussein, M., & Saleem, A. (Eds.), *Rethinking the pedagogy of sustainable development in the AI era* (pp. 17–36). IGI Global Scientific Publishing.

Kommineni, M., Chundru, S., Maroju, P. K., & Selvakumar, P. (2025). Ethical Implications of AI in Sustainable Development Pedagogy. In Chinedu, C., Mafarja, N., Hussein, M., & Saleem, A. (Eds.), *Rethinking the Pedagogy of Sustainable Development in the AI Era* (pp. 17–36). IGI Global Scientific Publishing.

Koo, L., Trokanas, N., & Cecelja, F. (2017). A semantic framework for enabling model integration for biorefining. *Computers & Chemical Engineering*, *100*, 219–231.

Koshy, L., & Shyry, S. P. (2025). Detection of tampered real time videos using deep neural networks. *Neural Computing & Applications*, *37*(11), 7691–7703. DOI: 10.1007/s00521-024-09988-1

Kotte, K. R., Thammareddi, L., Kodi, D., Anumolu, V. R., Kumar, A., & Joshi, S. (2025, February). Integration of Process Optimization and Automation: A Way to AI Powered Digital Transformation. In *2025 First International Conference on Advances in Computer Science, Electrical, Electronics, and Communication Technologies (CE2CT)* (pp. 1133-1138). IEEE.

Krajewski, P., Solecka, I., & Mastalska-Cetera, B. (2017). Landscape change index as a tool for spatial analysis. *IOP Conference Series. Materials Science and Engineering*, *245*, 072014.

Kranz, J. J., Hanelt, A., & Kolbe, L. M. (2016). Understanding the influence of absorptive capacity and ambidexterity on the process of business model change – the case of on-premise and cloud-computing software. *Information Systems Journal*, *26*(5), 477–517. DOI: 10.1111/isj.12102

Kravchenko, T., Bogdanova, T., & Shevgunov, T. (2022). Ranking requirements using MoSCoW methodology in practice. In Silhavy, R. (Ed.), *Cybernetics Perspectives in Systems. CSOC 2022. Lecture Notes in Networks and Systems, 503*. Springer., DOI: 10.1007/978-3-031-09073-8_18

Kristia, K., & Rabbi, M. F. (2023). Exploring the synergy of renewable energy in the circular economy framework: A bibliometric study. *Sustainability*, *15*(17), 13165.

Kristoffersen, E., Blomsma, F., Mikalef, P., & Li, J. (2020). The smart circular economy: A digital-enabled circular strategies framework for manufacturing companies. *Journal of Business Research*, *120*, 241–261.

Kumar, A., Tyagi, P. K., Tyagi, S., & Ghorbanpour, M. (2024). Integrating green nanotechnology with sustainable development goals: A pathway to sustainable innovation. *Discover Sustainability*, *5*(1). Advance online publication. DOI: 10.1007/s43621-024-00610-x

Kumar, N. M., Chand, A. A., Islam, F. R., Prasad, K. A., Malvoni, M., Mamun, K. A., & Chopra, S. S. (2020). Distributed Energy Resources and the Application of AI, IoT, and Blockchain in Smart Grids. *Energies*, *13*(21), 5739. DOI: 10.3390/en13215739

Kuru, K., & Khan, W. (2020). A Framework for the Synergistic Integration of Fully Autonomous Ground Vehicles With Smart City. *IEEE Access : Practical Innovations, Open Solutions*, *9*, 923–948. DOI: 10.1109/access.2020.3046999

Kusumastuti, A. (2017). *MULTI STAKEHOLDER INITIATIVE PRACTICES: PROMOTION OF GOOD GOVERNANCE (A CASE OF COMMUNITY EMPOWERMENT PROJECT IN PESANGGARAHAN VILLAGE, BATU DISTRICT, CITY OF BATU, EAST JAVA, INDONESIA).*

Kusumastuti, F., Kurnia, N., Astuti, S. I., Birowo, M. A., Hartanti, L. E. P., Amanda, N. M. R., & Kurnia, N. (2021). Modul Etis Bermedia Digital. In *Modul Etis Bermedia Digital.*

Kutaula, S., Chowdhury, S., Dey, P. K., Gillani, A., & Budhwar, P. S. (2024). Linking HRM with Sustainability Performance Through Sustainability Practices: Unlocking the Black Box. *British Journal of Management*, *36*(2), 615–632. DOI: 10.1111/1467-8551.12861

Kutscher, V., Ruland, S., Müller, P., Wasser, N., Lochau, M., Anderl, R., & Hähnle, R. (2020). Towards a circular economy of industrial software. *Procedia CIRP*, *90*, 37–42.

Lago, P., Funke, M., & Fatima, I. (2024). Architecting for Sustainability with the SAF Toolkit. *Proceedings IEEE 21st International Conference on Software Architecture Companion Icsa C 2024*, 379–380. https://doi.org/DOI: 10.1109/ICSA-C63560.2024.00070

Lago, P., Kazman, R., Meyer, N., Morisio, M., Müller, H. A., & Paulisch, F. (2013). Exploring initial challenges for green software engineering: Summary of the first GREENS workshop, at ICSE 2012. *Software Engineering Notes*, *38*(1), 31–33. DOI: 10.1145/2413038.2413062

Lang, C., Michos, O., & Conrad, L. (2018). Mathematical Approaches of Branching Morphogenesis. *Frontiers in Genetics*, *9*(e41643). Advance online publication. DOI: 10.3389/fgene.2018.00673

Larsen, E. R. (2017). The importance of excellent definition of project objectives. *Liaison Functions 2017 Core Programming Area at the 2017 Aiche Annual Meeting, 2017-Octob*, 235–248.

Larsen, E. R. (2018). The importance of excellent definition of project objectives. *Management Division 2018 Core Programming Area at the 2018 Aiche Annual Meeting*, 82–95.

Larsen, V. G., Tollin, N., Sattrup, P. A., Birkved, M., & Holmboe, T. (2022). What are the challenges in assessing circular economy for the built environment? A literature review on integrating LCA, LCC and S-LCA in life cycle sustainability assessment, LCSA. *Journal of Building Engineering*, *50*, 104203.

Laschi, C., Cianchetti, M., Mazzolai, B., Margheri, L., Follador, M., & Dario, P. (2012). Soft robot arm inspired by the octopus. *Advanced Robotics*, *26*(7), 709–727.

Latifah, F. N., & Widiatmoko, J. (2022). PENGARUH STRUKTUR KEPEMILIKAN TERHADAP CORPORATE SOCIAL RESPONSIBILITY DAN DAMPAKNYA PADA NILAI PERUSAHAAN. In *Jurnal Ilmiah Mahasiswa Akuntansi) Universitas Pendidikan Ganesha* (Vol. 13, Issue 03). www.wbcsd.org

Lawrenz, S., Leiding, B., Mathiszig, M. E. A., Rausch, A., Schindler, M., & Sharma, P. (2021). Implementing the circular economy by tracing the sustainable impact. *International Journal of Environmental Research and Public Health*, *18*(21), 11316.

Lee, A. C. K., & Maheswaran, R. (2011). The health benefits of urban green spaces: A review of the evidence. *Journal of Public Health*, *33*, 212–222. PMID: 20833671

Lee, J. K. Y., Gholami, H., Saman, M. Z. M., Ngadiman, N. H. A. B., Zakuan, N., Mahmood, S., & Omain, S. Z. (2021). Sustainability-oriented application of value stream mapping: A review and classification. *IEEE Access : Practical Innovations, Open Solutions*, *9*, 68414–68434.

Lee, S., & Lee, D. (2018). Improved prediction of harmful algal blooms in four major South Korea rivers using deep learning models. *International Journal of Environmental Research and Public Health*, *15*, 1322. PMID: 29937531

Lehmann, S. (2014). Low carbon districts: Mitigating the urban heat island with green roof infrastructure. *City, Culture and Society*, *5*, 1–8.

Lejcuś, K., Dąbrowska, J., Garlikowski, D., & Śpitalniak, M. (2015). The application of water-absorbing geocomposites to support plant growth on slopes. *Geosynthetics International*, *22*, 452–456.

Leong, J., May Yee, K., Baitsegi, O., Palanisamy, L., & Ramasamy, R. K. (2023). Hybrid project management between traditional software development lifecycle and agile based product development for future sustainability. *Sustainability*, *15*(2), 1121.

Lewandowski, S., Ullrich, A., & Gronau, N. (2021). Normen zur Berechnung des CO_2-Fußabdrucks (pp. 17–20).

Li, L., ... (2021). Membership inference attacks against language models. *arXiv preprint arXiv:2102.06514*.

Liang, X., Liu, M., & Huang, Y. (2023). Studying financial development with low-carbon architecture development and green technological innovation: Sustaining SDG-9. *Environmental Science and Pollution Research International, 31*(2), 2009–2025. DOI: 10.1007/s11356-023-31155-7

Liao, J., Liu, X., Zhou, X., & Tursunova, N. R. (2023). Analyzing the role of renewable energy transition and industrialization on ecological sustainability: Can green innovation matter in OECD countries? *Renewable Energy, 204*, 141–151.

Liaskos, C., Tsioliaridou, A., & Ioannidis, S. (2019, May). Organizing network management logic with circular economy principles. In *2019 15th International Conference on Distributed Computing in Sensor Systems (DCOSS)* (pp. 451-456).

Liberati, A., Altman, D. G., Tetzlaff, J., Mulrow, C., Gøtzsche, P. C., Ioannidis, J. P. A., Clarke, M., Devereaux, P. J., Kleijnen, J., & Moher, D. (2009). The PRISMA statement for reporting systematic reviews and meta-analyses of studies that evaluate health care interventions: Explanation and elaboration. *Journal of Clinical Epidemiology, 62*, e1–e34. PMID: 19631507

Li, H., Pang, F., Xu, D., & Dong, L. (2023). New Optimization Framework for Improvement Sustainability of Wastewater Treatment Plants. *Processes (Basel, Switzerland), 11*(11), 3156. DOI: 10.3390/pr11113156

Li, J., Song, G., Cai, M., Bian, J., & Mohammed, B. S. (2022). Green environment and circular economy: A state-of-the-art analysis. *Sustainable Energy Technologies and Assessments, 52*, 102106.

Li, J., & Trivic, Z. (2024). Impact of "blue-green diet" on human health and well-being: A systematic review of potential determinants in shaping the effectiveness of blue-green infrastructure (BGI) in urban settings. *The Science of the Total Environment, 926*, 171397. PMID: 38438033

Li, M., & Rasiah, R. (2024). Can ESG Disclosure Stimulate Corporations' Sustainable Green Innovation Efforts? Evidence from China. *Sustainability, 16*(21), 9390. DOI: 10.3390/su16219390

Limbore, N. V., Anute, N., Ahluwalia, G. K., Chordiya, P. B., Kalshetti, P., & Selvakumar, P. (2025). Ethical leadership and corporate responsibility. In Harriott, S. (Ed.), *Innovative approaches to managing conflict and change in diverse work environments* (pp. 193–218). IGI Global Scientific Publishing.

Lin, M., & Zhao, Y. (2020). Artificial intelligence-empowered resource management for future wireless communications: A survey. *China Communications*, *17*, 58–77.

Lin, Z., Wang, H., Li, W., & Chen, M. (2023). Impact of green finance on carbon emissions based on a two-stage LMDI decomposition method. *Sustainability (Basel)*, *15*(17), 12808. DOI: 10.3390/su151712808

Liquete, C., Kleeschulte, S., Dige, G., Maes, J., Grizzetti, B., Olah, B., & Zulian, G. (2015). Mapping green infrastructure based on ecosystem services and ecological networks: A pan-European case study. *Environmental Science & Policy*, *54*, 268–280.

Li, S., Zhang, H., Yan, W., & Jiang, Z. (2020). A hybrid method of blockchain and case-based reasoning for remanufacturing process planning. [if DOI is available]. *Journal of Intelligent Manufacturing*, •••, 1–11. https://doi.org/xx.xxx/xxxxx

Liu, Q., Trevisan, A. H., Yang, M., & Mascarenhas, J. (2022). (in press). A framework of digital technologies for the circular economy: Digital functions and mechanisms. *Business Strategy and the Environment*.

Liu, Y., Lei, J., & Zhang, Y. (2021). A study on the sustainable relationship among the green finance, environment regulation and green-total-factor productivity in China. *Sustainability*, *13*(21), 11926.

Li, W., Li, W., Zhu, Y., Wang, F., Huang, F., Wang, F., Zhu, Y., Huang, F., Dong, Z., & Zhao, Y. (2024). Research progress in water quality prediction based on deep learning technology: A review. *Environmental Science and Pollution Research International*, *31*(18), 26415–26431. DOI: 10.1007/s11356-024-33058-7

Lounis, Z., & Mcallister, T. P. (2016). Risk-Based Decision Making for Sustainable and Resilient Infrastructure Systems. *Journal of Structural Engineering*, *142*(9). Advance online publication. DOI: 10.1061/(asce)st.1943-541x.0001545

Lubos, S., ... (2024). Leveraging LLMs for the quality assurance of software requirements. In *2024 IEEE 32nd International Requirements Engineering Conference (RE)* (pp. 389-397). IEEE. https://doi.org/DOI: 10.1109/RE59067.2024.00046

Lu, J.-W., Chang, N.-B., & Liao, L. (2013). Environmental Informatics for Solid and Hazardous Waste Management: Advances, Challenges, and Perspectives. *Critical Reviews in Environmental Science and Technology*, *43*(15), 1557–1656. DOI: 10.1080/10643389.2012.671097

Lu, L., Zhu, X., Peters, C. A., Rau, G. H., Ren, Z. J., & Guest, J. S. (2018). Wastewater treatment for carbon capture and utilization. *Nature Sustainability*, *1*(12), 750–758. DOI: 10.1038/s41893-018-0187-9

Lundqvist, S. A. (2015). Why firms implement risk governance – Stepping beyond traditional risk management to enterprise risk management. *Journal of Accounting and Public Policy*, *34*, 441–466.

Luo, Y., Ye, M., Zhou, Y., Su, R., Huang, S., Wang, H., & Dai, X. (2024). Assessing the Environmental Impact of Municipal Waste on Energy Incineration Technology for Power Generation Using Life Cycle Assessment Methodology. *Toxics*, *12*(11), 786. DOI: 10.3390/toxics12110786

Mageed, N. N., Alsultani, R., & Abbas, A. W. N. (2024). The Impact of Using Advanced Technologies in Sustainable Design to Enhance Usability and Achieve Optimal Architectural Design. *International Journal of Sustainable Development and Planning*, *19*(11), 4273–4280. DOI: 10.18280/ijsdp.191116

Magrini, C., Nicolas, J., Berg, H., Bellini, A., Paolini, E., Vincenti, N., Campadello, L., & Bonoli, A. (2021). Using Internet of Things and distributed ledger technology for digital circular economy enablement: The case of electronic equipment. *Sustainability*, *13*, 4982.

Mahmood, A., Farooq, A., Akbar, H., Ghani, H. U., & Gheewala, S. H. (2023). An Integrated Approach to Analyze the Progress of Developing Economies in Asia toward the Sustainable Development Goals. *Sustainability (Switzerland)*, *15*(18). Advance online publication. DOI: 10.3390/su151813645

Mairiza, D., Zowghi, D., & Gervasi, V. (2014). Utilizing TOPSIS: A multi-criteria decision analysis technique for non-functional requirements conflicts. In Zowghi, D., & Jin, Z. (Eds.), *Requirements Engineering. Communications in Computer and Information Science, 432*. Springer., DOI: 10.1007/978-3-662-43610-3_3

Makhloufi, L., Siddik, A. B., & Zhou, J. (2023). Why green absorptive capacity and managerial environmental concerns matter for corporate environmental entrepreneurship? *Environmental Science and Pollution Research International*, *30*(46), 102295–102312. DOI: 10.1007/s11356-023-29583-6

Mamudu, U. U., Obasi, C. D., Awuye, S. K., Danso, H., Ayodele, P., & Akinyemi, P. (2024). Circular economy in the manufacturing sector: Digital transformation and sustainable practices. *International Journal of Science and Research Archive*, *12*(02), 129–141.

Mangutana, A. Y., Bisnis, P. M., Manajemen, P. S., Petra, U. K., & Siwalankerto, J. (2016). Implementasi Prinsip - Prinsip Good Corporate Governance Untuk Strategi Keberlanjutan Perusahaan Konstruksi Di Sumba. *Ágora*, *4*(1).

Marar, H. W. (2024). Advancements in software engineering using AI. *Computer Software and Media Applications*, *6*(1). Advance online publication. DOI: 10.24294/csma.v6i1.3906

Marijan, D., & Gotlieb, A. (2020). Industry-Academia research collaboration in software engineering: The Certus model. *Information and Software Technology*, *132*, 106473. DOI: 10.1016/j.infsof.2020.106473

Marx, K., & Engels, F. (2004). *Tesis Sobre Feuerbach*. El Cid Editor.

Masi, F., Bresciani, R., Rizzo, A., Edathoot, A., Patwardhan, N., Panse, D., & Langergraber, G. (2016). Green walls for greywater treatment and recycling in dense urban areas: A case study in Pune. *Journal of Water, Sanitation, and Hygiene for Development : a Journal of the International Water Association*, *6*, 342–347.

Massonet, A., Kiesel, R., & Schmitt, R. H. (2020). Der digitale Zwilling über den Produktlebenszyklus. Zeitschrift für wirtschaftlichen Fabrikbetrieb, 115(s1), 97–100.

Matsiola, M., Lappas, G., & Yannacopoulou, A. (2024). Generative AI in Education: Assessing Usability, Ethical Implications, and Communication Effectiveness. *Societies (Basel, Switzerland)*, *14*(12). Advance online publication. DOI: 10.3390/soc14120267

Matthew, U. O., Asuni, O., & Fatai, L. O. (2024). Green Software Engineering Development Paradigm: An Approach to a Sustainable Renewable Energy Future. In *Advancing Software Engineering Through AI, Federated Learning, and Large Language Models* (pp. 281-294). IGI Global.

Matthew, U. O., Asuni, O., & Fatai, L. O. (2024). *Green software engineering development paradigm*. IGI Global., DOI: 10.4018/978-8-3693-3502-4.ch018

Mbokane, L., & Modley, L. A. (2024). Green Consumerism in Young Adults: Attitudes and Awareness in University Students in Johannesburg, South Africa. *Sustainability (Switzerland)*, *16*(5). Advance online publication. DOI: 10.3390/su16051898

Md Khudzari, J., Kurian, J., Tartakovsky, B., & Raghavan, G. S. V. (2018). Bibliometric analysis of global research trends on microbial fuel cells using Scopus database. *Biochemical Engineering Journal*, *136*, 51–60. DOI: 10.1016/j.bej.2018.05.002

Mehra, R., Sharma, V. S., Kaulgud, V., Podder, S., & Burden, A. P. (2022). *Towards a green quotient for software projects*. https://doi.org/DOI: 10.1145/3510457.3513077

Meiden, C., & Silaban, A. (2023). Exploring the Measurement of Environmental Performance in Alignment with Environmental, Social, and Governance (ESG): A Qualitative Study. *Information Sciences Letters*, *12*(9), 2287–2297. DOI: 10.18576/isl/120932

Melesse, T. Y., Di Pasquale, V., & Riemma, S. (2020). Digital twin models in industrial operations: A systematic literature review. *Procedia Manufacturing*, *42*, 267–272.

Mi, C., Gou, X., Ren, Y., Zeng, B., Khalid, J., & Ma, Y. (2024). Seasonal electricity consumption forecasting: An approach with novel weakening buffer operator and fractional order accumulation grey model. *Grey Systems: Theory and Application*, *14*, 414–428.

Mishra, N. K., Mishra, N., & Sharma, P. P. (2025). Unraveling the relationship between corporate governance and green innovation: A systematic literature review. *Management Research Review*, *48*(5), 825–845.

Moktadir, M. A., Sultana, R., Madaan, J., Dwivedi, A., Rahman, A., Chiappetta Jabbour, C. J., & Paul, S. K. (2020). An investigation of key performance indicators for operational excellence towards sustainability in the leather products industry. *Business Strategy and the Environment*, *29*(8), 3331–3351. DOI: 10.1002/bse.2575

Moreira, A., Capilla, R., Leifler, O., Penzenstadler, B., Betz, S., Duboc, L., Nguyen, N.-T., Coroamă, V. C., Brooks, I., Porras, J., Peters, A.-K., Fernandes, J. P., Lago, P., Oyedeji, S., Heldal, R., & Venters, C. C. (2024). A roadmap for integrating sustainability into software engineering education. *ACM Transactions on Software Engineering and Methodology*. Advance online publication. DOI: 10.1145/3708526

Morsy, K. M., Mostafa, M. K., Abdalla, K. Z., & Galal, M. M. (2020). Life cycle assessment of upgrading primary wastewater treatment plants to secondary treatment including a circular economy approach. *Air, Soil and Water Research*, *13*, 1178622120935857.

Mosadegh, B., Polygerinos, P., Keplinger, C., Wennstedt, S., Shepherd, R. F., Gupta, U., Shim, J., Bertoldi, K., Walsh, C. J., & Whitesides, G. M. (2014). Pneumatic networks for soft robotics that actuate rapidly. *Advanced Functional Materials*, *24*(15), 2163–2170. gmwgroup.harvard.edu+1

Moshnyaga, V. G. (2013). An assessment of software lifecycle energy. *2013 23rd International Workshop on Power and Timing Modeling Optimization and Simulation Patmos 2013*, 112–119. https://doi.org/DOI: 10.1109/PATMOS.2013.6662163

Motamedimoghadam, M., Amaral, M., & Mira Da Silva, M. (2024). Organizational capabilities for digital innovation: A systematic literature review. *European Journal of Innovation Management*. Advance online publication. DOI: 10.1108/ejim-02-2024-0227

Mougenot, B., & Doussoulin, J. P. (2024). A bibliometric analysis of the Global Reporting Initiative (GRI): Global trends in developed and developing countries. *Environment, Development and Sustainability*, *26*(3). Advance online publication. DOI: 10.1007/s10668-023-02974-y PMID: 36788933

Mourtzis, D. (2018). Design of customised products and manufacturing networks: Towards frugal innovation. *International Journal of Computer Integrated Manufacturing*, *31*, 1161–1173.

Muguerza, J. (2004). *Ethics and perplexity: Toward a critique of dialogical reason.* Rodopi.

Muralidhar, R., Borovica-Gajic, R., & Buyya, R. (2022). Energy Efficient Computing Systems: Architectures, Abstractions and Modeling to Techniques and Standards. *ACM Computing Surveys*, *54*(11s). Advance online publication. DOI: 10.1145/3511094

Mushi, G. E., Di Marzo Serugendo, G., & Burgi, P. Y. (2022). Digital technology and services for sustainable agriculture in Tanzania: A literature review. *Sustainability*, *14*, 2415.

Nadjib, M., Moedjari, S., Nasrullah, H., Hadiputro, A. N., Bonakarta, K., Blok, B., Sa, J., No, T., & Jombang, K. (2019). Penentuan Faktor Kritis Keberhasilan Implementasi ERP di Perusahaan Baja Menggunakan Formulasi Keberhasilan Dari DeLone & McLean. *Jurnal IKRA-ITH Informatika, 3*(3).

Naranjo, A., Colonia, A., Maury-Ramírez, A., Mesa, J., & Maury, H. (2020). State-of-the-Art Green Roofs: Technical Performance and Certifications for Sustainable Construction. *Coatings*, *10*(1), 69. DOI: 10.3390/coatings10010069

Naumann, S., Dick, M., Kern, E., & Johann, T. (2011). The GREENSOFT model: A reference model for green and sustainable software and its engineering. *Sustainable Computing : Informatics and Systems*, *1*(4), 294–304. DOI: 10.1016/j.suscom.2011.06.004

Nazim, M., Ahmad, S., Arif, M., Mishra, V., & Ahmad, J. (2024, Moradabad, India). Optimizing software requirements selection: A hybrid K-means and intuitionistic fuzzy TOPSIS approach. In *2024 13th International Conference on System Modeling & Advancement in Research Trends (SMART)* (pp. 750-755). IEEE. https://doi.org/DOI: 10.1109/SMART63812.2024.10882593

Nazim, M., Mohammad, C. W., & Sadiq, M. (2022). Analysis of fuzzy AHP and fuzzy TOPSIS methods for the prioritization of the software requirements. In Kulkarni, A. J. (Ed.), *Multiple Criteria Decision Making. Studies in Systems, Decision and Control, 407*. Springer., DOI: 10.1007/978-981-16-7414-3_4

Nazim, M., Mohammad, C. W., & Sadiq, M. (2022). Fuzzy-based methods for the selection and prioritization of software requirements: A systematic literature review. In Bhateja, V., Tang, J., Satapathy, S. C., Peer, P., & Das, R. (Eds.), *Evolution in Computational Intelligence. Smart Innovation, Systems and Technologies, 267*. Springer., DOI: 10.1007/978-981-16-6616-2_11

Negri, E., Fumagalli, L., & Macchi, M. (2017). A review of the roles of digital twin in CPS-based production systems. *Procedia Manufacturing*, *11*, 939–948.

Neogi, S., Sharma, V., Khan, N., Chaurasia, D., Ahmad, A., Chauhan, S., & Bhargava, P. C. (2022). Sustainable biochar: A facile strategy for soil and environmental restoration, energy generation, mitigation of global climate change and circular bioeconomy. *Chemosphere*, *293*, 133474. PMID: 34979200

Nerurkar, P., Shirke, A., Chandane, M., & Bhirud, S. (2018). Empirical analysis of data clustering algorithms. *Procedia Computer Science*, *125*, 770 ?"779. DOI: 10.1016/j.procs.2017.12.099

Neto, A. A., & Deschamps, F., Silva, da, Ribeiro, E., & Lima, E. P. de. (2020). Digital twins in manufacturing: An assessment of drivers, enablers and barriers to implementation. *Procedia CIRP*, *93*, 210–215.

Neves Da Silva, A., & Novo, P. (2017). Hubgrade smart monitoring centers: Measuring resource consumption and moving towards a circular economy. *Field Actions Science Reports*, *17*, 32–37.

Ngo, T., Ullah, S., Le, T., & Trinh, H. H. (2022). Climate risk disclosures and global sustainability initiatives: A conceptual analysis and agenda for future research. *Business Strategy and the Environment*, *32*(6), 3705–3720. DOI: 10.1002/bse.3323

Noe, R., Hollenbeck, J., Gerhart, B., & Wright, P. (2006). *Human Resources Management: Gaining a Competitive Advantage, Tenth Global Edition*. kansaigaidai.ac.jp. https://www.kansaigaidai.ac.jp/asp/files/academics/course-syllabi/fall-semester-2019/BUS9F19.pdf

Norouzi, M., Chàfer, M., Cabeza, L. F., Jiménez, L., & Boer, D. (2021). Circular economy in the building and construction sector: A scientific evolution analysis. *Journal of Building Engineering*, *44*, 102704.

Noszczyk, T. (2018). A review of approaches to land use changes modeling. *Human and Ecological Risk Assessment*, •••, 1–29.

Novák, V., Perfilieva, I., & Mockor, J. (2012). *Mathematical principles of fuzzy logic* (Vol. 517). Springer.

Nurmalasari. (2013). Pengukuran Tingkat Kematangan Tata Kelola Teknologi Informasi Menggunakan Maturity Level Domain Po Dan Ai Framework Cobit 4.1. *Pilar Nusa Mandiri, Vol. IX*(2).

Ogunkan, D. V. (2022). Achieving sustainable environmental governance in Nigeria: A review for policy consideration. In *Urban Governance* (Vol. 2, Issue 1). https://doi.org/DOI: 10.1016/j.ugj.2022.04.004

Ogutu, H., Adol, G. F. C., Bujdosó, Z., Andrea, B., Fekete-Farkas, M., & Dávid, L. D. (2023). Theoretical nexus of knowledge management and tourism business enterprise competitiveness: An integrated overview. *Sustainability*, *15*(3), 1948.

Okamura, A. M., Simone, C., & O'leary, M. D. (2004). Force modeling for needle insertion into soft tissue. *IEEE Transactions on Biomedical Engineering*, *51*(10), 1707–1716. PMID: 15490818

Okorie, O., Salonitis, K., Charnley, F., Moreno, M., Turner, C., & Tiwari, A. (2018). Digitisation and the circular economy: A review of current research and future trends. *Energies*, *11*, 3009.

Olatunji, O. O., Akinlabi, S. A., Ayo, O. O., Madushele, N., Adedeji, P. A., & Fatoba, S. O. (2019). Drivers and barriers to competitive carbon footprint reduction in manufacturing supply chain: A brief review. *Procedia Manufacturing*, *35*, 992–1000.

Oliver, D., & Lainhart, J. (2012). COBIT 5: Adding Value Through Effective Geit. *Edpacs*, *46*(3), 1–12. DOI: 10.1080/07366981.2012.706472

Orieno, O. H., Ndubuisi, N. L., Eyo-Udo, N. L., Ilojianya, V. I., & Biu, P. W. (2024). *Sustainability in project management: A comprehensive review*. World Journal of Advanced Research and Reviews., DOI: 10.30574/wjarr.2024.21.1.0060

Oyedeji, S., Shamshiri, H., Porras, J., & Lammert, D. (2021). Software Sustainability: Academic Understanding and Industry Perceptions. In *Lecture Notes in Business Information Processing: Vol. 434 LNBIP*. https://doi.org/DOI: 10.1007/978-3-030-91983-2_3

Ozili, P. K. (2022). Green finance research around the world: A review of literature. *International Journal of Green Economics*, *16*(1), 56–75.

Pacana, A., Ulewicz, R., Siwiec, D., & Ulewicz, M. (2024). A Novelty Model Employing the Quality Life Cycle Assessment (QLCA) Indicator and Frameworks for Selecting Qualitative and Environmental Aspects for Sustainable Product Development. *Sustainability*, *16*(17), 7821. DOI: 10.3390/su16177821

Padilla-Rivera, A., Güereca-Hernandez, L. P., Morales Brizard, M., & Merveille, N. (2024). Barriers, Challenges, and Opportunities in the Adoption of the Circular Economy in Mexico: An Analysis through Social Perception. *Recycling*, *9*(5), 71. DOI: 10.3390/recycling9050071

Page, M. J., McKenzie, J. E., Bossuyt, P. M., Boutron, I., Hoffmann, T. C., Mulrow, C. D., Shamseer, L., Tetzlaff, J. M., Akl, E. A., & Brennan, S. E.. (2021). The PRISMA 2020 statement: An updated guideline for reporting systematic reviews. *BMJ (Clinical Research Ed.)*, *372*, 89. PMID: 33782057

Pan, C., Hu, J., & Xie, M. (2018). ENZYME: An Energy-Efficient Transient Computing Paradigm for Ultralow Self-Powered IoT Edge Devices. *IEEE Transactions on Computer-Aided Design of Integrated Circuits and Systems*, *37*(11), 2440–2450. DOI: 10.1109/tcad.2018.2858478

Pang, C.-Y. (2015). A cross-platform architecture with intelligent agents for dynamic processes and services composition. In *Achieving Enterprise Agility Through Innovative Software Development*. https://doi.org/DOI: 10.4018/978-1-4666-8510-9.ch003

Pantović, V., Jovanović-Milenković, M., Vujičić, S., Vidojević, D., & Sofijanić, S. (2024). Data-Driven Decision Making for Sustainable IT Project Management Excellence. *Sustainability*, *16*(7), 3014. DOI: 10.3390/su16073014

Panza, L., Faveto, A., Bruno, G., & Lombardi, F. (2022). Open product development to support circular economy through a material lifecycle management framework. *International Journal of Product Lifecycle Management*, *14*(2-3), 255–281.

Pap, S., & Morar, L. (2013). Procurement approaches in different supply chains. *AMM*, *436*, 551–556.

Parfitt, C. (2024). A foundation for ‘ethical capital’: The Sustainability Accounting Standards Board and Integrated Reporting. *Critical Perspectives on Accounting*, *98*. Advance online publication. DOI: 10.1016/j.cpa.2022.102477

Park, H., Easwaran, A., & Andalam, S. (2019). Challenges in digital twin development for cyber-physical production systems. In Chamberlain, R., Taha, W., & Torngren, M. (Eds.), *Cyber physical systems, model-based design* (Vol. 11615, pp. 28–48). Springer International Publishing.

Park, J., Choi, W., & Jung, S. U. (2022). Exploring Trends in Environmental, Social, and Governance Themes and Their Sentimental Value Over Time. *Frontiers in Psychology, 13*. Advance online publication. DOI: 10.3389/fpsyg.2022.890435 PMID: 35837641

Pastor-Escuredo, D., Morales-Guzmán, A., Torres-Fernández, Y., Bauer, J.-M., Wadhwa, A., Castro-Correa, C., Romanoff, L., Lee, J. G., Rutherford, A., & Frias-Martinez, V. (2014). Flooding through the lens of mobile phone activity. In *Proceedings of the IEEE Global Humanitarian Technology Conference (GHTC 2014)* (pp. 279–286). San Jose, CA, USA.

Patel, P., Gregersen, T., & Anderson, T. (2024). An agile pathway towards carbon-aware clouds. *ACM SIGENERGY Energy Informatics Review, 4*(3), 10–17.

Patil, R. A., Ghisellini, P., & Ramakrishna, S. (2020). Towards Sustainable Business Strategies for a Circular Economy: Environmental, Social and Governance (ESG) Performance and Evaluation. In *An Introduction to Circular Economy*. https://doi.org/DOI: 10.1007/978-981-15-8510-4_26

Patros, P., Rana, O., Spillner, J., Varghese, B., Dustdar, S., & Papadopoulos, A. V. (2021). Toward Sustainable Serverless Computing. *IEEE Internet Computing, 25*(6), 42–50. DOI: 10.1109/mic.2021.3093105

Paulraj, D., Prakash, M., Neelakandan, S., Baburaj, E., & Sethukarasi, T. (2023). An Efficient Hybrid Job Scheduling Optimization (EHJSO) approach to enhance resource search using Cuckoo and Grey Wolf Job Optimization for cloud environment. *PLoS One, 18*(3), e0282600. DOI: 10.1371/journal.pone.0282600

Peña, C., Civit, B., Gallego-Schmid, A., Druckman, A., Pires, A. C., Weidema, B., & Motta, W. (2021). Using life cycle assessment to achieve a circular economy. *The International Journal of Life Cycle Assessment, 26*, 215–220.

Penzenstadler, B., Raturi, A., Richardson, D., & Tomlinson, B. (2014). Safety, security, now sustainability: The nonfunctional requirement for the 21st century. *IEEE Software, 31*(3), 40–47. DOI: 10.1109/MS.2014.29

Perno, M., Hvam, L., & Haug, A. (2022). Implementation of digital twins in the process industry: A systematic literature review of enablers and barriers. *Computers in Industry, 134*, 103558.

Pesqueira, A., & Sousa, M. J. (2024). Exploring the role of big data analytics and dynamic capabilities in ESG programs within pharmaceuticals. *Software Quality Journal, 32*(2). Advance online publication. DOI: 10.1007/s11219-024-09666-4

Piila, N., Sarja, M., Onkila, T., & Mäkelä, M. (2022). Organisational drivers and challenges in circular economy implementation: An issue life cycle approach. *Organization & Environment, 35*(4), 523–550.

Pimonenko, T., Bilan, Y., Horák, J., Starchenko, L., & Gajda, W. (2020). Green brand of companies and greenwashing under sustainable development goals. *Sustainability (Switzerland), 12*(4). Advance online publication. DOI: 10.3390/su12041679

Pinto, L. V., Inácio, M., & Pereira, P. (2023). Green and blue infrastructure (GBI) and urban nature-based solutions (NbS) contribution to human and ecological well-being and health. *Oxford Open Infrastructure and Health, 1*, ouad004.

Pirola, F., Boucher, X., Wiesner, S., & Pezzotta, G. (2020). Digital technologies in product-service systems: A literature review and a research agenda. *Computers in Industry, 123*, 103301.

Pitchai, R., Tiwari, S., Viji, C., Kistan, A., Puviarasi, R., & Gokul, S. (2024). Green Technologies, Reducing Carbon Footprints, and Maximizing Energy Efficiency With Emerging Innovations: Green Computing. In Jain, V., Raman, M., Agrawal, A., Hans, M., & Gupta, S. (Eds.), *Convergence Strategies for Green Computing and Sustainable Development* (pp. 86–110). IGI Global Scientific Publishing., DOI: 10.4018/979-8-3693-0338-2.ch005

Plesker, C., Kutscher, V., Knobloch, R., & Schleich, B. (2023). Modularisation and containerisation of the digital process twin. *Procedia CIRP, 120*, 57–62.

Plociennik, C., Pourjafarian, M., Nazeri, A., Windholz, W., Knetsch, S., Rickert, J., & Weidenkaff, A. (2022). Towards a digital lifecycle passport for the circular economy. *Procedia CIRP, 105*, 122–127.

PMI (Project Management Institute). (2017). *A guide to the Project Management Body of Knowledge (PMBOK® Guide)* (6th ed.). Project Management Institute.

Polygerinos, P., Correll, N., Morin, S. A., Mosadegh, B., Onal, C. D., Petersen, K., & Shepherd, R. F. (2017). Soft robotics: Review of fluid-driven intrinsically soft devices; manufacturing, sensing, control, and applications in human-robot interaction. *Advanced Engineering Materials, 19*(12), 1700016.

Polygerinos, P., Wang, Z., Galloway, K. C., Wood, R. J., & Walsh, C. J. (2015). Soft robotic glove for combined assistance and at-home rehabilitation. *Robotics and Autonomous Systems, 73*, 135–143.

Polygerinos, P., Wang, Z., Overvelde, J. T., Galloway, K. C., Wood, R. J., Bertoldi, K., & Walsh, C. J. (2015). Modeling of soft fiber-reinforced bending actuators. *IEEE Transactions on Robotics, 31*(3), 778–789.

Prado Muci de Lima, I., & Costa Fernandes, D. (2024). ESG 2.0: The New Perspectives for Human Rights Due Diligence. In *Csr Sustainability Ethics and Governance: Vol. Part F3171*. https://doi.org/DOI: 10.1007/978-3-031-56619-6_14

Preut, A., Kopka, J.-P., & Clausen, U. (2021). Digital twins for the circular economy. *Sustainability*, *13*, 10467.

Pribadi, M. R., & Irsyad, H. (2018). Model Konseptual Penerapan Tata Kelola TI PLN Pembangkitan Sumbagsel Berdasarkan COBIT 5. *Jurnal Ilmiah Informatika Global*, *9*(1). Advance online publication. DOI: 10.36982/jig.v9i1.440

Procaccianti, G., Fernández, H., & Lago, P. (2016). Empirical evaluation of two best practices for energy-efficient software development. *Journal of Systems and Software*, *117*, 185–198. DOI: 10.1016/j.jss.2016.02.035

Putra, K. R., & Anggreani, F. (2022). Perancangan Arsitektur Enterprise Pada Instansi Pemerintahan: Systematic Literature Review. *Computing and Education Technology Journal (CETJ)*. https://ppjp.ulm.ac.id/journals/index.php/cetj

Qian, Y., Zhou, W., Yu, W., & Pickett, S. T. (2015). Quantifying spatiotemporal pattern of urban greenspace: New insights from high-resolution data. *Landscape Ecology*, *30*, 1165–1173.

Qing, C., & Jin, S. (2023). Does ESG and Digital Transformation affects Corporate Sustainability? The Moderating role of Green Innovation. *ArXiv.Org*, *3*.

Quesado, P., Silva, R., & Oliveira, H. C. (2024). Management Control Systems and Sustainability: A Bibliometric Analysis. *Sustainability*, *16*(12), 5067. DOI: 10.3390/su16125067

Radovanović, A., Talukdar, S., Roy, B., Mullen, E., Hung, P., Chen, B., Duarte, A., Care, N., Xiao, D., Schneider, I., Smith, K., Koningstein, R., Cirne, W., Haridasan, M., & Cottman, M. (2023). Carbon-Aware Computing for Datacenters. *IEEE Transactions on Power Systems*, *38*(2), 1270–1280. DOI: 10.1109/tpwrs.2022.3173250

Raffel, C.. (2020). Exploring the limits of transfer learning with a unified text-to-text transformer. *Journal of Machine Learning Research*.

Rahimian, V., & Ramsin, R. (2008). Designing an agile methodology for mobile software development: A hybrid method engineering approach. *Proceedings of RCIS*, *10*, 337–342. DOI: 10.1109/RCIS.2008.4632123

Rahwan, I., Cebrian, M., Obradovich, N., Bongard, J., Bonnefon, J.-F., Breazeal, C., Crandall, J. W., Christakis, N. A., Couzin, I. D., & Jackson, M. O.. (2019). Machine behaviour. *Nature*, *568*, 477–486. PMID: 31019318

Rai, P. K., Mishra, V. N., & Singh, P. (2022). *Geospatial technology for landscape and environmental management: sustainable assessment and planning*. Springer.

Rajkumar, M., Mahanta, P., Adige, V. S., & Pole, A. K. (2016). DevOps culture and its impact on cloud delivery and software development. *Proceedings of ICACCA, 56*, 1–6. DOI: 10.1109/ICACCA.2016.7578902

Rajput, S., & Sharma, T. (2024, June). Benchmarking emerging deep learning quantization methods for energy efficiency. In *2024 IEEE 21st International Conference on Software Architecture Companion (ICSA-C)* (pp. 238-242). IEEE.

Rall, E., Hansen, R., & Pauleit, S. (2019). The added value of public participation GIS (PPGIS) for urban green infrastructure planning. *Urban Forestry & Urban Greening, 40*, 264–274.

Ramya, K., & Ayothi, S. (2023). Hybrid dingo and whale optimization algorithm-based optimal load balancing for cloud computing environment. *Transactions on Emerging Telecommunications Technologies, 34*(5). Advance online publication. DOI: 10.1002/ett.4760

Rancea, A., Anghel, I., & Cioara, T. (2024). Edge computing in healthcare: Innovations, opportunities, and challenges. *Future Internet, 16*(9), 329.

Rao, N. R. (2025). Optimizing Enterprise Application Deployment Strategies for Package Distribution and Installation With a Focus on Sustainability and Education. In *Integrating AI and Sustainability in Technical and Vocational Education and Training (TVET)* (pp. 279-298). IGI Global Scientific Publishing.

Rapach, S., Riccardi, A., Liu, B., & Bowden, J. (2024). A taxonomy of earth observation data for sustainable finance. *Journal of Climate Finance, 6*, 100029. DOI: 10.1016/J.JCLIMF.2023.100029

Rashid, N., Ilyas, M., Khan, H. U., & Khan, S. U. (2021). Green-Agile Maturity Model: An Evaluation Framework for Global Software Development Vendors. *IEEE Access : Practical Innovations, Open Solutions, 9*, 71868–71886. DOI: 10.1109/access.2021.3079194

Rashid, N., Khan, S. U., Khan, H. U., & Ilyas, M. (2021). Green-agile maturity model: An evaluation framework for global software development vendors. *IEEE Access : Practical Innovations, Open Solutions, 9*, 71868–71886.

Raymond, C. M., Frantzeskaki, N., Kabisch, N., Berry, P., Breil, M., Nita, M. R., Geneletti, D., & Calfapietra, C. (2017). A framework for assessing and implementing the co-benefits of nature-based solutions in urban areas. *Environmental Science & Policy, 77*, 15–24.

Raza, S. A., & Khan, K. A. (2022). Impact of green human resource practices on hotel environmental performance: The moderating effect of environmental knowledge and individual green values. *International Journal of Contemporary Hospitality Management, 34*(6), 2154–2175.

Ren, W., & Ji, J. (2021). How do environmental regulation and technological innovation affect the sustainable development of marine economy: New evidence from China's coastal provinces and cities. *Marine Policy, 128*, 104468.

Ribeiro, M., Singh, S., & Guestrin, C. (2016, August). ?oWhy should I trust you? ?? Explaining the predictions of any classifier. In *Proceedings of the 22nd ACM SIGKDD International Conference on Knowledge Discovery and Data Mining (KDD ?(tm)16).*

Rivas-Asanza, W., Celleri-Pacheco, J., Andrade-Garda, J., García-Vázquez, R., Mato-Abad, V., Rodríguez-Yáñez, S., & Suárez-Garaboa, S. (2018). Environmental sustainability in information technologies governance. *Sustainability (Switzerland), 10*(12). Advance online publication. DOI: 10.3390/su10124792

Rizvi, S. W. H., Agrawal, S., & Murtaza, Q. (2021). Circular economy under the impact of IT tools: A content-based review. *International Journal of Sustainable Engineering, 14*(2), 87–97.

Rodgers, W., Murray, J. M., Stefanidis, A., Degbey, W. Y., & Tarba, S. Y. (2023). An artificial intelligence algorithmic approach to ethical decision-making in human resource management processes. *Human Resource Management Review, 33*, 100925.

Rosa, P., Sassanelli, C., Urbinati, A., Chiaroni, D., & Terzi, S. (2020). Assessing relations between Circular Economy and Industry 4.0: A systematic literature review. *International Journal of Production Research, 58*(6), 1662–1687.

Rossi, C., Byrne, J. G., & Christiaen, C. (2024). Breaking the ESG rating divergence: An open geospatial framework for environmental scores. *Journal of Environmental Management, 349*. Advance online publication. DOI: 10.1016/j.jenvman.2023.119477 PMID: 37944316

Ruckelshaus, M. H., Guannel, G., Arkema, K., Verutes, G., Griffin, R., Guerry, A., Silver, J., Faries, J., Brenner, J., & Rosenthal, A. (2016). Evaluating the benefits of green infrastructure for coastal areas: Location, location, location. *Coastal Management, 44*, 504–516.

Rus, D., & Tolley, M. T. (2015). Design, fabrication and control of soft robots. *Nature, 521*, 467–475. DOI: 10.1038/nature14543

Russo, I., Confente, I., Holmström, J., Öhman, M., & Tokar, T. (2024). Embracing methodological evolution and diversity in logistics and supply chain management research. *International Journal of Physical Distribution & Logistics Management, 54*(7/8), 653–672. DOI: 10.1108/IJPDLM-05-2024-0205

Ruza, C., & Caro-Carretero, R. (2022). The Non-Linear Impact of Financial Development on Environmental Quality and Sustainability: Evidence from G7 Countries. *International Journal of Environmental Research and Public Health, 19*(14), 8382. DOI: 10.3390/ijerph19148382

Saari, U. A., Baumgartner, R. J., & Mäkinen, S. J. (2017). Eco-friendly brands to drive sustainable development: Replication and extension of the brand experience scale in a cross-national context. *Sustainability (Switzerland), 9*(7). Advance online publication. DOI: 10.3390/su9071286

Saaty, R. W. (1987). The analytic hierarchy process ?" What it is and how it is used. *Mathematical Modelling, 9*(3-5), 161 ?"176. DOI: 10.1016/0270-0255(87)90473-8

Sachs, J. D. (2012). From Millennium Development Goals to Sustainable Development Goals. *Lancet, 379*, 2206–2211. PMID: 22682467

Saetang, W., Puttinaovarat, S., Saeliw, A., Chai-Arayalert, S., Kajornkasirat, S., Kongcharoen, J., & Puangsuwan, K. (2024). Eco-Friendly Office Platform: Leveraging Machine Learning and GIS for Carbon Footprint Management and Green Space Analysis. *Sustainability, 16*(21), 9424. DOI: 10.3390/su16219424

Salata, S., Garnero, G., Barbieri, C. A., & Giaimo, C. (2017). The integration of ecosystem services in planning: An evaluation of the nutrient retention model using InVEST software. *Land (Basel), 6*, 48.

Samal, A., & Misra, L. I. Mohit, Pougajendy, S., Chandel, P. S., Manjunath, T. C., & Selvakumar, P. (2025). Musealization and tourism practices. In S. Oflazoğlu & M. Dora (Eds.), Preserving cultural heritage in post-disaster urban renewal (pp. 115-142). IGI Global Scientific Publishing.

Samal, A., & Misra, L. I. Mohit, Pougajendy, S., Chandel, P. S., Manjunath, T. C., & Selvakumar, P. (2025). Musealization and Tourism Practices. In S. Oflazoğlu & M. Dora (Eds.), *Preserving Cultural Heritage in Post-Disaster Urban Renewal* (pp. 115-142). IGI Global Scientific Publishing.

Samuel, & Augustine, Y. (2019). Competitive Advantage and Corporate Governance in Indonesia with Enterprise Risk Management as Mediating. *Journal of Economics and Sustainable Development*. https://doi.org/DOI: 10.7176/jesd/10-8-05

Sangwan, K. S., Digalwar, A. K., & Bhakar, V. (2019). A sustainability assessment framework for cement industry – A case study. *Benchmarking*, *26*(2), 470–497. DOI: 10.1108/BIJ-01-2018-0021

Sani, B., & Jan, S. (2024). Empirical Analysis of Widely Used Website Automated Testing Tools. *EAI Endorsed Transactions on AI and Robotics*, *3*. Advance online publication. DOI: 10.4108/airo.7285

Santarius, T., Dencik, L., Diez, T., Ferreboeuf, H., Jankowski, P., Hankey, S., & Staab, P. (2023). Digitalization and sustainability: A call for a digital green deal. *Environmental Science & Policy*, *147*, 11–14.

Sarfraz, M., Ozturk, I., Yoo, S., Raza, M. A., & Han, H. (2023). Toward a new understanding of environmental and financial performance through corporate social responsibility, green innovation, and sustainable development. *Humanities & Social Sciences Communications*, *10*(1). Advance online publication. DOI: 10.1057/s41599-023-01799-4

Sartre, J.-P., Camus, A., Sprintzen, D., & Van den Hoven, A. (2004). *Sartre and Camus: A historic confrontation*. Humanities Press.

Sassanelli, C., Rosa, P., Rocca, R., & Terzi, S. (2019). Circular economy performance assessment methods: A systematic literature review. *Journal of Cleaner Production*, *229*, 440–453.

Sauvola, T., Lwakatare, L. E., Karvonen, T., Kuvaja, P., Olsson, H. H., Bosch, J., & Oivo, M. (2015). Towards customer-centric software development: A multiple-case study. *Proceedings 41st Euromicro Conference on Software Engineering and Advanced Applications Seaa 2015*, 9–17. https://doi.org/DOI: 10.1109/SEAA.2015.63

Saxena, A., Singh, R., Gehlot, A., Akram, S. V., Twala, B., Singh, A., Montero, E. C., & Priyadarshi, N. (2022). Technologies Empowered Environmental, Social, and Governance (ESG): An Industry 4.0 Landscape. *Sustainability 2023, Vol. 15, Page 309, 15*(1), 309. https://doi.org/DOI: 10.3390/SU15010309

Schleich, B., Anwer, N., Mathieu, L., & Wartzack, S. (2017). Shaping the digital twin for design and production engineering. *CIRP Annals*, *66*(1), 141–144.

Schneider, P., Gottschalk, N., Löser, R., & Scharbrodt, T. (2011). Integrated climate protection program for the city of Chemnitz—Climate diagnosis, climate change prognosis and conception of adaptation measures in the urban area. In *Resilient Cities: Cities and Adaptation to Climate Change—Proceedings of the Global Forum 2010* (pp. 299–310). Berlin, Germany: Springer.

Schoen, J. H., Burdette, J. H., West, T. G., Geer, C. P., Lipford, M. E., & Sachs, J. R. (2024). Savings in CT Net Scan Energy Consumption: Assessment Using Dose Report Metrics and Comparison With Savings in Idle State Energy Consumption. *AJR. American Journal of Roentgenology*, *222*(1). Advance online publication. DOI: 10.2214/ajr.23.30189

Schroeder, P., Anggraeni, K., & Weber, U. (2019). The relevance of circular economy practices to the Sustainable Development Goals. *Journal of Industrial Ecology*, *23*, 77–95.

Seele, P., & Lock, I. (2017). The game-changing potential of digitalization for sustainability: Possibilities, perils, and pathways. *Sustainability Science*, *12*(2), 183–185.

Selicati, V., Intini, F., Rospi, G., & Dassisti, M. (2022). Addressing heterogeneity sources in manufacturing sustainability assessment using the system design view. *CIRP Journal of Manufacturing Science and Technology*, *37*, 319–331.

Seo, C., Yoo, D., & Lee, Y. (2024). Empowering Sustainable Industrial and Service Systems through AI-Enhanced Cloud Resource Optimization. *Sustainability*, *16*(12), 5095. DOI: 10.3390/su16125095

Septriadi, R., Firdaus, F., & Cholil, W. (2019). Evaluasi Tata Kelola Teknologi Informasi Menggunakan Framework Simcobit, Studi Kasus pada Sekolah Tinggi Ilmu Kesehatan Bina Husada Palembang. *Jurnal Ilmiah Informatika Global*, *10*(1). Advance online publication. DOI: 10.36982/jiig.v10i1.747

Seuring, S., & Müller, M. (2008). From a literature review to a conceptual framework for sustainable supply chain management. *Journal of Cleaner Production*, *16*, 1699–1710.

Shah, S. M. A., Ahmed, Z., Ullah, I., Jiang, Y., Adebayo, T. S., & Wu, H. (2021). Linking Green Human Resource Practices and Environmental Economics Performance: The Role of Green Economic Organizational Culture and Green Psychological Climate. *International Journal of Environmental Research and Public Health*, *18*(20), 10953. DOI: 10.3390/ijerph182010953

Shao, J., Liu, Y. D., Alam, F., Ahmad, H., Butt, A. H., & Shao, H. (2024). Optimizing Sustainable Performance Green Talent Management Strategies Focused on Core Competencies. *Journal of Global Information Management*, *32*(1), 1–24. DOI: 10.4018/jgim.352495

Shapsugova, M. (2023). ESG principles and social responsibility. *E3s Web of Conferences, 420*. https://doi.org/DOI: 10.1051/e3sconf/202342006040

Sharma, R., Lopes de Sousa Jabbour, A. B., Jain, V., & Shishodia, A. (2022). The role of digital technologies to unleash a green recovery: Pathways and pitfalls to achieve the European Green Deal. *Journal of Enterprise Information Management, 35*(1), 266–294.

Sharma, V., Chatterjee, P., Kumar, M., & Gonzalez, E. D. R. S. (2023). Modelling of green manufacturing barriers using a survey-integrated decision-making approach. *Reports in Mechanical Engineering*, *4*(1), 256–275. DOI: 10.31181/rme040117112023s

Shawon, A. R., Kottmann, L., Feike, T., Hackauf, B., Uptmoor, R., & Memic, E. (2024). Comprehensive evaluation of the DSSAT-CSM-CERES-Wheat for simulating winter rye against multi-environment data in Germany. *Agronomy Journal, 116*(4), 1844–1868. DOI: 10.1002/agj2.21590

Shepherd, R. F., Ilievski, F., Choi, W., Morin, S. A., Stokes, A. A., Mazzeo, A. D., Chen, X., Wang, M., & Whitesides, G. M. (2011). Multigait soft robot. *Proceedings of the National Academy of Sciences, 108*(51), 20400–20403. DASH+1DOI: 10.1073/pnas.1116564108

Shoeibi, A., Khodatars, M., Ghassemi, N., Jafari, M., Moridian, P., Alizadehsani, R., Panahiazar, M., Khozeimeh, F., Zare, A., & Hosseini-Nejad, H.. (2021). Epileptic seizures detection using deep learning techniques: A review. *International Journal of Environmental Research and Public Health, 18*, 5780. PMID: 34072232

Shokri, R.. (2017). Membership inference attacks against machine learning models. In *Proceedings of IEEE Symposium on Security and Privacy*.

Siddiq, M., Ullah, I., & Khan, M. I. (2023). Clustering software requirements using transformer-based models. *IEEE Access : Practical Innovations, Open Solutions*.

Siddiqui, M. S., Ruhe, G., & Nguyen, T. N. (2019). Decision support for requirements reprioritization in software release planning. *Automated Software Engineering*.

Silva, A. S., Araujo, A., Palomino, P., Araujo, R., & Dermeval, D. (2024). *Mastering Requirements Volatility: Strategies for Dynamic Environments and Multiple Stakeholders in Government Software Projects*. IEEE., DOI: 10.1109/ACCESS.2024.3510056

Silvius, A. J. G., & Schipper, R. (2014). Sustainability in project management: A literature review and impact analysis. *Social Business*, *4*(1), 63–96. DOI: 10.1362/204440814X13948909253866

Simonaitis, A., Daukšys, M., & Mockienė, J. (2023). A comparison of the project management methodologies PRINCE2 and PMBOK in managing repetitive construction projects. *Buildings (Basel, Switzerland), 13*(7), 1796. DOI: 10.3390/buildings13071796

Singhal, N., & Konguvel, E. (2022). An Approach for Restaurant Management System during Covid-19. *2022 International Conference on Computer Communication and Informatics Iccci 2022*. https://doi.org/DOI: 10.1109/ICCCI54379.2022.9740862

Siregar, I. F., Soleha, N., Ismail, T., & Taqi, M. (2024). Influence of ESG on Sustainability Reporting: Mediation Rule of Green Innovation and Investor Sentiment. *International Journal of Energy Economics and Policy, 14*(1), 452–463. DOI: 10.32479/ijeep.14988

Soares, I. V., Yarime, M., & Klemun, M. M. (2025). Estimating GHG emissions from cloud computing: Sources of inaccuracy, opportunities and challenges in location-based and use-based approaches. *Climate Policy*. Advance online publication. DOI: 10.1080/14693062.2025.2450054;SUBPAGE:STRING:ABSTRACT;REQUESTEDJOURNAL:JOURNAL:TCPO20;WGROUP:STRING:PUBLICATION

Sohail, M. R., Mughal, S., Abiha, U., Abbas, A., Ali, M., & Khan, S. U. (2024). An empirical study to investigate the impact of sustainable practices in agile software development. *Proceedings of FIT63703, IEEE*, 1–6. https://doi.org/DOI: 10.1109/FIT63703.2024.10838460

Soliman, M., Ali, R. A., Khalid, J., Mahmud, I., & Assalihee, M. (2023). Modeling the continuous intention to use the Metaverse as a learning platform: PLS-SEM and fsQCA approach. In *Current and Future Trends on Intelligent Technology Adoption* (Vol. 1, pp. 41–62). Springer Nature.

Soongpol, B., Rukhiran, M., & Netinant, P. (2024). Practical Sustainable Software Development in Architectural Flexibility for Energy Efficiency Using the Extended Agile Framework. *Sustainability, 16*(13), 5738. DOI: 10.3390/su16135738

Sörensen, J., Persson, A. S., & Olsson, J. A. (2021). A data management framework for strategic urban planning using blue-green infrastructure. *Journal ofEnvironmental Management, 299*, 113658. PMID: 34523536

Soundariya, A., Behera, N. K., Selvakumar, P., Chandel, P. S., Gupta, S., & Manjunath, T. C. (2025). AI and environmental ethics: The role of AI in addressing climate change ethical considerations in AI-driven environmental solutions. In Chakraborty, S. (Ed.), *Human values, ethics, and dignity in the age of artificial intelligence* (pp. 321–346). IGI Global Scientific Publishing.

Soundariya, A., Behera, N. K., Selvakumar, P., Chandel, P. S., Gupta, S., & Manjunath, T. C. (2025). AI and Environmental Ethics: The Role of AI in Addressing Climate Change Ethical Considerations in AI-Driven Environmental Solutions. In Chakraborty, S. (Ed.), *Human Values, Ethics, and Dignity in the Age of Artificial Intelligence* (pp. 321–346). IGI Global Scientific Publishing.

Spišáková, M., Mandičák, T., Mésároš, P., & Špak, M. (2022). Waste management in a sustainable circular economy as a part of design of construction. *Applied Sciences (Basel, Switzerland)*, *12*(9), 4553.

Sreekanthaswamy, N., Anitha, S., Singh, A., Jayadeva, S. M., Gupta, S., Manjunath, T. C., & Selvakumar, P. (2025). Digital tools and methods. In Çela, E., Paliktzoglou, V., Sengar, S., Eappen, P., & Vajjhala, N. (Eds.), *Enhancing school counseling with technology and case studies* (pp. 25–48). IGI Global Scientific Publishing.

Srivastav, S., Mustyala, A., & Allam, K. (2023). Software automation enhancement through the implementation of DevOps. *International Journal of Research Publication and Reviews*, *4*(6), 2050–2054. DOI: 10.55248/gengpi.4.6.23.45947

St Flour, P. O., & Bokhoree, C. (2021). Sustainability assessment methodologies: Implications and challenges for SIDS. *Ecologies*, *2*(3), 285–304. DOI: 10.3390/ecologies2030016

Stillitano, T., Spada, E., Iofrida, N., Falcone, G., & De Luca, A. I. (2021). Sustainable agri-food processes and circular economy pathways in a life cycle perspective: State of the art of applicative research. *Sustainability*, *13*(5), 2472.

Stojčić, M., Mardani, A., Zavadskas, E. K., Pamučar, D., & Stević, Ž. (2019). Application of MCDM Methods in Sustainability Engineering: A Literature Review 2008–2018. *Symmetry*, *11*(3), 350. DOI: 10.3390/sym11030350

Sun, Y. (2025). Cloud and Edge Computing as Effective Trends in Business Model Innovation: A Bibliometric Review. *Journal of Software (Malden, MA)*, *37*(1), e2754.

Surbeck, C. Q., & Tyson, L. (2024). Leveraging Envision and ESG for Improved Sustainability Performance in Projects and Engineering Companies. *World Environmental and Water Resources Congress 2024 Climate Change Impacts on the World We Live in Proceedings of the World Environmental and Water Resources Congress 2024*, 1220–1228. https://doi.org/DOI: 10.1061/9780784485477.108

Szopińska, E., Kazak, J., Kempa, O., & Rubaszek, J. (2019). (in press). Spatial form of greenery in strategic environmental management in the context of urban adaptation to climate change. *Polish Journal of Environmental Studies*, *29*.

Szulczewski, W., & Jakubowski, W. (2018). The application of mixture distribution for the estimation of extreme floods in controlled catchment basins. *Water Resources Management, 32*, 3519–3534.

Talati, D. (2025). AI-Generated code for cloud DevOps: Automating infrastructure as code. *International Journal of Science and Research Archive, 14*(3), 339–345. DOI: 10.30574/ijsra.2025.14.3.0608

Taylor, C., & Sours, A. (2018). *Materials stewardship: A framework for managing and preserving materials in the circular economy*. NACE International.

Tehrani, A., Heidar-Zadeh, F., & Richer, M. (2024). CuGBasis: High-performance CUDA/Python library for efficient computation of quantum chemistry density-based descriptors for larger systems. *The Journal of Chemical Physics, 161*(7). Advance online publication. DOI: 10.1063/5.0216781

Tencati, A. (2016). Corporate Reporting Frameworks. In *A Handbook of Corporate Governance and Social Responsibility*. https://doi.org/DOI: 10.4324/9781315564791-27

Tola, F., Mosconi, E. M., Marconi, M., & Gianvincenzi, M. (2023). Perspectives for the development of a circular economy model to promote ship recycling practices in the European context: A systemic literature review. *Sustainability, 15*(7), 5919.

Trzeciak, M., Sienkiewicz, Ł. D., & Bukłaha, E. (2022). Enablers of Open Innovation in Software Development Micro-Organization. *Journal of Open Innovation, 8*(4). Advance online publication. DOI: 10.3390/joitmc8040174

Tufek, N.. (2025). Validating semantic artifacts with large language models. In MeroA o PeA uela, A. (Eds.), Lecture Notes in Computer Science: Vol. 15344. *The Semantic Web: ESWC 2024 Satellite Events*. Springer., DOI: 10.1007/978-3-031-78952-6_9

Udhayakumar, S. P., & Sivasubramanian, M. (2024). Impact of demographic attributes on requirement elicitation and quality software development. *International Journal of Intelligent Enterprise, 11*(4), 317–334. DOI: 10.1504/IJIE.2024.141869

Uludağ, Ö., Putta, A., Matthes, F., & Paasivaara, M. (2021). Evolution of the agile scaling frameworks (pp. 123–139). Springer. https://doi.org/ United Nations. (2015). *Transforming our world: The 2030 agenda for sustainable development.* https://sdgs .un.org/2030agendaDOI: 10.1007/978-3-030-78098-2_8

Vacchi, M., Siligardi, C., Cedillo-González, E. I., Ferrari, A. M., & Settembre-Blundo, D. (2021). Industry 4.0 and smart data as enablers of the circular economy in manufacturing: Product re-engineering with circular eco-design. *Sustainability, 13*, 10366.

Vahidi, A., & Aliahmadi, A. (2018). Describing the necessity of multi-methodological approach for viable system model: Case study of viable system model and system dynamics multi-methodology. *Systemic Practice and Action Research, 32*(1), 13–37. DOI: 10.1007/s11213-018-9452-0

Väisänen, J. M., Ranta, V., & Aarikka-Stenroos, L. (2019). Enabling circular economy with software: A multi-level approach to benefits, requirements and barriers. In *Software Business: 10th International Conference, ICSOB 2019, Jyväskylä, Finland, November 18–20, 2019* [Springer International Publishing.]. *Proceedings, 10*, 252–259.

van Lamsweerde, A. (2001). Goal-oriented requirements engineering: A guided tour. In *Proceedings of the Fifth IEEE International Symposium on Requirements Engineering* (pp. 249-262). IEEE. https://doi.org/DOI: 10.1109/ISRE.2001.948567

van Lamsweerde, A. (2004). Goal-oriented requirements engineering: A roundtrip from research to practice. In *Proceedings of the 12th IEEE International Requirements Engineering Conference* (pp. 4-7). IEEE. https://doi.org/DOI: 10.1109/ICRE.2004.1335648

Van Wynsberghe, A. (2021). Sustainable AI: AI for sustainability and the sustainability of AI. *AI and Ethics, 1*, 213–218.

Vanderborght, B., Albu-Schäffer, A., Bicchi, A., Burdet, E., Caldwell, D. G., Carloni, R., & Wolf, S. (2013). Variable impedance actuators: A review. *Robotics and Autonomous Systems, 61*(12), 1601–1614.

Velaoras, K., Polyzos, S., Menegaki, A. N., & Gotzamani, K. (2025). The Role of Environmental Certification in the Hospitality Industry: Assessing Sustainability, Consumer Preferences, and the Economic Impact. *Sustainability, 17*(2), 650. DOI: 10.3390/su17020650

Venters, C. C., Capilla, R., Betz, S., Crick, T., Crouch, S., Koc, H., & Lago, P. (2018). Software sustainability: Research and practice from a software architecture viewpoint. *Journal of Systems and Software, 138*, 174–188. DOI: 10.1016/j.jss.2017.12.010

Verdecchia, R., Lago, P., Ebert, C., & De Vries, C. (2021). Green IT and green software. *IEEE Software, 38*(6), 7–15.

Vergallo, R., D'Alò, T., Matino, S., Mainetti, L., & Paiano, R. (2024). Evaluating Sustainable Digitalization: A Carbon-Aware Framework for Enhancing Eco-Friendly Business Process Reengineering. *Sustainability, 16*(17), 7789. DOI: 10.3390/su16177789

Vinuesa, R., Azizpour, H., Leite, I., Balaam, M., Dignum, V., Domisch, S., Felländer, A., Langhans, S. D., Tegmark, M., & Nerini, F. F. (2020). The role of artificial intelligence in achieving the sustainable development goals. *Nature Communications, 11*, 233. PMID: 31932590

Völker, S., Baumeister, H., Claßen, T., Hornberg, C., & Kistemann, T. (2013). Evidence for the temperature-mitigating capacity of urban blue space—A health geographic perspective. *Erdkunde, 67*, 355–371.

Volpato, T., Oliveira, B. R. N., Garcés, L., Capilla, R., & Nakagawa, E. Y. (2017). Two perspectives on reference architecture sustainability. *ACM International Conference Proceeding Series, Part F1305*, 188–194. https://doi.org/DOI: 10.1145/3129790.3129815

VoPham, T., Hart, J. E., Laden, F., & Chiang, Y. Y. (2018). Emerging trends in geospatial artificial intelligence (geoAI): Potential applications for environmental epidemiology. *Environmental Health : A Global Access Science Source, 17*, 1–6. PMID: 29665858

Wang, C. (2023). *The effect of mandatory GHG Disclosure regulation on GHG disclosure quality, corporate financial and environmental performance: a UK study*. Doctoral dissertation.

Wang, G., & Ye, L. (2022). Spatial-temporal pattern of mismatch degree of high-quality tourism development and its formation mechanism in Taihu Lake Basin, China. *Sustainability, 14*, 4812.

Wang, Y., Lu, J., Zhu, X., Ye, J., Kong, Y., & Hao, W. (2023). A GM-based energy management strategy of hybrid power system for hydrogen fuel cell buses. *Journal of Advanced Transportation, 2023*, 6656612.

Wehner, M., Truby, R. L., Fitzgerald, D. J., Mosadegh, B., Whitesides, G. M., Lewis, J. A., & Wood, R. J. (2016). An integrated design and fabrication strategy for entirely soft, autonomous robots. [OUCI]. *Nature, 536*, 451–455. DOI: 10.1038/nature19100 PMID: 27558065

Wen, S., & Qiang, G. (2022). Managing stakeholder concerns in green building projects with a view towards achieving social sustainability: A Bayesian-network model. *Frontiers in Environmental Science, 10*, 874367.

Widiastuti, A., & Nurhayati, A. S. (2019). *Faktor-Faktor Yang Mempengaruhi Pengembangan Desa Wisata Nganggring Sleman*.

Wiesner, P., Grinwald, D., Weiß, P., Wilhelm, P., Khalili, R., & Kao, O. (2025, June). Carbon-Aware Quality Adaptation for Energy-Intensive Services. In *Proceedings of the 16th ACM International Conference on Future and Sustainable Energy Systems* (pp. 415-422).

Willem, T., Bak, M., Müller, R., Fritzsche, M.-C., Ruess, A. K., Breuer, S., Tigard, D., Sierawska, A., Meier, L. J., Buyx, A., Mclennan, S., Zimmermann, B. M., Braun, M., Schönweitz, F. B., & Fiske, A. (2024). Embedded ethics in practice: A toolbox for integrating the analysis of ethical and social issues into healthcare AI research. *Science and Engineering Ethics*, *31*(1). Advance online publication. DOI: 10.1007/s11948-024-00523-y

Wong, J. K. W., & Li, H. (2008). Application of the analytic hierarchy process (AHP) in multi-criteria analysis of the selection of intelligent building systems. *Building and Environment*, *43*(1), 108 ?"125. DOI: 10.1016/j.buildenv.2006.11.019

Wong, L. W., Tan, G. W. H., Ooi, K. B., Lin, B., & Dwivedi, Y. K. (2024). Artificial intelligence-driven risk management for enhancing supply chain agility: A deep-learning-based dual-stage PLS-SEM-ANN analysis. *International Journal of Production Research*, *62*(15). Advance online publication. DOI: 10.1080/00207543.2022.2063089

Wu, L., & Jin, S. (2022). Corporate Social Responsibility and Sustainability: From a Corporate Governance Perspective. *Sustainability (Switzerland)*, *14*(22). Advance online publication. DOI: 10.3390/su142215457

Xie, Q., & Li, J. (2021). Detecting the cool island effect of urban parks in Wuhan: A city on rivers. *International Journal of Environmental Research and Public Health*, *18*, 132. PMID: 33375462

Xu, K., Yang, M., Yang, J., Nataliia, B., Cai, Y., Zhang, H., & Wang, Y. (2024). Mapping scholarly publications of energy conservation and emission reduction in support of the sustainable development goals (SDGs). In *Frontiers in Environmental Science* (Vol. 12). Frontiers Media SA. https://doi.org/DOI: 10.3389/fenvs.2024.1421990

Xue, B., Liu, B., & Sun, T. (2018). What matters in achieving infrastructure sustainability through project management practices: A preliminary study of critical factors. *Sustainability*, *10*(12), 4421. DOI: 10.3390/su10124421

Yadav, N., Gupta, V., & Garg, A. (2024). Industrial automation through ai-powered intelligent machines—enabling real-time decision-making. In *Recent Trends in Artificial Intelligence Towards a Smart World: Applications in Industries and Sectors* (pp. 145–178). Springer Nature Singapore.

Yang, M., Chen, L., Wang, J., Msigwa, G., Osman, A. I., Fawzy, S., & Yap, P. S. (2023). Circular economy strategies for combating climate change and other environmental issues. *Environmental Chemistry Letters*, *21*(1), 55–80.

Yang, X., Chen, A., & PourNejatian, N.. (2022). A large language model for electronic health records. *NPJ Digital Medicine*, *5*, 194. DOI: 10.1038/s41746-022-00742-2 PMID: 36572766

Yang, Z., Na, J., & Dong, X. (2024). Corporate governance for sustainable development: A study on mechanism configuration. *Journal of Cleaner Production*, *458*, 142509.

Yilmaz, Y., Bandi, V., Mondal, D., Wang, S., Woods, R. A., Chan, T. M., Carey, R., & Thoma, B. (2021). Developing a dashboard for faculty development in competency-based training programs: A design-based research project. *Canadian Medical Education Journal*, *12*(4). Advance online publication. DOI: 10.36834/cmej.72067

Yrjönkoski, K., Jaakkola, H., Systä, K., Mikkonen, T., & Henno, J. (2019). Software business: A short history and trends for the future. *CEUR Workshop Proceedings*, •••, 2508.

Yuan, F., Ye, C., Peng, Y., Zuo, Z., Huang, X., Mao, Z., Tian, Z., Shu, W., Gu, S., Yang, J., & Jiang, Y. (2025). AI-Driven Optimization of Blockchain Scalability, Security, and Privacy Protection. *Algorithms*, *18*(5), 263. DOI: 10.3390/a18050263

Yu, W., & Ramanathan, R. (2014). An empirical examination of stakeholder pressures, green operations practices and environmental performance. *International Journal of Production Research*, *53*(21), 6390–6407. DOI: 10.1080/00207543.2014.931608

Zanotti, T., Puglisi, F. M., & Pavan, P. (2020). Smart Logic-in-Memory Architecture for Low-Power Non-Von Neumann Computing. *IEEE Journal of the Electron Devices Society*, *8*, 757–764. DOI: 10.1109/jeds.2020.2987402

Zavieh, H., Sangaiah, A. K., & Javadpour, A. (2024). Efficient task scheduling in cloud networks using ANN for green computing. *International Journal of Communication Systems*, *37*(5). Advance online publication. DOI: 10.1002/dac.5689

Zervakis, G., Soudris, D., Pekmestzi, K., & Xydis, S. (2019). Multi-Level Approximate Accelerator Synthesis Under Voltage Island Constraints. *IEEE Transactions on Circuits and Systems. II, Express Briefs*, *66*(4), 607–611. DOI: 10.1109/tcsii.2018.2869025

Zetzsche, D. A., & Anker-Sørensen, L. (2022). Regulating sustainable finance in the dark. *European Business Organization Law Review*, *23*(1), 47–85.

Zhang, C., & Ji, W. (2019). Big data analysis approach for real-time carbon efficiency evaluation of discrete manufacturing workshops. *IEEE Access : Practical Innovations, Open Solutions*, *7*, 107730–107743.

Zhang, H., Berg, A. C., Maire, M., & Malik, J. (2006). SVM-KNN: Discriminative nearest neighbor classification for visual category recognition. In *2006 IEEE Computer Society Conference on Computer Vision and Pattern Recognition (CVPR ?(tm)06).*

Zhang, L., Ning, L., Yang, X., Zeng, S., Yuan, T., Li, G., Ke, C., & Zhang, J. (2023). Half-power prediction and its application on the energy management strategy for fuel cell city bus. *Automotive Innovation*, *6*, 131–142.

Zhang, P., Yang, A., Pang, M., Zhang, L., Hao, Y., Wang, C., Xu, M., & Voinov, A. (2024). Food–energy–water nexus optimization brings substantial reduction of urban resource consumption and greenhouse gas emissions. *PNAS Nexus*, *3*(2). Advance online publication. DOI: 10.1093/pnasnexus/pgae028

Zhang, Q., Smith, K., Wang, S., Shen, J., Zhao, X., Jin, X., & Ren, Z. J. (2021). Greenhouse gas emissions associated with urban water infrastructure: What we have learnt from China's practice. *WIREs. Water*, *8*(4). Advance online publication. DOI: 10.1002/wat2.1529

Zhang, X., Geng, Y., Tong, Y. W., Kua, H. W., Tian, X., Wu, R., Zhao, X., & Chiu, A. S. F. (2021). Spatial characteristics and its driving factors of low-carbon energy technology innovation in China: A gravity movement and exploratory spatial data analysis. *Journal of Cleaner Production*, *295*. Advance online publication. DOI: 10.1016/j.jclepro.2021.126481

Zhang, Y., Wang, J., & Liu, Y. (2017). Game theory based real-time multi-objective flexible job shop scheduling considering environmental impact. *Journal of Cleaner Production*, *167*, 665–679.

Zhao, J., & Gómez Fariñas, B. (2023). Artificial intelligence and sustainable decisions. *European Business Organization Law Review*, *24*(1), 1–39.

Zheng, Z., Ning, K., & Zhong, Q.. (2025). Towards an understanding of large language models in software engineering tasks. *Empirical Software Engineering*, *30*, 50. Advance online publication. DOI: 10.1007/s10664-024-10602-0

Zhou, C., & Wu, Y. (2020). A planning support tool for layout integral optimization of urban blue–green infrastructure. *Sustainability*, *12*, 1613.

Zhou, Z., Chen, X., & Xiao, X. (2013). On evaluation model of circular economy for iron and steel enterprises based on support vector machines with heuristic algorithm for tuning hyper-parameters. *Applied Mathematics & Information Sciences*, *7*, 2215–2223.

Zhu, J., Zheng, Z., He, P., & Lyu, M. R. (2017). Online QoS Prediction for Runtime Service Adaptation via Adaptive Matrix Factorization. *IEEE Transactions on Parallel and Distributed Systems*, *28*(10), 2911–2924. DOI: 10.1109/tpds.2017.2700796

Zhu, X., Zhao, S., Pang, X., & Jia, Z. (2024). Joint Optimization of Task Caching and Computation Offloading for Multiuser Multitasking in Mobile Edge Computing. *Electronics (Basel)*, *13*(2), 389. DOI: 10.3390/electronics13020389

Zufiria, P. J., Pastor-Escuredo, D., Úbeda-Medina, L., Hernandez-Medina, M. A., Barriales-Valbuena, I., Morales, A. J., Jacques, D. C., Nkwambi, W., Diop, M. B., & Quinn, J. (2018). Identifying seasonal mobility profiles from anonymized and aggregated mobile phone data: Application in food security. *PLoS One*, *13*, e0195714. PMID: 29698404

About the Contributors

Sherif Mohamed A. Ismail With over 25 years of experience in the software industry, Dr. Sherif Ismail brings a wealth of expertise and a proven track record in Business Information Systems. His comprehensive skill set, and practical insights have established him as a seasoned professional in the field. Throughout his career, he has excelled in various roles, including developer, designer, analyst, project manager, and quality expert. This extensive experience has honed his abilities and equipped him with a deep understanding of software engineering principles. In addition to his remarkable industry background, Dr. Ismail has made significant contributions to the academic community. He has held prestigious positions as a lecturer at Maritime Academy for Science and technology, the University of Hail, assistant professor at the University of Dammam, Currently, he serves as a Professor at the American University, and professor at Umm Al-Qura University. where his expertise is highly valued. Dr. Ismail's research interests encompass several cutting-edge domains, including Artificial Intelligence (AI), Natural Language Processing, Knowledge Management, and Sentiment Analysis. His innovative work in these areas has garnered attention and recognition from peers and professionals alike. As a result, he has published over 100 research papers across various domains, demonstrating his intellectual prowess and dedication to advancing knowledge. By seamlessly integrating his theoretical expertise with his extensive practical experience, Dr. Ismail has solidified his position as an accomplished software engineering professional. His comprehensive skill set, remarkable research contributions, and academic qualifications make him an invaluable asset to both the industry and academia.

***

Munir Ahmad is a seasoned professional in the realm of Spatial Data Infrastructure (SDI), Geo-Information Productions, Information Systems, and

Information Governance, boasting over 25 years of dedicated experience in the field. With a PhD in Computer Science, Dr. Ahmad's expertise spans Spatial Data Production, Management, Processing, Analysis, Visualization, and Quality Control. Throughout his career, Dr. Ahmad has been deeply involved in the development and deployment of SDI systems specially in the context of Pakistan, leveraging his proficiency in Spatial Database Design, Web, Mobile & Desktop GIS, and Geo Web Services Architecture. His contributions to Volunteered Geographic Information (VGI) and Open Source Geoportal & Metadata Portal have significantly enriched the geospatial community. As a trainer and researcher, Dr. Ahmad has authored over 50 publications, advancing the industry's knowledge base and fostering innovation in Geo-Tech, Data Governance, and Information Infrastructure, and Emerging Technologies. His commitment to Research and Development (R&D) is evident in his role as a dedicated educator and mentor in the field.

M. Irvanni Bahri is an academic at Institut Teknologi Batam, Indonesia. He focuses on research in management science, regional planning, public policy, and social humanities.

Souvik Banerjee, PhD. He is a faculty at Management Development Institute (MDI) Murshidabad. His research interests include Corporate Finance, Corporate Governance, Behavioral Finance, and Financial Economics. His work has been published in Scopus-indexed and ABDC-listed journals. At present, he is the Editor of the MDIM Journal of Management Review and Practice (Sage). He has developed several business cases for MBA and executive education. He has trained executives from Fortune 500 companies in Corporate Finance and Corporate Valuation.

Abhijeet Das is a dedicated faculty member in the Department of Civil Engineering at C.V. Raman Global University (CGU), Bhubaneswar, Odisha, India. Based in the Khordha district, Dr. Das contributes actively to academic excellence and research in the field of civil engineering. His work focuses on advancing knowledge and practical applications that support the development of sustainable infrastructure. With a strong commitment to teaching and innovation, Dr. Abhijeet Das continues to inspire students and peers alike in the pursuit of engineering excellence.

Aulia Agung Dermawan is a lecturer and doctoral student (S3) at Universiti Tun Hussein Onn Malaysia (UTHM). Currently, he serves as the Head of the Engineering Management Study Program at the Batam Institute of Technology (ITEBA), while also being active in the academic world and research. With an educational background in industrial engineering and management, Aulia is known as a figure who is highly dedicated to curriculum development and research innovation. His commitment to the development of science is reflected in various scientific publications and his contributions to national and international conferences. (agung@iteba.ac.id)

S. Ida Evangeline, presently working as an Assistant Professor in the Department of Electrical and Electronics Engineering at the Government College of Engineering, Tirunelveli, Tamilnadu, India. She obtained her Bachelor's in Electrical and Electronics Engineering from Manonmaniam Sundaranar University in 2003, and Master's in Power Systems Engineering from Anna University, Chennai, Tamilnadu, India in 2005. She completed her PhD degree in 2023 at Anna University, Chennai, Tamilnadu, India. She has published six research papers in international journals. Her current research interests include optimal power flow, renewable energy, soft computing, machine learning, and deep learning.

Jonathan Joseph, PhD, is an Associate Professor at the Thakur College of Engineering and Technology Mumbai, India. As a researcher Dr. Joseph has published 30 national and international research papers in various journals and conferences. He has also received a copyright from the Govt. of India. He earned his PhD in Commerce and Management from Rashtrasant Tukadoji Maharaj Nagpur University, Nagpur. He also holds MBA, MCom, and and BCom degrees from Rashtrasant Tukadoji Maharaj Nagpur University, Nagpur, India.

Tarun Madan Kanade, PhD, is a member of the faculty of operations management at the Symbiosis Institute of Operations Management, which is a constituent of Symbiosis International (Deemed University) in India. Through his deep thoughts and numerous works, he has made a significant contribution to the academic and literary realms, making him a young author who stands out as a respected figure. His enormous achievements include contributions to several books, incisive chapters, research articles that explore new ground, and keynote speeches at a variety of conferences both nationally and internationally. Dr. Kanade is a person who is passionate about traveling and has a strong desire to learn new things and experience new places. His excursions, which have brought him to more than eleven different nations, are more than just vacations; they are quests for knowledge, which he makes sure to properly chronicle for the benefit of both educators and practitioners. Because of his extensive expertise, which spans nine years and encompasses a wide range of subjects, he has a distinctive point of view that he applies to his work. Because of his strategic vision and his ability to prepare for

Ansarullah Lawi is an industrial engineering lecturer at Batam Institute of Technology, Indonesia.

T.C. Manjunath was born on 6th February 1967. He did his B.E. from RV College of Engg. in 1989 (B'lore Univ), M.E. in Robotics & Automation from Govt.'s LD College of Engg., (Gujarat Univ., Ahmedabad) in 1992 with FCD-First Rank & PhD in Systems & Control Engg. from IIT Bombay in the year 2007, got best research scholar award for the entire IITB. He is currently working as the Dean Research (R & D) and as Professor in Dept. of Computer Science & Engg. with specialization in IoT, Cyber Security, Blockchain Technology in Rajarajeswari College of Engineering, Bengaluru, Karnataka. He has got a teaching (academic), research & administrative experience of more than 35+ years (10 years as Principal & 8 years as HoD, 1 year as Dean Research & rest as faculty) and has published more than 1500+ research papers in various national & international journals & conferences, with 175+ patents, 100+ book-chapters, 25 awards, 100s of Keynote talks and also published 25 text books in various field of science, engineering & technology, completed projects worth Rs. 9 Crores till date & guided 10 PhD scholars in VTU. He is a member of 30 Professional Society Chapters and is a fellow of IE, IETE, AMIEE, Sr. Member of IEEE and a chartered engineer.

P. Selvakumar is currently an Associate Professor in the Department of Science and Humanities at Nehru Institute of Technology, Coimbatore, Tamil Nadu, India. Prior to joining Nehru Institute of Technology, he held positions as an Assistant Professor in the Department of Science and Humanities various engineering colleges in Coimbatore, Tamil Nadu, India, spanning from 2011 to 2023. Dr.P. Selvakumar's academic and research interests lie primarily in the field of phytochemistry. He has made significant contributions to his field, with an impressive record that includes 30 journal publications, 12 patents, and 20 conference papers. Additionally, he has organized 5 seminars and conferences, further demonstrating his commitment to academic and scientific exchange. Throughout his career, Dr. P.Selvakumar has been recognized for his dedication and excellence in teaching, having been honored with several awards, including the Best Teacher Awards. He holds a prominent position in the academic community, contributing actively to research.

Jogen Sharma is a Research Scholar (PhD) in the Department of Library and Information Science at KIIT Deemed to be University, Bhubaneswar, India. He holds an M.A. in Bengali, M.L.I.Sc. and PGDLAN. His research interests include Bibliometric Analysis, library digitalization, RFID and sustainable library practices. He has published several papers in reputed journals.

Indumathi Srinivasan's career spans healthcare, consulting, and technology sectors, delivering impactful results at Smiligence, HCL Technologies, Sodexo India, Juran Academy, and Apollo Hospitals. Her expertise in SQL, Tableau,

Power BI, JIRA, and Confluence enables her to develop data-driven strategies for business optimization. Her academic background includes an MBA in Health Service Management, a Bachelor's in Microbiology, and a Post Graduate Diploma in Strategic Digital Marketing. At SIMATS University, her Ph.D. research in Healthcare Management focuses on EHR Data Quality Management, examining data integrity and interoperability to improve clinical decision-making accuracy. As a certified Lean Six Sigma practitioner from ASQ and Indian Statistical Institute, she has trained professionals in process optimization. Indumathi combines analytical skills with technology expertise to advance business intelligence and healthcare informatics.

Subramani AK brings 18 years of teaching experience to the classroom. Holding a Ph.D. in Business Administration from Manonmaniam Sundaranar University, Tirunelveli, Dr. Subramani A K has contributed significantly to the field with 70 articles published in international journals, including 28 in Scopus indexed journals, 4 in Anna University Annexure journals, and 2 in national journals.

Mohammed Abdul Wajeed works as Professor in Computer Science & Engineering Dept., in Lords Institute of Engineering and Technology, Hyderabad. He holds PHD in CSE from Jawaharlal Nehru Technological University.

Power BI, Excel, and Confluence enables her to develop data-driven strategies for business optimization. Her academic background includes an MBA in Health Service Management, a Bachelor's in Microbiology, and a Post Graduate Diploma in Supply Digital Marketing. At NMIMS University, her PhD research in Healthcare Management focuses on enhancing Data Quality Management, examining data integrity and interoperability to improve clinical decision-making accuracy. As a certified Lean Six Sigma practitioner from KPMG and a(n) international institute, she has trained professionals in process optimization and mentoring, combines analytical skills with technology expertise to advance business intelligence and healthcare informatics.

Subramani A.K. brings 15 years of academic experience to the classroom, holding a Ph.D. in Business Administration from Manonmaniam Sundaranar University, Tirunelveli. Dr. Subramani A.K. has contributed significantly to the field with 70 articles published in international journals, including 28 in Scopus indexed journals, 4 in Anna University Annexure journals, and 2 in national journals.

Mohammed Abdul Wajeed works as a Professor in Computer Science & Engineering Department, Lords Institute of Engineering and Technology, Hyderabad. He holds PhD in CSE from Jawaharlal Nehru Technological University.

Index

Symbols

A

B

C

D

E

F

G

H

I

L

N

P

R

S

V

www.ingramcontent.com/pod-product-compliance
Lightning Source LLC
LaVergne TN
LVHW080909300926
849162LV00003B/615
* 9 7 9 8 3 3 7 3 4 6 5 2 6 *